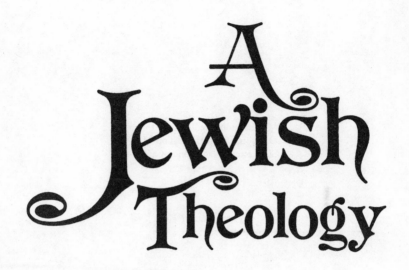

A Jewish Theology

LOUIS JACOBS

BEHRMAN HOUSE, INC. PUBLISHERS NEW YORK, N.Y

FOR SHULAMIT

First published in 1973 by
Darton, Longman & Todd Ltd
85 Gloucester Road, London SW7 5SU

Published in the United States by
Behrman House, Inc., 1261 Broadway, New York, New York 10001

Library of Congress Cataloging in Publication Data

Jacobs, Louis.
  A Jewish theology.

  1. Jewish theology. I. Title.
BM601.J28 1973   296.3   73-17442

ISBN 0-87441-248-x
ISBN 0-87441-226-9 pbk.

10 9 8 7 6 5 4 3 2 1

TABLE OF CONTENTS

Chapter

		Page
	PREFACE	v
1.	WHAT IS JEWISH THEOLOGY?	1
2.	THE UNITY OF GOD	21
3.	THE *Via Negativa* AND GOD AS *Person*	38
4.	TRANSCENDENCE AND IMMANENCE	56
5.	OMNIPOTENCE AND OMNISCIENCE	72
6.	ETERNITY	81
7.	CREATION	93
8.	PROVIDENCE	114
9.	THE GOODNESS OF GOD	125
10.	EXCURSUS: THE NAMES OF GOD	136
11.	THE LOVE OF GOD	152
12.	THE FEAR OF GOD	174
13.	WORSHIP AND PRAYER	183
14.	REVELATION	199
15.	TORAH AND MITZVAH	211
16.	JEWISH ETHICS	231
17.	SIN AND REPENTANCE	243
18.	REWARD AND PUNISHMENT	260
19.	THE CHOSEN PEOPLE	269
20.	PEOPLEHOOD AND STATEHOOD	276
21.	JUDAISM AND OTHER RELIGIONS	284
22.	THE MESSIANIC HOPE	292
23.	THE HEREAFTER	301
	BIBLIOGRAPHY	323
	INDEX	333

PREFACE

THIS book attempts a systematic presentation of the main themes of Jewish theology. Kaufmann Kohler's pioneering work in the field *Jewish Theology: Systematically and Historically Considered*, was published in 1918 (re-published by Ktav in 1968) and is now out of date. Samuel S. Cohon's *Jewish Theology*, published posthumously from an incomplete manuscript, was evidently compiled in the main a long time ago and now has the same dated air as Kohler's work. Many Jewish thinkers have written on theological topics since Kohler but there is a real lack of systematic treatment which this book seeks, however inadequately, to fill. The material presented here has not been published before except for some passages which have appeared in other books of mine (especially *Principles of the Jewish Faith*, which covers some of the same ground) and in the column I wrote regularly for the journal *Judaism*. The passages in smaller type in the body of the text contain more technical details and fuller bibliographical notes. If the reader wishes to skip these he can do so without detriment to the argument.

The first chapter of this book surveys the attitudes towards theology in the contemporary Jewish scene and argues for a more positive approach to this important branch of Jewish thought. That there are serious obstacles to the working out of a viable Jewish theology is not to be denied but this should not prevent us from making the effort, always with the proviso that the results are put forward with no exaggerated claims as to their significance. The subjective element must frankly be recognised; the attempt being seen as *a* Jewish theology, a possible statement, acceptable to some minds, unacceptable to others. Tentativeness is a virtue in theological thinking and if speculation is the more suitable word so be it.

The unity of God is the subject of the second chapter. Judaism dissociates itself entirely from all dualistic philosophies and from every compromise with pure monotheism. Implied in the doctrine of God's unity is that of His uniqueness. God is totally different from any of His creatures. But since the only language we have to speak of God is human language the problem of what can legitimately be said of God has always loomed large in any philosophical treatment of the Jewish faith. Chapter three considers this problem. The *via negativa* is accepted in essence but the idea of God as Person, i.e. as not less than a person, is defended against those thinkers who pronounce too readily the demise of the "supernatural". Traditional Theism, in which God is more than a vague "Force" or "Power" or "Process" in the universe, is still valid and is both more satisfying to the religious mind and has greater logical coherence than its naturalistic rivals.

Chapters four to six continue with the theme of religious language and its meaning. What is it that Theists are trying to say when they affirm that God is both transcendent and immanent, that He is omnipotent and omniscient and that He is eternal? The Jewish faith is neither deistic nor pantheistic. Whether it is compatible with panentheism is considered and it is suggested that the difficulty is chiefly one of semantics. The semantic confusion in the mystical idea of the "eternal Now" is noted in the chapter on "Eternity" but, then, the whole question of God in His relationship to time and space is a mystery.

Chapters seven to nine treat God as Creator and of His relationship to the world. The most acute problem here is the existence of evil, a problem which bears down with unparalleled intensity on contemporary Jewry with the horrors of the holocaust fresh in its memory to allow no rest. Since evil is real and God wholly good the theist has to grapple with the meaning of omnipotence as applied to God but when all that can be said has been, the theist can only walk through the darkness by his faith. It is hard to believe in God but even harder not to believe in Him.

Chapter ten is an excursus on the names of God, inserted here because the names given to God at various stages in the history of Judaism demonstrate how men thought of God in his relationship to them and in theirs to Him. This latter is discussed in chapters eleven to thirteen in its general aspects of love, fear and worship. There are various levels at which each of these operates from that unreflective type of observance without inwardness which borders on behaviourism to the mystic's intense longing. The Hasidic advice for each man to discern the "root of his soul" and follow the path to which he finds himself drawn is wise. The great temptation is self-delusion.

The detailed obligations which Judaism imposes on its adherents and their source in relevation is the theme of chapters fourteen to sixteen. The acknowledgement that Judaism is a developing faith and that a fundamentalist understanding of revelation is no longer tenable demands a new approach to the philosophy of the Halakhah. But the *mitzvot* still provide the Jew with his vocabulary of worship and should consequently be seen, even in the new scheme, as divine commands.

The human situation is such that man is ever confronted with the challenge of the *ought to be* to the *what is*. He is acutely aware of his failings and needs to find atonement. Chapters seventeen to nineteen study the perennial themes of sin and repentance. These, and even those of reward and punishment (provided that they are not construed so as to suggest despotism in the Deity), are as relevant to the modern Jew as they were to his ancestors.

The special role of the Jewish people and the new challenge to Jewish thinking on the question posed by the establishment of the State of Israel, as well as the attitude of Judaism to other religions, are examined in chapter nineteen through to chapter twenty one. The doctrine of chosenness is defended but not in its qualitative interpretation in which the Jewish soul is seen as inherently superior.

Eschatology has its place in any presentation of Jewish theology. Chapter twenty-two considers the doctrine of the Messiah as the culmination of human history here on earth, while chapter twenty three urges the acceptance of the traditional view that this life is not all and that there is an Hereafter, though in this area especially crudity of concept is to be avoided.

Some readers will no doubt be critical that a number of topics have been treated less than fully. I am particularly conscious that the critique can be levelled against the chapter on ethics and on the role of Jewish peoplehood with reference to the State of Israel. My excuse is that these topics, of the utmost importance to Jewish life, do not fall directly under the scope of Jewish theology. A cursory treatment of these great themes would be inexcusable in a work on Judaism as a whole. It is more intelligible in a work limited in scope to theology. The details of how a Jew should conduct himself and his attitude to the State of Israel are in all probability the most important a Jew today has to consider. But both these themes demand separate works to be treated comprehensively. Here only those aspects of them which touch directly on theology are examined.

A feature of the book to which I should like to call attention is the prominence given to the Kabbalah. This is not because I believe that

the Kabbalah can be swallowed whole. The modern Jew who finds
inadequate many of the mediaeval formulations of faith is likely to
find specially acute problems when reading the works of the Kabbalists. For all that the daring speculations of the Kabbalists deserve to be
recorded in a work on Jewish theology. God is at the centre of their
thought. Mysticism has rightly been described as religion in the most
intense form and there is an awakened interest in Jewish mysticism in
our day. Dean Inge's remark that personal religious experience is
bound to be attractive in an age which has seen the breakdown of
authoritarianism in religion commends itself to many thoughtful
people.

That more attention has not been paid to the moderns—Hermann
Cohen, Baeck, Buber, Rosenzweig, Kaplan and Heschel—in comparison with the amount of space given to the views of the pre-
moderns is not because I imagine that Jewish religious thought came
to an end at the close of the 18th century. It is rather that the chief aim
of this book is to describe the tradition and to note the reservations
regarding this tradition of one Jew among the many who have
grappled with this theme. Where the views of the moderns are germane to the argument they have been invoked and at times criticised.
For a closer examination of modern Jewish theological thought a very
different book would have to be written. Nevertheless, I am aware
that I may be faulted for neglecting some of the more significant
insights provided by more recent writers. I can only plead that my
anthology of the moderns, entitled: *Jewish Thought Today* published
by Behrman House be considered as a complementary volume to
this one. An author ought not to be guilty of writing the same book
twice.

The book refers frequently to the "modern Jew". That there is such
a creature is a fact of daily experience. We are different from our
forebears. Even the Jew who is finding his way back to tradition is,
in the vivid simile of Franz Rosenzweig, at the periphery of the circle
bent on approaching its centre. That many modern Jews are bothered
by the conflict between certain traditional formulations and the new
knowledge and insights is equally well-established. No apology is
needed, then, for trying to spell out the details of the conflict and how
it might be resolved in a synthesis of the old with the new. This task
has been undertaken with varying degrees of success by thinking
Jews belonging to different schools over the past hundred and fifty

years and more. The particular synthesis advocated in this book places greater reliance on tradition than some would be prepared to accept. The book might even qualify as "Orthodox" were it not that the majority of Orthodox Jews today would repudiate its attitude towards revelation and the question of authority in Judaism.

The idea of a quest for the Torah is basic to the book's approach. For all its conviction that theology is important and wedded though it is to the attempt—foolhardy some would say—at systematising Jewish beliefs, it acknowledges, as we all must, that theological problems, or, for that matter, any other problems of significance to the way men live, are not solved within the pages of the books. But there is a grand Jewish tradition of Midrash, the root of which word means, after all, "to search". The search itself belongs to the life of religion as conceived by Judaism. In the old tale, when the dervish repeatedly entreats Allah to say: "Here am I". Allah eventually replies that He had already done so in the dervish's very quest.

It is a pleasure to record my thanks to the members of the discussion group of the New London Synagogue for much stimulating discussion of the topics considered here. Professor Eugene Borowitz was kind enough to read through the whole manuscript and offer a detailed critique. Many of his suggestions for the improvement of the work have been acted upon. While I am deeply indebted to him the views presented in the book are my responsibility alone.

CHAPTER ONE

WHAT IS JEWISH THEOLOGY?

JEWISH theology is an attempt to think through consistently the implications of the Jewish religion. In its contemporary version such thinking through is to be done in accordance with the state of knowledge and information available at the present epoch in human history. Jewish theology differs from other branches of Jewish learning in that its practitioners are personally committed to the truth they are seeking to explore. It is possible, for instance, to study Jewish history in a completely detached frame of mind. The historian of Jewish ideas or the Jewish people or Jewish institutions need have no wish to express Jewish values in his own life. He need not be a Jew at all. Some of the best work in the discovery of what the Jewish past was really like has been done by non-Jews. Involvement (apart from the necessary degree of interest in the subject) is not essential for competence in historical study. It can be argued that too much personal concern for the subject is detrimental to such studies in that the danger of a surrender to bias will always be present. It is otherwise with theology. The theologian must avail himself of the accurate findings of the historians, otherwise his speculations will belong to fantasy. But while the historian asks what has happened in the Jewish past, the theologian asks the more personal question, what in traditional Jewish religion continues to shape my life as a Jew in the here and now? The historian uses his skills to demonstrate what Jews have believed. The theologian is embarked on the more difficult, but, if realised, more relevant, task of discovering what it is that a Jew can believe in the present.

The kind of questions the theologian asks and seeks to answer are chiefly concerned with God. Theology is the science of God. The Jewish theologian deals with questions such as: What is the Jewish concept of God? *Is* there a Jewish concept of God? What does Judaism teach about God's nature? Does God reveal Himself to

mankind and if so how? How is God to be worshipped? But as soon
as questions of this nature are raised the element of absurdity in the
whole theological enterprise becomes overwhelming. The best
religious thinkers have been unanimous in declaring that God is
unknowable. "If I knew Him I would be Him" remarked the sage
quoted by the 15th century Jewish theologian Joseph Albo.[1] Judging
by the experience of the most subtle of religious thinkers, the more
one reflects on the tremendous theme the more one is inclined to
reject all faltering human attempts to grasp the divine. Does this not
mean that the whole exercise is futile, that theology is doomed to
commit suicide by its very success? "For man may not see Me and
live" (Ex. 33 : 20).

There is much point to the objection and the theologian who
abandons his humility loses his vocation. Yet the theologian follows
respectable antecedents when he replies that his concern is chiefly
with God in manifestation, in His relationship with man, and this
can be discussed unless the theistic faith itself is ruled out of court.

If, for example, prayer is engaged in, it becomes quite legitimate to
ask what it is we are doing when we pray and which kinds of prayer
are valid, which invalid. Furthermore, the doctrine that God is
unknowable is itself a matter of human knowledge, arrived at by
those who hold it after rigorous and sustained thought, and therefore
is itself a thesis embraced by the term theology.

Maimonides' analysis[2] is relevant. Maimonides is very thorough-
going in his determination to dissociate from God anything belonging
to the human. Maimonides' theology is one of negation. One cannot

---

1. *Sefer Ha-Ikkarim*, II, 30, ed. Husik. p. 206. Albo quotes Jedaiah Bedersi: *Behinat
   Olam*, Chapter 24: "The sum total of what we know of Thee is that we do not
   know Thee". Husik, note 1, points to a similar observation in Saadia: *Beliefs and
   Opinions*, I, 4, Rosenblatt, p. 84. Saadia remarks that only the Creator can comprehend what *creatio ex nihilo* means and that therefore a demand by a creature
   for a demonstration of how this is possible is a demand for the creature to be the
   Creator. Husik, note 2, refers to Maimonides, *Guide* I, 59, who writes: "All men,
   those of the past and those of the future, affirm clearly that God, may He be
   exalted, cannot be apprehended by the intellects, and that none but He Himself
   can apprehend what He is, and that apprehension of Him consists in the inability
   to attain the ultimate term in apprehending Him. Thus all the philosophers say:
   We are dazzled by His beauty, and He is hidden from us because of the intensity
   with which He becomes manifest, just as the sun is hidden to eyes that are too
   weak to apprehend it".
2. *Guide*, I, 59.

say what God is—since by using human language to do this the human associations are bound to obscure the truth—but only what God is not. If that is the case, argues Maimonides, what difference is there between the complete ignoramus and the most refined religious thinker since both arrive at the conclusion that we cannot know God's essential nature? In terms of our discussion Maimonides is asking what is the purpose of theological study if it can never produce positive results.

The objection is stated by Maimonides this way (in Pines's translation): "Someone may ask and say: If there is no device leading to the apprehension of the true reality of His essence and if demonstration proves that it can only be apprehended that He exists and that it is impossible, as has been demonstrated, to ascribe to Him affirmative attributes, in what respect can there be superiority or inferiority between those who apprehend Him? If, however, there is none, *Moses our Master* and *Solomon* did not apprehend anything different from what a single individual among the pupils apprehends, and there can be no increase in this knowledge".

Basically Maimonides' reply amounts to this. To know more about what God is not, is itself a very significant increase in positive knowledge. The unsophisticated believer entertains crude beliefs about the nature of God, depicting Him as a colossal human being and the like. The task of theological thinking is to refine the God concept so that more and more is understood of how God is wholly other. This is the position of one of the most uncompromising defenders of a negative theology in the history of Jewish thought. Other theologians may be prepared to say rather more than Maimonides and to defend the legitimacy of using even positive attributes when speaking of God. But, in any event, the very point at issue is a theological one and discussion of the topic need not be fruitless.

So much for theology in general. Jewish theology embarks on the task of understanding more fully the significance of the Jewish religion. It draws on the particular insights of the Jewish teachers of the past.

A Jewish theology to be relevant must grapple with the problems raised by modern thought but it cannot ignore the systematic presentations of the mediaeval giants. (Before the mediaeval period there was much theological discussion but not *systematic* treatment of Jewish theology.) The most important of these are the following. (The initials E.T. after a title denote that an

English translation is available, the details of which are given in the
Bibliography.) The first great systematic Jewish theologian is Saadia Gaon.
His work *Emunot Ve-Deot* [*Beliefs and Opinions*] (E.T.) was written in
Arabic in 933 and has been translated into Hebrew. Bahya Ibn Joseph Ibn
Pakudah (probably first half of the 11th century) wrote his *Hovot Ha-Levavot*
(E.T.) [*Duties of the Heart*] in Arabic but the work was translated into
Hebrew. It is largely an ethico-religious treatise but deals with theology
especially in the first of its ten Gates: *Shaar Ha-Yihud* [*Gate of Unification*].
Judah Ha-Levi (d. after 1140) wrote his *Kuzari* (E.T.) as a defense of
Judaism and this work, too, was written in Arabic and translated into
Hebrew. Similarly, the Jewish Aristotelean thinker Abraham Ibn David
(c. 1110–c. 1180) wrote his *Emunah Ramah* [*Sublime Faith*] in Arabic and it was
translated into Hebrew. Practically all of Maimonides' (1135–1204) works
have theological import. The most important are his *Commentary to the
Mishnah*, his *Moreh Nevukhim* (E.T.) [*Guide for the Perplexed*] both written
in Arabic and translated into Hebrew, and his great Code written in
Hebrew *Yad Ha-Hazakah* [*The Strong Hand*] of which the first Book
especially considers theological topics. The boldest of the mediaeval
thinkers Levi b. Gershon, Gersonides (1288–1344) wrote his *Milhamot
Adonai* [*Wars of the Lord*] in Hebrew. The great critic of Aristotle, Hasdai
Crescas (1340–1416) wrote his *Or Adonai* [*Light of the Lord*] in Hebrew.
His pupil Joseph Albo (c. 1380–1435) wrote his *Sefer Ha-Ikkarim* (E.T.)
[*Book of the Principles*] in Hebrew.

If we delineate as one of the main tasks of Jewish theology the
thinking through of the Jewish religion so that its teachings cohere
with our present state of knowledge, this does not mean that we set
up the nebulous thing called modern thought as rival to Judaism, or
as a judge of it. Since the object of all theological investigation is God,
the Author of all that there is, it means quite simply that it will not do
to construct a theology based solely on the traditional sources. We
must also take into account the new knowledge which has accumu-
lated under God's guidance, especially where this runs counter to
statements in the traditional sources. Maimonides, for instance, can
hardly be ignored in any Jewish theological presentation but it would
be folly to attempt to swallow Maimonides whole including his
mediaevalism, his Aristotelian notions of science, for instance.

The contemporary Jewish theologian must endeavour, however,
inadequately, to do for our age what the great mediaeval theologians
sought to do for theirs. He must try to present a coherent picture of
what Jews can believe without subterfuge and with intellectual
honesty.

In addition to having contemporaneity, theology must be consistent. Whatever is said in one area must not contradict what is said in another. This is notoriously difficult in theology in general. It is especially difficult with regard to Jewish theology. A rich variety of views has come down to us from the past and many diverse views have been advocated by Jewish thinkers. It is, therefore, extremely tempting to quote from the Jewish sources without taking the necessary steps to determine whether the different views adopted are compatible. In all probability a degree of eclecticism cannot be avoided but the most strenuous efforts must be made in order to avoid a hopeless muddle. The maxim quoted by Solomon Schechter[3] that the best theology is that which is not consistent has some force. It serves as a warning against facile solutions to profound problems and as a reminder that we cannot fit God into any of our tidy schemes. If it is taken as justifying loose and woolly thinking in the area of religion it can easily lead to a glorification of the absurd and to a tacit admission that religion has nothing to do with truth. Holy nonsense is still nonsense. Even if the religious believer is ready to admit—as he must—that there are limits to human reasoning about the divine he must be capable of defending his position as a reasonable one and he must try to sketch the boundaries of his reasoning if he is to remain intelligible. A theology of silence is also a theology.

The pitfalls surrounding any attempt to construct a Jewish theology are numerous. No single person today can hope, for example, to acquire expertise in all the branches of Jewish thought ancient and modern. The linguistic equipment for this is alone daunting. Hebrew, Aramaic and the other ancient Semitic tongues are required for the understanding of the Bible and Rabbinic literature; Greek for Philo; Arabic for the mediaeval thinkers; German for much of the best that has been produced by modern Westernised thinkers; the languages of Asia for a correct assessment of the Far Eastern religions for comparative purposes; and one would have to add Latin for Aquinas and the other famous Christian theologians. Even if one relies on good translations the sobering fact remains that there is hardly any corner

---

3. *Studies in Judaism*, Vol. I. p. 231. Schechter's illustration is from Rabbinic views on retribution for sin. Retribution is taught so as to make man feel the responsibility of his actions but the principle is never carried so far as to deny the sufferer our sympathy. It can be doubted whether, in fact, this is evidence of inconsistency.

of these vast areas of human thought that has not been critically examined by diligent scholars ready to pounce, and with justification, on fatuous errors due to unfamiliarity with the material. If the theologian wishes his work to be contemporary he must, at the very least, also know something of what is being done today in astronomy, psychology, biophysics, para-psychology and many other subjects which impinge on his chosen subject. He must have an appreciation of scientific method and its aims; of the history of the modern world; of linguistic philosophy and its discussion of religious language. With regard to method the prospect is even more alarming. How does the theologian learn to tread the tightrope between smooth self-assurance and the timidity which refuses to express any but the most conventional views, between dogmatism and scepticism, between attraction for the novel and the startling and abject servility to the past, between hyper-criticism and blind loyalty? In the Jewish tradition even a Moses is compelled to bow to the wisdom of "For the task is too heavy for you; you cannot do it alone" (Ex. 18: 18). What, then, can be more presumptuous than to attempt to write a Jewish theology today?

What then is to be done? Can Judaism afford to encourage religious behaviourism by implying that it is right to practise Judaism but not to consider the beliefs which endow the observances with their significance? One of the most revealing features of Jewish life today is the keen interest in theological questions by many sensitive Jews who wish to know not alone what Judaism would have them do but what Judaism would have them believe.

The inescapable conclusion appears to be that work on theology by Jews should be encouraged but that those foolhardy enough to undertake it should declare their incompetence, not out of false modesty but because the subject demands nothing less. They should present their views as an invitation to others to consider, to criticise, to improve on, to challenge. At present the important thing is to get theology on the move once again in Jewish circles. Perhaps the name "theologian" is too grandiose for one who undertakes haltingly the re-examination of Jewish beliefs in the light of experience. Every writer on the subject can only repeat what the Jewish preachers of old were fond of saying when they faced squarely the question: Who am I to preach to others? They protested: I am speaking to myself. If others wish to overhear what I say I cannot object.

If there is a need for a Jewish theology in this century it is one that has
hardly been satisfied. There are, of course, many works on theological ideas
and on problems of Jewish faith in the modern world. One might
mention in particular: the writings of Martin Buber, Franz Rosenzweig,
Mordecai Kaplan, Ignaz Maybaum and A. J. Heschel; Milton Steinberg's
Anatomy of Faith; Ever Since Sinai by Jacob J. Petuschoswski and the other
writings of this thinker; *Foundations of Faith* by Simon Greenberg;
Arthur A. Cohen: *The Natural and the Supernatural Jew*; Emil L. Fackenheim:
Quest for Past and Future; Leon Roth: *Judaism*; Will Herberg: *Judaism and
Modern Man*; Samuel Belkin: *Essays in Traditional Jewish Thought* and
In His Image; J. B. Agus: *Guideposts to Modern Judaism*; Robert Gordis:
Judaism for the Modern Age; Samuel S. Cohon: *Theology Lectures*; Richard
L. Rubenstein: *After Auschwitz* and *The Religious Imagination*. Special
reference should be made to the following symposia on Jewish belief:
A Treasury of Tradition ed. Lamm and Wurzburger; *Rediscovering Judaism;
Reflections on a New Jewish Theology* ed. Arnold J. Wolf; *Varieties of Jewish
Belief* ed. Ira Eisenstein; *The Condition of Jewish Belief*, a symposium
compiled by the editors of *Commentary* magazine. The *Commentary*
symposium consists of the replies by Rabbis and theologians of the
Orthodox, Conservative and Reform groups in the United States to a list
of questions which in essence are as follows: (1) In what sense do you
believe the Torah to be divine revelation? (2) In what sense do you believe
that the Jews are the chosen people of God? (3) Is Judaism the one true
religion? (4) Does Judaism as a religion entail any particular political viewpoint? (5) Does the "God is dead" question have any relevance to
Judaism? The quote on the jacket blurb of the *Commentary* symposium
from Milton Himmelfarb's Introduction is highly significant: "Historically,
some Jewries were more theological than others. The more advanced the
culture they lived in and the more vigorous its philosophical life, the
more they had to theologise. Mediaeval Spanish Judaism was more
theological than Franco-German Judaism, Maimonides more than Rashi.
In these terms, we live in Spanish and not Franco-German conditions,
and we too need theology. *How much? More, I would say, than we are getting*"
(*italics* mine). The works treating this scheme systematically and comprehensively can be counted on one hand. M. Friedländer's *The Jewish
Religion* is elementary and not a little naive. Morris Joseph's *Judaism as
Creed and Life* is more sophisticated and contains a good deal of material
in a well-presented manner. Both these works are very "Victorian" in
outlook and are now dated. Leo Baeck's *The Essence of Judaism* is justly
celebrated but ponderous and rather vague. Isidore Epstein's *The Faith of
Judaism* is attractively written. It surveys Jewish beliefs from the strictly
Orthodox point of view but is inadequate in coping with the challenges
presented, for example, by historical criticism. The standard work on the
whole theme is Kaufmann Kohler's *Jewish Theology*. This and Samuel S.
Cohon's *Jewish Theology* are the only two works with this title. Kohler's
book is a splendid pioneering effort and is indispensable for the study of the

subject but is heavily coloured by Protestant thought in the period when
the book was compiled. The same applies more or less to Cohon's book.
More recently Eugene B. Borowitz has published his *A New Jewish Theology
in the Making* but this, while very helpful as regards the problems of theological
method, is not a systematic treatment of Jewish theology. While various
topics in the field are treated in the companion volume, *How Can A Jew
Speak of Faith Today*, these must be considered preliminary investigations
rather than a coherent account of Judaism. Solomon Schechter's *Aspects
of Rabbinic Theology* is essential reading for the understanding of the
thought of the Talmudic Rabbis on theological themes but it is almost
entirely a purely historical study with hardly any emphasis on Jewish theology
for the present. The same applies to the splendid, *The Sages, Their Concepts
and Beliefs* (Heb.) by Ephraim E. Urbach. Montefiore and Loewe's *A
Rabbinic Anthology*, on the other hand, does contain many notes on debates
by the editors of contemporary theological significance. On the general
theme the articles *Theology* by J. Z. Lauterbach (*Jewish Encyclopedia*,
Vol. XII, pp. 128–137) and Samuel S. Cohon (*Universal Jewish Encyclopedia*,
Vol. 10, pp. 242–244) should be consulted.

The detailed topics with which a Jewish theology should be concerned are: the Jewish approach to God and how this differs from the
approaches of other religions; the relationship between God and
man; the meaning and significance of worship; the doctrine of
reward and punishment; the doctrines of the Messiah and the Hereafter; the idea of the Chosen People and the theological implications
of the State of Israel; the problem of evil; the question of divine
providence and miracles; in short all those topics which have to do
with Jewish belief in contradistinction to Jewish practice. A work on
Jewish theology will consequently be more limited than a work on
Judaism as a whole. Its concern will be with Judaism as a religion.
Naturally, however, other aspects of Judaism will find their
place in such a work insofar as they are relevant to the central
theme.

The question of dogma in Judaism about which so much has been
written can be evaded by Jewish theology only by being untrue to
its aim. The author of a Jewish theology ought to describe which
Jewish beliefs, as he sees it, are both Jewish and true. The difficult
question of what the Jewish dogmas are has been studied historically
in the remarkable essay by Solmon Schechter entitled: *The Dogmas
of Judaism*.[4] Schechter is surely right when he observes: "Political

4. *Studies in Judaism*, Vol. I, pp. 147–181. Schechter's note should be consulted for
   a full bibliography on the subject.

economy, hygiene, statistics, are very fine things. But no sane man would make for them those sacrifices which Judaism requires from us. It is only for God's sake, to fulfil His commands and to accomplish His purpose, that religion becomes worth living and dying for. And this can only be possible with a religion which possesses dogmas". True, yet it is a pity that Schechter did not feel it to be within his terms of reference to consider what these dogmas are for the modern Jew. It is essential to take up the matter from where Schechter left off and it is here that a modern Jewish theology can come into its own. The topic will be treated directly as we proceed.

The following are the principles of the Jewish faith as drawn up by different thinkers. Maimonides in his *Commentary to the Mishnah*, Sanh. 10: 1 has 13 principles (these became the foremost of the Jewish creeds): (1) Belief in the existence of God; (2) God's unity, (3) His incorporeality, (4) His eternity, (5) God alone is to be worshipped, (6) Prophecy, (7) Moses is the greatest of the prophets, (8) The Torah was given by God to Moses, (9) The Torah is immutable, (10) God knows the thoughts and deeds of men, (11) Reward and Punishment, (12) The Messiah, (13) The Resurrection. Simon b. Zemah Duran (1361–1444): *Magen Avot* end of Introduction p. 2b: (1) The Existence of God, (2) The Torah is divine, (3) Reward and Punishment. Abba Mari b. Moses of Lunel (d.c. 1250) in his *Minhat Kenaot*, Chapters 4f, pp. 7f: (1) Belief in God, (2) Creation of the world by God, (3) Providence. Joseph Albo: *Ikkarim* (the book as a whole): (1) The existence of God, (2) The Torah is divine, (3) Reward and Punishment. Isaac Arama (c. 1420–1494) in *Akedat Yitzhak*, Gate 55: (1) *Creatio ex nihilo*, (2) Revelation, (3) The World· to Come. The Spanish Theologian, hostile to philosophy, Joseph Jabez (15th–16th century) in his *Maamar Ha-Ahdut* states that there are 3 principles: (1) The Unity of God, (2) Providence, (3) That in the future all men will acknowledge His unity. (Schechter op. cit. p. 173, gives them incorrectly as: *Creatio ex nihilo*, Individual Providence and the Unity of God). Moses b. Joseph di Trani (called *Mabit*, 1505–1585) in his *Bet Elohim, Shaar Ha-Yesodot*, follows Maimonides that there are 13 principles but observes that these are all embraced by 3 main principles: (1) The existence of God, (2) The Torah is from Heaven, (3) Providence = Reward and Punishment. Isaac Abarbanel (1437–1508) in his *Rosh Amanah*, Chapter 23, argues that there are no special principles of the faith but that every part of the Torah is of equal value. The same view is adopted by David b. Solomon Ibn Abi Zimra (1479–1573) in his *Responsa*, No. 344. Reference might here be made to the Samaritan Creed (see John Macdonald: *The Theology of the Samaritans*, I, 6, pp. 49–55): (1) One God, (2) Moses, (3) The Law, (4) The Holy mount of Gerizim, (5) Judgement Day, e.g. in the Defter (The Samaritan Liturgy): "My Lord, we shall never worship any but Thee, nor have we any faith but in Thee and in Moses Thy prophet, and in Thy true Scriptures and in the place of worshipping Thee, Mount Gerizim, Bethel, the mount of rest and of the divine presence, and in the Day of Vengeance and Recompense".

It has been argued, however, that Judaism is opposed to theology on two grounds. The first of these is because Jewish thinking in its classical and formative periods—those of the Bible and the Rabbinic literature—was "organic" rather than systematic,[5] a response to particular concrete situations rather than a comprehensive account of what religious belief entails. Secondly, the emphasis in Judaism is on action, on doing the will of God not on defining it. There is truth in both these contentions but it is far from the whole truth. A concern with systematic thinking about Judaism did not emerge until Greek modes had made their impact upon the Jewish teachers. Once this had happened sustained reflection on the nature of the Jewish faith was seen as an imperative, at least in those circles which experienced the full force of the collision. Unless Philo of Alexandria, Saadia, Bahya, Maimonides, Gersonides, Crescas and Albo among the ancient and mediaeval thinkers; Cordovero and Luria, R. Schneor Zalman of Liady and R. Hayim of Volozhyn among the Kabbalists; and, in modern times, Moses Mendelssohn, Schechter, Rabbi Kook, Kaufmann Kohler, Buber, Rosenzweig and Leo Baeck; are to be read out of Judaism, theology is a legitimate pursuit for Jews. Indeed if the example of such outstanding Jewish thinkers is followed, the attempt to work out a theology for our age as they did for theirs is more than a reluctant dispensation. As they saw, and frequently maintained, a refined, intellectually respectable faith is the only one possible for men who have been trained to apply their reason in other areas of human life.[6] One can understand, though disagree with the secular Jewish nationalist when he pronounces on the un-Jewish nature of theological thinking. His interest is in the Jewish culture and ethics and he has no need for the God hypothesis. But it is curious what happens when Jewish religious teachers roundly make this declaration. First they say that Judaism has no theology and many of them

5. The best statement of Rabbinic Judaism as "organic" is to be found in the words of Max Kadushin, see especially his: *The Rabbinic Mind*. Kadushin adds further subtleties but these are not our concern.
6. Bahya Ibn Pakudah: *Duties of the Heart, Shaar Ha-Yihud*, Chapter 2, quotes with approval the saying of "a philosopher" that only the prophet, who knows God intuitively, and the philosopher, whose ideas about God have been refined in the crucible of his thought, worship God. All others worship something other than God.

proceed to state in detail what it is that Judaism would have us believe —generally, the acceptance as infallible truth of every traditional view. A good case can be made out for reliance on tradition or experience rather than reason on the basic issues of belief in God but if such a position is argued for it is theology that is being done. If, however, all that is implied in the rejection of Jewish theology is that the mediaeval thinkers were too much influenced by Greek and Arabic thought, this might be conceded. Nonetheless, our age has both produced new insights and recaptured some old ones (such as the Biblical) and these must become part of an adequate Jewish theology for today.

One of the quotes frequently heard nowadays in the accusation that theology is un-Jewish is from the Midrash: "God said: Would that they had forsaken Me and kept My Torah".[7] Needless to say this is a misquotation. The Midrash clearly does not wish to imply that God wants us not to think about Him. The meaning is rather that God is prepared, as it were, to settle for uninformed, self-seeking observance of the Torah because, such is the spiritual power of the Torah, even this will eventually lead Israel to Him. As the passage from this Midrash concludes: "The light she (the Torah) contains will restore them to the good".

Nor is it true that theology is a harmless but irrelevant pastime, a luxury we can ill afford in our age when so many practical problems press in on us. Even on purely pragmatic grounds theology is important, because how Jews lead their lives depends on how they conceive of the purpose of their existence. "Show me a man's philosophy", said Chesterton, "and I'll show you the man". Is it not correct, for instance, that all the divisions among religious Jews on the scope and obligation of Jewish observances depend ultimately on differing views regarding a basic theological question, the meaning of revelation?

Rabbi Solomon Goldman expressed many years ago, in a commencement address to young Rabbis,[8] a mistrust of theology that is typical of many of its Jewish opponents. There are profoundly committed Jews whose concern it is to preserve the unity of the Jewish

---

7. Jer. Talmud, Hag. 1: 7; Lam. R. Introduction 2. M. Friedländer: *The Jewish Religion*, p. 3, note 1, quotes this and, with very dubious historical warrant, paraphrases it as: "theologians would do better if they were less eager to investigate into the essence of God and His attributes and were more anxious to study and to do God's commandments".

8. *The Function of the Rabbi* in *Crisis and Decision*, pp. 79–99.

people and fear too much theology as a divisive force. Goldman writes:[9] "We will, friends, be wholly within the spirit of Jewish tradition if we are more concerned with how men live than with what they believe. It is more important that you be concerned with details than with generalities, with *Mizvot* than with *Ani Maamins*". But of which Jewish tradition is Goldman speaking? Certainly not that of Bahya Ibn Pakudah, for instance, who deplored the very emphasis which Goldman advocates. Bahya's "Duties of the Heart" (the title of his famous book) cover all the inner life of man and these are considered "in detail" and are upheld by Bahya as supreme *Mitzvot*. How can one be concerned only with the details of Jewish life unless one has a philosophy of Judaism? Goldman himself seems to be aware of the problem when he admits:[10] "I do not want to be misunderstood. Mine is not the temper to belittle the value of earnest speculative thought. I do not seek to eliminate metaphysics from our preoccupations. You do not belong to the society of men if you are not questing for certainty. You are what the cabbalists called *pagum* or defective if you do not every so often ascend the philosopher's ivory tower to seek the lever that will balance the Cosmos. I speak only of the delusion and conceit which assume that what is spiritually satisfying and intellectually convincing to oneself must needs become the cornerstone for all".

As a warning against over-confidence Goldman, and those who think like him, is worth listening to. In any event the theologian ought not be concerned to seek his lever in the philosopher's ivory tower but in Judaism as he seeks to co-ordinate its teachings and establish coherence between them and what he and others feel to be true. The dangers of pride and dogmatism should act as a check to theological smugness. They ought not to frustrate theology itself.

So much for the objection that theology is un-Jewish. It is impossible, however, for a work on theology to proceed without recognising that theological thinking, together with metaphysics in general, has been subjected to a severe hammering in the second third of this century. This has come from linguistic analysis on the one hand and from existentialism on the other. Many linguistic philosophers, especially in Great Britain and the United States, have become extremely suspicious of theological formulations. Theological

9. See *supra* p. 87–88.
10. Pp. 85–86.

language they declare to be frequently meaningless and its problems only pseudo-problems. The contemporary theologian, if he is wise, will heed their demand that he show how his statements are to be "cashed". The need for precision in language and the avoidance of obscurity are requisites for any theological presentation. The tendency of some continental theologians to reject clear, easily understood words in favour of a high-flown vocabulary which only darkens counsel is extremely unfortunate. The discussion of profound matters is hampered not assisted when carried out in a ponderous, elusive style. (On the Jewish theological scene, it is sad to record, Buber, Rosenzweig and Leo Baeck are especially guilty on this score.) As has been said in this connection, one does not have to be fat in order to drive fat oxen.

The existentialists, even (perhaps one should say especially) the religious existentialists, tend to scorn theology as so much "cosmic talk" with no relevance to the religious and spiritual predicament of the individual desperately searching for that which is true for him. Man needs God, it is claimed, as the living heart of his faith not talk about Him as a pleasant intellectual exercise. But the search for truth is also an important part of a man's life and he can engage in this, too, with passion. Religious existentialists write books to put forward their point of view; they defend their philosophy against attack, they argue for existentialism as a valid outlook; and, insofar as they do these things, they, too, are doing theology. To say, as some of them do, that it is pointless to consider ultimate reality apart from man's involvement in it is in itself to make a significant statement about ultimate reality.

Every attempt at constructing a Jewish theology must face up to the problem of methodology. The materials for the construction are the teachings about God and His relationship to man contained in the Bible and extended, elaborated on and interpreted in the Rabbinic literature, in post-Talmudic thought down to the present day, and in the living experience of the Jewish people throughout the ages. The central methodological problem is that of discrimination. Not everything that has come down to us from the past is durable. For instance, Maimonides (a thinker who, as we have already emphasised, must on any showing have a voice in any Jewish theological scheme) solemnly rules[11] that if Jewish authorities enjoy the power to do so various

11. *Yad, Avodah Zarah* 10: 1; *Rotzeah* 4: 10.

types of unbelievers are to be deprived of their lives. The whole temper of our times based on sounder knowledge of the horrors to which religious intolerance can lead and a deeper respect for individual conscience is against Maimonides who was a child of his day in this and in other mediaeval attitudes he firmly adopted. Even the strictly Orthodox compilers of the latest Talmudic Encyclopaedia (*Encyclopedia Talmudit*] currently being published in Israel record the views of Orthodox Rabbis that these rules have had their day[12] either because this is not the way to win souls nowadays or because the old type of unbeliever is no more. Historical investigations into the nature of Judaism have revealed that it is a developing faith, influenced at every step in its growth by the ideas and cultural patterns of the various civilisations with which Jews came into contact. The result is that contradictions abound in the traditional sources, to the extent that matters some teachers consider to be essential to Judaism others consider inessential or even harmful. Saadia Gaon[13] rejects the doctrine of the transmigration of souls while for the Kabbalists it is a basic Jewish doctrine.[14]

The criteria for determining which beliefs are to be embraced by a Jewish theology and which rejected can only be those of consistency within the tradition and coherence with the rest of our knowledge. Where there are contradictions in the traditional sources the contemporary Jewish theologian must try to decide which of the views is closest to the spirit of the tradition as a whole, no easy task to be sure. Where there are contradictions between traditional formulations and more recent views he must try to decide which is closest to the truth, an even more difficult exercise. Obviously there will be a degree of agnosticism in areas where a simple decision for or against is ruled out by the nature of the problem. Equally obvious will be the strong element of subjectivity in the presentation and at times of arbitrariness. Provided all this is frankly acknowledged—and the theologian is content to call his essay *a* Jewish theology not *the* Jewish theology—no great harm is done. Speculation has its place. Theology can and should be a creative endeavour. The historian of the Jewish religion tells us what it is that Jews believed in former ages. The task

---

12. Article *Apikoros*, Vol. 2, p. 137 *cf.* Samuel Morell: *The Halachic Status of the Non-Halachic Jew* in *Judaism*, Fall, 1969.
13. *Beliefs and Opinions*. VI, Chapter 8.
14. See Manasseh b. Israel: *Nishmat Hayim*, IV, Chapters 6–16.

of the theologian is to draw on the findings of the historian but to ask what it is that Jews can believe today. Since his material will be culled from Jewish sources the resulting edifice will succeed in providing a Jewish spiritual home for some. It will almost certainly fail to provide a home for those with different theological approaches and these will be called upon to construct a more suitable dwelling for themselves out of the same raw materials.

At the centre of any Jewish theology is the doctrine of God. This traditional Jewish view is nowadays called *theism*. Whether, as Y. Kaufmann maintains[15] the doctrine of the one God erupted spontaneously in ancient Israel or whether as a majority of scholars hold,[16] there can be detected in the Bible a gradual evolution from polytheism through henotheism to pure monotheism, is a matter for Biblical research to decide. The relevant factor for the Jewish theologian is that theistic belief became the unqualified Jewish belief held by all believing Jews. *Theism* is the doctrine that God is both transcendent and immanent. He is in the universe and involved in all its processes but He is also beyond the universe. If there were no universe there would still be God. But without God there could be no universe. *Theism* involves the rejection as untrue of: *deism*, the doctrine that God is only transcendent; *pantheism*, that God is wholly immanent; *polytheism*, that there are many gods; *dualism*, that there are two gods, one good the other evil; *atheism*, that there is no God; and *agnosticism*, that man by his nature cannot know whether or not there is a God. Traditional *theism* says of God that He exists, that He is one, that He is both transcendent and immanent, that He is omnipotent, that He is omniscient, that He is eternal, that He is the Creator of the universe, and that He is wholly good. All these ideas are either explicit in the picture regarding God which emerges eventually in classical Judaism or would seem to follow from reflection on the significance and nature of that picture. Each of them requires further study for its detailed meaning and for whether it can be qualified in some way, if necessary, and yet remain Jewish doctrine. A work on Jewish theology must address itself to these themes.

The Jewish theologian accepts as the basis of all his work the belief that God exists. He must say something about how he has arrived at

15. *The Religion of Israel*. This point is the continuing theme of the whole work.
16. A comprehensive survey of the whole problem is H. H. Rowley's *Moses and Monotheism* in *From Moses to Qumran*, Chapter 2, pp. 35–63.

his sense of conviction but *qua* theologian he is not called upon to engage in the different discipline known as the philosophy of religion. As a believer in God the theologian must try to convey what he understands to be the content of this belief. In the remainder of this chapter, then, the question of God's existence will be discussed. But it must be repeated that the theologian has attained to a belief in God because this seems to him to be the most satisfactory philosophy of human existence in terms of whatever experience he has of life and truth. He begins his work with the traditional affirmation:[17] "I believe with perfect faith that the Creator, blessed be His name, is the Author and Guide of everything that has been created, and that He alone has made, does make, and will make all things", though his own formulation of what is implied may differ in some respects from this particular one.

This kind of avowal will no doubt disappoint some prospective readers who wish to turn to books of this nature for an undeniable demonstration that God exists. The theologian can only reply that his work is undertaken with a different aim in mind. It is not his purpose to convert the non-believer but to try to give to the believer an account of what it is that he believes. The hypothetical believer addressed includes, of course, the poor theologian himself. Yet the non-believer may gain an idea of what belief properly involves. Often it turns out, his non-belief is shared by the believer for Judaism does not affirm much nonsense that people take it to. Hence it may turn out that though this book is not written to persuade, the supposed non-believer may be more within the circle of faith than he has thought.

Some religious thinkers, both mediaeval and modern, have found the statement "God exists" to be offensive.[18] To say that someone exists is to imply that he might not have existed. It is to treat him as one of the many beings in the universe whom it is possible to conceive of as not having existence. Thus, it is possible to think of the universe itself as not having come into existence. But God, in Tillich's phrase, is *being-itself*. It is impossible to imagine *being-itself* as not existing.

17. *Singer's Prayer Book*, p. 93.
18. See the discussion in Albo: *Sefer Ha-Ikkarim*, II, 30 and Paul Tillich's statement (*Systematic Theology*, Vol. I, p. 227): "God does not exist. He is being-itself beyond essence and existence. Therefore, to argue that God exists, is to deny him".

For thinkers who argue in this way it is as absurd to say that God exists as to say that God has died or is blind. Whatever meaning we give to the word "God" it must by definition imply (or, at least, most people who use the word would hold it to imply) that He is the Being who cannot die. He is the one for whom terms with human associations like death and blindness are totally inapplicable. But all this is to make rather heavy weather of what most people readily understand. Neither believers nor unbelievers generally take "God exists" to be a description of God's nature but an affirmation that the term "God" has a reference, that there really is a God, that He is not a figment of the imagination.

In the history of theism there are four different ways to faith in God, ways by means of which men have attained to complete and utter conviction that God is.[19] These are: (1) the way of reason, in which proofs are offered for God's existence; (2) the way of experience, the mystical approach, in which God is directly apprehended; (3) the existentialist "leap of faith", in which man opts for belief in God as a personal decision; (4) the way of tradition, in which a man follows the theistic beliefs of predecessors to whom, they claim, God revealed Himself.

The attempt to prove God's existence by rational demonstration goes back to Plato[20] (although his proof was for deity, conceived of in pluralistic terms, not for the God of traditional theism).[21] This approach to faith was followed by Philo of Alexandria[22] and was popular among the mediaeval thinkers, Christian, Islamic and Jewish. The three main "arguments" or "proofs" for the existence of God are: (1) The *ontological*, invented by St. Anselm of Canterbury, in which the very definition of God as the most perfect being embraces His existence, since an existing being is more perfect than a non-existing being. (2) The *cosmological*, in which God's existence is affirmed as the only explanation of why things *are*. God is the Cause of causes, the Prime Mover. (3) The *teleological*, or *argument from* (or "to") *design*, in which the order evident in the universe points to a Designing Mind. Two further arguments advanced in more recent times are: the *moral argument*, in which God is affirmed as the ground of the moral

19. These are considered in detail in my book *Faith*.
20. *The Laws*. Book X.
21. See Walter Kaufmann: *Critique of Religion and Philosophy*, pp. 137–139.
22. *Legum Allegoria*, III, 32, pp. 367–369; *De Fuga et Inventione*, 2, p. 17; *De Specialibus Legibus*, I, 6, p. 119.

life, as the only explanation of the idea of duty; and the *argument from religious experience*, in which God is affirmed as the only explanation of the widely attestated experiences of the mystics and other men who have had religious experiences in which they have claimed to have been in contact with a transcendental reality.[23]

The mediaeval thinkers had no doubts regarding the capacity of the arguments to do what they set out to do, prove the existence of God. To be sure some mediaeval Jewish thinkers were suspicious of the attempt to arrive at God's existence by means of the unaided human reason when faith by tradition was available. The debate really centred on the question of which way—that of tradition or of reason—was the more secure. The traditionalists pointed to the notorious capacity of the human mind to fall into error. Once give reason its head, they argued, and men might mistakenly be led by it into doubt. The exponents of the way of reason countered that the opposite is true. The man who relies solely on tradition will always be haunted by the fear that the tradition might be wrong, whereas the way of reason was sure, convincing and free from all subsequent doubt. But both the traditionalists and reasoners were basically agreed that, leaving aside the question of failure to attain the truth, the way of reason, if properly followed, did lead to God. If only man used his reason correctly it could prove to him that God exists. To this day it seems to be the official view of the Roman Catholic Church that it is not only necessary for man to believe in God but necessary for him to believe that the existence of God is capable of rational demonstration. That this whole view has been severely challenged in modern times is due to the thinking of the philosophers Hume and Kant.[24]

Hume's critique of the cosmological argument is based on his empirical approach. He argues that we have no right to conclude from our observations of what we call cause and effect that *effect B*

23. The literature on the proofs for God's existence is immense. A good selection from the thinkers for and against and a comprehensive bibliography is provided in *The Existence of God* edited by John Hick.

24. Hume's works on religion are: *The Natural History of Religion; Dialogues Concerning Natural Religion; An Enquiry Concerning Human Understanding.* Useful is Richard Wollheim's *Hume on Religion.* Kant's main works on religion are: *Critique of Pure Reason; Critique of Practical Reason.* The important sections of these are given in Caldecott and Mackintosh: *Selections from the Literature of Theism,* pp. 179–255. A useful small book on the arguments of Hume, Kant and others is Ninian Smart's *Philosophers and Religious Truth.*

must follow on cause *A*, only that in all the cases investigated *B does* follow *A*. Consequently, all we can say about causes and their effects are in terms of our observations regarding the relationship between things in the universe. To speak of a cause of the universe itself would mean that we have observed a number of universes to discover that effect *B* always follows on cause *A*, which is patently absurd. Therefore, there is no meaning to the question: What is the cause of the universe? Hume's critique of the teleological argument is based on the evidence there is of lack of design we would expect if it had Supreme Mind as its Author.

Kant's critique is based on his theory of knowledge. On Kant's view human reasoning is the tool we have for seeing the world in the relationship between its various parts. The human mind coordinates the impressions it receives through the senses and gives these form. We can never know the *noumena*—as things are in themselves, only the *phenomena*—the impressions we receive of them. Consequently, the human mind is not endowed with the capacity to discover by pure reason the truth about that which is beyond the universe, beyond the phenomena. It follows that the attempt to invoke God as the explanation of the universe is bound to fail. Kant does, however, believe that man's "practical reason" must convince him of God's existence since otherwise the sense of duty and obligation would have no ground. Kant therefore rejects the cosmological and teleological proofs (and also finds the ontological proof unsatisfactory) but does accept a version of the moral argument.

Even after Hume and Kant some thinkers down to the present day still treat the traditional arguments for the existence of God with respect and have tried to defend them against the critics. But for the majority of thinkers all confidence has departed that proofs can be found for the existence of God. Religious existentialists, from Kierkegaard onwards, far from being dismayed at the prospect, have rejoiced in it. In a famous saying of Kant, knowledge is denied in order to make room for faith. Kierkegaard considered it a gross impertinence to try to prove God's existence much as it would be if someone addressing a king on his throne stopped to prove that the king existed.[25] Recent works on the philosophy of religion generally

25. *Concluding Unscientific Postscript*, p. 485.

take great pains to examine all the arguments, including the existentialist approach, with great subtlety. They have added many
criticisms and refinements. The result has been a strengthening faith
for some minds. However, in general it must be said that there has
been an abandonment of the mediaeval confidence that anyone who
has the intellectual capacity and the mental stamina can demonstrate
that God exists.

The way of faith most typical of Judaism is the way of tradition.
The Jew is one who is either born into or adopts of his own free choice
a community which has constantly made sense of its existence and
survival in terms of a God-given guidance. Ultimately the Jewish
believer opts for God in complete conviction that this belief makes
sense of human life with all its difficulties in a way in which no other
philosophy does. It was on the basis of this, for example, that Judah
Ha-Levi begins his argument for faith. He does not argue for God
as Creator of the world but as the Deliverer of Israel from Egyptian
bondage.[26]

Jewish theology, then, starts with an affirmation that God is. It
proceeds to examine in detail what this entails in terms of human
beliefs and demands on human life, seeking always to set forth the
ideas of the great Jewish thinkers of the past but examining these
critically as well as analytically so that they can provide an adequate
philosophy of Jewish belief to be embraced by Jews today.

26. *Kuzari*, I, 10–13.

CHAPTER TWO

THE UNITY OF GOD

"HEAR, O Israel! The Lord our God, the Lord is One" (Deut. 6: 4). This, the *Shema* ("Hear"), is the great text of monotheism. For over two thousand years it has been recited twice daily by devout Jews. The Jewish child is taught the verse as soon as he can learn to speak. The Jew repeats it on his death-bed if he is able to utter any sound at all. The Jewish martyrs recited it as they made ready to give their lives for their faith. It has been throughout the ages the most powerful single declaration of the significance of the Jewish religion. Of later and lesser use in the liturgy but of similar import is the verse: "And the Lord shall be King over all the earth; In that day shall the Lord be One, and His name one" (Zech. 14: 9).

What is the meaning of the word "One" (Hebrew *ehad*) in Deuteronomy? In the first instance it means one and not many and is therefore a denial of polytheism. There is only one God and there are no others. Allied to this is the idea that God in His essence is indivisible. A deity like Baal could be split up, as it were, into various local deities, hence the plural form Baalim and Ashterot found in the Bible when speaking of the pagan gods. God is one and indivisible. He is Lord of all. He cannot be united syncretistically with other gods.

But there is a second meaning to the word "One". The Hebrew *ehad* can also mean "unique", the *one* unlike any other. If this is the idea contained in the *Shema* its significance is that God is different from all that men name as gods. He alone possesses the attributes of deity. He is totally different from all His creatures so that no creature can be compared with Him. "To whom then will ye liken Me, that I should be equal? saith the Holy One" (Is. 40: 25). This second meaning —of uniqueness—is really implied in the first. Monotheism is not a mere mathematical reduction of gods until only one is left. Monotheism does not simply affirm that there is, as a matter of fact, only one God although theoretically there might have been more than one. It teaches that the proper understanding of what "God" means can only result in the belief that there *can* only be one God. The polytheistic deities were thought of as separate beings, frequently in conflict with one another, each having a part of the universe for his or her domain. Monotheism denies the existence of such beings. There is only one Supreme Being who is Lord of all that there is. To speak of the possibility of the existence of more than one Supreme Being would be to talk nonsense for then none of the suggested beings would be supreme. The uniqueness of God is implied in the very term "God" as monotheism uses it. In this sense certainly it is correct to adopt Tillich's formulation that God is not *a* being among others but *being-itself*.[1]

To repeat what has been said in the previous chapter,[2] whether these ideas erupted in ancient Israel spontaneously or whether there can be traced in the Biblical record a gradual evolution from polytheism through henotheism to pure monotheism, is a matter for Biblical scholarship. Theology is concerned with what eventually emerged as the monotheistic idea. In any event in the Bible and in the Rabbinic literature monotheism is not speculative, that is to say, the implications of what can be subsumed under the heading of the unity of God was not fully explored in a systematic way. Reflection on what is implied in pure monotheism was reserved for the mediaeval period in Jewish religious thought. Before proceeding to an examination of the mediaeval thinkers we must first examine, however, what were felt to be the two great challenges to Jewish monotheism in the Rabbinic period—Zoroastrian dualism and Christianity.[3]

The great struggle against polytheism, begun in the Bible, continued right down through the Rabbinic period. The Talmud is full of detailed rules aimed against *avodah zarah*, "strange worship" = idolatry. However, the main intellectual challenge to monotheism was the Persian doctrine that there are two Gods—Ormuzd, the god

---

1. On the meaning of "One" in the *Shema* see especially S. R. Driver's analysis in his *Deuteronomy*, pp. 89–91. The date of Deuteronomy is generally considered to be earlier than the reforms of Josiah in 621 B.C.E. *Cf.* the Hebrew article *Ahdut ha-elohim* by Isaac Heinemann in *Encyclopedia Mikrait*, Vol. I, pp. 202–205.
2. See *supra* p. 15.
3. For the Rabbinic statements on the unity of God see Israel Konovitz's anthology: *Ha-Elohut, Chapter 2*, pp. 9–15.

of goodness and light, and Ahriman, the god of evil and darkness.[4]
It is possible that Deutero-Isaiah preaches against Persian dualism:

> "That they may know from the rising of the sun,
> and from the west,
> That there is none beside Me;
> I am the Lord, and there is none else;
> I form the light, and create darkness;
> I make peace, and create evil;
> I am the Lord, that doeth all these things"
>
> (Is. 45: 6–7)

It is probable that Persian dualism had, in fact, an influence on
Jewish thought in the emergence of the doctrine of Satan, though in
Rabbinic thought Satan is completely subordinate to God and is in
no way a real rival to Him.[5] At a later period the Sassanian dynasty
(211–640 C.E.) made Zoroastrianism the State religion. Since the rule
of this dynasty largely coincided with the activities of the Babylonian
Amoraim it is not surprising that in the Babylonian Talmud in
particular there are many references to the dualistic challenge.

A few examples may here be adduced of the struggle against
dualism as expressed in the Rabbinic literature.[6] The Rabbinic term
for dualism is *shete reshuyot*, "two powers" or "two authorities" i.e.
two gods in control of the world. The Sifre to Deuteronomy 32: 39:
"See now that I, even I, am He, and there is no god with Me" comments: "If anyone says that there are two powers in Heaven the
retort is given to him: 'There is no god with Me'".[7] In another passage
a refutation of the "two powers" doctrine is given from the fact that
when God said: "I am the Lord thy God" (Ex. 20: 2) who protested?[8]
The Mishnah[9] rules that if a man says in his prayers "We acknowledge
Thee, we acknowledge Thee" (i.e. he repeats the formula *modim
anahnu lakh*) he is to be silenced. While the Mishnah does not state

4. See article *Zoroastrianism* in Hastings' *Encyclopedia of Religion and Ethics*, Vol. XII,
  pp. 862–868 and G. F. Moore: *History of Religions*, Vol. I, pp. 357–405.
5. See article *Satan* in *Jewish Encyclopedia*, Vol. XI, pp. 68–71 and *infra* pp. 129–131.
6. See G. F. Moore: *Judaism*, Vol. I, p. 367 and Vol. II, pp. 115–116.
7. *Sifre*, 329; *Yalkut*, 946.
8. *Mekhilta, Ba-Hodesh.* 5.
9. *Ber.* 5: 3; *Meg.* 4: 9.

the reason this is given in the Gemara that it appears as if he acknowledges "two powers".[10] In a curious passage[11] it is said that Elisha b.
Abuyah who became a Jewish sectarian, was misled when he saw the
high angel Metatron[12] and believed that there were "two powers".

On this whole question of dualism in the Rabbinic period G. F.
Moore has well said:[13] "The difficulty of reconciling the evils of the
world with the goodness of God was so strongly felt in the early
centuries of our era in the East and the West, and a dualistic solution
of one kind or another was so widely accepted in philosophy and
religion, that it is idle to attempt to identify the Jewish circles which
accepted this solution. It must suffice that we know there were such
circles; that they tried to fortify their position with texts of Scripture;
and that the rabbis refuted them with their own weapons.[14] It is
certain also that, whatever leanings there may have been in this
direction, Judaism, with its inveterate monotheism, was not rent by
dualistic heresies as Christianity was for centuries".

Dualistic traces did, indeed, linger on in the doctrines of Satan and
Metatron and in the Kabbalistic views on the *sitra ahara*[15] ("the other
side", the demonic realm) but as Jewish monotheistic thought
developed, the complete subordination of the powers of evil to God
became dominant in Judaism. For all the terrible problem of why the
wholly good God should tolerate evil in His creation, Jewish monotheism consistently affirmed that God alone is in control of the world.
Today dualism as a religious philosophy has virtually vanished from
the scene as a live option. This is partly for the same reason that
monotheism came to be seen as superior to polytheism. In a world
divided up among the various gods it is hard to explain the evidence
of unity in the world. It has often been noted that modern science,
based on the idea that there is such a unity, could not have arisen
against a polytheistic background. And by the same token dualism is
an unacceptable philosophy. The Rabbis put this quaintly in the
Talmudic story[16] of a Zoroastrian Magus who declared to a Rabbi

10. See Jer. Talmud Meg. 4: 9; Babylonian Talmud Meg. 25a; Ber. 33b.
11. Hag. 15a.
12. See article *Metatron* in *Jewish Encyclopedia*, Vol. VIII, p. 519 and E. Urbach: *The
    Sages*, p. 118-119.
13. *Judaism*, Vol. I, pp. 366-367.
14. See, for example, the story of the *min* (not Sadducee as in the current editions) in
    Hull. 87a.
15. See I. Tishby: *Mishnat Ha-Zohar*, Vol. I, pp. 285-307.
16. Sanh. 30a.

that the upper part of the body (containing the brain and the heart) belongs to Ormuzd and the lower part to Ahriman. The Rabbi replied that if this were the case why does Ahriman permit Ormuzd to send water through his territory, i.e. if the dualism alleged to be present in the universe is reflected in man's body how are the digestive processes possible?

To turn to Christianity, while it is true that in the Jewish–Christian polemics of the middle ages the Christian doctrine of the Trinity was attacked by Jews as a breach in pure monotheism, even as tritheism, this was not the cause of offence in the Rabbinic period. At this period Christianity was attacked for its dualism, i.e. for its doctrine of the Incarnation which Jews saw as dualistic in content, a belief in God the Father and Jesus the Son as "two powers". This is why there are no polemics against the Trinity in the Rabbinic literature but against the Incarnation, especially in third century Caesarea, where the Rabbis were in close contact with Christians. Two of the best-known preachments of R. Abahu of Ceasarea have frequently been quoted. Commenting on the verse: "God is not a man that He should lie; Neither the son of man, that He should repent: When He hath said, will He not do it? Or when He hath spoken, will He not make it good?" (Num. 23 : 19), R. Abahu takes the last part of the verse not as a question but as a statement and the pronoun in the first part of the verse as referring not to God but to man. Thus R. Abahu said: "If a man says to you, 'I am a god', he is lying; 'I am the Son of Man', he will end by being sorry for it; 'I am going up to heaven', he will not fulfil what he has said'.[17] On the verse: 'I am the first, and I am the last, and beside Me there is No God' " (Is.44: 6) R. Abahu comments[18], in a polemic against both Christianity and other forms of dualism: " 'I am the first', for I have no father; 'and I am the last', for I have no brother; 'and beside Me there is no God', for I have no son". (In all probability the original reading here was:[19] " 'and I am the last' for I have no son; 'and beside Me there is no God' for I have no brother").

In the middle ages, however, the doctrine of the Trinity came under fire from the Jewish side. Christian exegesis in the middle ages interpreted the *Shema* itself, with its three references to deity, referring to

17. Jer. Talmud Taan. 2: 1.
18. Ex. R. 29: 5.
19. See the note of David Luria in the Vilna ed. p. 51 note 15.

the Trinity.[20] Jewish exegetes declared that the opposite was true
and they made the *Shema* yield the thought that there is only one
God and not three Persons in the Godhead.[21] There are, however,
curious references in the Zohar to the three divine names in the
Shema. These represented the unity of three powers in the Godhead,
i.e. the *Sefirot* ("numbers", "qualities", "attributes of deity"—see
further) of Lovingkindness, Judgement and Beauty (*Hesed, Gevurah,
Tiferet*), symbolised by the colours white, red and green, or the
Sefirot of Wisdom, Understanding and Beauty (*Hokhmah, Binah,
Tiferet*).[22] The Christian Kabbalists read into these Zoharic interpretations the Christian doctrine of the Trinity but this is absurd since
the Zohar is strongly anti-Christian in intent and repeatedly stresses
the unity of the *Sefirot* with *En Sof* (God as He is in Himself).[23] But
the possibility that the formal Zoharic interpretation was influenced
by the mediaeval Christian exegesis of this verse cannot be ruled out.[24]

Christian thinkers frequently assert that Jewish polemics against
Trinitarianism are based on an inadequate understanding of what the
doctrine really means. It is no doubt true that crude attacks on
Christianity as tritheism are unfounded (tritheism is, in fact, heresy
from the Christian point of view) and there are subtleties in the
doctrine which Christians have tried to uncover. But the fact remains
that all Jewish thinkers have rejected trinitarianism as incompatible
with monotheism as Judaism understands it. Jewish martyrs in the
middle ages gave their lives rather than embrace Christianity.
Nowadays there are many areas in which the adherents of Judaism
and Christianity can fruitfully cooperate to their mutual advantage
and for the sake of the things, and they are many, which they hold in
common. But there are real differences between the two faiths which
both ackowledge and no good can come from any attempt to conceal
these.

On the Jewish attitude to Trinitarianism see my *Principles of the Jewish
Faith*, pp. 85–89; Jewish Encyclopedia, Vol. XII, pp. 260–261; M. Goldstein:
Jesus in the Jewish Tradition, pp. 202f; O. S. Rankin: *Jewish Religious*

20. See *Jewish Encyclopedia*, Vol. XII, p. 261 and J. Katz: *Exclusiveness and Tolerance*,
    p. 19.
21. See e.g. Bahya Ibn Asher to Deut. 6: 4.
22. Zohar I, 18b; III, 263a.
23. See *infra* pp. 149–150.
24. See I. Tishby: *Mishnat Ha-Zohar*, Vol. II, pp. 278–280.

Polemics, Chapter IX, pp. 157f; and J. D. Eisenstein: *Otzar Vikhuhim* for a collection of polemics and disputations. Among the mediaeval thinkers the Trinity is combated by Saadia: *Beliefs and Opinions*, II, 5-8; Bahya Ibn Pakudah: *Duties of the Heart, Shaar Ha-Yihud*, Chapter 7; Crescas: *Bittul Ikkere Ha-Notzerim*; and the list recorded by Baron: *Social and Religious History of the Jews*, Vol. IX, Chapter XXXIX, note 7, pp. 293-297. Leon de Modena: *Magen Va-Herev*, Part II, Chapter 4, pp. 25-27, suggests that the main Jewish objection to Trinitarianism is the doctrine of the Incarnation which suggests that there are three persons in the Godhead rather than three aspects of God's thought to which there would be little objection. For a description of how, in the thought of the Church Fathers, the absolute unity of God taught by Philo, as well as in Judaism generally, gradually became the relative unity of the Trinity, see H. A. Wolfson: *The Philosophy of the Church Fathers*, Chapter XV, pp. 305.

Among the mediaeval Jewish thinkers the unity of God was a constant theme. For many of them the idea of God's unity embraced the further idea that there is no multiplicity in His Being, that, as they expressed it, His was an "absolute simplicity" (*pashut be-takhlit ha-peshitut*). Thus the question of the divine attributes—good, wise, powerful—loomed very large in mediaeval thought. Do these attributes tend to suggest a multiplicity in God? This led the mediaeval thinkers frequently to adopt a theology of negation, in which one can only say what God is not, never what He is. This is why the doctrine of God's unity is generally discussed in the mediaeval works in the context of His incorporeality. The corporeal has the qualities of quantity and multiplicity, not so the incorporeal. The "unification of God" means, therefore, for many of the mediaeval thinkers, the complete refinement of the God concept so as to negate from it all multiplicity. This led to severe abstraction, to great austerity in the formulation of the God concept, to which the rise of the Kabbalah can be seen as a reaction.

For the mediaeval thinkers on the unity of God see: Saadia: *Beliefs and Opinions*, II, 1; Bahya Ibn Pakudah: *Duties of the Heart, Shaar Ha-Yihud;* Maimonides: *Guide* I, 50-59 and *Yad, Yesode Ha-Torah:* 1: 7-12; Crescas: *Or Adonai*, I, 3: 3-4; Albo: *Ikkarim*, II, 6 and 30. Maimonides' (*Yad, Yesode Ha-Torah* 1: 7) Statement of the Unity of God is: "This God is One, not two or more than two, but One whose unity is different from all other unities that there are. He is not one as a genus, which contains many species, is one. Nor is He one as a body, containing parts and dimensions, is one. But His is a unity than which there is no other anywhere". Ibn Gabriol famous statement of the unity (*The Kingly Crown*, II, pp. 28-29) is:

"Thou art One, the beginning of all computation,
   the base of all construction.
Thou art One, and in the mystery of Thy
   Oneness the wise of heart are astonished,
   for they know not what it is.
Thou art One, and Thy Oneness neither diminishes
   nor increases, neither lacks nor exceeds.
Thou art One, but not as the one that is counted
   or owned, for number and chance cannot
   reach Thee, nor attribute, nor form.
Thou art One, but my mind is too feeble to set
   Thee a law or a limit, and therefore I
   say: "I will take heed to my ways, that
   I sin not with my tongue".
Thou art One, and Thou art exalted above
   abasement and falling—not like a
   man, who falls when he is alone".

The Kabbalists appear to have been impressed by the philosophers' concept of the divine unity, but at the same time, they longed for a less abstract approach to the Deity. The result was the Kabbalistic doctrine of *En Sof* and the *Sefirot*. God as He is in Himself is *En Sof* ("That which Is Without Limit").

This aspect of deity is entirely unknown and unknowable. Indeed, in their negation of all associations of human speech from *En Sof* the Kabbalists are more radical than the philosophers.[25] But God in manifestation, God as He reveals Himself to others, emerges from concealment in the ten emanations known as the *Sefirot*. A detailed account of the Sefirotic doctrine is beyond the scope of this chapter[26] but it can be sketched here very briefly in outline. Basically the Kabbalists substitute for the impassive, static concept of deity the idea of a dynamic Godhead functioning under ten different aspects. Thus it is easy to see why this doctrine had to bear the brunt of anti-Kabbalistic ire as a severe departure from traditional monotheism.

The *Ten Sefirot* are: (1) *Keter*, "Crown", the divine will to create; (2) *Hokhmah*, "Wisdom", in which all God's creative activity is contained in *potentia*; (3) *Binah*, "Understanding", the unfolding in the divine Mind of the details of creation; (4) *Hesed*, "Lovingkindness", the divine goodness in its uncontrolled flow; (5) *Gevurah*, "Power", the

25. See *infra* pp. 149–150.
26. By far the best analysis of the Sefirotic doctrine is that of I. Tishby: *Mishnat Ha-Zohar*, Vol. I, pp. 131–161. Cf. G. Scholem: *Major Trends*, pp. 205–243.

divine judgement which arrests the flow of Lovingkindness so that creatures can endure and not be engulfed in the splendour of the divine grace; (6) *Tiferet*, "Beauty", the harmonising principle affecting the necessary balance between *Hesed* and *Gevurah*; (7) *Netzah*, "Victory" and (8) *Hod*, "Splendour", the two supporting principles; (9) *Yesod*, "Foundation", the generative principle; and 10) *Malkhut*, "Sovereignty", the governing principle, the prototype of God's rule over His creatures. God thus unfolds Himself to His creatures by means of ten emanations. He emerges from His concealment in order to bring His creatures into being that they might share in His goodness.

Keter, the link as it were, between *En Sof* and the Sefirotic realm, is too elevated for human thought to reach. (Sometimes *Keter* is not even counted among the *Sefirot* but is apart from them. In this scheme the *Sefiah Daat*, "Knowledge", mediating between *Hokhmah* and *Binah*, makes up the number ten.) Something of this remoteness applies also to the *Sefirot* of *Hokhmah* and *Binah*. Of *Binah* it is said in the Zohar[27] that one can ask what it is but expect no answer whereas of *Hokhmah* one cannot even put the question. The seven lower *Sefirot*, from *Hesed* to *Malkhut*, are, however, legitimate objects of human contemplation. *Tiferet* is also called "The Holy One, blessed be He" while *Malkhut* is called "The *Shekhinah*". Man, by his deeds, can influence the higher worlds and help to bring down the flow of divine grace if he is virtuous. When this happens there is harmony and balance in the Sefirotic realm, otherwise the *Shekhinah* (a kind of female element in the Godhead) is in exile. There are references in the Kabbalistic literature to the sacred marriage between "The Holy One, Blessed be He" and His *Shekhinah*. We are thus presented in the Kabbalah with a highly-charged mythology and it is easy to see why objections were raised to the whole Kabbalistic concept.

In fact, the charge of *decatheism* was hurled against the Kabbalah. Specific reference was made in this connection to the Christian doctrine of the Trinity and it was argued that the Kabbalistic doctrine of the Ten who are One is a more serious heresy than the Christian doctrine of the Three who are One. The Kabbalists reply in terms strongly reminiscent of the Church Fathers on the Trinity. The Kabbalists stress again and again that the *Sefirot* are united with *En Sof;* that while Kabbalistic prayer is directed to this or that *Sefirah* it is to *En Sof* as revealed in the *Sefirot* to which it is directed, not to the *Sefirot*

27. I, 1b.

themselves; that to detach any of the *Sefirot* from the others and from *En Sof* is to be guilty of mystical heresy. Among the illustrations the Kabbalists use is that of the human psyche which expresses itself in thought, emotions and deeds but which is in essence a unity: or that of the different coloured lights in one ember of a coal fire; or that of water poured into bottles of different colours.[28]

Opponents of the Kabbalah have not been slow in pointing to its mythological nature. S. Rubin: *Heidenthum und Kabbala* goes so far as to suggest that the whole Kabbalistic system is no more than a Jewish attempt to retain such pagan ideas as the birth of the gods. Rubin compares the Sefirotic doctrine with the myths of Brahma, Siva and Vishnu in Indian religion and Osiris, Isis and Horus in the ancient Egyptian religion and he sees the *Seforah Yesod* as a cosmic phallic symbol. For the mythological elements in the later Lurianic Kabbalah (shortly to be considered in this chapter) see G. Scholem's essay: *Kabbalah and Myth* in his: *On the Kabbalah and Its Symbolism*, Chapter 3, pp. 87–117. On the objection to the recital, before carrying out the precepts, of the formula: "For the sake of the unification of the Holy One, Blessed be He, and His *Shekhinah*" (*le-shem yihud*, found in the Lurianic Kabbalah and which is based on Zohar III, 51b) see the famous Responsum of Ezekiel Landau (*Noda Bi-yudah, Yoreh Deah*, No. 93) and A. Wertheim: *Halakhot Ve-Halikhot Ba-Hasidut*, pp. 71–72. Among the Hasidic replies is that of Hayim Tchnerowitz in his *Shaar Ha-Tefillah*, beg., pp. 3–10. A well-known Responsum on the *Sefirot* is that of R. Isaac b. Sheshet Barfat (*Ribash*, 1326–1408). In Responsum No. 157 he discusses the Sefirotic doctrine and whether it is permitted to pray to the *Sefirot*. He remarks that he once heard someone influenced by philosophy attack the Kabbalists on the grounds that while the Christians believe in "three" the Kabbalists believe in "ten". The author describes a meeting he had with the elderly sage Don Joseph Ibn Shoshan, who is described as a Talmudic sage, familiar with philosophy, and a great Kabbalist and saint. *Ribash* put the question to him: How can the Kabbalists have one *Sefirah* in mind when reciting one benediction and another *Sefirah* in mind when reciting another benediction? Is it not forbidden for a Jew to pray to the *Sefirot* and thereby incur the suspicion that he treats them as deities? Don Joseph replies that of course the prayer of the Kabbalists is directed to the Cause of causes but concentration on the different *Sefirot* in prayer can be compared to a petition presented to a king in which the monarch is entreated to command that the suppliant's wish be carried out through the particular lord appointed for that purpose. Thus when the Kabbalist thinks of the *Sefirah* of *Hesed* when praying on behalf of the righteous and when he thinks of the *Sefirah* of *Gevurah* when praying for the downfall of

28. See I. Tishby: *Mishnat Ha-Zohar*, loc. cit., and Joseph Gikatila's Introduction to his *Shaare Orah*.

the wicked, his intention is to pray to God to draw down His influence into
the requisite *Sefirot*. Ribash praises the ingenuity of the reply but expresses
his dissatisfaction with it. Surely, he argues, it is far better to pray to God
with simple intention without appearing to advise God how to grant the
request! *Ribash* concludes that he personally favours simple, uncomplicated
intention in his prayers. It would be incorrect to conclude from this that
Ribash was an opponent of the Kabbalah. As he remarks in this Responsum,
since he had not had the advantage of learning the system at the feet of a
master he prefers to avoid the subject. Cf. Joseph Ergas: *Shomer Emunim*,
I, 67, pp. 39–43. Elijah's mystical prayer (*Tikkune Zohar*, Second Introduction)
is relevant in this connection: "Elijah began to praise God saying: Lord
of the universe! Thou art One but are not numbered. Thou art Higher
than the highest. Thou art the Mystery above all mysteries. There is no
thought that can grasp Thee at all. It is Thou who produced the Ten
Perfections which we call the *Ten Sefirot*. With them Thou guidest the
secret worlds which have not been revealed and the worlds which have
been revealed, and in them Thou concealest Thyself from humans. But
it is Thou Who bindest them together and uniteth them. Since Thou art
in them, whoever separates any of these *Ten* from the others it is as if He had
made a division in Thee".

If it be asked whether a modern Jew can believe in the Sefirotic
doctrine, the matter is not, of course, capable of proof one way or the
other but it can be said surely that, in fact, very few modern Jews do
believe in it. Unless one believes, as the Kabbalists did, that the doctrine
is a direct divine revelation concerning the mystery of God's being,
one sees the Kabbalah as a gigantic speculative scheme in which Jews
meditated on ideas—Neo-Platonic and Gnostic—which had come
down from the past. To be sure ideas which come from without can
also be true but what can be quite adequately explained as a purely
human development of thought is unlikely to be accepted as revealed
truth in our historically-minded age. Most modern Jews would
certainly conclude that the Kabbalistic scheme is not a true reflection
of ultimate reality. They would, therefore, if their bent lies in this
direction, find the Kabbalistic doctrines fascinating in themselves
and even of indirect significance for the mystical approach to Judaism
but largely irrelevant to an acceptable Jewish theology. However, it
cannot be left simply at that. These profound speculations are as much
part of Jewish thinking on the unity of God as the different speculations of the mediaeval philosophers. At least, these ideas deserve
examination, even though the inquiry is conducted with a degree
of scepticism the orthodox Kabbalist would reject in horror.

We have examined in this light the earlier Kabbalistic doctrines as found in the Zohar. We must now turn to the later Kabbalah of the famous sixteenth century Kabbalist R. Isaac Luria (known as the *Ari*, the Lion). The *Ari's* system is based on the great question paraphrased as follows by G. Scholem:[29] How can there be a world if God is everywhere? If God is "all in all" how can there be things which are not God? How can God create out of nothing if there is no nothing? The *Ari* replies with the doctrine of *Tzimtzum* ("withdrawal") i.e. that God "withdrew from Himself into Himself" in order to leave room for the world. In the Zoharic scheme the *Ten Sefirot* are emanations of God. In the Lurianic Kabbalah the first impulse, as it were, in God's unfolding is this withdrawal and the *Ten Sefirot* only emerge after this withdrawal. The Lurianic Kabbalah without doubt displays tremendous ingenuity amounting to genius in developing the extremely complicated system by means of which the many come from the One.[30]

> Here is not the place to describe these ideas in detail. For this many
> volumes would be required. But the central themes can briefly be stated.
> After the *Tzimtzum* an "empty space" was left. This is not to be taken
> literally, of course. The reference is to the primordial "space" into which
> the Sefirotic realm evolved by a process of emanation and from which there
> eventually emerged space and time as we know these. Into this "empty space"
> a thin ray of light from *En Sof* emerged. This is the sustaining power of all
> that subsequently emerged. From this there emerged what is known in
> the Lurianic Kabbalah as *Adam Kadmon* ("Primordial Man"). (The idea of
> *Adam Kadmon* is very ancient. Man on earth is, as it were, the counterpart
> of the creative processes on high. Man is the apex of creation because the
> structure of his body in the physical world mirrors those spiritual potencies
> by which God brought the world into being.) Subtle lights then emerged
> from the "ear", "nose" and "mouth" of *Adam Kadmon*. These produced
> *in potentia* the "vessels" with which to contain the light of the *Sefirot* which
> were later to emerge. Lights then proceeded from the "eyes" of *Adam
> Kadmon* and while the "vessels" of the three higher *Sefirot*—*Keter*, *Hokhmah*
> and *Binah*—were able to contain these lights the "vessels" of the seven lower
> Sefirot were unable to do so. The result was the cosmic catastrophe
> known in the Lurianic Kabbalah as *shevirat ha-kelim*, "the breaking of the
> vessels". Ultimately this was necessary in order for the "other side" (*sitra
> ahara*) to emerge. This is the demonic side of existence, necessary if the world

29. *Major Trends*, pp. 260–261.
30. For the Lurianic Kabbalah see I. Tishby: *Torat Ha-Ra Ve-Ha-Kelipah;* M. H. Luzzatto: *K'lah Pithe Hokhmah;* J. Oshlag: *Talmud Eser Sefirot;* I. S. Ratner: *Le-Or Ha-Kabbalah.*

was to become an arena in which man could freely choose the good and reject the evil. Only in this way could he make the good his own. For it is the will of the All-good to benefit His creatures and only the highest good, which is that freely chosen and not given as a gift, will suffice for man to be God-like. The catastrophe represented by the breaking of the vessels is essential in that through it the finite can come into being and be tolerated by the Infinite. As a result of the breaking of the vessels the light of En Sof became, as it were, fragmented. "Holy sparks" from the Infinite light were scattered to form the vital power to sustain the Sefirotic realm and the "worlds" beneath it. But now that the vessels are broken everything is in a state of disarray. Nothing is in its proper place. The gigantic task allotted to man is that of reclaiming and releasing the "holy sparks" by restoring them to their Source. This is the process known as *tikkun*, "putting right", "perfecting". When the task of *tikkun* is complete, redemption will come not only to Israel and not only to mankind as a whole but to the entire cosmic process, in fact, to God Himself in His aspect of manifestation.

After the breaking of the vessels it was now necessary to put the *Sefirot* together again, as it were, so that they might contain the light. This was done by grouping the *Sefirot* in "configurations" or "faces" (partzufim) in which all *ten Sefirot* unite in order to give strength one to the other. The five main *partzufim* are: (1) *arikh* (or *arikh anpin*, the "long face" or "long suffering"), corresponding to *Keter*; (2) *Abba*, "father" and (3) *Imma*, "mother", corresponding to *Hokhmah* and *Binah*; (4) *zeer* (or *zeer anpin*, the "little face" or "impatience") corresponding to *Tiferet* (and the other five lower *Sefirot* apart from *Malkhut*); and *nukvah*, the "female", corresponding to *Malkhut*. There is a bewildering array of configurations, associations of the *partzufim* one with the other. The term used for this is *zivvug*, which really means "copulation". *Zeer* and *nukvah* are especially associated in this way. Again it is man who influences the higher worlds in this way by his deeds. He helps to bring about this unification, since he is marvellously formed after the pattern of the upper worlds and whatever he does has cosmic significance. Man helps to produce harmony in the Sefirotic realm and assists the *tikkun* process so that eventually the complete unity of God is seen through all the multiplicity of things. Once the *Sefirot* have been arranged in the form of *partzufim* they could contain most of the light with the exception of a kind of overspill. This descended from the World of Emanation, the Sefirotic realm, to provide the power to sustain the world beneath it, the World of Creation, which has its own *Sefirot* arranged as *partzufim*. Here, too, there is an overspill which provides the power for the world beneath it, the World of Formation, and the process is again repeated to provide the power for the World of Action, the source on high of this world and including this world. There is an overspill even here but at this stage it emerges from the realm of the sacred to provide the power for the demonic side, which feeds, as it were, on the holy, since without God's sustaining power nothing can endure. The four worlds are; (1) *olam ha-atzilut*, "the world of emanation"; (2) *olam ha-beriah*, "the world of creation"; (3) *olam ha-yetzirah*, "the world of formation"; (4) *olam ha-asiyah*, "the world of action". The lowest stage of each world is known as the *Malkhut* of that world (on the analogy of the *Sefirah Malkhut*, the lowest of the *Sefirot*, representing God's desire to reign over His creatures). The *Malkhut* of each world becomes the *Keter* (the highest of the *Sefirot*) of the world immediately beneath it. (Above and beneath are not thought of in spatial terms but in terms of spiritual rank and degree.) One can therefore speak of *Malkhut* of *En Sof* which becomes *Keter* of *Adam Kadmon*. There is thus a great chain of being extending from *Malkhut* of *En Sof* = *Keter* of *Adam Kadmon* through *Malkhut* of *Adam Kadmon* = *Keter atzilut* to *Malkhut* of *atzilut* = *Keter* of *beriah* and so on to the lowest stages of this world. Man in this world at the lowest end of the chain, and beset by the forces of the *sitra ahara*, has the tremendous task of elevating all these worlds, of restoring them to their primordial unity by lifting up the holy sparks both by his dedication to God when using the things of this world and by rejecting evil, the domain of the *sitra ahara*.

As with regard to the Sefirotic doctrine, the Lurianic ideas will be accepted as revealed truth by very few modern Jews. But one can see the Lurianic Kabbalah as a most powerful attempt at grasping the idea of God's unity while accounting for the multiplicity and diversity of things in the world as we experience it. All this, the Kabbalists are saying in so many words, must have its source in the "worlds on high".

The *Tzimtzum* idea received many different interpretations among the Kabbalists. In the 18th century Hasidic movement, and particularly in the branch of it known as *Habad* (founded by R. Schneor Zalman of Liady), it is interpreted in such a way that the doctrine of God's unity means not alone that there is only one God and that God is unique, but that there *is* only God. In this philosophy God is all. There are no creatures, from His point of view, as it were, only the One. All the multiplicity of things we observe in the universe as well as we ourselves are due to the screening of the divine light. *Tzimtzum* does not, in fact, really take place. Its meaning is rather that the divine light is progressively concealed so that creatures eventually enjoy existence from their point of view but not from God's.[31] This is acosmism with a vengeance and would seem to be a surrender to Far Eastern monistic views on the nature of ultimate reality. But there are two important differences between monotheism conceived of in this way and monism. The first is that in a monistic scheme the world of the senses is an illusion whereas in *Habad* monotheism the world is

31. See M. Teitelbaum: *Ha-Rav Mi-Ladi;* and for a detailed treatment of this theme see Menahem Mendel of Lubavitch: *Derekh Mitzvotekha*, pp. 118–124.

real enough from the point of view of creatures. The multiplicity of things, on the *Habad* view, is said to be "included in God's unity". This leads to the second difference between Hasidic monotheism and monism (and pantheism). In Hasidic monotheism it is God alone who embraces all and is in all, so that, in fact, from His point of view, He is the all and there is none else. On the other hand both monism and pantheism are basically atheistic. That is, in these philosophies, the ultimate "stuff" or "substance" of the universe is not God or, at the most, God is merely a synonym for the ultimate "stuff" or "substance" of the universe. A possible term for the Hasidic view is *panentheism*—all is *in* God. The "all" is not identified *with* God in such a way that it would be meaningless to speak of the possibility of God without the "all". It is rather that the "all" is *in* God.

Not long after the rise of Hasidism this doctrine was severely attacked by the traditional defenders of Jewish monotheism. It was claimed that the panentheistic doctrine tends to obliterate the demarcation lines between the holy and the unholy, between good and evil. It would lead, as the opponents of Hasidism quaintly put it, to thinking on words of Torah in unclean places.[32]

There is nothing in the Hasidic idea to cause it to be rejected as opposed to the unity of God. On the contrary the doctrine of God's unity is stretched here to its utmost limits, far beyond any previous Jewish thinkers have ever attempted. The serious objection to this kind of panentheism is rather on the question of what meaning one can give to it. How can it make sense to say that from God's point of view there are neither creatures nor universe and yet to hold that from our point of view these do exist? Or to put the objection in another way, once one admits that the universe and creatures do exist, as one must, in what way can they be said to be non-existent from God's point of view? To say that they do not *really* exist is to indulge in a meaningless play on words. The word "exists" denotes something. What is added to the connotation of this word by the further statement that they do not *really* exist or that they are "included in God's unity?" The Habad thinkers gave much thought to this question but eventually they fall back on the idea of a sublime

---

32. See the letters of anathema which were written against the Hasidim in E. Zweiful's *Shalom Al Yisrael*, Vol. II, pp. 37-60 and R. Hayim of Volhozhyn: *Nefesh Ha-Hayim*, pp. 69–70, quoted *infra* p. 68–69.

mystery too deep for human understanding.[33] It is beyond the finite mind of man to comprehend how there can be a universe and creatures and yet only God. But while the notion of sublime mystery beyond all human comprehension can be applied to such questions as God's nature it does not make sense to apply it to what, after all, is a question of logic. If in our language, the only language we have, it is not a logically meaningful statement to say that creatures both enjoy and do not enjoy existence then nothing significant has been said at all. The mystery left for God to solve, as it were, is no mystery at all but a meaningless jumble of words. Once all the meaning that can be extracted from the term "exist" has been extracted and it is clearly seen what is covered by the term, any further attempt at qualification in terms of non-existence tells us nothing further about God or for that matter about creatures. I can say, for example, that Sherlock Holmes is only a character in fiction and did not really exist because our language knows of the distinction between real and fictitious existence. But I cannot say, without contradicting myself, that a fictitious character does not exist fictitiously or that a real person does not really exist. Nor will it do to say that from God's point of view we are only fictitious characters whereas from our point of view we are real persons. Since both terms, fictitious and real, now refer to the same entities—creatures—we are simply using two different words for the same thing.

One can see what the Hasidic thinkers were trying to do. God-intoxicated men find it hard to admit that there is anything anywhere that is not-God. But the realities of the human situation as we know it and of the language we use demand that our conception of the unity and omnipresence of God be not invoked to deny the existence of the universe and its creatures. This is not necessarily to reject the Kantian distinction between the *noumena* and the *phenomena*. It may well be the case that we never have knowledge of things as they really are. But that which we do perceive we do perceive, our perception, at least, is real, and there is a "we" to do the perceiving unless we are to deprive the term perception of all its meaning.

We have surveyed in this chapter the range of Jewish thought on the unity of God from the Biblical rejection of polytheism through the philosophical explorations of uniqueness and the dynamism of the

33. See my *Seeker of Unity* (on the *Habad* thinker Aaron of Starosselje), Index s.v. "marvel".

Kabbalistic concept down to Hasidic panentheism. Modern Jewish monotheistic belief-has been so thoroughly explored in the previous centuries that a consensus has emerged among believers as to what it implies and what it rejects. Judaism stands or falls on the rejection of polytheism as it is incompatible with dualism or trinitarianism. Beyond that there is room for speculation on the lines of the mediaeval thinkers but moderns will be sceptical, to say the least, regarding the Kabbalistic systems and will regard Hasidic panentheism as logically obscure. The believing Jew still recites the *Shema* as implying the pure monotheistic doctrine on which Judaism as a religion is based.

CHAPTER THREE

THE *VIA NEGATIVA* AND GOD AS *PERSON*

AT THIS stage in our inquiry it is necessary to consider in greater detail the point that has been mentioned more than once—how far it is legitimate to speak at all of God's nature. In the previous chapter on the unity of God we saw how, for the mediaeval thinkers, the idea of a simple unity demands a negation so far as different aspects of deity are concerned. In the history of Jewish religious thought there is, indeed, to be observed a definite tendency among some thinkers to negate all attributes from God. He is to be described, if He is to be described at all, as unknowable. In the history of religious thought such an attitude is known as the *via negativa.*[1]

The theist who gives thought to this question of talking about God's nature soon becomes aware that if he says too much about it he is guilty of trying to impose human limits on the infinite. Familiarity is the great temptation. It has been said that theologians frequently speak as if they had just had lunch with the Deity. They make gigantic claims of admission into the great secret which are comical in their pretentiousness. It was in reaction to these claims that the well-known limerick was composed:

> *O God, for as much as without Thee*
> *We are not able to doubt Thee,*
> *Lord, give us the grace*
> *To convince the whole race*
> *We know nothing whatever about Thee.*

On the other hand, if too little is said about God there is danger of belief shading off into atheism. Theologians are here surely right in

1. The first part of this chapter is based on my paper: *The Via Negativa in Jewish Religious Thought.*

their refusal to give up all talk about God. Leaving aside the very significant question of revelation, theistic faith cannot dispense with every concept of Deity unless it abandons that which it holds to be true and which gives life meaning.

Most theists, in the interests of a vital faith, have preferred to take the risk of saying too much than too little. But some theists, concerned with the refinement of their religious ideas, have preferred to adopt a theology of negation which sometimes goes so far as to say that the only thing we can say about God is that we cannot say anything about God.

On the face of it, it might be assumed that such a negative theology is negative in a pejorative sense. That is it is bound to feed the prospective adherent of theistic faith with a diet of bloodless abstraction, depriving him of all the warmth and passion associated with religion in its most intense moods. Such a reading of the matter would be false if only because the *via negativa* has historically been most favoured by the mystics, strange God-seekers and world-losers whose fervour for God and hunger for His presence cannot seriously be doubted. The Object of the mystic's contemplation is, to be sure, "closer than breathing and nearer than hands and feet". Yet his fascination for it derives in no small measure from the fact that, for him, It is so wonderful, so majestic, so utterly different from anything in heaven and earth, that It cannot be contained in human speech and is to be worshipped in silence. The *via negativa* is only a negation of religion for those limited in vision. The mystic bows before God in adoration not in spite of God's ineffability but because of it.

Bahya Ibn Pakudah in his *Duties of the Heart* devotes a whole section (*Shaar Ha-Yihud*, "Gate of Unity") to the meaning of the unity of God. Since God is unique, the use of reason in the religious life, of which Bahya is a strong advocate, only begins with attaining to complete certainty that there is a God. It is equally important in order to refine one's ideas about God, that He be not depicted mentally in terms which suggest that He really resembles anything in His creation. The "unification of God" means for Bahya that man negates from God all human and finite limitations. If, says Bahya,[2] we wish to determine the nature of a thing, we must ask concerning that thing two questions—*if* it is and *what* it is. But of God one can only ask *if*

2. *Shaar Ha-Yihud*, Chapter 4.

He is. Once having established that God is we cannot go on to ask
what He is for His true nature is beyond all human comprehension.
In that case, what are we to make of the descriptions of God's attributes
found in Scripture and used in the liturgy? Bahya claims that the
three main attributes are to be understood in a negative not a positive
sense.[3] These are: His existence, His unity and His eternity. Even
when these three are expressed in positive form, they are really to be
understood negatively, they are negative attributes. Thus to say that
God exists means that He is not non-existent; to say that He is one is
to say that there is no plurality or multiplicity in Him; to say that He
is eternal is to say that He is not bound by time and is not transient.
Inscrutable though God's nature is, this we do know and affirm, that
it is wrong to deny His existence, that there is no plurality in Him and
that He is not bound by the temporal process. As for the other attributes, such as God's goodness and His wisdom, these can be expressed
and understood even in a positive way because, unlike the first three,
they deal with God's acts, not with His essence. They have psychological value[4] in that they afford man a vocabulary of worship. If all
use of divine attributes were to be disallowed men would have no
means of communicating with God.

Maimonides takes up the question of negative attributes and
develops the doctrine at length in his *Guide for the Perplexed*.[5] For
Maimonides, to ascribe to God positive attributes is a form of polytheism because it suggests that other beings, namely His attributes,
are co-existent with Him for all eternity.[6] Hasdai Crescas[7] disagrees
with Maimonides. It is impossible, Crescas argues, to avoid the use of
positive attributes (and those who claim to do so are themselves
inconsistent in this matter). There is nothing offensive, observes
Crescas, in the use of positive attributes since there is a relation between
God and His creatures even though God is infinite and His creatures
finite. Many moderns would side with Crescas in this debate and
would certainly refuse to treat the use of positive attributes as a kind
of polytheism. Moreover, if one can speak at all of a "normative"
Jewish view on this matter it would be that of Crescas. However,

3. *Shaar Ha-Yihud*, Chapter 10.
4. *Shaar Ha-Yihud*, Chapter 10.
5. *Guide*, I, 51–60.
6. *Guide*, I, 58.
7. *Or Adonai*, Book I, section 3, Chapter 3.

Maimonides' view, as we shall see, has its followers, some of whom go even further in the way of negation than Maimonides himself appeared ready to go.

According to Maimonides, even to say that God is One is not to say anything significant about His true nature but only to negate all plurality from His being. Even to say that God exists is simply to say that His non-existence is impossible. Like Bahya, Maimonides does permit positive attributes to be used if these refer to God's acts but attributes referring to God's nature are only permissible in their negative form. Furthermore, those attributes which refer to God's acts imply only the acts themselves not the emotions responsible for such acts when performed by humans.[8] Thus the many Biblical references to God's mercy do not imply that God is influenced by feelings of mercy but "that acts similar to those which a father performs for his son, out of pity, mercy and real affection, emanate from God solely to the benefit of His pious men, and are by no means the result of any impression or change".

Linguistic analysis certainly has something to say on this whole question of negative attributes. Is there any difference linguistically between the statement that a being exists and that it is not non-existent? Is it not simply a case of using a different set of words to express exactly the same thing?[9] A possible defence of these views of the mediaeval thinkers, if not of the thinkers themselves, is in order. Indeed, the meaning is the same whether positive or negative attributes are used but the negative form is preferable. It provides us with the suggestion of total inadequacy we require if we are not to imagine that in using the attributes we are really coming closer to an understanding of God's true nature.

Albo (*Ikkarim*, II, 23-23) follows Maimonides. Attributes referring to God's nature are to be used only in a negative sense; attributes referring to God's acts can be used in a positive sense. Albo (II, 22) adds: "But even the attributes of this class (i.e. those taken from God's acts) must be taken in the sense involving perfection, not in the sense involving defect. Thus, although these attributes cause emotion in us and make us change from one of the contraries to the other, they do not necessitate any change

8. *Guide*, I, 54.
9. This point was, in fact, made by Crescas: *Or Adonai*, Book I, section 3, Chapter 3, who observes that to say that God is not not-knowing is to say that He is knowing, cf. M. Waxman: *The Philosophy of Don Hasdai Crescas*, pp. 68–69.

or emotion in God, for His ways are not our ways, nor are His thoughts
our thoughts". Albo (*Ikkarim* II, 23) purports to find the complete negation
of attributes concerning God's nature in Psalm 103:1 where the Psalmist
says: "Bless the Lord, O my soul; and all that is within me, bless His
holy name". According to Albo this means: "My soul, bless the Lord
with the brevity of praise that befits Him, in view of the excellence of His
nature and of His holy name, i.e. Himself. As to this, one must not multiply
words, nay, one must not even pronounce them with his lips unless he
understands them in a negative sense. Hence the Psalmist expresses himself
briefly and without any explanations. The expression, 'All that is within
me, bless His holy name', signifies the praise which is becoming to Him
in view of the excellence of His holy name, which is ineffable" (Husik's
translation). The question of attributes is discussed, too, by Isaiah Horowitz
(*Shelah*, Part II, end, p. 84) who quotes especially Maimonides and Albo.
He follows the Kabbalistic view to be discussed in the next paragraphs but
he adds an interesting observation of his own on why Jewish tradition
forbids the recitation of the special psalms of praise (*Hallel*) except on the
festivals when tradition enjoins us to recite it. According to his explanation
the recitation of Hallel on the festivals is, in fact, a recounting of the
marvels which God wrought for our ancestors and this is permitted. But one
who recites *Hallel* on other days thereby demonstrates that he is engaged not
in simply recounting God's mighty acts but in praising God and implying
that the attributes mentioned in the Psalms can really be applied to God.
This, he insists, is a kind of blasphemy.

The philosophical exponents of the doctrine of negative attributes
do, then, allow, albeit reluctantly, the use of certain attributes in
speaking of God. A much more radical theory of negation is found
among the Kabbalists. The Kabbalists make the distinction between
God as He is in Himself and God as He becomes manifest to His
creatures, between *deus absconditus* and *deus revelatus*. For the Kabbalists God is revealed to others through the "instruments" or "powers"
which are emanated from Him, the *Ten Sefirot*.[10] God as He is in
Himself is called, as we have seen, *En Sof* ("That which is without
limit"). The Kabbalists make every effort to avoid the faintest suggestion of a dualistic doctrine. They are ever on guard against the
faintest hint of anything approaching the idea that any but God is in
control of the universe, that there are two gods, one hidden, one
revealed, as in Gnostic theories. *En Sof* and the *Sefirot*, the Kabbalists
never tire of saying, are One, though how this is possible remains for
them the profoundest mystery.

10. See *supra* pp. 28–31.

It is important to recognise the psychological need, to which reference has been made in connection with Bahya's views, and which acted as a spur to the Kabbalists. On the one hand the Kabbalists appear to have been impressed by the arguments of the philosophers in the direction of negation. Indeed, they went much further than the philosophers in this direction. On the other hand they appear to have held that only positive affirmations can be helpful in worship if one is to practice his religion with piety. Consequently, they tried to seize both horns of the dilemma. Positive attributes are permissible in speaking of God as He makes Himself manifest and these are provided by the doctrine of the *Sefirot*. Unlike Maimonides, the Kabbalists hold that it is permissible to ascribe even emotions and not alone acts to God in manifestation. But of God as He is in Himself, of *En Sof*, not even negative attributes are allowed. The distinction is no longer between two types of attributes but between two aspects of Deity.

The impersonal nature of *En Sof* is stressed. The later Kabbalists emphatically deny that any psychological processes can be ascribed to *En Sof*.[11] Yet there is no real consistency in this matter. Terms such as "*En Sof*, blessed be He" abound. The term *En Sof* was first used by Azriel of Gerona (1160–1238) who remarks[12]: "Know that *En Sof* cannot be thought of, much less spoken of, even though there is a hint of *It* in all things, for there is nothing else apart from It. Consequently, *It* can be contained neither by letter nor name nor writing nor anything". Another writer, contemporaneous with the Zohar, writes:[13] "Know that the *En Sof* we have mentioned is hinted at neither in the Pentateuch nor the Prophets nor the Hagiographa nor in the Rabbinic literature but the masters of worship (= the Kabbalists) received a faint hint of *It*". The Zohar itself speaks but rarely of *En Sof* and when it does it is to declare than En Sof is incomprehensible.[14] Even of the higher reaches of God in manifestation, that is to say of the stages represented by God's will, His wisdom and His understanding (*Keter*, *Hokhmah* and *Binah*) the Zohar prefers to speak in negative terms. God's will, represented by the *Sefirah Keter* is

---

11. Joseph Ergas: *Shomer Emunim*, Part II, No. 71, pp. 84–85.
12. *Perush Eser Sefirot* in Meir Ibn Gabbai's *Derekh Emunah*, p. 4a.
13. *Maarekhet Ha-Elohut*, Mantua, 1558, Chapter 8 beg., quoted by G. Scholem: *Major Trends*, p. 353 note 8.
14. Zohar I, 22b; III, 225a, cf. I. Tishby: *Mishnat Ha-Zohar*, Vol. I. pp. 95f.

called *Ayin*, "Nothingness".[15] So elevated is this beyond all human thought that it can only be represented by complete negation. Of the divine wisdom, represented by *Hokhmah*, the Zohar remarks that one cannot even ask what it is since it is beyond all human questioning. Of *Binah* one can ask what it is but one cannot expect any answer. One can only approach this aspect of Deity with a question as to its nature but it is too far above human thoughts for humans to expect an intelligible reply.[16] The eighteenth century Kabbalist, the Gaon of Vilna, carries this doctrine of the ineffability of *En Sof* to the uttermost limits when he remarks that strictly speaking one can so little speak of *En Sof* that one cannot even give It the name *En Sof* ![17]

If we search for the sources of the negative theology as it appears among the mediaeval thinkers, and, in more radical form, among the Kabbalists, we discover two main influences at work. These are the current mediaeval tendency towards a theology of negation, particularly stressed in Neo-Platonism, and the suggestions of negation found in the classical sources of Judaism—the Bible and the Rabbinic literature.

Neo-Platonism is especially emphatic that very little can be said of God as He is in Himself. The views of Plotinus on this subject are well known. In Plotinus the "One" is unknowable. If it is called the "Good" this is not intended to affirm any quality within itself. To affirm its existence means no more than that it does not fall within the realm of non-existents. For Plotinus it is false even to say that the "One" exists because it is beyond all essence and existence.[18] "Its definition, in fact, could only be 'the indefinable': what is not a thing is not some definite thing. We are in agony for a true expression; we are talking of the untellable; we name, only to indicate for our own use as best we may. And this name, The One, contains really no more than the negation of plurality: Under the same pressure the Pythagoreans found their indication in the symbol 'Apollo' (*a* = not; *pollon* = many) with its repudiation of the multiple. If we are to think positively of The One, name and thing, there would be more truth in silence; the designation, a mere aid to inquiry, was never

---

15. Zohar II, 239a.
16. See Zohar I, 1a. Scholem: *Major Trends*, p. 220, calls this "a thought which suggests the apotheosis of the well-known Jewish penchant for putting questions".
17. See Ratner: *Le-Or Ha-Kabbalah*, p. 39 note 40.
18. *Enneads*, V, 5. 6, ed. Stephen Mackenna, p. 408, cf. p. xxiv.

intended for more than a preliminary affirmation of absolute simplicity to be followed by the rejection of even that statement; it was the best that offered, but remains inadequate to express the nature indicated. For this is a principle not to be conveyed by any sound; it cannot be known on any hearing, but, if at all, by vision; and to hope in that vision to see a form is to fail even in that". Here we have all the ideas which appear later among the mediaeval Jewish philosophers and the Kabbalists so that the direct influence of Neo-Platonism cannot be doubted.

The *via negativa*, it has frequently been noted, bears strong resemblances, also, to ideas found in the Upanishads. The doctrine is also found in pseudo-Dionysius and in him owes much to the Neo-Platonist Proclus who was lecturing in Athens in the year 430.[19] Pseudo-Dionysius prefers to use the non-personal *It* when speaking of the Godhead: "Now concerning this hidden Super-Essential Godhead we must not dare, as I have said, to speak, or even to form any conception Thereof, except those things which are divinely revealed to us from the Holy Scriptures. For as It has lovingly taught us in the Scriptures concerning Itself, the understanding and contemplation of Its actual nature is not accessible to any being; for such knowledge is super-essentially exalted above them all. And many of the Sacred Writers thou wilt find who have declared that It is not only invisible and incomprehensible, but also unsearchable and past finding out, since there is no trace of any that have penetrated the hidden depths of Its infinitude. Not that the Good is wholly incommunicable to anything; nay, rather, while dwelling alone by Itself, and having there firmly fixed Its super-essential Ray, It lovingly reveals Itself by illuminations corresponding to each separate creature's powers and thus draws upwards holy minds into such contemplation, participation and resemblance of Itself as they can attain—even them that holily and duly strive thereafter and do not seek with impotent presumption the Mystery beyond that heavenly revelation which is so granted to fit their powers, nor yet through their lower propensity slip down the steep descent, but with unwavering constancy press

19. See the section on Dionysius the Aeropagite in A. C. Bouqet: *Sacred Books of the World*, part III, 7 (iv), pp. 218–220. Cf. the remarks of E. R. Dodd in his edition of *Proclus—The Elements of Theology*, p. 195, in which he refers to the influence of Proclus on Dionysius, and Appendix I: *The Unknown God in Neo-Platonism*, pp. 310–313.

onward toward the Ray that casts its light upon them and, through the
love responsive to these gracious illuminations, speed their temperate
and holy flight on the wings of a godly reverance". The parallel
between all this and the writings of the Kabbalists is so striking that
with few alterations we might almost be reading a passage from the
Zohar.

Ideas such as these were attractive to many Jewish minds, nurtured
on a religious tradition which prohibited in the strongest terms the
fashioning of any image of the divine. For all the anthropomorphisms
in the Bible, the theologians of negation could not have been unaware
of verses such as: "For your own sake, therefore, be most careful—
since you saw no shape when the Lord your God spoke to you at
Horeb out of the fire" (Deut. 4: 15). A fertile soil for the growth of
the Neo-Platonic ideas in this matter was provided even in one of the
most anthropomorphic passages in the Bible—the account of God's
reply to Moses when he requested God to show him His glory: "And
He said, thou canst not see My face; for man shall not see Me, and
live. And the Lord said, Behold there is a place by Me, and thou shalt
stand upon the rock. And It shall come to pass, while My glory
passeth by, that I will put thee in a cleft of the rock, and will cover thee
with My hand until I have passed by. And I will take away My hand,
and thou shalt see My back; but My face shall not be seen" (Ex. 32:
20–23). To be sure this passage as it stands is anthropomorphic in the
extreme but once it came to be interpreted metaphorically—as
happened in the later Jewish teaching—it yielded ideas close to those
of Neo-Platonists. Once a term like "back" in the passage was treated
metaphorically to convey the idea that man can comprehend some
aspects of divine manifestation, it followed that "face" was to be
interpreted to mean other aspects which can never be comprehended
by mortal man.

The passage in Ex. 33: 18–23 was, of course, a puzzle to the philosophically-
minded commentators and there is a long history of its interpretation.
Saadia (*Beliefs and Opinions*, II, 12) remarks that some people are confused
by Moses' request to see God's glory, are even more confused at God's reply
that man cannot see God's "face" and live and still more confused at the
distinction between God's "face" and His "back". Saadia, in his effort
to solve the problem, appears to take "seeing" literally. When God reveals
Himself to the prophet He creates a special light, which the prophets refer
to as "the glory of the Lord". All references in Scripture to the prophets
"seeing the Lord" are to this light. When Moses requested God to let him

see this light God replied that the first rays of this light were so powerful
that he could not gaze upon it with his naked eyes lest he perish. But he
was allowed to look at the back of the light. Saadia concludes: "As for
for Creator Himself, however, there is no means whereby anybody
might see Him. Aye, that is in the realms of the impossible". On this theory
of Saadia see A. Altmann: *Saadya's Theory of Revelation*, and on the influence
of the theory on mediaeval Jewish thought generally see Joseph Dan:
The Esoteric Theology of Ashkenazi Hasidism, Chapter 5, pp. 104–170. Judah
Ha-Levi (*Kuzari*, IV, 3) follows this line of thinking. Quite different is
Maimonides' understanding of the passage in Exodus. For Maimonides
(*Yad, Yesode Ha-Torah*, I: 10) Moses wished to have such a clear knowledge
(to "see") of God's nature that such knowledge would be quite distinct in his
mind from the knowledge he had of created things. This intense and
clear knowledge of God is described metaphorically as "see the face"
because when a man sees his neighbour's face he can henceforth easily
distinguish him from other men. God replies that such intense and clear
knowledge is not possible for man. However to Moses was given a depth of the
knowledge of God given to no other man so that in some faint way he was
able to distinguish God from His creatures. This fainter type of knowledge
is compared to "seeing the back" since when a man sees another from
behind he cannot distinguish him as clearly from others as if he saw him
from the front but he is still able to distinguish him in some way by the
different build of his body, the colour and fit of his clothes, and the
like. Thus, according to Maimonides (cf. *Guide*, I, 21) Moses demanded a
certain apprehension of God and this was refused him but he was given
an inferior apprehension. The Talmudic interpretation of seeing the "back"
that God showed Moses the "knot of the *Tefillin*" (Ber. 7a) was hardly
intended to be taken literally, though its precise meaning is unclear.
It possibly refers to the notion of "binding", i.e. that there is a connection
between that which Moses was shown and that which he was not shown.
Cf. Baruch Epstein: *Torah Temimah* to Ex. 33: 23.

Turning to the Rabbinic literature we find very few references to
anything like a theology of negation but there are, nonetheless, some
significant passages on the basis of which it is possible to construct
such a theology. We read[20] that the Palestinian teacher R. Abin said:
When Jacob of the village of Neboria was in Tyre, he interpreted the

20. Jer. Talmud Ber. 9: 1; Midrash to Psalm 19. Maimonides (*Guide*, I, 59) quotes
the verse from Psalms in support of his position. Cf. Zohar I, 2b. R. Joseph Karo
(*Bet Joseph* to *Tur, Orah Hayim*, 113) remarks in the name of R. Joseph of Gerona
that there is no objection to repeating Biblical verses which speak of God's
praises and, in the name of R. Aaron Ha-Levi of Barcelona, that the objection
to many praises only applies in any event, to praising God by recounting His
attributes not to the re-telling of His marvels and wonders.

verse: "For Thee, silence is praise, O God" (Psalms 65: 2) to mean
that silence is the ultimate praise of God. "It can be compared to a
jewel without price: however high you appraise it, you still under-
value it". The parallel passage in the Babylonian Talmud[21] adds the
popular proverb: "A word is worth a *sela*, silence two".

Another famous Talmudic passage, so helpful to Maimonides'
doctrine that he comments on it at length,[22] is the story[23] of the
prayer-reader who was rebuked by R. Hanina. We are told that a
prayer-reader praised God by listing at length all the attributes of
God of which he could think. When he had finished, R. Hanina
asked him if he had now exhausted the praises of God. R. Hanina
said that even the three attributes "The Great", "The Valiant" and
"The Tremendous" could not lawfully be used were it not for the
fact that Moses had used them and they have been incorporated into
the liturgy by the "Men of the Great Synagogue". The passage
concludes with a parable. A king possessing millions of gold pieces
is praised for possessing millions of silver pieces. This does not praise
him but disparages him.

Maimonides comments that in the parable the King is praised for
possessing silver pieces when, in reality, he possesses gold. The
parable does not say that the king is praised for possessing thousands
of gold pieces when, in reality, he possesses millions, for this would
suggest that the difference is one of degree not of kind. Whatever is
said of God in praise is so remote from the reality that the parable can
only use the simile of gold and silver pieces. The very coin of praise is
different.

The *via negativa* is undoubtedly unconventional in Jewish thought
but, as we have seen, it has, nonetheless, a respectable history and
numbers some great Jewish names among its adherents. Ideas left
vague and presented unsystematically in earlier sources became
revitalised under the impact of Neo-Platonism in the mediaeval period,

21. Meg. 18a. The translation "silence is the ultimate praise of God" follows Jastrow
    who takes the word *samma* as derived from *siyum* = "conclusion". Rashi, Meg.
    18a s.v. *samma*, understands the word to mean "medicine" and translates "silence
    is the best medicine". Levy, Wörterbuch, connects the word with Greek *soma*
    = "body" and translates: "the main thing is silence". Cf. Ibn. Ezra and Rashi
    to Ex. 15: 11: God is called "awesome in praises" because men are always in awe
    at praising God since whatever they say of Him is inadequate.
22. *Guide*, I, 59.
23. Ber. 33b.

to emerge as a definite theological approach. This approach is wrongly characterised as vaporous and lacking warmth and commitment. In an age in which we are repeatedly being told, and rightly so, that it is untenable to think of a God "up there" or "out there" there is positive value in the way of negation. Now God is not thought about at all as He is in Himself but only as He is manifested in His creation. He is only to be approached in wondrous worship as an Object (it would be better to say beyond subject and object) altogether too sublime to be imprisoned in the poor vehicle that is human speech.

The *via negativa* was, in fact, used by thinkers like Maimonides as part of their struggle against a corporeal concept of the Deity. We know that even among the learned in Maimonides' day and before it there were not lacking believers who took the anthropomorphic descriptions of the Bible and the Talmud literally. They held that it was incumbent for the Jew to believe that God has a form or, at least, could assume a form at will. That this was so can be seen from the curious case of the learned Talmudist of the 13th century Moses of Taku. He was severely critical of the whole philosophical enterprise as represented by Saadia and Maimonides. God is described in the Bible as sitting on a throne surrounded by His angels and appearing to man. Therefore, argues Moses of Taku,[24] the attempts of the philosophers not only contradicts the plain meaning of Scripture but sets arbitrary limits on God's power. If a magician can turn himself into a hare why should it be considered impossible for God to assume various forms and guises?

For Maimonides such a belief as that of Moses of Taku was rank heresy. It is setting no arbitrary limits on God to say that He cannot be other than God any more than it would be to state categorically that God cannot will Himself out of existence. That the ideas of a Moses of Taku strike the modern Jew as the height of absurdity is due to the refinement of the God concept undertaken by thinkers like Saadia[25] and Maimonides. Even thinkers like Crescas who saw no objection to the use of positive attributes agreed, of course, that God is incorporeal.

24. Moses of Taku's work: *Ketav Tamim* has been published from the manuscript with an Introduction and notes by R. Kircheim in *Otzar Nehmad*, Vol. III, pp. 54–99.
25. *Beliefs and Opinions*, II, 1–13. Cf. Simon Rawidowicz: *Saadya's Purification of the Idea of God* in *Saadya Studies*, pp. 139–165.

Maimonides goes so far as to read out of Judaism anyone who entertains the notion of God's corporeality. He observes[26] that anyone
who believes that there is only one God but that he has a body or form
is a heretic (*min*) and has no share in the World to Come. Maimonides'
great critic, Abraham Ibn David, comments: "Why does he call such
a person a heretic? Many greater and better than he have followed
this line of thought because of what they had seen in Scripture and
even more from that which they had seen in the legendary material of
the Talmud (*divre aggadot*) which confuses the mind". The debate
only concerns the exclusion of such crude believers from the Jewish
faith. Abraham ibn David would agree that the corporeal doctrine is
untenable.

Modern religious thinkers hardly need to be reminded of the total
inadequacy of a corporeal conception of God. Some of them, in their
horror of corporeality, have gone far beyond even the *via negativa* to
interpret the whole God concept in naturalistic terms. God, for these
thinkers, is the name we give to the Force or Power or Process, to be
observed at work in the world, which "makes for righteousness'. The
belief in a "Personal God" has been abandoned by these thinkers. But
it is difficult to see how such views really differ from an out and out
atheism or, at least, one might ask, what, according to these thinkers,
would a man have to disbelieve in order to qualify as an atheist? To
describe God as a "Person" is to be sure totally inadequate in describing
His true nature. But there is personality in the universe, we are "persons", and it is very difficult to see how this can have emerged from the
workings of a blind Force. Human personality is the highest thing we
know in the universe. Man is greater than the most powerful force
outside him in the universe in that he has an intellect and a moral
sense. The beauty of the Niagara Falls, for instance, is in the eye of the
human beholder. He can love and think and practise justice and they
can do none of these. While learning the lesson taught by the pro-
ponents of the *via negativa* we are still obliged to describe God, if we
speak of Him at all, in terms of the highest we know. This has been
expressed by saying that God is not less than personal.

The best-known Jewish exponent of a non-supernaturalistic theism is Mordecai
M. Kaplan, see especially his: *The Meaning of God in Modern Jewish Religion.*
Cf. the chapter on God's Incorporeality in my *Principles of the Jewish*

26. *Yad, Teshuvah,* 3: 7.

Faith, pp. 118–134. The literature which has grown up around the "death of God" controversy is relevant to our theme in that it discusses the whole question of having religion without the God of traditional theism. *Cf.* in particular the books of John Robinson, the Bishop of Woolwich, and the controversy surrounding them, e.g. *Honest to God*; *The New Reformation?*; *Exploration into God*; *The Honest To God Debate*; and the statement of Michael Ramsey, the Archbishop of Canterbury: *Image Old and New*. On the "death of God" see: Paul van Buren: *The Secular Meaning of the Gospel*; T. J. J. Altizer: *The Gospel of Christian Atheism* and (with William Hamilton) *Radical Theology and the Death of God*; H. Cox: *The Secular City*; Daniel E. Jenkins; *Guide to the Debate about God*; and C. F. D. Moule and others: *Faith, Fact and Fantasy*. In the latter book (pp. 47–78) P. R. Baelz points out that various "moves" are adopted by the "death of God" theologians, i.e. some say that the word "God" is no longer adequate or that this word refers to something other than it seems or that both the belief and the word be dropped and that it is difficult to be sure which of these moves some of our contemporary theologians are making. On the Jewish side the exponent of a "death of God" theology is Richard L. Rubenstein. On the whole subject of God as "personal" see I. Epstein's *The Faith of Judaism*, Chapter VIII, pp. 134f.

Rejecting then both extremes, of Moses Taku's corporeality and naturalism, we are left with the affirmation that God *is* and the negation of all human limitations from His being. Within this range the question of how far one goes in the way of negation still remains. This is not a matter to be decided by vote or by a consensus of opinion among Jewish thinkers. Some will prefer to follow Crescas, others Maimonides, and others again may prefer to go the whole way with the *En Sof* doctrine. Two statements of a theological position held by devout Jewish thinkers of the past may be quoted. The first of these is found in the mediaeval hymn *Shir Ha-Kavod* ("The Song of Glory") attributed to the school of Judah the Saint (12th–13th century):[27]

> *I will declare Thy glory, though I have not seen Thee;*
> *Under images will I describe Thee, though I have not known Thee.*
> *By the hand of Thy prophets, in the mystic utterance of Thy Servants,*
> *Thou hast imaged forth the grandeur and the glory of Thy majesty.*
> *Thy greatness and Thy might they described*
> *In accordance with the power made manifest in Thy acts.*
> *In images they told of Thee, but not according to Thine essence;*

27. Singer's Prayer Book, pp. 81–84.

They but likened Thee in accordance with Thy works.
They figured Thee in a multitude of visions;
Behold Thou art One under all images.

The second statement is from the writings of R. Moses Cordovero in the 16th century:[28] "When your intellect conceives of God, do not permit yourself to imagine that there is a God as depicted by you. For if you do this you will have a finite and corporeal conception, God forfend. Instead your mind must dwell only on the affirmation of God's existence and then recoil. To do more than this is to allow the imagination to reflect on God as He is in Himself and such reflection is bound to result in imaginative limitation and corporeality. Put reins, therefore, on your intellect and do not allow it too great a freedom, but assert God's existence and deny your intellect the possibility of comprehending Him. The mind should run to and fro—running to affirm God's existence and recoiling from any limitations produced by the imagination, since man's intellect is pursued by his imagination".

Hastings Rashdall,[29] though writing many years ago, can be allowed to have the last word here: "If we are justified in thinking of God after the analogy of the highest existence within our knowledge, we had better call him a Person. The word is no doubt inadequate to the reality, as is all the language we employ about God; but it is at least more adequate than the terms employed by those who scruple to speak of God as a Person. It is at least more adequate and more intelligent than to speak of Him as a force, a substance, a "something not ourselves that makes for righteousness"; and in using the term Person we shall at least make it clear that we do not think of Him as a 'thing', or a collection of things, or a vague substratum of things, or even a mere totality of minds like our own".

So far our discussion has been concerned with the metaphysics of the *via negativa* and of God as Person. More than any other modern thinker, Martin Buber has shown how a non-metaphysical, existentialist approach can be extremely helpful in extracting meaning from the whole concept of God as Person. Buber does not explore the actual concept of God as Person. He does not believe that such an exploration can get us very far. His emphasis is on *meeting* God as a Person. This is the theme of Buber's famous book *I and Thou*.

28. *Elimah Rabbati*, I, 10, p. 4b.   29. *Philosophy of Religion*, p. 56.

Buber's distinction between two kinds of relationship—*I–It* and *I–Thou* is well known. In the *I–It* relationship a man stands apart from the things or persons he approaches. He examines them in a detached manner. He sees them as being of use to him and he is not involved with them except in terms of this use. The *I–It* relationship is entirely proper in many areas of life. Scientific investigation, for example, requires a measure of detachment. The scientist, to be true to his task, must be an *observer* of the phenomena he studies. But there is another type of relationship—the *I–Thou* in which man is deeply involved with another. Here he sees the other as a "Thou" whom he meets as a person.

Buber himself has described vividly how the distinction made itself felt to him when he was still a child:[30] "When I was eleven years of age, spending the summer on my grandparents' estate, I used, as often as I could do it unobserved, to steal into the stable and gently stroke the neck of my darling, a broad dapplegray horse. It was not a casual delight but a great, certainly friendly, but also deeply stirring happening. If I am to explain it now, beginning from the still very fresh memory of my hand, I must say that what I experienced in touch with the animal was the Other, the immense otherness of the Other, which, however, did not remain strange like the ox and the ram, but rather let me draw near and touch it. When I stroked the mighty mane, sometimes marvellously smooth-combed, at other times just as astonishingly wild, and felt the life beneath my hand it was as though the element of vitality itself bordered on my skin, something that was not I, was certainly not akin to me, palpably the other, not just another, really the Other itself; and yet it let me approach, confided itself to me, placed itself elementally in the relation of *Thou* and *Thou* with me. The horse, even when I had not begun by pouring oats for him into the manger, very gently raised his massive head, ears flicking, then snorted quietly, as a conspirator gives a signal meant to be recognisable only by his fellow conspirator; and I was approved. But once—I do not know what came over the child, at any rate it was childlike enough—it struck me about the stroking, what fun it gave me, and suddenly I became conscious of my hand. The game went on as before, but something had changed, it was no longer the same thing. And the next day, after giving him a rich feed, when I stroked my friend's

30. *The Philosophy of Martin Buber*, p. 10.

head he did not raise his head. A few years later, when I thought back to the incident, I no longer supposed that the animal had noticed my defection. But at the time I considered myself judged".

According to Buber, whenever a man has this *I-Thou* relationship he is, in fact, addressing God, the *Thou* behind all *Thous*. This is the significance of speaking of God as Personal, although Buber would add that the whole point of the distinction is that one does not speak of God but only *to* God. As Buber explains it: "The extended lines of relations meet in the eternal *Thou*. Every particular *Thou* is a glimpse through to the eternal *Thou*; by means of every particular *Thou* the primary word addresses the eternal *Thou*. Through this mediation of the *Thou* of all beings fulfilment, and non-fulfilment, of relations comes to them: the inborn *Thou* is realised in each relation and consummated in none. It is consummated only in the direct relation with the *Thou* that by its nature cannot become *It*. Men have addressed their eternal *Thou* with many names. In singing of Him who was thus named they always had the *Thou* in mind: the first myths were hymns of praise. Then the names took refuge in the language of *It*; men were more and more strongly moved to think of and to address their eternal *Thou* as an *It*. But all God's names are hallowed, for in them He is not merely spoken about, but also spoken to."

What Buber offers us is an approach to God that is non-anthropo-morphic and intensely personal. Issue can be taken, however, with Buber and his followers in their refusal to engage in any sustained metaphysical discussion of God as non-anthropomorphic and yet personal. There appears to be no valid reason why the kind of meta-physical approach sketched in the earlier part of this chapter should not be used as a complement to Buber's insight.

Buber is also anti-mystical. The mystical approach, typified by the Habad thinkers whose views we have noted, tends to see the loss of selfhood in the divine as the highest aim. The habad Hasidim speak in fact of the "annihilation of the self". Buber is very suspicious of this in that it encourages an attitude of dualism between the Creator and His creatures. Man cannot live all the time, the majority of men for most of the time, lost to the divine. After the mystical flight he returns to become even more conscious than ever of the gulf between God and the universe. Followers of Buber have for this reason claimed that his vision is the deeper. Perhaps it is a matter of temperament. In favour of the mystical approach it can be argued that some of the most sublime creations of the human spirit, in art, literature and music, for example, have been attained through the artist's forgetfulness of self. A good case can be made out that, from the religious point of view, this is what the great mystics were thinking of when they tried haltingly to describe how man's true self meets the Self of the universe when the ego is transcended. Against this it can be said that the mystical soul is rare and that for the majority of men who live in the world and are involved in it Buber is, indeed, the more profound guide.

CHAPTER FOUR

TRANSCENDENCE AND IMMANENCE

A THOROUGH-GOING pantheism, in which God is only immanent in the universe and not transcendent, can really have no other meaning than that God is identified with the totality of things, that He is the universe and the universe is He. (The Hasidic doctrine of panentheism, fundamentally different from pantheism, has been discussed in Chapter 2 of this book and will be further considered later in this Chapter.) Deism, on the other hand, is the doctrine that God is entirely beyond the universe. It leaves no room for any interaction between the divine and the universe and hence no possibility of divine intervention in the affairs of the universe. Deism rules out divine providence and revelation. Traditional theism rejects both pantheism and deism, affirming that God is both transcendent and immanent, beyond the universe and apart from it but working within it.

Now when it is said of God that He is "beyond" or "outside" the universe this immediately raises questions and can be very misleading in that such terms suggest a spatial location. God is not removed from the universe to inhabit remote outer space on any sophisticated view of traditional theism. When terms like "beyond" or "outside" or "apart from" the universe are used of God by theists they can only mean that He is other than the universe, that if there were no universe God would still be.

It is certainly very precarious to read later philosophical ideas into the words of the Talmudic Rabbis, but, whatever the original meaning of the following Talmudic passage, it can serve (and has so served in Jewish thought) as a peg on which to hang what would appear to be the normal way of understanding the idea of God's transcendence and immanence. In the passage[1] God is compared to the soul and there are said to be five points of resemblance. God "fills the

1. Ber. 10a.

world" and the soul "fills the body". God "sees, but is not seen" and the soul "sees, but is not seen". God "sustains the world" and the soul "sustains the body". God is "pure" and the soul is "pure". God "resides in the innermost recesses" and the soul "resides in the innermost recesses".

One way of describing the difference between a corpse and a living person is to say that the latter, unlike the former, has a soul within him. But "within" here cannot refer to any spatial location. (Of course it is true that in primitive thought the soul was held to be located in a part of the body—some of the early Greeks, for example, thought of the soul as being located in the heel—but few people think of it in this way today. Nor is it relevant to our argument to point out the ambiguities in the whole concept of the "soul". The point we are trying to make is that when people do speak of the soul *in* the body they do not normally think of it as inhabiting part of the body in the way in which, for example, wine which has just been imbibed resides in a definite part of the body.) If the "soul" is thought of as in some way invading the body, which is located in space, it is not thought of as coming there from somewhere in outer space but from a spiritual realm which is "beyond" the spatial universe altogether. There is obviously no spatial location outside the universe for any space we can imagine belongs to the universe. When we use terms like "outside" or "beyond" (or, for that matter, "depth") in speaking of God's transcendence, it is clear, or ought to be, that these terms are used for spiritual realities and are not to be understood literally. This has sometimes been put as that God is present in the universe in the sense in which an author is present in his book, although this analogy, too, must not be pressed too far.

The transcendence of God is taught in many a Biblical passage. In the creation narrative with which the book of Genesis opens (Gen. 1: 1–2: 4a) God is Creator of heaven and earth and all their hosts. He brings the world into being by "saying" "Let there be". The prophet of exile declares (Is. 40: 21–26):

Know ye not, hear ye not?
Hath it not been told to you from the beginning?
Have ye not understood the foundations of the earth?
It is He that sitteth above the circle of the earth,

> And the inhabitants thereof are as grasshoppers;
> That stretcheth out the heavens as a curtain,
> And spreadeth them out as a tent to dwell in . . .
> To whom then will ye liken Me, that I should be equal?
> Saith the Holy One.
> Lift up your eyes on high,
> And see: who hath created these?
> He that bringeth out their hosts by number.
> He calleth them all by name;
> By the greatness of His might, and for that He is
>   strong in power,
> Not one faileth.

And again (Is. 55: 8–9):

> For My thoughts are not your thoughts,
> Neither are your ways My ways, saith the Lord.
> For as the heavens are higher than the earth,
> So are My ways higher than your ways,
> And My thoughts than your thoughts.

The Psalmist (Ps. 95: 4–5) says:

> In His hand are the deep places of the earth;
> The heights of the mountains are His also
> The sea is His, and He made it;
> And His hands formed the dry land.

That God is far distant from man and cannot be reached by man's thought is expressed in the book of Job (11: 7–9):

> Canst thou find out the deep things of God?
> Canst thou attain unto the purpose of the Almighty?
> It is high as heaven; what canst thou do?
> Deeper than the nether-world; what canst thou know?
> The measure thereof is longer than the earth,
> And broader than the sea.

And again (Job 35: 5–7):

> Look unto the heavens, and see;
> And behold the skies, which are higher than thou.
> If thou hast sinned, what doest thou against Him?
> And if thy transgressions be multiplied, what doest
>   thou against Him?
> If thou be righteous, what givest thou Him?
> Or what receiveth He of thy hand?

The book of Ecclesiastes declares (5: 1):
> *Be not rash with thy mouth, and let not*
> *thy heart be hasty to utter a word before*
> *God; for God is in heaven, and thou upon earth;*
> *Therefore let thy words be few.*

But this is by no means the whole story. The truth is that it is not really possible to speak of *the* Biblical view, as if there is no development of thought at all among the Biblical authors and no different emphases in the various Biblical books. Moreover, the Bible is not a series of philosophical treatises. Indeed, the very concepts of transcendence and immanence, which are philosophical terms, are far removed from Biblical forms of thought and expression. What does emerge from a study of the relevant Biblical passages is that while there are numerous statements in which God is regarded as apart from the universe there are also many statements in which He is said, so it is implied, to be involved in the processes of the universe. He is described, frequently as Father, for example, and as King. The question of miracles will be considered separately in this book but the many Biblical references to miracles surely imply that God intervenes in the universe He has created. The Psalmist, speaking of God's omnipresence, says (Ps. 139: 7–12):

> *Whither shall I go from Thy spirit?*
> *Or whither shall I flee from Thy presence?*
> *If I ascend up into heaven, Thou art there;*
> *If I make my bed in the netherworld, behold, Thou art there.*
> *If I take the wings of the morning,*
> *And dwell in the uttermost parts of the sea;*
> *Even there would Thy hand lead me,*
> *And Thy right hand would hold me.*
> *And if I say: "Surely the darkness shall envelope me,*
> *And the light about me shall be night";*
> *Even the darkness is not too dark for Thee,*
> *But the night shineth as the day;*
> *The darkness is even as the light.*

Again the Psalmist says (Ps. 19: 2):
> *The heavens declare the glory of God,*
> *And the firmament showeth His handiwork.*

And when the prophet (Is. 6: 3) speaks of the seraphim declaring that God is "holy", that is, utterly apart from and different from man, he speaks yet of these declaring that God's glory fills the world:

> And one called unto another, and said:
> Holy, holy, holy, is the Lord of Hosts;
> The whole earth is full of His glory.

There is a Talmudic passage[2] of relevance to the theme of transcendence and immanence in the Bible. There we read that the third century Palestinian teacher R. Johanan said that wherever you find recorded in the Bible the "greatness" of God there you find His "humility". R. Johanan supports his case with quotations from all three parts of the Bible, the Pentateuch, the Prophets and the Hagiographa. In the Pentateuch there is the verse: "For the Lord your God, He is the God of gods and the Lord of lords" (Deut. 10: 17), and immediately afterwards it says: "He doth execute justice for the fatherless and widow". In the Prophets there is the verse (Is. 57: 15): "For thus saith the High and Lofty One, that inhabiteth eternity, whose name is holy", and immediately afterwards it says: "(I dwell) with him that is of a contrite and humble spirit". In the Hagiographa (Ps. 68: 5) there is the verse: "Extol Him that rideth upon the skies, whose name is the Lord" and immediately afterwards it is written "A Father of the fatherless and a judge of the widows".

On the general question of transcendence and immanence in the Bible C. G. Montefiore (quoted by Abelson: *The Immanence of God*, p. 49 note 2) is probably correct that in the earlier passages God was thought of as very near. "God became far off rather *late*, and then by Immanence He had to be made 'near' again". But even in the earliest passages the idea of immanence is implied in rudimentary form. The famous passage in Gen. 28: 10-22 (Jacob's dream) is germane. S. R. Driver (*Genesis*, p. 268) after pointing to the more primitive ideas in the narrative (e.g. the annointing of the sacred stone) remarks that the truths which find expression in it are: "that heaven and earth are not spiritually parted from one another, that God's protecting presence accompanies His worshippers, and that He is ever at their side, even when they are away from their accustomed place of worship, and are otherwise tempted by circumstances not to realise the fact." More especially the question of transcendence and immanence is behind the institutions of Tabernacle and Temple. Modern Biblical scholarship traces a long process of development behind the account of the

2. Meg. 31a.

Priestly writers in the final chapters of Exodus. Behind the whole idealistic institution, i.e. one which in its Exodus form is an imaginary structure but based on very early material, is the idea of God as dwelling in the Tabernacle. The root *shakhan*, used of the Tabernacle (*mishkan*), goes back to a very ancient idea, that the god dwells in his house. But eventually in Biblical monotheism it came to express the paradox of transcendence and immanence. As Frank M. Cross Jr. remarks (*The Priestly Tabernacle*, p. 64), after an acute analysis of the literary and historical problem: "The Priestly writers were struggling with the problem of divine immanence and transcendence, in other words, the problem of the covenant-presence of Yahweh in the sanctuary. Israel's cosmic and omnipotent (*sic*, surely "omnipresent"?) God could not be confined to any earthly sanctuary. Yet the supreme object and benefit of the covenant relationship—of Isreal's election in the great events following the Exodus—was God's new 'closeness' in the tabernacles. It seems clear that this old word *skn* has been taken as the technical theological term to express this paradox. The Priestly writers retrieved a 'desert' terminology that was genuinely archaic. Yahweh does not 'dwell' on earth. Rather he 'tabernacles' or settles impermanently as in the days of the portable, ever-conditioned tent".

The Rabbinic views on transcendence and immanence have been adequately surveyed in the excellent work on this subject by J. Abelson.[3] Of special significance is the Rabbinic doctrine of the Shekhinah. The Shekhinah (from the root *shakhan*, "to dwell', used, as above, in the account of the Tabernacle) is the Divine Presence, the indwelling Presence of God. For a full statement of the doctrine Abelson's work should be consulted. Here we need only refer to some typical Rabbinic passages regarding the Shekhinah.

The Shekhinah is compared to light. Thus the verse: "May the Lord cause the light of His countenance to shine upon thee" (Num. 6: 25) is paraphrased by the Midrash "May He give thee of the light of the Shekhinah".[4] The "shining" (*ziv*) of the Shekhinah is referred to in the Midrashic passage[5] in which it is said that the shining of the Shekhinah in the Tent of Meeting can be compared to a cave by the sea. The sea rushes in to fill the cave, but the sea suffers no diminution of its waters. Similarly, the Divine Presence filled the Tent of Meeting, but it filled the world just the same. The third century Babylonian teacher Rab said:[6] "In the World to Come there is no eating nor

3. *The Immanence of God in Rabbinical Literature.*
4. *Sifre*, 41, to Num. 6: 25.
5. Num. R. 12: 4; Cant. R. 3: 8.
6. Ber. 17a.

drinking nor propagation nor business nor jealousy nor hatred nor competition, but the righteous sit with their crowns on their heads and enjoy the brightness (*ziv*) of the Shekhinah". Sometimes, too, the Shekhinah is personified, as when R. Meir says:[7] "When a man is sore troubled, what does the Shekhinah say? My head is ill at ease, my arm is ill at ease". But even when the Shekhinah is personified it is, as it were, the symbol of God's manifestation in the universe. Nowhere in the Rabbinic literature is there to be found anything like the later Kabbalistic idea of the Shekhinah as a female element in God, treated as in some way separate from "The Holy One, blessed He", the male element. (In the Kabbalah the Shekhinah represents the Sefirah *Malkhut* and "The Holy One, blessed by He" the *Sefirah Tiferet*).[8]

In an oft-quoted Talmudic passage[9] it is said: "Come and see how beloved Israel is before God; for wherever they went into exile the Shekhinah went with them. When they were exiled to Egypt, the Shekhinah went with them; in Babylon the Shekhinah was with them; and in the future, when Israel will be redeemed, the Shekhinah will be with them".[10]

From such passages, which could easily be multiplied, it seems clear that while the Rabbinic doctrine of the Shekhinah does touch on the question of divine immanence it is not quite what immanence as a philosophical term means. It is probably true to say that the idea of God at work in and through the processes of the universe is expressed in the Bible and the Rabbinic literature but it is incipient and implied rather than stated explicitly. Bearing this in mind there is

7. Mishnah Sanh. 6: 5.
8. See *supra* pp. 29–30. The sole exception so far as the Rabbinic literature is concerned is the very late Midrash (Prov. ed. Buber, p. 47a): "The Shekhinah stood before the Holy One, blessed be He". See Scholem: *Reshit Ha-Kabbalah*, p. 51, note 1. Urbach: *The Sages*, Chapter 3, p. 34 n. 1 quotes Sifre, Num. 94 in which the Shekhinah is spoken of as separate from *Ha-Makom*. Urbach, however, op. cit., p. 51 takes issue with Scholem in his interpretation of the late Midrash quoted above. Here the term "Shekhinah" is used loosely as a synonym for *bat kol*, a heavenly voice. Saadia (*Beliefs and Opinions*, II, 10, ed. Rosenblatt, p. 121) understands the references to the Shekhinah as a special form created for that purpose, see *supra*, p. 46.
9. Meg. 29a.
10. In the Kabbalah the "exile of the Shekhinah" means the exile of the Shekhinah from "The Holy One, blessed be He", i.e. the disharmony produced, as it were, in the Sefirotic realm when Israel (the counterpart of the Shekhinah on earth) is in exile.

no reason to quarrel with Abselon's summary:[11] "It has now, I hope, sufficiently been proved that Rabbinic theology is deeply ingrained with a mystical element. The quintessential feature of all mysticism— the belief in the Immanence of God—is a characteristic of the Rabbinic Judaism. The incoming of God into human life, the implanting of the Divine life within the human soul, the permanent presence of the Divine Spirit accompanying or acting in fellowship with, a whole body of men or a whole race,—I have quoted sufficient illustrations from the vast domains of Talmudic and Midrashic literature to demonstrate the tenacity with which the authors of the latter held these truths, and their unshakable belief in the fact that the people on whose behalf they spoke experienced them". To this it might, however, be added that the religious experience of the Rabbis was not found in "solitariness', it was not apart from the daily experience of life and had a social character. In the words of Max Kadushin Rabbinic mysticism is "normal mysticism".[12]

Among the mediaeval thinkers the concept of Nature began to be used and this led to detailed consideration of how Nature is related to God. The views of the mediaeval thinkers in this connection will be examined in the section in this book on Providence.[13] But reference should be made to Judah Ha-Levi's expression of the paradox of transcendence and immanence in his famous poem:[14]

> Lord where shall I find thee?
> High and hidden is thy place:
> And where shall I not find thee?
> The world is full of thy glory.

We now must turn to the reaction of Judaism towards the more recent challenges of pantheism and deism as rivals to traditional theism.

The great exponent of pantheism is, of course, Benedict Spinoza. It appears that in Spinoza's system God and Nature are treated as

11. *The Immanence of God*, p. 278.
12. See the Chapter on *Normal Mysticism* in Kadushin's *The Rabbinic Mind*, Chapter 6, pp. 194–272.
13. See *infra*, pp. 114–116.
14. *Selected Poems of Jehudah Ha-Levi*, trans. Nina Salaman.

different names for the same thing. God is not "outside" or apart from
Nature. He did not *create* Nature but *is* Nature. Neither intellect nor
will can be ascribed to God. Indeed, in Spinoza's thought, it seems
that God is the name given to the totality of things. At the opposite
pole from Spinoza were the Deists.[15] Deism was a popular philosophy
in the 18th century. With the rise of modern science and the conse-
quent vividness of a causal explanation of phenomena, it seemed
plausible to some to draw a distinction between God, the Author and
Creator of all that exists, and Nature, which proceeds by its own laws
without divine intervention. God, in His relationship to Nature, is
thought of as the maker of a machine. The influence of the maker is
limited to the manufacture of the machine, which is then left to work
by itself with no more than an occasional check by the maker to see
if the machine is functioning properly. Carlyle[16] described the Deistic
God as "an absentee God, sitting idle, ever since the first Sabbath, at
the outside of his universe, and seeing it go".

One of the most learned scholars Anglo–Jewry has ever had was
the Haham David Nieto (1654–1728). In a sermon delivered at the
Spanish and Portuguese Synagogue in London on Nov. 20th, 1703,
Nieto attacked the Deist view[17] which regards Nature as a metaphysical entity apart from God. Nieto observed that the term
"Nature" was of fairly recent coinage and is, in reality, only another
name for God's providential control over the world He has created.
Therefore, Nieto declared, God and Nature were one and the same.
Nieto's concern was to refute the Deist view that Nature is an intermediary between the world and God. Such a view, stated Nieto, was
at variance with Judaism. Nature is simply a modern term for which
the Rabbis used the word "God". Opponents of Nieto seized upon
this sermon as evidence that Nieto had accepted Spinozism and a

15. On deism see: George Galloway: *The Philosophy of Religion*, pp. 458–460; N. L.
    Torrey: *Voltaire and the English Deists*; J. Orr: *English Deism: Its Roots and Fruits*.
    Kaufmann Kohler (*Jewish Theology*, Preface, beg.) claims that Moses Mendel-
    ssohn was "rather a deist that a theist" and that this is why Mendelssohn stated
    bodly that Judaism "is not a revealed religion but a revealed law intended solely
    for the Jewish people as the vanguard of universal monotheism". This is, of course,
    to speak very loosely. Strictly speaking the deists acknowledged neither a revealed
    religion nor a revealed law since, for them, revelation of any kind was ruled out
    by their philosophy.
16. *Sartor Resartus*, Book II, Chapter 7.
17. On Nieto and his views see especially the excellent treatment of Jacob J. Petuch-
    owski: *The Theology of Haham Dacid Nieto*, pp. 118–127.

query was addressed to Zevi Ashkenazi, the famous Rabbi of Amsterdam, for his opinion. The conclusion arrived at by both Nieto and Zevi Ashkenazi was that the fundamental difference between Spinoza and what Nieto considers to be the authentic Jewish view is that for Spinoza God is the name given to the totality of things, whereas, on the Jewish view, God created Nature and He governs the world. On the Jewish view God is transcendent as well as immanent and particular parts of Nature such as vegetation, clouds and rain, are God's creatures, not part of God Himself.

The distinction becomes clearer if a few passages, in Cecil Roth's translation *Anglo-Jewish Letters*, pp. 89–95 are given from the letter addressed by Nieto's Wardens to Zevi Ashkenazi and from the latter's reply.

(1) *From the letter of the Wardens.*
"Rabbi David Nieto, president of the Rabbinical court and guide and teacher of our community, gave a sermon in the synagogue in which he said: "I am reputed to have stated in the Rabbinical college that *God and Nature, and Nature and God, are one and the same*. It is true that I have made this statement and I now repeat and confirm it; and I gave as my authority the words of the Psalmist in the 147th Psalm: He who covereth the heaven with clouds; he who prepareth rain for the earth; he who maketh grass to grow upon the mountains. You must know, however, as the first principle of our faith, that the word Nature is a modern expression, no more than four or five hundred years old, and is not found in the words of the Talmudic Sages, who said that it is God who *causeth the wind to blow*; and God who *causeth the rain to fall*; and God who *causeth the dew to come forth*. From these passages it is clear that everything attributed by modern thinkers to Nature is due to the action of God; so that in fact there is no such thing as Nature, what they call Nature being nothing more than the providence of God. And so, as I said, God and Nature, and Nature and God, are one and the same". This sermon has given rise to a charge of heterodoxy . . . Such is the case. We ask you to decide with whom is the right".

(2) *From the reply of Zevi Ashkenazi.*
"I have listened to the complaints of his (Nieto's) opponents but I do not understand them. If they take exception to his statement that apart from God there is no Nature comprehending all existing things, and make this objection on the ground that it is a derogation from the glory of God, the King of Kings, that he should act without an intermediary; they must learn that it is those who seek for the mediation of Nature in the general world-order who are likely to fall into perplexity, whereas those who believe in the direct action of God's providence in all things do so securely

whithersoever they turn. If, secondly, they think that the words of the
sermon referred not to Nature in general but to particular natural things—
the heat of fire, for example, or the wetness of water—and from this
understanding force the interpretation that in their natural action fire and
water are themselves the Godhead (an opinion which would not be held
by the most foolish and brutish of unbelievers, much less by a sage and
learned man among the people of God who believe in God and in His holy
law)—on this count the words of the sermon are perfectly clear, without
the need of the defence, seeing that they are centred upon the fundamental
principle of the world order; as he says: *it is God who causeth the winds to
blow and bringeth down the rain and dews; from which passage it is clear that
everything attributed by modern thinkers to Nature is due to the action of God.*
On this point only wilful misconstruction can raise a doubt".

The reply of Zevi Ashkenazi has been printed in his Responsa collection:
Teshuvat Haham Tzevi, No. 18. See Solomon B. Freehof: *A Treasury of
Response*, pp. 176–81.

Another attack on deism, though without mentioning the deists
by name (the author in all probability was not aware of their existence)
is found in the work *Tanya* by the Hasidic master R. Schneor Zalman
of Liady (1747–1813), founder of the Habad movement of Hasidism.
R. Schneor Zalman writes:[18] "Here lies the answer to the heretics and
here is uncovered the root of their error, in which they deny God's
providence over particular things and the miracles and wonders
recorded in Scripture. Their false imagination leads them into error,
for they compare the work of the Lord, Creator of heaven and earth,
to the works of man and his artifices. These stupid folk compare the
work of heaven and earth to a vessel which comes from the hands of a
craftsman. Once the vessel has been fashioned it requires its maker no
longer. Even when the maker has completed his task and goes about
his own business, the vessel retains the form and appearance it had
when it was fashioned. Their eyes are too blind to notice the important
distinction between the works of man and his artifices—in which
"something" is made from "something", the form alone being
changed from a piece of silver into an ornament—and the creation of
heaven and earth, which is the creation of "something" out of
"nothing". This latter is a marvel greater even than the division of the
Red Sea, for instance, when the Lord caused a strong east wind to blow
all through the night, until the waters were divided to stand up as a
heap and a wall. If the Lord had stopped the wind for but a moment,

18. *Tanya*, *Shaar Ha-Yihud Ve-Ha-Emunah*, Chapter 2, pp. 153–4.

the waters, undoubtedly, would have begun to flow again in their normal, natural way and would no longer have stood upright like a wall. Although this nature implanted in the waters is also a "something" created out of "nothing", yet for all that a stone wall does stand upright without the help of the wind, only this is not true of the nature of water. It follows *a fortiori* that with regard to *creatio ex nihilo* —higher than nature and a much greater marvel than the division of the Red Sea—it is certain that the creature would revert to the state of nothingness and negation, God forfend, if the Creator's power over it were to be removed. It is essential, therefore, for the power of the Worker to be in His work constantly if that work is to be kept in existence". For Schneor Zalman it is impossible to suggest, as do the deists, that God has created Nature and left it, as it were, to its own devices, since from God's point of view Nature itself is "unnatural", contrary to the "nothingness' from which it emerged. As the stone drops to the ground when the restraining hand relinquishes its hold, Nature would "naturally" revert to nothingness were it not for the hand of God, which keeps Nature permanently suspended over the void. It follows that it is an absurdity to speak of Nature being left to its own devices, for if Nature were "left alone" by God it would become "no-Nature", vanishing into the abyss whence it came.

In reality Schneor Zalman is alluding here to the idea that from God's point of view, as it were, there is no universe at all. Hence God alone can make the universe appear real to us and it is absurd to speak of the universe being left to its own devices. We touch here, then, on the Hasidic doctrine of panentheism, to which we have alluded and criticised in an earlier chapter.[19] In deism God is apart from the world. In pantheism He is only *in* the world or identified with it. In panentheism the world is *in* God. (As we have noted earlier a good deal depends on how *in* is to be understood here and the difficulties of the panentheistic idea have been sufficiently noted.)

Hasidic panenthenism, though especially prominent in *Habad*, has its roots in early Hasidism. In *Habad* in particular, but to some extent in early Hasidism generally, the Lurianic doctrine of *Tzimtzum* (see *supra*, pp. 32–34) is interpreted in such a way that God does not really "withdraw" so that ultimately there is only God. God in His relation to the universe is described in Hasidic thought in terms suggesting that the world is an emanation from God. The very suggestive early Hasidic illustration (see,

19. See *supra*, pp. 34–37.

for example, *Keter Shem Tov*, I, pp. 51-b) is "like a snail whose shell is formed
of itself". This saying is found in the Midrash (Gen. R. 21: 5) but there
refers only to the garments of the "generation of the wilderness" which
grew with them as they grew older. It would appear that the use of the
illustration to refer to the relationship between God and the universe is
peculiar to Hasidism. Cf. *Keter Shem Tov*, I, p. 8b, that the meaning of the
verse: "Know this day, and lay it to thy heart, that the Lord He is God
in heaven above and in the earth beneath; *there is none else*" (Deut. 4: 39),
is that, in reality, there is *nothing but God*, for otherwise the world would
be "separate" from *En Sof* and this would imply limitation in God. This
text became a favourite *Habad* text. Frequently in early Hasidic literature
the Midrashic saying (Num. R. 12: 4) that there is no place empty of the
Shekhinah is paraphrased in Aramaic—*let atar panui minne*—"no place is empty
of Him". Cf. Dubnow: *Toledot Ha-Hasidut*, pp. 52 F. The verse: "The
whole earth is full of his glory" (Is. 6: 3) was interpreted in early Hasidism
to mean that all is God, as was the verse: "Blessed be the glory of the
Lord from His place" (Exek. 3: 12). The verse: "And Thou preservest them
all" (Neh. 9: 6) was interpreted to mean: "And Thou giveth being to them
all", i.e. that their being is in God (*mehavveh* instead of *mehayeh*). On this see
the letters of anathema against the Hasidim published by E. Zweiful in
his *Shalom Al Yisreal*, Vol. II, pp. 37-60, here it is said: "They interpret
unlawfully the verse: 'Blessed be the glory of the Lord from His place' and
the verse: 'And Thou preservest them all'." Eventually, it is interesting to
note, even a man like R. Hayim of Volozhyn, disciple of the Gaon of Vila,
the chief opponent of the Hasidim, can write (*Nefesh Ha-Hayim*, Shaar 3,
p. 67f): "Apart from Him, blessed be He, there is nothing else whatsoever,
in reality, in all the worlds, from the highest of the high to the lowest depths
of the earth. So that one can say that there is no creature or world at all
but all is filled with the essence of His pure unity, blessed be He." And
again: "From His point of view, blessed be He, they are all as if they had
no existence whatsoever, even now, as before creation." The only difference
between R. Hayim and *Habad* is that the former does not consider it
meritorious to dwell long on this theme in contemplation. R. Hayim's
words, clearly directed against Hasidism, are worth quoting (pp. 69-70):
"This tremendous matter is intended only for the sage, who can understand
on his own the inner meaning of the subject by allowing his heart to run
to and fro, for the whole purpose of inflaming the purity of his heart
for God's worship in prayer, But there is the greatest danger in too much
contemplation on this theme . . . In fact, I would have withheld myself altogether
from speaking of this, for the earlier teachers, of blessed memory, greatly
concealed this subject . . . But, on the other hand, I observed that although
this was proper in their generation yet nowadays we have been without a
guide (= the Gaon of Vilna) for many days. The way of each man is upright
in his own eyes; to follow the tendency of reason and the whole inclination
of man's thoughts is only to fly with his thoughts to wherever reason
directs. More than anything, this has become a popular doctrine so that

even fools speak in parables, saying that real divinity is in all places and in all things; and all their days their eyes and hearts are turned in deep contemplation on this theme, to the extent that even the hearts of empty youths draw them to conduct themselves in accordance with this reasoning of theirs. How great is the care man should take in this matter to guard himself with protection after protection! For if, God forfend, his heart will persuade him to fix this thought so firmly as to act in accordance with it even in practice (i.e. as opposed to the holding of it merely in theory) then, God forfend, there can result the destruction of many of the foundations of our holy Torah, may the All-Merciful deliver us. It is easy for man to be snared, God forfend, in the trap of his evil inclination, which may suggest to him, for instance, on the basis of this idea, that it is permissible brazenly to think on words of Torah even in unclean places because it has become fixed firmly in the mind that all is real divinity . . ." On this theme see M. Teitelbaum: *Ha-Rav Mi-Ladi*, Vol. II, Chapters 1-3, pp. 37-94 and Tishby and Dan: *Torah Ha-Hasidut*, p. 775.

While both deism and pantheism are incompatible with theism as Judaism understands it, panentheism, though dubbed heresy by opponents of the Hasidim, has been advanced by many thinkers of this movement. The mystical mind tends to see God in all things. The doctrine of His omnipresence is extended to its uttermost limits. This tendency in Hasidism agrees with Elizabeth Barrett Browning:

> *Earth's crammed with heaven,*
> *And every common bush afire with God;*
> *But only he who sees, takes off his shoes.*

The paradox of divine transcendence and immanence is resolved in this system by declaring that God is the all, that if only man learns to penetrate deeper into ultimate reality he will see only the divine power by which all things are sustained. And although this way of looking at it is most typical of the *Habad* movement in Hasidism, to a large extent it is implicit, as we have noted, in Hasidism in general. The song of the Hasidic master, R. Levi Yitzhak of Berditchev, has frequently been repeated:[20]

> *Where I wander—You!*
> *Where I ponder—You!*
> *Only You, You again, always You!*

20. See e.g. Buber: *Tales of the Hasidim*, Vol. I, p. 212.

You! You! You!
When I am gladdened—You!
When I am saddened—You!
Only You, You again, always You!
You! You! You!
Sky is You! Earth is You!
You above! You below!
In every trend, at every end,
Only You, You again, always You!
You! You! You!

Much space has been given in this chapter to Hasidic panentheism because it can serve as a pointer for the modern Jew who accepts, as this book does, theistic supernaturalism. These mystical writers were grappling with a real problem. How can one understand the universe as God's creation and as the sphere of His continuous solicitude while recognising that at the same time it enjoys autonomy? The problem will be discussed further in the chapter on Providence but it must be considered, too, in any discussion of transcendence and immanence. The particular Hasidic solution is to suggest that "in reality" there is only God and that creatures "do not really" enjoy any independent existence. We have noted above[21] the logical difficulties in speaking of creatures as having independent existence and yet not "really" doing so. This is so weighty an objection that the Hasidic view cannot be sustained. Is it, then, no more than high-flown poetry or can we extract from it some insight of help to us without total acceptance of its illogical world view? It seems that we can.

Traditional theism affirms that the transcendent God is yet immanent in the universe He has created. The mystics among the theists say that this must imply that in some measure things are not what they seem to be. In the eyes of the mystics the "solidity" of things tend to dissolve in the more ultimate reality of the divine. The semantic question here is how to "cash" a term like "more ultimate". To be sure one cannot deny all reality to the universe, as some of the mystics appear to do, for, then, we are back to the logical confusion involved in both affirming and denying a reality at the same time. But it is not illogical to affirm that the solid realities we encounter in sense perception are not really what they seem to be. From Bishop Berkeley

21. See *supra*, pp. 35–36.

through Hume and Kant down to the theories of modern physicists the opinion that we know things as they really are has been challenged. It is startling but true, for instance, that when a television set is switched on and left in an empty room there is no picture to be seen without the human eye and no sound to be heard without the human ear. On the theistic premise it is but a step to affirm that the ultimate stuff of things is the divine energy and vitality which keeps them in being.

An illustration sometimes given by those who favour the mystical approach is of a man ascending a mountain and looking down on a village in the valley below. While he is on the lower slopes of the mountain, with the village close to his vision, every detail of the houses, roads, bridges and rivers can be seen distinctly. But the higher he ascends the more do these details merge into a single entity, the village, which, in turn, merges into the wider landscape seen as the climber reaches the summit. This is no more than an analogy but why should it not be assumed, granted the theistic position, that the "higher" one climbs in spiritual perception the greater is the force of realisation of the unifying power of God?

If one tries to see it in this way the autonomy of the universe is preserved even while one responds to the "Dudele" of R. Levi Yitzchak. That there are problems no one will deny. These must be considered as we pursue our investigation further.

CHAPTER FIVE

OMNIPOTENCE AND OMNISCIENCE

A DISCUSSION of the doctrine of God's omnipotence can fruitfully begin with a consideration of two Biblical passages in which practically the same words are used to denote the idea that nothing is too difficult for God to do. The first of these is the story in which Abraham is told that his wife Sarah, aged ninety, will give birth to a child (Gen. 18: 1–15). Sarah laughs at the very thought but her laughter is rebuked: "Is anything too hard for the Lord?" (Gen. 18: 14). The second passage deals with Jeremiah's purchase of a field at the command of God when the city is being threatened by the Chaldeans (Jer. 32: 6–27). Virtually the same words are used as in the Abraham narrative: "Behold, I am the Lord, the God of all flesh; is there anything too hard for Me?" (Jer. 32: 27).

The Hebrew word translated as "hard" in both passages, is *yippale*, with a root meaning of "separation", i.e. something extraordinary, totally different from normal human experience (cf. Deut. 17: 8 for the use of the same word). The authors of the two passages are saying, and it is an implication shared by all the Biblical writers, that God can do anything He chooses. Nothing is too marvellous for Him. His power is exalted far above that of humans. That which seems impossible for humans is not impossible for Him.

The Biblical writers were not bothered by the kind of problems regarding divine omnipotence discussed with much subtlety by mediaeval thinkers, Jewish, Christian and Muslim. The Biblical writers were content to affirm that God can do everything and leave it at that. But, under the impact of Greek philosophy, the mediaeval thinkers began to explore the scope of *all* in the term *all-powerful*. Is it really true to say that God can do anything He chooses? If He can, does this mean that He can, for example, create a stone which even He cannot lift up? Can He create another God? Can He will Himself out of existence? The answer to all these questions will surely be in the negative but is not then this negative answer a denial or qualification of divine omnipotence?

Since we are concerned in this book with Judaism, we can pause to examine how representative Jewish thinkers in the middle ages dealt with this kind of problem. Saadia[1] states that the soul will not praise God for being able to cause five to be more than ten without adding anything to the former; nor for being able to put the world through the hollow of a signet ring without making the one narrower and the other wider; nor for being able to bring back the day gone by in its original condition. For all these things are absurd. Saadia continues: "Of course, certain heretics often ask us about such matters, and we do indeed answer them that God is able to do everything, This thing, however, that they ask of Him is not anything because it is absurd, and the absurd is nothing. It is, therefore, as though they were to ask: 'Is God capable of doing what is nothing?' which is, of course, a real question." (This last sentence is not too clear. What Saadia probably means is that the question really means "Is God capable of not doing anything?" And this is a real question).

Centuries after Saadia, Joseph Albo[2] discusses the same question. Albo notices two kinds of impossibility. Some things are impossible in themselves so that we cannot imagine even God making them possible. For example, the whole is greater than a part of it and the diagonal of a square is greater than one of its sides. We cannot imagine that even God can make a part equal to the whole; or a diagonal of a square equal to one of its sides; or the angle of a triangle equal more than two right angles; or two contradictory propositions true at the same time of the same subject; or the affirmative and the negative true at the same time of the same thing in the same relation. It is impossible for our senses to testify that these or similar things are possible, says Albo, since our minds cannot imagine them. For this reason it is impossible to believe that God can create another being like Himself in every respect. For that would involve one being a cause and the other its effect, so that they would not be similar in every respect. The other kind of impossibility is that which contradicts a law of nature, e.g. the resurrection of the dead. Since the mind can imagine this God can do it.

---

1. *Beliefs and Opinions*, II, 13, p. 134.
2. *Ikkarim*, I, 22.

What both Saadia and Albo appear to be saying is that a physical impossibility is possible for God but not a logical impossibility. The same thought was expressed by Aquinas when he said:[3] "Nothing that implies a contradiction falls under the scope of God's omnipotence." What it all amounts to is that nonsense words do not make sense simply because the word "God" is tagged on to them. As Albo shows, to ask the question: "Can God make another being like Himself in every respect" is really to ask: "Can God make another being like himself in every respect who is not like Him in every respect?" This is to use a meaningless jumble of words and is no different from asking: "Can God. . .?" without completing the sentence. Saadia holds, for instance, that God can, if He so desires, make the whole world pass through a signet ring either by making the world small enough to pass through the ring or by making the ring large enough to pass round the world. But to ask whether He can make the world pass through the ring without making the one smaller or the other larger makes no sense at all. To speak of one thing passing through another *means* that one is smaller than the other. Similarly to make five into ten without adding to the former or to bring back the day gone by in its original condition is to talk nonsense. To make five into ten *means* adding to the former and to bring back the day gone by *means* that it is not left in its former condition. It is not as if there really were an entity called "the absurd" concerning which it is possible solemnly to ask whether God can do it. To say of a thing that it is absurd is to say that there is no such thing. Even when some religious thinkers have declared that God can do the absurd they can only mean that He can do that which *seems* absurd. If they do mean that God can do the logically impossible they are talking nonsense. And to acknowledge this is not to impose limits on divine omnipotence. God can do anything but, as Saadia says, the absurd is not anything.

See my book *Faith*, pp. 201–209 for the Jewish thinkers like R. Nahman of Bratzlav who take issue with the mediaeval denial that God can do the logically impossible and argue that God can make a square triangle. But the logical fallacy we have noted is only too obvious. No meaning can be given to the words "a square triangle". The recently published book in English translation by Lev Shestov (1866–1938) entitled *Athens and Jerusalem* makes great play on the essential differences between Greek and Hebraic

3. *Summa Theologica*, Part I, Quest. 25, 4. Cf. Maimonides *Guide*, II, 13 and also I, 75 end.

thought and implies frequently that for the latter God can do the logically impossible, e.g. in the example from Descartes (discussed on pp. 50f) God could have made a mountain without a valley. The logical difficulty is overlooked entirely. What meaning can be given to the word "mountain" without a "valley", in what would its "mountainness" consist? The jacket blurb of Shestov's book roundly declares: "Like Kierkegaard and the other Existentialists, Shestov views subjectivity or inwardness as the source of final truth, and feels that this truth—passionately held, self-contradictory and even absurd—is more meaningful than logical and abstract truth. Like other Existentialists, he protests against the brutalization of human values by modern science and technology." One can protest against the brutalization referred to and appreciate that abstract truth is not enough and see the value in the "true for me". But to embrace in the process the "self-contradictory and the absurd" is to reduce the whole exercise to nonsense. The word "meaningful" in the blurb is used in the sense of morally significant but can that which is not logically meaningful be morally meaningful? It is hard to see how it can since there is no such thing as the logically impossible. The sentence: "The self-contradictory can be morally meaningful' is a pseudo-sentence, no different from "can be morally meaningful".

Whatever else the doctrine of omnipotence means, therefore, it does not mean that nonsense propositions can be predicated of God. But traditional theism does insist that God is omnipotent and that a being lacking the power to do anything he chooses would not be God. However, there have been, and are, religious thinkers who would deny that God is omnipotent, though they would affirm that He is exceedingly powerful. On various grounds the doctrine of a limited or finite God has been advanced by these thinkers as the only adequate way of coping with our experience.

In the last century John Stuart Mill[4] argued that the idea of God as the Designer of the universe implies that He is only able to work on the stuff out of which the universe is formed. Otherwise why should God have had to design or plan the universe? Does not the idea of a "design" imply that there are obstacles to be overcome? If this is so then God is limited by the material on which He works. If there are no such limitations why could God not have brought the universe into being by a simple *fiat*? The idea of a designing mind implies that chaos of a kind is already "there" upon which order has to be imposed. The answer to this was given by Albo[5] long ago. Albo observes that

4. *Three Essays on Religion.*   5. *Ikkarim*, II, 4.

God could indeed have created the world all at once, as it were. However, the stages of the creative process, as depicted, for example, in the first chapter of Genesis, are necessary not for God's needs but in order to impress upon man that there is reality to the divine will and wisdom. Without such a concept there could be no meaning to the whole idea, upon which Judaism is based, of doing God's will. Albo quotes in this connection the passage from the Mishnah:[6] "By ten sayings was the world created. And what does Scripture teach thereby? Could it not have been created by one saying? But this was to requite the ungodly who destroy the world that was created by ten sayings, and to give goodly reward to the righteous who sustain the world that was created by ten sayings".

More recent thinkers like E. S. Brightman,[7] Charles Hartshorne,[8] and, on the Jewish side, Levi Olan,[9] have thought of God as limited by His own nature so that while He is infinite in some respects He is finite in others. Views of this kind are very attractive in that they purport to provide a solution to the most stubborn and intractable problem the theist has to face, why God tolerates evil in His creation. If God is not omnipotent the answer is that He does not desire this evil and would eradicate it if He could but He cannot. Man is, as it were, a partner with God in the struggle, in which He is engaged, against evil and imperfection.[10] To be sure the majority of Jewish thinkers have repeatedly affirmed that God is omnipotent but at least one of them, Gersonides, has expressed views not dissimilar from those of these modern thinkers. He did so, moreover, in the name of Judaism, i.e. as implied in the classical Jewish sources. Thus, Gersonides holds that there is a primal formless material co-existent with God from all eternity upon which God has to work[11] and that God only

---

6. Avot 5: 1.
7. *The Problem of God* and the Chapter: *Is God Finite?* in his: *A Philosophy of Religion*, Chapter X, pp. 170–180. Cf. P. A. Bertocci: *Introduction to the Philosophy of Religion*, Chapter 17, pp. 420–421; William K. Wright: *A Student's Philosophy of Religion*, pp. 394–401; and James Collins: *God in Modern Philosophy*, pp. 315–324.
8. See Charles Hartshorne and William L. Reese: *Philosophers Speak of God*.
9. See his essays in: *Varieties of Jewish Belief*, ed. Ira Eisenstein, pp. 149–159; and *New Resources for a Liberal Jewish Faith* in *Contemporary Reform Jewish Thought*, ed. Martin, pp. 21–38. Cf. Henry Slonimsky: *Essays*.
10. The problem of evil is discussed in Chapter 9 of this book, *infra*, pp. 125–135.
11. See *infra*, p. 94.

knows the future in a general sense but not how individual men will exercise their choice in particular circumstances.[12]

For all that, the doctrine of a finite God is hardly satisfying to the religious mind. It leaves the cosmic drama incomplete, with no certainty whatever that evil will eventually be vanquished. It leaves unexplained how "The Given", as Brightman calls this element in God over which He has no control, comes to be in God. It invites the suspicion that such a limited God has no reality but is a figment of the acute human imagination. For these reasons, and in spite of its brilliant advocates, the doctrine of the finite God has succeeded in winning few adherents. The stark alternatives for man are belief in God as traditionally conceived, that is the God who is omnipotent, or out and out atheism.

Traditional theism holds that God is omniscient as well as omnipotent. The doctrine that God knows everything and is not ignorant of anything is implied in a number of Biblical passages. With regard to human deeds and thoughts the Psalmist declares (Ps. 33 : 14–15):

> *From the place of His habitation*
> *He looketh intently upon all the*
> *inhabitants of the earth; He that*
> *fashioneth the hearts of them all,*
> *that considereth all their doings.*

Jewish teachers applied this not alone to events in the past and present but also to those still in the future. God knows not alone everything that has happened and is happening but also that which is to happen. The famous second-century teacher Rabbi Akiba expressed it as follows:[13] "All is foreseen, but freedom of choice is given."

This gave rise to the most difficult problem considered by the mediaeval thinkers. How can freedom of choice be given if all is foreseen? If God knows before a man is born all that he will do in his lifetime how can that man help doing whatever he does? It will not do to reply—as many have tried to do—that God's foreknowledge is not determinative, that while God *knows* what man will do this does not compel him to do it any more than our *knowledge* of what a man has done in the past exerts any compulsion on him to do it. For this is

12. See *infra*, pp. 78–79.   13. Avot 3: 16.

precisely the difficulty, how can *foreknowledge* fail to be determinative? It is not as if God is said to *assume* or *guess approximately* or *assess with great probability* how men will behave in the future. God is said to *know* how they will behave in the future. Such knowledge must preclude any possibility of error and it is hard to see how, granted this understanding of divine omniscience, a man can be free.

The three views put forward in the middle ages were: (1) Maimonides:[14] God has foreknowledge and man is free; (2) Gersonides:[15] Man is free and consequently God does not have complete foreknowledge; (3) Crescas:[16] God has complete foreknowledge and consequently man is not really free.

Both Gersonides and Crescas are convinced that it is logically impossible for God to have foreknowledge and yet for man to be free. (We have noted[17] that the mediaeval thinkers generally accept the view that a logical impossibility does not fall within the scope of God's omnipotence.) Gersonides, therefore, seizes one horn of the dilemma, Crescas the other. For Gersonides God knows things in general and has so constituted His world that a range of possible actions open up for man. But, since man is free to choose, these are only *possibilities*, not certainties, as they would be if God knew them beforehand. It follows that while God knows everything it is possible to know, He is not omniscient in any absolute sense. He does not know beforehand how man will use the possibilities open to him precisely because these are only possibilities. The great difficulty here is that if such a view were to be accepted it would virtually annul any idea of purpose in God's creation. It would presumably mean that God is so limited in His functions that He does not and cannot know how the human experiment will turn out. If it be argued that God does know in general terms the outcome of the whole process, it is still very hard to see how this can be since He is ignorant of the particular, individual decisions of which the process as a whole consists.

Crescas, on the other hand, holds that man only appears to be free but that, in reality, he is not free since all his deeds are determined by virtue of God's foreknowledge. Crescas is the only mediaeval Jewish thinker of note to embrace such a ("Calvinistic") view. It would make nonsense of the whole idea of blame and merit, of pursuing the good and rejecting evil, of reward and punishment, all of which seems

14. *Yad, Teshuvah* 5: 5.   16. *Or Adonai*, II: 4, 5.
15. *Milhamot*, III, 6.   17. *Supra*, pp. 73–74.

basic to Judaism. Crescas is aware of the difficulty and seeks bravely to grapple with it but without any conspicuous success.

For a comparison of the views of Crescas with those of Spinoza see Waxman: *Philosophy of Don Hasdai Crescas*, Chapter V, pp. 116–138; and for an account of Crescas's views in this matter see Julius Guttman: *Philosophies of Judaism*, pp. 238–240. Guttmann remarks that Crescas deviates even more decidedly from the unanimous doctrine of all previous Jewish religious philosophy by settling the conflict in favour of determinism. Although Crescas is generally considered to be the only Jewish thinker of note whose views approach religious determinism, the Hasidic master R. Joseph Mordecai of Izbica (d. 1854) has an even more radical deterministic view. R. Mordecai Joseph quotes the Talmudic passage (Ber. 33b): "Everything is in the hands of Heaven *except* the fear of Heaven" but observes that in reality: "Everything is in the hands of Heaven *even* the fear of Heaven." In this world the full truth that in reality only the will of God prevails is hidden from man so that the illusion of free will is maintained as an inducement to man to worship his Creator. In the Messianic age the truth will be revealed in all its splendour and in that age there will be neither virtue nor sin since all is due solely to the will of God. See his *Me Ha-Shiloah* to *Korah*, p. 98; to *Haazinu*, p. 127 bot., and to *Va-yera*, p. 15. See the fine article by J. G. Weiss: *The Religious Determinism of Joseph Mordecai of Izbica*.

Maimonides seizes both horns of the dilemma. God has foreknowledge and yet man is free. In order to understand how this might be possible, Maimonides examines what meaning we can give to the concept of God's knowledge. In God, says Maimonides, the knower, the thing known, and the process of knowing, are all one since God cannot be said to acquire knowledge of something outside of Himself of which He was hitherto ignorant. It is logically impossible for *human* foreknowledge of A's deeds to be compatible with A's freedom to do them but since divine knowledge is so different from human knowledge and so mysterious (so that, in fact, it is as impossible for humans to have any idea of what is meant by God's knowledge as to have any idea of what is the true nature of God) that, in a way we cannot hope ever to understand, divine foreknowledge is compatible with human freedom.

Maimonides leaves it at that. But subsequent attempts have been made to explore the subject more deeply, particularly by referring to the mystery of time and eternity. To say that God knows today what man is to do tomorrow is an invalid way of expressing the idea of God's foreknowledge. It should rather be said that God sees in the eternal "Now" man making his choice "tomorrow".[18] This idea is, however, extremely hard to grasp. We shall examine it further in our discussion of God's eternity.[19] In any event, Maimonides exhibits a far closer approximation to the demands of the religious conscience than either Gersonides, who would impose limits on God, or Crescas, who would deny human freedom.

18. See Moses Almosnino's remarks quoted in Tos. Yom Tov to Avot 3: 15.
19. *Infra*, pp. 86–92.

CHAPTER SIX

ETERNITY

THAT God has neither beginning nor end is stated implicitly in a number of Biblical passages. In some of these the stress is on the idea that God has no beginning, in others that He has no end, in others again that He has neither. Examples in which both ideas are mentioned are:

> *Before the mountains were brought forth,*
> *Or ever Thou hadst formed the earth and the world,*
> *Even from everlasting to everlasting, Thou art God*   (Psalms 90: 2);

and:

> *Thus saith the Lord, the King of Israel,*
> *And His Redeemer the Lord of hosts:*
> *I am the first, and I am the last,*
> *And beside Me there is no God*   (Isaiah 44: 6).

That God has no beginning appears to be emphasised in the somewhat obscure verse:

> *The ancient God (elohe kedem) is a refuge,*
> *A support are the everlasting arms*   (Deuteronomy 33: 27).

That He has no end is stated in the verse:

> *The Lord will reign for ever and ever!*   (Exodus 15: 18);

and in the verse:

> *The Lord will reign for ever,*
> *The God, O Zion, unto all generations. Hallelujah.*
>
> (Psalms 146: 10).

The book of Genesis opens with the majestic account of God's creation of the world. Unlike the pagan mythologies, there is silence on the whole question of the divine before the creative process begins. It was completely foreign to the ancient Hebrew genius to apply terms like "birth" and "death" to God.

The Psalmist speaks of all generations passing before God:

For a thousand years in Thy sight
Are but as yesterday when it is past   (Psalms 90: 4);

when all else has perished God will still be:

They shall perish, but Thou shalt endure;
Yes, all of them shall wax old like a garment;
As a vesture shalt Thou change them, and they shall pass away;
But Thou art the selfsame,
And Thy years shall have no end.   (Psalms 102: 27–28).

The word most frequently used in the Bible to denote the concept of eternity is *olam* (possibly from a root meaning "to be hidden"). The Biblical writers, when using the word of God, obviously wish to refer to His eternity. In other Biblical contexts the word simply denotes an extremely long duration of time, particularly ancient time, that is, the days of old. Thus the word is used of the slave who is to serve his master "for ever" (Ex. 21: 6); of ancient times (Deut. 32: 7); the old waste places (Is. 58: 2); and those long dead (Ps. 143: 3). God is described as the eternal God, *el olam* (Gen. 21: 33); He lives for ever, *le-olam* (Deut. 32: 40); He reigns for ever, *olam va-ed* (Ex. 15: 18; Ps. 10: 16); His throne is established for ever (Ps. 45: 7); He is the living God and everlasting King (Jer. 10: 10); His counsel endures for ever (Ps. 33: 11) as well as His mercy (Ps. 106: 1). It is clear that the term *olam* does not in itself imply eternity. In addition to the examples given above, King David is blessed with the conventional Oriental greeting that he should live "for ever", *le-olam* (1 Kings 1: 31). However, the usage in relation to God must be viewed differently. The Biblical writers would have viewed with horror the notion that God has come into existence at a given point of time or passes out of it. All the evidence points as clearly as possible to a special use of the term for God. Thus we may argue that when *olam* is used of God its significance lies in the implicit concept of eternity, understood as permanent duration of time without either beginning or end.

Another word used in the Bible to denote eternity is *netzah* (from a root meaning "to shine", "to be bright", and hence suggesting "everlastingness"). God is called *netzah yisrael* (1 Sam. 15: 29) which is generally translated as "the Glory of Israel" but may mean "The Eternal One of Israel". The word *netzah* is certainly used to express the idea of permanence in a number of Biblical passages (e.g. Amos 1:

11; Ps. 49: 20; Job 20: 7). The term *netzah* as an attribute of God is found together with other attributes in 1 Chronicles 29: 11 but here, too, the probable meaning is "Glory" or "Eminence". Of God it is said that at His right hand is bliss for evermore (*netzah*, Ps. 16: 11); that He will not forsake the needy for ever (*la-netzah*, Ps. 9: 19); that His mercy will not be witheld for ever (*la-netzah*, Ps. 77: 9); that He will not contend for ever (Ps. 103: 9) and that He will make death to vanish for ever (Is. 25: 8).

In all this it is, however, possible that our English translations have been influenced by mediaeval abstraction and that in the Bible, while God is certainly different from man, the full concept of eternity is left unexplored as foreign to Biblical thought.

The Biblical teachings on God's eternity were elaborated on by the Rabbis.[1] The usual Rabbinic contrast between God and man is made in this connection:[2] "Come and see! The measure of the Holy One, blessed be He, is unlike the measure of flesh and blood. The things fashioned by a creature of flesh and blood outlast him but the Holy One, blessed be He, outlasts the things He had fashioned." Inevitably, considering the dependence of Jews in Rabbinic times on the frequently arbitrary goodwill of powerful rulers, the contrast between God and man is often drawn in terms of the eternal, reliable God and the mortal unreliable king or emperor. Constantinople outlasts by far Constantine, Antioch outlasts Antiochus, Alexandria outlasts Alexander, but the Lord lives for ever and will rebuild Jerusalem and Zion and the cities of Judah.[3] When Pharaoh is ordered by Moses and Aaron in the name of God to let the people go, Pharaoh retorts that the Lord's name is not found in his list of gods. Moses and Aaron reply: "O fool! The dead can be sought among the living but how can the living be sought among the dead? Our God lives but those you mention are dead. Our God is 'The living God, and the everlasting King' (Jer. 10: 10)". Pharaoh then asks them whether God is young or old and how old He is, how many cities has He conquered, how many provinces has He subdued, how many years is it since He became King. To which they reply: "The power and might of our

1. A survey (comprehensive but unhistorical) of Rabbinic views on time is: M. M. Kasher's *The Problem of Time in Rabbinic Literature* (Heb.) in *Talpiot*, Vol. V, pp. 799–827.
2. Ber. 9a.
3. Midrash Psalms 9: 8.

God fill the world. He was before the world was created and He will be when all the world comes to an end and He has created thee and gave thee the spirit of life".[4] When Rabban Johanan b. Zakkai was about to die he wept. When his disciples asked him why he wept he replied: "If I were being taken before a king of flesh and blood who is here today and tomorrow in the grave, whose anger does not last for ever, who cannot imprison me for ever, who cannot kill me for ever even if he sentences me to death, and whom I can persuade and bribe to reconsider his judgement, even so I would weep. Now that I am being taken before the supreme King of kings, the Holy One, blessed be He, who lives and endures for ever and ever, whose anger, if He is angry with me, is everlasting, who, if He imprisons me, the imprisonment is for ever, who, if He puts me to death, puts me to death for ever, and whom I cannot persuade or bribe . . . shall I not weep?"[5] The account of the disciples who took leave of their master and blessed him that he should see his world (olam) in his lifetime,[6] has been understood to mean that he should see something of eternal life even while in this world[7] but it is questionable whether the blessing recorded can bear this meaning. "Thy world" may simply mean something like "life's ambition" and their blessing was for him to realise his desires during his life's span on earth.

The Rabbis had quite literally a down-to-earth attitude in this matter. God is eternal but it is not given to man to explore the full meaning of this idea. Aimed at contemporary attempts to pierce the veil is the famous ruling found in the Mishnah:[8] "Whoever reflects on four things it were better for him that he had not come into the world: what is above? what is beneath? what is before? and what is after?" No doubt there are echoes of the Gnostic controversies behind this statement and it is even possible that "before" and "after" do not refer to time at all but to space, i.e. to what is in one direction beyond the earth and what is in another direction. One cannot, therefore, expect to find in the Rabbinic literature anything like a detailed examination of what is meant by divine eternity. The mediaeval

4. Ex. R. 5: 14.
5. Ber. 28b.
6. Ber. 17a.
7. Leo Baeck: *The Essence of Judaism*, p. 190 (The reference in the note on p. 289 is incorrectly given as Ber. 17b).
8. Hag. 2: 1.

Jewish thinkers, on the other hand, were greatly concerned with philosophical questions regarding time and eternity and their relationship to God.

There are two views in mediaeval Jewish thought on the relationship between time and eternity. The philosophers tend to distinguish between God's time and the succession of years, days, hours and minutes that we call time, whereas the Kabbalists tend to think of God as outside time altogether.

Maimonides[9] believes that time is created so that expressions such as that God *was before* He created the world (suggesting a time span "before" time was created) are to be understood as a supposition regarding time or an imagining of time and are not to be understood as referring to the true reality of time. However, Maimonides[10] also argues for the indestructibility of the universe, which implies endless duration in time. His view would seem, therefore, to be that "once" time has been created it endures for ever. Ideas such as these go back to Plato's *Timaeus* in which time is distinguished from what is in time,[11] though it has been remarked that a difficulty is involved in the idea of time as a kind of box into which is placed that which is in time. The idea of time as a creation is taken up by Crescas[12] and Albo who follows Crescas.[13] Albo remarks that the concepts of priority and perpetuity can only be applied to God in a negative sense, that is they deny non-existence *a parte ante* and *a parte post*. This means that when we speak of God as being "before" or "after" some period it means no more than He was not non-existent before or after that period but that, in reality, terms like "before" and "after" indicating a time-span cannot be applied to the Eternal One. Following Maimonides, Albo distinguishes between two kinds of time. The first is measured time, which depends on motion and to which the terms prior and posterior can be applied. The second is not measured or numbered but is a duration existing prior to the "sphere". This is time in the abstract and is possibly eternal. Consequently, the difficulty of whether or not time originates in time is avoided. The second type of time has no origin. It is only the "order of time" (seder zemanim),

9. *Guide*, II, 13.
10. *Guide*, II, 27–29.
11. See C. D. Broad in Hastings' *Encyclopedia cf. Religion and Ethics*, Vol. 12, p. 343.
12. *Or Adonai*, I, 2, 11.
13. *Ikkarim*, II, 18–19.

to which Maimonides also refers, that originates in time. It is, indeed, difficult if not impossible to conceive of a "duration" before the creation of the world, but says Albo, it is similarly difficult to conceive of God as "outside" space. This is why, Albo concludes, the Rabbis declare that one must not ask what is above, what is below, what is before and what is behind.

The view found in the literature of the Kabbalah is that God is outside time or beyond time (le-maalah min ha-zeman). The Neo-Platonic idea of the "eternal Now", in which past, present and future are telescoped, as it were, is found in various mediaeval writers. St. Anselm[14] writes: "Thou wast not, then, yesterday, nor wilt Thou be tomorrow; but yesterday and today and tomorrow Thou art; or, rather, neither yesterday nor today nor tomorrow Thou art; but simply, Thou art, outside all time." Boethius[15] similarly writes: "Since God lives in the eternal present, His knowledge transcends all movement of time and abides in the simplicity of its immediate present. It encompasses the infinite sweep of past and future, and regards all things in its simple comprehension as if they were now taking place. Thus, if you will think about the foreknowledge by which God distinguishes all things, you will rightly consider it to be not a foreknowledge of future events, but knowledge of a never changing present".

On the Jewish side, Bahya Ibn Asher[16] comments on the verse "The Lord will reign for ever and ever!" (Ex. 15: 18): "All times, past and future, are in the present so far as God is concerned, for He was before time and is not encompassed by it". R. Moses Almosnino[17] (1510–c.1580) comments on "For now I know" (Gen. 22: 12) that this means in the "eternal Now" and he uses the idea of the "eternal Now" to solve the problem of God's foreknowledge and human free will.[18] The Hasidic master R. Nahman of Bratzlav[19] has this to say: "God, as is well-known, is above time. This is a truly marvellous notion, utterly incomprehensible, impossible for the human mind to grasp. You must appreciate, however, that basically time is the

---

14. *Proslogion*, trans. S. W. Deane, Chapter 19, p. 25.
15. *The Consolation of Philosophy*, Book 5, 6, p. 116.
16. *Commentary to the Pentateuch*, Vol. 2, ed. Chavel, p. 134.
17. *Tefillah Le-Mosheh* to Gen. 22: 12.
18. Quoted by *Tos. Yom Tov* to Avot 3: 15, see *supra*, p. 80.
19. *Likkute Maharan, Tinyana*, No. 61, p. 29.

product of ignorance, that is to say, time only appears real to us because our intellect is so puny. The greater the mind the smaller and less significant does time become for it. Take, for instance, a dream, in which the mind is dormant and the imaginative faculty takes over. In the dream it is possible for a seventy year span to pass by in a quarter of an hour. In the dream it seems as if a great length of time has elapsed but in reality only a very short space of time has been traversed. On awakening, the dreamer senses that the whole seventy year period of the dream occupied in a reality only a fraction of time. This is because man's intellectual capacity has been restored to him in his waking like and so far as his mind is concerned the whole seventy year period of the dream is no more than a quarter of an hour . . . There is a Mind so elevated that for It the whole of time is counted as naught, for so great is that Mind that for It the whole time span is as nothing whatever. Just as, so far as we are concerned, the seventy years which pass by in the dream are no more than a quarter of an hour in reality, as we have seen, so it is with regard to that Mind which is so far above anything we know as mind that for It time has no existence at all." The Kabbalists tend to explain the numerous references to time in the Sefirotic realm as meaning not prior and posterior, since there is no time span in the spiritual realm, but cause and effect.[20]

Saadia Gaon (*Beliefs and Opinions*, II, 13) asks how it is conceivable by the mind that God knows everything that has happened in the past as well as all that will happen in the future. He replies that humans find this hard to grasp because their knowledge comes to them through the senses. But God requires no intermediary, He has no senses, His knowledge is His essence and by its means He is cognizant of things. Consequently, for Him past and future are on the same level and He knows them both equally. Saadia quotes Is. 46: 10 in support of the idea that God knows the future as the present. Cf. Menaham Mendel of Lübavitch: *Derekh Mitzvotekha, mitzvat haamanut elokut,* 11-12, pp. 113-118. Menahem Mendel remarks: "In truth He does not exist in time, but time is only so far as creatures are concerned". He observes further that the human mind cannot grasp this idea any more than it can grasp the idea of God as "outside" space for this belongs to the comprehension of God's essence which is impossible for man. At the beginning of section 12 R. Menahem Mendel uses the expression "He is in the category of the eternal present" (*hoveh tamid*). He explains the whole idea on the basis of the Kabbalistic doctrine of God's withdrawal (*Tzimtzum,* see *supra,* pp. 32-34), as it were, in order to make room for the world,

20. See J. Oshlag: *Talmud Eser Sefirot,* Vol. I, Part 1, p. 26.

i.e. that this takes place outside time and space and that time and space
as we know them emerge into the "empty primordial space" left after God's
withdrawal. The celebrated Talmudist R. Joseph Rosen (d. 1936) frequently
treats of the idea of God as outside time in his Halakhic works, see M. S. Kasher:
Ha-Gaon Ha-Ragadshovi Ve-Talmdudo, Chapter 8, pp. 57–59. In philosophical
literature there has been much discussion of the nature of time and eternity
and the idea of the latter as beyond time altogether There is important
and interesting material in: Adolf Grunbaum: *Philosophical Problems of Space
and Time*; Michael Whiteman: *Philosophy of Space and Time*; and Richard
Swinburne: *Space and Time*; and the three symposia: *Man and Time*, ed.
Joseph Campbell; *The Philosophy of Time*, ed. Richard Gale; and the less
satisfactory: *The Voices of Time*, ed. J. T. Fraser. The religious doctrine of
eternity as timelessness and the arguments for and against have been
studied by Nelson Pike: *God and Timelessness*.

Even in our own day there are references in the writings of Rabbis of the
old school to the "eternal Now". In his essay on the problem of foreknowledge and free will, R. Joseh Laib Bloch, principal of the Yeshiva
of Telz in Lithuania, invokes the "eternal Now" as a solution to the
problem. (*Shiure Daal*, Vol. 2, pp. 93–103, Cf. *supra* pp. 77–80) Rabbi
Bloch refers to the comment of R. Schneor Zalman of Liady in his
Shulhan Arukh that the sabbath is kept at different times in different parts
of the world because the source of the sabbath is on high and there is no
time there, hence sabbath observance depends on human time and this
differs from place to place (c.f. R. Schneor Zalman's *Tanya, Shaar Ha-Yihud*,
Chapter 7, pp. 162f, that the Tetragrammaton represents God as He who
was (*Hayah*) is (*hoveh*) and will be (*yiheyeh*) in one moment (*be-rega ehad*),
i.e. in the "eternal Now". He quotes the Zohar (III, 257b) but the words
"in one moment" do not occur there. Rabbi E. Dessler (*Mikhtav Me-
Elijahu*, pp. 292–293) reflects on the idea of spiritual progress in the Hereafter
since the World to Come is beyond time and progress implies a time
sequence. His solution is that the soul is endowed with the capacity to
experience time when it has left the material world behind. This capacity,
as well as that of comprehension, both of which prevent the soul from
becoming absorbed in the divine and hence incapable of spiritual progress,
belong to the "bodily element" (*guf*) of the soul which the soul inhabits
even in eternal life.

A modern Catholic theologian, Karl Rahner, similarly explores
the eschatological implications of the doctrine of eternity as outside
time altogether. Fr. Rahner writes :[21] "In reality, it is *in* time, as its
own mature fruit, that 'eternity' comes about. It does not come
'after' the time we experience, in order to prolong time: it eliminates

21. *The Life of the Dead*, Chapter 14 in his: *Theological Investigations*, Vol. 4
pp. 347–354.

time by being released from the time that was for a while so that the definitive should come about in freedom. Eternity is not an immeasurably long-lasting mode of pure time, but a mode of the spirit and freedom which are fulfilled in time, and hence can only be comprehended in the light of a correct understanding of spirit and freedom. A time, such as that of the beasts for instance, which is not pregnant with these things, does not bring forth eternity. But when we try to think of man's spiritual and free existence as something definitive, we have to extract the notion from time, and we are almost forced to portray it as endless duration. To overcome this difficulty we must do what is done in modern physics and learn to think imaginatively, and to this extent perform a process of 'de-mythising'. We must say; through death—not after it—*there is* (not: begins to take place) the achieved definitiveness of the freely matured existence of man. What he has come to be is there as the hard-won and untrammelled validity of what was once temporal; it progressed as spirit and freedom, in order to be."

Rahner is speaking "existentially" but the "eternal Now" of the mystics is also "existential" as well as "essentialist" in that the condition they seek to describe is not one of place but of state. It would not evidently be far from their thought to have them speak of man, after his death, becoming part of the "eternal Now".

Is the mystical concept of the "eternal Now" philosophically respectable? This question was discussed by Aldous Huxley in his book: *The Perennial Philosophy*.[22] Huxley first records the views of Hobbes and other "enemies of the Perennial Philosophy" who argue that God cannot have any knowledge of future events since these are completely indeterminate. (It was, indeed, on these grounds that Gersonides, alone among Jewish thinkers, denied that God can have foreknowledge of particular contingent events. God knows the possible as possible not as certainty so that the doctrine of God's omniscience is limited to the affirmation that He knows all that can be known.)[23] Huxley relies on the alleged evidence for ESP according to which even human beings can have foreknowledge at times. "And if a finite consciousness can know what card is going to be turned up three seconds from now, or what shipwreck is going to take place next week, then there is nothing impossible or even intrinsically

22. Chapter XII, *Time and Eternity*, pp. 192–207.
23. See *supra*, pp. 78 –80.

improbable in the idea of an infinite consciousness that can know events indefinitely remote in what, for us, is future time." Whether there is evidence for ESP is still hotly debated but even if conclusive it is possible that telepathy or some other strange means of cognition is the explanation of the phenomena rather than precognition. And in any event there appears to be a fallacy in Huxley's argument. The "eternal Now" of the mystics surely does not mean that God sees the remote future in *our* present (as the analogy from human precognition would suggest) but that He sees past, present and future "all at once". It is very difficult indeed to see how knowledge can "now" be had of a "future" event without that event being already present in some sense, i.e. as in a completely deterministic scheme. The question is really one of logic. Is it at all logically meaningful to speak of past, present and future as "Now"? It is not a question of whether God can or cannot do this or that but a question of what precisely is it that we are asking Him to do. How does one "cash" the word "Now" in this context?

Exponents of the "eternal Now" use spatial illustrations to convey the idea. Huxley quotes this from Nicholas of Cusa: "The concept of a clock enfolds all succession in time. In the concept the sixth hour is not earlier than the seventh hour or the eighth, although the clock never strikes the hour, save when the concept biddeth". Now it is true that on the clock face all the hours are together but this is only because the "concept" of the clock is a spatial representation of time. In the reality of time the sixth hour is, of course, *earlier* than the seventh or the eighth. A more recent defence of the "eternal Now" is G. D. Yarnold's *The Moving Image*. Yarnold, too, operates with spatial imates, e.g. the familiar type of diagram in which successive events in time— A1, A2, A3, A4 . . . —are displayed on a single page with vertical slanting lines meeting a point above them, this point representing the Observer in the "eternal Now". But what is readily imaginable when presented in this way on the printed page becomes far less accessible when applied to the actual time process.

The logical problem of time is studied in: *Fate, Logic and Time* by Steven M. Cahn. Cahn writes as a philosopher, not a theologian, though he bases his argument on the theological discussion of determinism versus free will. To the idea of the "eternal Now" Cahn[24] objects that there are some events which cannot be performed

24. P. 78.

simultaneously, e.g. raising an arm and lowering it. One must happen *before* the other and God must know this. How, then, can God know them both in the "immediate present"? But this seems to repeat the misunderstanding of which Huxley was guilty. God cannot know now in *our* present two events which cannot occur simultaneously because this involves a logical contradiction. To say that they cannot occur simultaneously is to say that they cannot both occur now, i.e. in our present. But the claim of the mystics' "eternal Now" is that God sees events which are for us truly past, present and future in *His* "Now". He does not see the two events of raising the arm and lowering it as occurring simultaneously but as occurring one after the other in His "eternal Now". Whether *this* is logically meaningful is another question, as we have noted, but nothing is added to the argument by invoking events which cannot be performed simultaneously,

Cahn follows Charles Hartshorne who, interestingly enough, relies on Gersonides whom we have quoted earlier. Hartshorne[25] labels the view that "omniscience sees the future as it is, that is, as partially indeterminable" the "Principle of Gersonides". In this connection it is pertinent to quote Isaac Husik, who, surely correctly, remarks:[26] "Levi ben Gerson's solution, whatever we may think of its scientific or philosophic value, is surely very bold as theology, we might almost say it is a theological monstrosity. It practically removes from God the definite knowledge of the outcome of a given event so far as that outcome is contingent. Gersonides will not give up the contingent, for that would destroy freedom. He therefore accepts free will with its consequences, at the risk of limiting God's knowledge to events which are determined by the laws of nature. Maimonides was less consistent, but had the truer theological sense, namely, he kept to both horns of the dilemma. God is omniscient and man is free. He gave up the solution by seeking refuge in the mysteriousness of God's knowledge. This is the true religious attitude."

To sum up, the problem of time is one of the great mysteries. The mind reels at the thought of time flowing endlessly along. The notion of eternity has been understood by many religious thinkers as conveying the thought of existence outside time. An illustration sometimes given is of fictitious two-dimensional creatures who may be able with difficulty to imagine a third dimension but who would be

25. *Man's Vision of God*, p. 139.
26. *A History of Mediaeval Jewish Philosophy*, pp. 345-346, see *supra*, pp. 78-80.

obliged to think of it in terms of the two dimensions they know and would be incapable of grasping the nature of the third dimension. In H. G. Well's story *The Time Machine* this is said of the time traveller who vanished in the time machine of the title: "Will he ever return? It may be that he swept back into the past, and fell among the blood drinking, hairy savages of the Age of Unpolished Stone; into the abysses of the Creataceous Sea; or among the grotesque saurians, the huge reptilian brutes of the Jurassic time. He may even now, if I may use the phrase—be wandering on some plesoisaurus-haunted Oolithic coral reef, or beside the lonely saline lakes of the Triassic Age. Or did he go forward, into one of the nearer ages, in which men are still men, but with the riddles of our own time answered and its wearisome problems settled?" "If I may use the phrase"—and, of course, it is not permissible to use the phrase and time travel itself is *logically* impossible. But Maimonides reminds us that in speaking of God's knowledge we are altogether outside of the realm of any of our experiences and the sense of mystery remains. In whatever way we think of time we are bound to fall back on the insoluble. Even if we think of time as duration alone, our minds are presented with the alternatives of either postulating that time will eventually come to an end or that it will last for ever. We cannot grasp either of these ideas. Whenever we try to think of time as coming to an end we find ourselves asking: And what will happen *then?* Endless duration in time is similarly quite beyond our imagination. When theists call God the "Timeless' or the "Eternal" they are, in part, acknowledging that time is an impenetrable mystery for the human mind and that any deep reflection on the mystery brings us back to the nature of the Supreme Being who is Lord of space and time.

CHAPTER SEVEN

CREATION

IT IS a basic Jewish belief that God is Creator of the universe. The Biblical term *Boré*, "Creator",[1] is frequently used for God in subsequent Jewish literature.[2] In the synagogue hymn recited before readings from the Psalms, God is described as:[3]

> *Blessed be He who spake, and the world existed:*
> *Blessed be He;*
> *Blessed be He who was the Master of the world in the beginning.*

In another Synagogue hymn[4] it is said:

> *Thou wast the same before the world was created;*
> *Thou hast been the same since the world hath been created.*

In the 16th century formulation of the Jewish Creed (*Ani Maamin*) the first principle of the Jewish faith is given as:[5]

> *I believe with perfect faith that*
> *the Creator, blessed be His name, is*
> *the Author and Guide of everything*
> *that has been created, and that He alone*
> *has made, does make, and will make all things.*

Maimonides[6] begins his great Code with these words: "The foundation of all foundations and the pillar of wisdom is to know that there is a First Being. He it is who brought all things into being and all the

1. Is. 4: 28; 42: 5; 43: 15; 45: 18; Amos. 4: 13; Eccl. 12: 1.
2. E.g. Avot 4: 22; Maimonides, *Yad, Yesode Ha-Torah*, 2: 8–10; Shulhan Arukh, *Orah Hayim*, 1: 1.
3. Singer's Prayer Book, p. 17.
4. Singer's Prayer Book, p. 10.
5. Singer's Prayer Book, op. 93.
6. Yad, *Yesode Ha-Torah*, 1: 1–3.

beings in heaven and earth and in between only enjoy existence by
virtue of His true being. If it could be imagined that He does not exist
nothing else could have existed. But if it could be imagined that no
other beings, apart from Him, enjoyed existence, He alone would
still exist and He could not cease because they have ceased. For all
beings need Him but he, blessed be He, does not need them, not any
of them. Consequently, His true nature is different from the truth
regarding the nature of any of them."

In the middle ages the doctrine of *creatio ex nihilo* was especially
stressed, many Jewish thinkers holding this to be essential to Jewish
faith.[7] No Jewish thinker accepted the Aristotelean view[8] that matter
is eternal and, with the exception of Gersonides,[9] Jewish thinkers
rejected, too, the Platonic view of a hylic substance upon which God
imposes form but does not create.[10] Creation means that God brought
the universe into being literally out of nothing.

Such *speculations*, however, are foreign to Biblical thought. It is a
moot point whether the creation narrative in Genesis (1: 1–2: 4a)
implies *creatio ex nihilo* but other Biblical passages do seem to convey
the idea.[11] The first verse in Genesis uses the word *bara* to describe
God's creative activity. Some mediaeval commentators do understand this to mean *creatio ex nihilo* but Ibn Ezra pointed out long ago
that in the Genesis narrative itself the word is used, too, of the creation
of animals (1: 21) and of man (1: 27). Modern scholars have noted that
the root seems to mean "to cut out" and does not therefore imply
creatio ex nihilo. However, the word is only used in the Bible when
speaking of God. Its significance, consequently is that God's power is
responsible for the emergence of something quite new in which this
power is especially to be seen. This would give added meaning to the
use of the word for the creation of matter in the first verse of Genesis,
of the creation of life and of the creation of man. As T. H. Robinson
has said:[12] "On the one hand we have a dignified, philosophical,

7. See Albo: *Ikkarim*, I, 23.
8. See Saadia: *Beliefs and Opinions*, I, 1–15; Maimonides, *Guide*, II, 13–31.
9. *Milhamot*, VI. In *The Wisdom of Solomon*, II: 17, it is similarly stated that God
   created the world "out of formless matter".
10. See Plato *Timaeus*, 29 and 53, Maimonides, *Guide*, II, 25. In Guide, II, 13,
    Maimonides argues against the philosophers who think of *creatio ex nihilo* as a
    logical impossibility and hence (see *supra*, pp. 72–74) impossible even for God.
11. See e.g. Ps. 33: 6–9; 102: 26; 121: 2; Jer. 10: 12; Is. 42: 5; 45: 7–9.
12. *The Old Testament and Modern Study* ed. Rowley, p. 351.

scientific, almost evolutionary statement, in which the divine act of 'creation', i.e. the introduction of a totally new factor which cannot be explained by anything earlier, occurs only at three crucial points, the provision of sheer matter, the introduction of animal life, and the formation of that personality which man shares with God Himself."

Naturally there is much discussion of creation in the Rabbinic literature.[13] The Platonic notion, for instance, of an idea of the world in the mind of God, a pattern, as it were, after which He created the world, is reflected in the well-known Rabbinic saying:[14] "God looked into the Torah and created the world" so that the Torah is thought of as a kind of primordial blue-print. There are numerous speculations on the manner of God's creation of the world scattered throughout the Rabbinic literature. Some of these can be mentioned here.

The School of Shammai said: the heavens were created first and then the earth (following the order in Gen. 1: 1) but the School of Hillel said: the earth first and then the heavens (following the order in Gen. 2: 4). The Sages said that heaven and earth were created simultaneously.[15] We are told that a philosopher said to Rabban Gamaliel: "Your God is a great Craftsman, but He found good materials to help Him in the work of creation, namely Tohu and Bohu, darkness, spirit, water, and the deep" (see Gen. Chapter 1). Rabban Gamaliel quoted other Scriptural verses which state that these materials, too, were created by God.[16] As late as the third century, however, R. Johanan could say that God took two coils, one of fire and the other of snow, wove them into each other and created the world.[17] The opinion that the primordial light was a garment with which God wrapped Himself before creation[18] is probably a reference to a theory of emanation which became especially prominent in the Kabbalah.[19] According to one Rabbinic theory[20] all things were created simultaneously on the first day of creation but made their appearance at

13. See especially A. Altmann: Studies in *Religious Philosophy and Mysticism*, pp. 128–139; A. Cohen: *Everyman's Talmud*, pp. 27–40.
14. Gen. R. 1: 1, Altmann op. cit. gives the literature on this topic in note 2.
15. Hag. 12a.
16. Gen. R. 1: 9.
17. Gen. R. 10: 3.
18. Gen. R. 3: 4.
19. Altmann op cit.
20. Gen. R. 12: 4.

different stages in the other six days just as figs are gathered simultaneously in one basket but each selected in its time.

The idea is found that God created several worlds and destroyed them before creating this one.[21] The purpose of creation is summed up in the saying that whatever the Holy One, blessed be He, created in His world, He created for His glory.[22] God is, as it were, proud of the world He has created. He declares that creation is "very good" (Gen. 1: 31). If the Creator praises His wonderful works who would dare to criticise them?[23]

The mediaeval Jewish philosophers, as above, understand *creatio ex nihilo* literally. The Kabbalists, however, give a completely different meaning to *creatio ex nihilo*. The universe comes into being through a series of emanations from God. God is referred to as *Nothing* because of God as He is in Himself nothing can be postulated so far as He from all human comprehension (see *supra*, pp. 42–44). *Creation ex nihilo*—in Heb. *yesh* ("that which is") *me-ayin* ("from that which is not")—means the creation of the universe out of God, the divine *Nothing* (see Scholem: *Major Trends*, p. 25). In general the Kabbalists interpret the first verses of Genesis as referring to the processes in the Godhead before the creation of the world, see e.g. The Zohar beg. In the Lurianic Kabbalah the Rabbinic idea of God creating and destroying worlds before He created this one, is said to refer to the spiritual "worlds", i.e. to the unfolding of God's creative activity, so that, for example, *Tohu* ("void") in Genesis refers to the stage of God's self-revelation known as olam *ha-tohu*, "the world of the void" which comes before the "world of perfection" (*olam ha-tikkun*). Cf. *supra*, pp. 32–34. As a typical example of how this line of interpretation was continued by the later Kabbalists see the remarks of the Hasidic master, R. Kalonymous Kalman of Cracow in his *Maor Va-Shemesh* to the first verse of Genesis. According to this teacher the "void" of Genesis is the primordial void left after God's withdrawal to make room for the world (*Tzimtzum*). God then said: "Let there be light", i.e. He caused His light to be emanated into the void so as to provide the sustaining power required for the worlds later to be created. The ancient and curious idea of "cycles" of creation is found in the early Kabbalah. The doctrine has it that after each cycle of 7,000 years the world is restored to chaos and re-created. In each cycle there is a different Torah! Later Kabbalists, notably Cordovero and Luria, reject this notion. For an acute study of the whole idea see I. Weinstock: *Be-Maagale Ha-Nigleh Ve-Ha-Nistar*, pp. 153–241.

Modern scientific theories regarding the origin of the universe such as the "big bang" theory (that an explosion occurred in the very

21. Gen. R. 9: 2.   22. Avot 6: 11.   23. Gen. R. 12: 1.

remote past to produce matter) are not strictly relevant to theology. They are interesting in themselves but have nothing to say one way or the other on the theological doctrine of creation. They are attempting at describing *how* the universe came into being whereas theology's concern is with the fact that it came into being by the divine *fiat*. As we have seen,[24] some religious thinkers have thought of time itself as a creation so that the creative process is set in motion, as it were, outside time altogether. The significance of the doctrine of God as Creator—and this is unaffected by any modern scientific theories—is that the whole universe is subordinate to Him, that He exercises control over and manages it, and that human beings hold their possessions in a stewardship deriving from Him. The Rabbinic doctrine of man as co-partner with God in the work of creation[25] is relevant here. God gives man the skills with which to master the world (see Gen. 1:28) but man must not use his powers destructively but to further God's creative purpose. This is the importance of the sabbath in the Jewish scheme. By refraining on the sabbath from creative activity[26] man demonstrates that he uses his skills not as of right but by permission of the Creator with the corollary that he uses them for the benefit of mankind not to its detriment. A further example of this co-partnership is the duty to procreate and so cause the world to be inhabited and not desolate.[27] Man has the supreme dignity of sharing the creative task with God Himself.

Naturally there are speculations, ancient and modern, on the manner and scope of creation. Modern scientific investigation has succeeded in demonstrating the immense size of the universe. But so far as we know at present there are no sentient creatures having

24. *Supra*, pp. 85–88.

25. Hamnuna said: He who prays on the eve of the sabbath and recites *and the heaven and the earth were finished* (Gen. 2: 1) Scripture treats of him as though he had become a partner with the Holy One, blessed be He, in the work of creation (Sabb. 119b). Every judge who judges with complete fairness even for a single hour Scripture gives him credit as though he had become a partner with the Holy One, blessed be He, in the work of creation (Sanh. 10a).

26. This interpretation of the sabbath laws is now a commonplace among Orthodox writers see e.g. S. R. Hirsch: *Horeb*, Vol. I, section 2, pp. 61f and Herman Wouk: *This is My God* p. 68 and p. 295. There is, of course, no reference to "creative activity" in the classical sources but the idea is possibly implicit in the Rabbinic definition of what constitutes "work" on the sabbath, cf. Ex. 20: 8–11.

27. See Mishnah Gittin 4: 5 "The world was only created for fruition and increase. As it is written, *He created it not a waste, He formed it to be inhabited*" (Is. 45: 18). On this see David M. Feldman: *Birth Control in Jewish Law*, pp. 48f.

intelligence and a moral sense anywhere in the universe. What would be the theological implications if it were, however, discovered that such creatures do exist? True at this stage such a discussion is purely academic but it is not without interest in itself and might shed some light incidentally on the whole doctrine of creation.

Professor E. L. Mascall in his Bampton lectures[28] devotes a section of the first lecture to a speculation on the implications for his faith if it is one day found that there are rational corporeal beings in parts of the universe other than earth. He concludes: "Theological principles tend to become torpid for lack of exercise, and there is much to be said for giving them now and then a scamper in a field where the paths are few and the boundaries indefined; they do their day-by-day work all the better for an occasional outing in the country. Outings, however, are outings and work is work, and it is very important not to confuse them with each other." It is in this spirit that the following observations are offered.

The Bible is silent on the question of whether intelligent beings exist on other planets. Biblical cosmology, however, is definitely geocentric, so that a literal understanding of the relevant texts would suggest that there are no such beings. Most theologians today, however, would not view this as a particularly difficult problem if it can be proved that there are sentient moral beings on other planets. The Biblical picture has, in any event, long been challenged on such questions as the age of the earth, the time span of man on it, and the emergence of animal and human life. The conventional solutions are applicable to our problem: the Biblical record is not to be taken literally; or its authors share the knowledge of their day on matters concerning the physical universe and its structure; or the Bible is not inerrant even though it is the word of God. The suggestion that the Bible does, in fact, know of the existence of extra-terrestrial intelligent life and actually refers to it (e.g. in Gen. 6: 4 the *nefilim*, "fallen ones", being invaders of earth from another planet) is too ridiculous to merit serious attention even in a discussion which some would consider to be fantastic in itself.

More serious are the problems raised by what may be termed the mechanics of salvation in the three theistic faiths—the Torah for the Jews, the Incarnation for Christians, the Koran for Muslims. What becomes of these if there are beings in the universe who, because they

28. *Christian Theology and Natural Science.*

are moral and intelligent, require "salvation" and yet cannot be helped by means relevant only to the human situation? I do not know whether Muslim theologians have discussed this question. A number of Christian thinkers have tried to deal with it from the standpoint of their faith, some of them postulating that it is compatible with the Christian view to hold that each race in the universe had its own, non-human incarnation. The analogy on the Jewish side would be a proliferation of non-human *Torot*!

First a word or two might be said on the background. The classical Jewish sources do refer, in fact, to the notion, derived from the Greeks, that there are other "worlds",[29] but there is no reference to these being inhabited by sentient moral creatures. The numerous references to the angelic hosts are irrelevant to our question. Of possibly greater relevance are the references in the sources to moral beings who live so distant from normal human habitation that the moral law as expressed in the "seven laws of the sons of Noah" does not reach them but who, nevertheless, lead moral lives—people who are, as it were, neither Jews nor Gentiles, and who are guided by neither the law for the Jew nor the law for the Gentile but by their own inner light.[30]

A very early discussion of our particular problem is to be found in the rather neglected work of Rabbi Phineas Elijah b. Meir Hurwitz of Vilna (d. 1821).[31] Hurwitz believes, on the basis of Isaiah 45: 18, that there are creatures on planets other than earth. He refers also to the passage in the Talmud[32] in which, according to one opinion, *Meroz* (Judges 5: 23) is a star and yet, says Hurwitz, *Meroz* is cursed, which indicates that it is inhabited. Hurwitz goes on to admit that the creatures on other planets may have intelligence, but he refuses to believe that they have free will, for this is only possible in creatures with a human constitution. He does not seem to be bothered with why, in that case, *Meroz* was cursed. He concludes: "Consequently, there is only room for Torah and worship in this world, for neither Torah nor worship has any meaning where there is no free will. It is only from this world that God obtains satisfaction (*nahat ruah*)".

29. E.g. in Ber. 32b and A.Z. 3b.
30. See e.g. Jer. Talmud, B.M. 2: 5 and the "sons of Cain" in Ginzberg: *Legends of the Jews*, Vol. V, p. 143.
31. *Sefer Ha-Berit*, Part I, *Maamar* 3, Chapters 2–4, pp. 30–32.
32. M.K. 16a.

It might be thought pointless and tactless for Jews to consider the specific Christian problem and *vice versa*, but on a question such as this, entirely different though the specific dogmas are, the theological gambits are more or less the same, so that we can learn from one another. Jerome Eckstein[33] fairly puts the question for both faiths: "Let our imagination roam, and let us speculate about the possible conflicts between future discoveries of space exploration and our old religious beliefs, if these religious beliefs are understood as offering knowledge of the kind given by science. Suppose a strangely figured race of creatures with the approximate intelligence of humans and a culture and ethics radically different from ours was discovered on some distant star, would this not pose serious problems to the dogmatic and authoritarian interpretations of the Judaeo–Christian religions? Would these creatures, who obviously were not descended from Adam and Eve be tainted with original sin? Would they too have souls? Would they be in need of grace and salvation? Did Jesus absorb their sins? Would they be in need of the Messiah? Why is there no mention of these creatures in the divinely written Scriptures? Would they be subject to all the laws and traditions of these earth-centred religions? Would they be eligible to life in the hereafter? How, generally, ought we to behave with them? Are they to be treated as 'things' or as 'persons'? Suppose again that their intelligence was vastly superior to ours, how would that effect the answers to the above questions?" Some of these questions are directed solely to Christians and others are not particularly cogent but there are problems here which are the legitimate concern of Jewish theology.

Christian thinkers seem to be divided on whether it is doctrinally sound to believe in more than one incarnation. Professor E. A. Milne[34] believes that it is not, and he seeks to avoid the difficulty by suggesting that one day the whole intergalactic universe may by intercommunication (e.g. by radio signals and the like) become one system. "In that case there would be no difficulty in the uniqueness of the historical event of the Incarnation. For knowledge of it would be capable of being transmitted by signals to other planets and the re-enactment of the tragedy of the crucifixion in other planets would be unnecessary" [*sic*].

33. *The Fall and Rise of Man*, p. 80.
34. *Modern Cosmology and the Christian Idea of God*, p. 153.

A less parochial view is taken by Arthur F. Smethurst[35] and C. D. F. Moule[36] both of whom quote a poem on the subject by Alice Meynell suggesting that there may be other non-human incarnations. Professor Mascall, who has been quoted earlier, is somewhat sceptical about the possibility that there might be corporeal beings in other parts of the universe but warns against dogmatism.[37] "Nevertheless, if we are inclined to be intimidated by the mere size of the universe, it is well to remember that on certain modern cosmological theories there is a direct connection between the quantity of matter in the universe and the conditions in any limited portion of it, so that in fact it may be necessary for the universe to have the enormous size and complexity which modern science has revealed, in order for the earth to be a possible habitation for living beings. It will thus be well for us to keep a perfectly open mind on the question of the existence in the universe of rational corporeal creatures other than man." Mascall, however, eventually accepts as a possibility the view that there may be more than one incarnation.

As might have been expected from his novels on the theme, C. S. Lewis has written on the problem of extra-terrestrial beings. His essay on the subject appears in the volume containing some of his collected writings entitled *Christian Reflections*. The editor tells us in his Preface that the piece was originally published in the American Periodical *Show* (Vol. III, Feb. 1963) under the title: *Onward Christian Spacemen*. But, he says, Lewis so disliked this title that the essay has been renamed: *The Seeing Eye*.[38]

Lewis begins by making short shrift of the Russians' claim that they had not found God in outer space,[39] the god who could be found in a spatial locality is the god of savages, a deity who can be contained in a particular temple or grove. "Looking for God—or Heaven—by exploring space is like reading or seeing all Shakespeare's plays in the hope that you will find Shakespeare as one of the characters or Stratford as one of the places. Shakespeare is in one sense present at every moment in every play but he is never present in the same way as Falstaff or Lady Macbeth. Nor is he diffused through the play like a gas".

35. *Modern Science and Christian Beliefs*, pp. 96–97.
36. *Faith, Fact and Fantasy*, pp. 111–112.
37. P. 43.
38. Pp. 167–176.
39. See *supra*, pp. 56–61.

Lewis has something to say, too, on the ethics of space exploration. Some writers are dubious of the whole enterprise from the religious angle. Lewis is not bothered by the "space race" between America and Russia. "Great powers might be more usefully, but are seldom less dangerously, employed than in fabricating costly objects and flinging them, as you might say, overboard. Good luck to it! It is an excellent way of letting off steam." It is not difficult to think of a Jewish position on this question which goes beyond Lewis, who merely gives a *heter* (dispensation) to the space race on the grounds of its harmlessness, and to think of such endeavours as part of God's command to master the earth (Gen. 1: 28), since, presumably, wherever man can reach in space is covered by the implications of the word "earth" in this context. The Rabbinic doctrine, to which reference has been made at the beginning of this chapter, of man as co-partner with God in the work of creation, is also relevant to the issue.

But, Lewis goes on to ask, if there are rational creatures on other planets, what becomes of the Christian doctrine of the Incarnation? He replies that for the moment the question is hypothetical, and he appears to be sceptical whether there are, in fact, such creatures elsewhere than on earth. But, if there are, various possibilities are open. The creatures found there might be wholly good, and in that case they would have no need to be redeemed. We might find a race like our own, containing both good and evil. They might have been given some other form of redemption—"At some point in their history some great interference for the better." (Note the Christian influence even in the admission). We might meet a species needing redemption. This, says Lewis, would be a task for Christian missionaries [*sic*]. Finally, we might find a race strictly diabolical with no tiniest spark felt in them from which any goodness could ever be coaxed into the feeblest glow. But, he says, Christians always believed that there were devils but thought that they were all incorporeal. "A minor readjustment then becomes necessary". It is not at all surprising to find the author of *The Screwtape Letters* believing in devils, but from the point of view of such a believer is the readjustment only minor?

There is hardly any discussion of the subject in contemporary Jewish writing. W. Gunther Plaut touches on it.[40] Rabbi Plaut asks: "Will the possibility that there are intelligent creatures on other

40. *Judaism and the Scientific Spirit*, pp. 36–39.

planets impose any strain on our religious beliefs?" He replies: "The modern Jew will answer this question with a firm 'No'. An earlier generation, rooted in beliefs in an earth-centred universe, might have had some theological difficulties, but we have them no longer. That God should, in his vast creation, have caused only one earth and one manlike genus to evolve, is in fact harder to believe than that His creative power expressed itself in other unfathomable ways. This does not in any way diminish our relationship to Him or His to ours. Just as a father may love many children with equal love, so surely may our Father on high spread His pinions over the vastness of creation." In a note[41] Plaut observes: "There is some reason to believe that even the Jewish ancients were already hinting at a wider view. Judaism knows various expressions for God. It calls Him 'King of the World' and also 'King of All Worlds'. A Midrash states that before our earthly creation God created and destroyed many worlds" (Gen. R. 3: 7). But, of course, the ancients had no notion of "worlds" inhabited by non-human, moral beings (other than angels) and the reference in the Midrash is surely to God destroying many worlds *before* the creation of this one.

The only full-scale consideration of our problem from the Jewish point of view is, so far as I am aware, that of Rabbi Norman Lamm.[42] Lamm begins by giving an adequate account of the history of the kind of speculation we are here considering and the state of present-day scientific opinion on the question. He warns against drawing too rash conclusions and wittily remarks: "Drinking deeply from the heady wines of amazing hypotheses and fascinating theories, most of them not proven, a number of scientists have become intoxicated with a sense of their own unimportance. Never before have so many been so enthusiastic about being so trivial." Yet he wisely continues:[43] "Nevertheless these exceptions having been noted, the fact remains that most of the highly respected scientists of our day eminent in their fields, do believe that intelligent life exists elsewhere in the universe, and some of them believe that such life is close enough to us for communication. The credentials of these scientists are impeccable and the weight of evidence sufficiently convincing for us to take their conjectures seriously, despite any reservations we may have."

41. P. 79.
42. *The Religious Implications of Extraterrestrial Life.*
43. P. 18.

Lamm sees three challenges with which Judaism is confronted by the new Conceptions. These are with regard to the uniqueness of man, the uniqueness of the Creator, and the relation between God and man. With regard to the first challenge, Lamm points out that Saadia[44] and Maimonides[45] were divided on whether man is the ultimate purpose of God's creation. If there are beings equal to man, or possibly superior to him, in other parts of the universe, it would only mean that Maimonides is vindicated, and while Maimonides' views are Jewishly unconventional, the adjustment can be made without too much difficulty, since no question of dogma is involved.[46]

The second challenge concerns the generation of life. If life has been generated on other planets by natural processes, what becomes of the doctrine of God as Creator? But here, too, Lamm has no difficulty in replying that there is nothing in the Jewish doctrine of creation which prevents us believing that God can create *through* natural processes, much as we say (the illustration is Lamm's) that Solomon built the Temple even though he engaged craftsmen to do the work.[47]

As for the third challenge, Lamm sees this as the temptation to regard God in non-personal terms in view of the vastnesses revealed in the new picture of the universe. But, Lamm argues, relying on some of the Kabbalists, Judaism has in any event faced the question of personality in God in the distinction between God as He is in Himself (*En Sof*) and God in His aspect of revelation (the *Sefirot*).[48] From God's point of view, as it were, there is, indeed, no universe and hence no personal relationships. But from the creaturely point of view these relationships can be attained through creaturely effort and are open to man no matter how vast the universe.[49] Lamm does not make it sufficiently clear that if there are sentient, moral beings on planets other than earth the whole Kabbalistic system is rendered null and void. For that system certainly differs from Maimonides in that in it every act of man has a cosmic influence since the form of man is the bodily expression here on earth of the heavenly realities. It is all very well to say, as Lamm does, that the Halakhah (the legal side of Judaism) is only concerned with man and his deeds on earth, but the

44. *Beliefs and Opinions*, I, 4.
45. *Guide*, III, 13.
46. Pp. 21–36.
47. Pp. 36–42.
48. See *supra*, pp. 28–31.
49. Pp. 42–45.

Kabbalistic interpretation of the significance of the Halakhah is that the Halakhic rules, reflecting great supernal mysteries, provide the power, as it were, by which the divine grace flows *through all creation*. This system clearly presupposes the uniqueness of man.

At the end of his stimulating essay Lamm, in recounting R. Hayim of Volozhyn's distinction between God's point of view and ours, says: "Hence, even as confirmed an anthropocentrist as R. Hayim of Volozhyn does not hold God to this one theatre as a divine audience —nor puppeteer—concerned 'primarily with human events'. God in His infinite Essence still remains aloof from all of creation, which, no matter how vast or ancient, remains for Him a non-event. Were R. Hayim to consider the possibility of extraterrestrial rational creatures, he could easily revise his system, limiting man's efficacy in affecting the Essence-Relatedness tension to the scene of earth. The shift from cosmological to existential terms—man influencing God's willingness to enter into dialogue with him alone, rather than managing the destiny of the entire cosmos and all the mystical worlds beyond it— can be made without injury to the main tenets of his thought."

There is a major fallacy here. R. Hayim's own thought (in which, incidentally, he was strongly influenced by R. Schneor Zalman of Liady)[50] is on the question of God in essence versus God in revelation. This can, indeed, be applied to man on earth. But R. Hayim, as an orthodox Kabbalist, accepts the other doctrine that God in His aspect of revelation allows man to influence the whole cosmos. To be sure, a rejection of this latter doctrine would do no damage to R. Hayim's *original* ideas, but it would destroy completely the Kabbalistic system which R. Hayim obviously accepts and upon which his own ideas are based. Thus the type of readjustment Lamm is thinking of could not possibly have been made by R. Hayim who accepts the Kabbalah as revealed truth. Lamm may not so accept it, and if there are sentient, moral beings in other parts of the universe, the doctrine will have to go, but it is difficult to see how this can be described as an *"easy"* revision or how it can be made "without injury to the main tenets of his thought". To put it in slightly different words, it will not do to deny that God is only concerned with earth and humans by pointing out that from one way of looking at things God is not concerned with anything at all or, indeed, that there *is* anything about which to be

concerned. If one speaks of the problem at all and invokes the idea of
God's concern, one is already speaking of God in His revalatory aspect
and here the question remains: If one can speak of God's concern, why
should that concern be limited to man?

An illustration from a similar problem may help to make the matter clearer.
Suppose someone is bothered by the Chosen People idea, by why God should
be especially concerned with the Jews. Various solutions are open to him,
but the one that is logically precluded is to declare that it is illegitimate to
speak of God being concerned because from the aspect of *En Sof* there is no
concern. The invocation of this aspect can only have as its aim the clari-
fication of the scope of a term like "concern" when used of God, but once
one is prepared to use the term the question remains why its implications
should be confined to the Jews or applied especially to them. The question
why God should be especially concerned with Jews is not a question about
concern but about its application. By the same token, the question why
God should be especially concerned with man on earth rather than with
moral beings on other planets comes no nearer its solution through a consideration of what concern means in this context. There is a similar
confusion in Lamm's concluding remarks: "We may yet learn that, as
rational, sentient, and self-conscious creatures, 'we are not alone'. But then
again, we never felt before nor need we feel today or in the future that
we are alone, 'For Thou art with me'." Now, if there is a problem when
we discover that "we are not alone" in the universe, it is no solution at
all to point out that we knew all along that we are not alone because we are
with God—"For Thou art with Me". If the reason the new situation
bothered us were because it made us feel lonely, it would be reassuring
to be reminded that we are not alone. In fact, what bothers us is the very
opposite, that hitherto we had imagined that we were alone with God,
and now we learn that we have to share His love with other creatures.
It may not be disturbing to discover this, but, if it is, what comfort can there
be in our knowing all along that we were not alone with ourselves but
with God? Apart from this, Lamm is rather tilting at windmills, because
the challenges he mentions are not the major ones. The question of the
divine personality, for instance, is posed by the vastness of the universe
in the new picture but not by the possibility of extraterrestrial life. The
existence of moral beings on planets other than earth would soften this
particular difficulty rather than otherwise because the moral sense, which
belongs to the personal, would then be written large not only upon earth.
The more serious difficulty, to which Lamm does not refer at all, is the one
to which we alluded at the beginning of this discussion, the question of
the uniqueness of the Torah. Lamm's arguments centre around what the Torah
means in the light of the new possible situation. But if this possibility is
real, the far more difficult and radical question to be faced is that there
are whole worlds for which the Torah, given to humans, can have no

meaning. In asking what Judaism has to say about extraterrestrial life, Lamm begs the question whether Judaism has any relevance in this context. It may be that if there really are rational and moral but non-human beings on other planets they will have been given a non-human Torah.

All this is speculation, some would consider futile speculation and fruitless. But as we suggested as we embarked on this inquiry, theological principles benefit from an occasional exercise in the purely speculative.

A theological inquiry into the doctrine of creation ought in any event to consider the role in creation of creatures other than man. In the traditional scheme man is midway between the animals who have no moral sense and the angels who cannot do evil and the demons who can only do evil. The purpose of the animal creation is very mysterious. We have noted earlier[51] Maimonides' view that it is incorrect to understand the sole purpose of all creation as being for the benefit of man. On this view God has His own purposes, unknown to us, for the myriads of creatures other than man that He has brought into being. It is certainly hard to believe that the animals in their rich and marvellous variety, are solely for the purpose of affording man delight, or other benefits, or even for awakening his sense of wonder. The problem of animal suffering is particularly acute, since animals have no moral sense, it is hard to see what purpose there can be in nature being "red in tooth and claw". Judah Ha-Levi[52] is one of the few Jewish thinkers to grapple with this problem. He declares that while man can see the wisdom of the Creator in the means He has provided for animals to find their food, why should this take the form of animals preying on one another. The wisdom evident in the spider's web only makes more acute the problem of why the fly should be doomed to be caught and eaten. Ha-Levi's answer is that if the wisdom of the Creator can be seen then man must bow in faith that somehow, in a way he cannot at present grasp, the facts of nature are not contrary to the belief in an all-benevolent Creator. It is, indeed, impossible to go further than Ha-Levi. We simply do not know. In fact, the consideration of why animals suffer is bound up with the much more penetrating and far more mysterious question of why there should be animals at all. What purpose do they serve?

51. *Supra*, p. 104.   52. *Kuzari*, III, 11.

Cf. the man-centred remarks of the Midrash (Gen. R. 8: 6) that animals, birds and fishes were created on the analogy of a king who had a tower stocked with all good things. If he had no guests what pleasure has the king in so stocking it? In similar vein it is said that God created nothing that is useless, the snail as a cure for scab, the fly as a cure for the sting of the wasp, etc. (Sabb. 77b). Two modern interesting speculations on the theme of the purpose of animals are: C. S. Lewis: *The Problem of Pain*, Chapter IX, pp. 117–131 and John Hick: *Evil and the God of Love, Animal Pain*, pp. 345–353, both of which, however, are strongly Christological in tone. Saadia (*Beliefs and Opinions*, III, end, cf. Henry Malter: *Life and Works of Saadia Gaon*, pp. 210–211, note 482) believes that there is reward for animals in the Hereafter but Maimonides (*Guide*, III, 17) ridicules such a notion. Certainly Judaism is strictly opposed to afflicting pain on animals (*tzaar baale hayim*), unless it be for the purpose of satisfying real and urgent human needs. Animals may be killed and hunted for food and clothes but the pain must be reduced to the minimum. The third century teacher Rab ruled (Ber. 40a) that a man must not eat before he gives food to his beasts, since Scripture (Deut. 11: 15) says: "And I will give grass in thy fields for thy cattle" and after that: "Thou shalt eat and be satisfied." In a remarkable Talmudic passage (B.M. 85a) it is said that a calf being led to the slaughter broke away and hid its head under the robes of Rabbi Judah the Prince and lowed in terror. He said to the calf: "Go, for it was for this thou was created," whereupon it was decreed in Heaven: "Since he has no pity, let suffering be brought upon him." This tale graphically emphasises that although animals may be killed for food it is heartless to accept this as anything but a necessary evil. The famous sixteenth century mystic R. Moses Cordovero writes (*Tomer Devorah*, Chapter III, end): "Furthermore, man's mercy should be extended to all creatures, neither destroying nor despising any of them. For the Supernal Wisdom is extended to all created things—minerals, plants, animals and humans. This is the reason for the Rabbinic warning us (Ber. 50b) against despising food. In this way man's pity should be extended to all the works of the Blessed One just as the Supernal Wisdom despises no created thing for all are created from that Source, as it is written: 'In Thy wisdom Thou hast made them all' (Ps. 104: 24). This is the reason why our holy teacher was punished for his failure to have pity on the young calf which tried to hide near him . . . In this way man should despise no created thing, for they were all created by Wisdom. He should not uproot anything which grows, unless it is necessary, nor kill any living thing unless it is necessary. And he should choose an easy death for them, with a knife that has been carefully examined (so that it contains no notches) to have pity on them as far as possible. To sum up, to have pity on all things and not to hurt them depends on Wisdom, unless it be to elevate them higher and higher, from plant to animal and from animal to human. For then it is permitted to uproot the plant and to kill the animal, to bring merit out of demerit." There is a well-known Responsum on hunting animals for sport in the Responsa collection of R. Ezekiel Landau (d. 1793) see *Noda*

Biyudah, Yoreh Deah, No. 10, trans. into English with notes by Solomon
B. Freehof: *A Treasury of Responsa,* pp. 216–219. A wealthy Jewish Magnate
had a large estate and wished to know the attitude of Jewish law on whether
it was permissible for him to hunt for sport the wild animals on this estate.
In the course of his lengthy reply, Rabbi Landau notes: "I cannot comprehend how a Jew would even dream of killing animals merely for the
pleasure of hunting. When the act of killing is prompted by sport, it is
downright cruelty."

There are numerous references to angels in the Rabbinic literature
and there is no doubt whatsoever that the Rabbis believed in their
existence, though some scholars have seen significance in the absence
of a single reference to angels in the whole of the Mishnah.[53] Angels,
are, of course, mentioned frequently in the Bible and folk-beliefs
about angels were widespread long before the Rabbinic period. The
following are some of the remarks regarding angels in the Rabbinic
literature.[54] (It has often been noted that there are far more references
to angels and demons in the Babylonian Talmud than in the Palestinian. The angels are never worshipped and it is clear from the whole
of the Rabbinic literature that such attempts at worship would have
been condemned in the strongest terms as idolatry.)[55] Angels are
immortal and do not propogate their species[56] and they have no evil
inclination.[57] With the exception of the names Gabriel (Dan. 8:
16:9:21) and Michael (Dan. 10:13:12:1) in the late book of Daniel,
the angels in the Bible have no name. There is, in fact, an interesting
Rabbinic observation[58] that the names of the angels came into the
possession of Israel from Babylon. A frequent device, evident in
many a Rabbinic passage, is to place apparent moral objections to
God's conduct of the world in the mouth of the ministering angels,
as if to say that these objections are weighty and have spiritual force.[59]
Good men are said to be higher in rank than the angels.[60] Israel is
dearer to God than the angels. Israel pronounces the divine name after
the two words *Shema Yisrael* ("Hear O Israel") whereas the angels can

53. See Neumark: *Toledot Ha-Ikkarim,* Vol. II, pp. 3–4.
54. See *Jewish Encyclopedia,* Vol. I, pp. 583–597; A Cohen: *Everyman's Talmud,*
    pp. 47–58.
55 See, e.g. Hull. 40a.
56. Gen. R. 8:11.
57. Gen. R. 68:11.
58. Jer. Talmud, R.H. 2:1.
59. Ber. 20b; 61b and freq.
60. Sanh. 93a.

only pronounce it after three: "Holy, holy, holy," and the angels are not permitted to sing their praises of God in Heaven until Israel has done so down below.[61]

The mediaeval thinkers believed in the existence of angels but tend to interpret the whole subject of angeology in highly spiritual and more or less rationalistic terms. Maimonides' statement[62] is typical. Angels are creatures possessing form without matter. They are pure spirits differentiated from one another not by any bodily distinctions but by spiritual form and purpose. When it is said, for instance, that some angels are higher than others the reference is to spiritual worth not to any spatial location. When the prophets speak of the angels as fire or as having wings they are using figurative language to explain the vision in which they saw these beings. Fire, for example, is the human way of expressing a substance without weight. The names of the different grades of angels, Ofanim, Serafim and the like, refer to their spiritual stages. The highest order of angels are the "holy beasts" (Ezek. Chapter 1), which are described as being under the Throne of Glory because these are the highest of all created things, God alone being above them. The lowest grade of angels, on the other hand, are sometimes called "men". It is these who converse with the prophets and are given this name because of all the celestial beings their spiritual stage is closest to the human. The higher the angel the greater is his apprehension of God. Maimonides[63] understands the cherubim on the ark cover (Ex. 25: 17–22) to be a constant reminder to man of the existence of "angels". This is important because, in Maimonides' view, the prophet receives his communication through an angel and hence belief in angels is the foundation of prophecy and ultimately, therefore, of the Torah. The two cherubim represent the angels. If there had been only one it might have been confused with an image of Deity. As it is two facts are established, that there are angels and that they are many. The Deity is One and He created the multiplicity of angelic beings.

For further reference to angels in the mediaeval writings see Saadia: *Beliefs and Opinions*, II, 9: 10 and; III, 10; IV, 2; VI, 4; VIII, 5; Halevi: *Kuzari*, I, 87. Jacob Anatoli (*Malmad Ha-Talmidim*, p. 68a) understands the second commandment as implying a prohibition against the invocation of angels

61. Hull. 91b.
62. *Yad, Yesode Ha-Torah*, Chapter 2, cf. *Guide*, I, 49 and II, 6.
63. *Guide*, III, 45.

and attacks the custom of reciting the prayer *makhnise rahamim* in which the angels are entreated to bring Israel's prayers to God. Anatoli says that in the prayers of Moses and the other prophets and in the liturgy there is not the slightest trace of prayers to angels. The difficulty of Jacob's prayer (Gen. 48: 16) he answers in two ways: (1) The meaning is: "God who sent His angel to redeem me"; (2) The term "angel" is used here of the will of God. Cf. Israel Abraham's note in his *Companion to the Authorized Daily Prayer Book*, pp. 44–47 and Zunz-Albeck: *Ha-Derashot Be-Yisrael*, p. 546, note 100, for some of the sources for the Rabbinic opposition to the invocation of angels. Naturally, the Kabbalah is full of references to angles. (See I. Tishby: *Mishnat Ha-Zohar*, Vol. I, pp. 447–454). A typical Zoharic statement (III, 152a) is that angels are pure spirits and in their natural form they cannot appear in this material world for the world could not contain them. They have to assume the garments of this world in order to be contained in it.

Belief in demons[64] was very widespread throughout the Rabbinic period. The Babylonian Talmud in particular contains stories of haunted houses, visitations by demons, spells and incantations of every kind. The struggle against superstition was fierce but it is undeniable that many superstitions did manage to find their way into Jewish life.

Maimonides waged constant war against these superstitious beliefs, interpreting the references to them in the Talmudic literature in a psychological manner or as merely figurative. For instance, the Talmud[65] permits one who was bitten by a snake to utter an incantation over the wound. Maimonides[66] codifies this ruling but adds: "even though it has no effect whatsoever the sages permitted it in order that he might keep his sanity since he is in danger". The Shulhan Arukh[67] follows Maimonides and records the ruling in the identical words. This roused the ire of the Gaon of Vilna who remarks:[68] "This is the view of Maimonides and he records the same opinion in his Commentary to the Mishnah on the fourth chapter of tractate Avodah Zarah. But all subsequent teachers disagree with him since numerous incantations are referred to in the Talmud. He (Maimonides) followed philosophy and he therefore wrote that magic, the use of divine names for magical purposes, incantations, demons and amulets are

64. See, J. Trachtenberg: *Jewish Magic and Superstition*, Chapters 3 and 4, pp. 25–60.
65. Sanh. 101a.
66. *Yad, Avodat Kokhavim*, 11: 11.
67. *Yoreh Deah*, 179: 6.
68. *Biur Ha-Gra ad loc.* note 13.

all false but they smote him on the head since we find many accounts
in the Talmud of the efficacy of divine names and magic . . . The
Torah itself testifies 'and they became serpents' (Ex. 7: 12), see the
Zohar to this passage. Amulets are referred to in the Talmud many
times and spells too numerous to count. Philosophy, with its many
words, misled him (Maimonides) to explain all these passages figuratively and to remove them completely from their plain meaning.
God forfend, I believe neither in them (i.e. the philosophers) nor their
followers. All these matters are to be understood literally but they do
have an inner meaning; not, however, the inner meaning given by
the philosophers, which is in reality only an external meaning, but of
the masters of truth (the Kabbalists)." Abraham Ibn Ezra, like
Maimonides, denies the existence of demons.[69] The legend is told
that as a punishment Ibn Ezra was set upon by evil spirits disguised as
black dogs when he was passing through a wood in England, from the
shock of which he never recovered.[70]

What should the attitude be of the modern Jew to angels and
demons? The obstacles to such beliefs are so weighty that most moderns have given up entirely any belief in either angels or demons. The
evidence of modern psychical research is convincing to a minority
that some kind of psychical disturbance and interference from
"outside" does take place occasionally. The theological difficulties
are tremendous. Why should God require these beings? What purpose do they serve? Is there not but a step from believing in their
existence to according them something of the divine power? Is not
such a belief a surrender to superstition and at variance with pure
religious faith? Thinkers like Maimonides valiantly tried to refine
Jewish beliefs in this area but were handicapped by the clearest
references to angels in the Bible and the numerous references to both
angels and demons in the Rabbinic literature. This fact, for them
though not for us, gave a kind of divine sanction to the beliefs, which
it was heresy to question. Again the advance of modern science
enables us to explain otherwise quite mysterious phenomena without
invoking supernatural forces, benevolent or malevolent. We no
longer attribute mental illness, for example, to the invasion of the
human mind by demons which have to be cast out before the patient

69. See his Commentary to Lev. 17: 7.
70. This story was told with glee by Ibn Ezra's opponent Moses of Taku: *Ketav
Tamim*, p. 97.

can recover. The whole area of the occult is viewed with great suspicion by sensitive thinkers, though it has its followers. And quite apart from all these very weighty considerations, angels and demons are simply irrelevant to our religious life. They do not form part of our religious consciousness. We fail to be at all moved by them even if they do exist. Most moderns see great gain and no loss in the new picture in terms of a more refined, less arbitrary, faith.

Can it be left at that or should moderns still keep an open mind on the question? To be sure the many superstitions associated with these beliefs have gone never to return or, when they are present, are generally acknowledged to be irrational vestiges of primitive beliefs. Yet some may still consider it rash to deny completely that there is any reality at all behind all the talk of angels and demons in the classical Jewish sources. Are the "heavenly hosts" which praise God only a beautiful piece of ancient poetry? Perhaps the soundest attitude after all is an open mind free from the grosser descriptions and conceptions but acknowledging that we cannot know all of God's purposes in His creation. For all we know to the contrary, there may be myriads of creatures of which we have no inkling, which have their place in this mysterious universe.

> *The angels keep their ancient places;—*
> *Turn but a stone, and start a wing!*
> *'Tis ye, 'tis your estranged faces*
> *That miss the many-splendoured thing.*

Fine poetry or halting expression of a reality? Most of us would opt solidly for the former. Yet perhaps, a very faint perhaps, the question mark is still there.

CHAPTER EIGHT

PROVIDENCE

THE Hebrew term for God's providence is *hashgahah*. This abstract term is not used before the middle ages but the idea that God controls and guides the universe He has created permeates the Bible and the post-Biblical literature. The term *hashgahah* is derived from the verse in Psalms (33: 14): "From the place of His habitation He *looketh intently* (*hishgiah*) upon all the inhabitants of the earth." As we shall see, the mediaeval discussions around the concept were concerned with the scope of divine providence. The mediaeval thinkers refer to two kinds of providence: (1) *hashgahah kelalit* ("general providence"), God's care for the world in general or for species in general; and (2) *hashgahah peratit* ("special providence"), God's care for each individual. We can profitably begin with the views of these thinkers.

Maimonides[1] defends not alone the doctrine of general providence (*hashgahah kelalit*) but also of special providence (*hashgahah peratit*), though he limits the latter to humans and argues that it is in direct proportion to man's intellect and piety. Gersonides[2] discusses the question at length and arrives at a similar conclusion. This means that, for instance, God takes care, as it were, that the species of spiders and flies are preserved but He does not ordain that a particular spider catch a particular fly. This happens purely by chance. Only man, when he rises in moral stature and intelligence, becomes linked, as it were, to the divine and so comes under the divine care for him as an individual. Crescas,[3] however, takes issue with this. God created man because of His love for man and love is not dependent on conditions such as the intellectual ability of its recipients. All men, argues Crescas, not only saints and philosophers, enjoy God's special providence.

1. *Guide*, III, 17–18.
2. *Milhamot*, Maamar IV.
3. *Or Adonai*, Maamar II, 2: 4.

The Kabbalists were especially preoccupied with this topic. Joseph Ergas, for example, devotes the final section of his *Shomer Emunim*[4] to the different types of providence and observes: "Nothing occurs by accident, without intention and divine providence, as it is written: 'Then will I also walk with you in chance' (*be-keri*) (Lev. 21: 24). You see that even the state of 'chance' is attributed to God, for all proceeds from Him by reason of special providence." Still, Ergas follows Maimonides, without mentioning him by name, in limiting special providence to the human species: "However, the guardian angel has no power to provide for the special providence of non-human species; for example, whether this ox will live or die, whether this ant will be trodden on or saved, whether this spider will catch this fly and so forth. There is no special providence of this kind for animals, to say nothing of plants and minerals, since the purpose for which they were created is attained by means of the species alone, and there is no need for providence to be extended to individuals of the species. Consequently, all events which happen to individuals of these species are by pure chance and not by divine decree, except, as we shall presently explain, where it is relevant for the divine providence regarding mankind." These remarks were a source of offence to the Hasidic teachers, otherwise admirers of the *Shomer Emunim*. For Hasidism there is divine providence over everything; nothing moves without direct divine control, no stone lies where it does unless God wills it so. This is a natural consequence of the Hasidic emphasis discussed above that the creation exists within God.

The Hasidic attitude to providence is referred to by the editor, I. Stern, of the latest edition of the *Shomer Emunim*, Jer., 1965, Introduction, pp. 31–33. Stern quotes a number of prominent Hasidic teachers who declare that the doctrine of the *Baal Shem Tov*, the founder of Hasidism, is opposed to the views of Maimonides and that special providence extends to all, e.g. R. Phineas of Koretz (*Peer La-Yesharim*, No. 38): "A man should believe that even a piece of straw that lies on the ground does so at the decree of God. He decrees that it should lie there with one end facing this way and the other end the other way"; R. Hayim of Sanz (*Divre Hayim* to *Mikketz*, beg.): "It is impossible for any creature to enjoy existence without the Creator of all worlds sustaining it and keeping it in being, and it is all through divine providence. Although Maimonides has a different opinion in this matter the truth is that not even a bird is snared without providence from above." Further on the Hasidic attitude see the anthologies *Derekh Hasidim*

4. II, 81.

and *Leashon Hasidim* by Nahman of Tcherin s.v. *teva*. The main idea here is
that God is unchanging and so nature follows its law without change.
But if a man rises to a high moral standard and acts contrary to his nature
then the natural laws are nullified. This is a Hasidic expression of the idea
found in Maimonides.

The mediaeval discussions had to do chiefly with the theological
justification of the evil in the universe, with Islamic fatalism, and with
the metaphysical problems connected with God's foreknowledge.
The first and last of these still pose problems for belief in divine
providence.[5] The rise and success of modern science pose the problem
in a new form. This can be stated as follows.

The Mishnah[6] rejects as a "vain prayer" a cry for that which is past,
citing as examples the prayer that a pregnant woman should give
birth to a male child and the cry of a man that the sound of lamentation
he hears from afar should not be from his house. A modern example
would be that of the student who receives a letter from his university
which he knows contains the results of his examinations. It would be
a "vain prayer" for him to pray when he opens the letter he should
find that it is to inform him that he has passed. It is too late to pray for
these things since they have already happened. Does not the scientific
picture of a long chain of cause and effect (even if, after Hume,[7] these
terms are no longer what they used to be) render every prayer for a
particular outcome in the physical world a prayer that is too late, a
crying over spilled milk? If God's providence extends to particulars,
what precisely is the relationship of this providence to the perceived
(and predictable) natural processes? There has been little enough
concern with these questions among our contemporaries, but recently
a number of studies have appeared in which the subject is freshly
examined.

It is obviously true that the modern problem could not have been known
to the Rabbis. There are, nonetheless, instances in the Rabbinic literature of
an awareness of the idea that the regularity of the natural order is itself a
kind of providence and that intervention from without is not necessary in
normal circumstances. In Avot 5: 6 it is said that ten things were created on
the eve of the first sabbath of Creation in the twilight: the mouth of

5. On the problem of evil see *infra*, pp. 125–135; on Foreknowledge see *supra*,
   pp. 77–80.
6. Ber. 9: 3.
7. See *supra*, pp. 18–19.

the earth (Num. 16: 32); the mouth of the well (Num. 21: 16); the mouth of the ass (Num. 22: 28); the rainbow; the manna; the rod (Ex. 4: 17); the Shamir (a miraculous stone of great hardness which Solomon used in building the Temple); the tablets of stone. Zangwill came near to the meaning of this when he commented "The Fathers of the Mishnah, who taught that Balaam's ass was created on the even of Sabbath, in the twilight, were not fantastic fools, but subtle philosophers, discovering the reign of universal law through the exceptions, the miracles that had to be created specially and were still a part of the order of the world, bound to appear in due time much as apparently erratic comets are." In another passage (Gen. R. 5: 6) it is said that at the time of Creation God imposed a condition on the sea that it be divided for the Israelites, on the lions not to harm Daniel, on the fish to vomit out Jonah. In the story of the poor man whose wife had died and whose breasts became as a woman's that he might suckle his child (Sabb. 53b) one of the Rabbis remarked: "How great this man must have been that such a miracle was performed for him" but his colleague retorted: "On the contrary! How unworthy this man must have been that the order of creation was changed on his behalf." On the other hand there are numerous miracle tales in the Rabbinic literature; the belief held universally by the Rabbis was that God does perform miracles for saintly men. In this connection it should be noted that generally speaking a distinction is made between these saintly miracle-workers and the famous scholars, see especially the story told in Ber. 34b bottom of the page. The late second century Palestinian teacher, R. Hanina, gave expression to the extreme view of special providence when he said (Hull. 7b): "No man bruises his finger here on earth unless it was so decreed against him in Heaven." The famous Rabbinic statement regarding God's providence as extending over all His creatures is the saying (A.Z. 3b) that God feeds the whole world from the horned buffalo to the brood of vermin. On the question of providence and miracles in the Rabbinic literature see: Kohler: *Jewish Theology*, Chapters XXVII–XXVIII, pp. 160–175; G. F. Moore: *Judaism*, Vol. I, Part 2. Chapter 1, pp. 357–385; Schechter: *Aspects of Rabbinic Theology*, pp. 5–8; Konovitz: *Ha-Elohut*, pp. 22–26; Montefiore and Loewe: *A Rabbinic Anthology*, Chapter XIII, pp. 334–341; and especially Max Kadushin: *The Rabbinic Mind*, Chapter V, section v, pp. 143–152 and section vi, pp. 152–167.

A work that has occasioned much debate is William G. Pollard's *Chance and Providence*. Pollard observes in the Preface that he became a minister of religion after an established career as a physicist. He found it exceedingly difficult, when he thought about events in scientific terms, to imagine any kind of loophole through which God could influence them. At the same time he found that he could not deny the reality of God's providence as taught in the Bible. The two worlds existed for him side by side, but when he tried to put them together their apparent incompatibility bothered him. The book, which seeks to offer a solution, is he says, the result of some eight years of wrestling with the problem.

Pollard rests his case on the statistical character of scientific knowledge. Scientific explanation employs probabilities in place of certainties. He claims (the claim has been made before more than once) that quantum physics has revealed that chance and indetermincy are real aspects of the fundamental nature of things, and not merely the consequence of our inadequate and provisional understanding. Hence his suggestion that chance is the key to the solution of the problem of providence. "What Israel perceived as a mighty act of God was to other peoples only a favourable combination of circumstances. What Israel called Providence, the Greeks called Fortune."

Scientific investigation thus confirms the element of chance and accident in history. The believer may be tempted to argue that God's activities in these realms can be objectively seen, i.e. that it can be empirically examined (so Lecomte du Nouy, for example).[8] But this is not so, for then there would be no chance or accident. Pollard's case is that when scientific investigation has gone as far as it can it recognises chance and accident and can say no more than that these are present. The believer sees with the eye of faith (not through empirical investigation), and thus what is called "chance" or "accident" is regarded as the working of God's providence. One is reminded of Ergas's statement quoted above that God walks with man in "chance".

A traditionalist solution to the problem, arrived at by an acute analysis of what is implied in the doctrine of God's transcendence and immanence as well as the methodology of modern science, is attempted by Charles K. Robinson.[9] Robinson rightly states that there is no problem so far as general providence is concerned, but what of special providence? Robinson makes use of the notion of "related fields". Man's field of action is brought into an encounter with the transcendent much as one man encounters objectively another man without any effacement of individual choice and decision: e.g. Sennacherib is provided by God with the possibility of fulfilling God's purpose even while he is free to pursue the choice for

8. *Human Destiny.*   9. *Biblical Theism and Modern Science.*

his own ends. As Robinson italicises Isaiaah 10: 6–7: "Against a godless nation *I send* him . . . But *he* does *not so intend*, and his mind does not so think; but it is in *his mind* to *destroy* and to cut off nations not a few."

Robinson[10] sums up the Biblical view: "The Sovereign Creator who—sustaining in being every creature—knows the innermost secrets of every heart and the fundamental goals and ends towards which each individual man in the power of his finite freedom is in fact orienting himself, is able, whenever and wherever He in his transcendent love and wisdom freely elects to do so, to introduce into the conscious awareness of any man possible modes of action which can function as appropriate instrumental means for the realisation of the ends that man freely desires, but which also lead to farther-reaching historical consequences not foreseen or intended by that man, but foreseen and intended by God in his gracious revelatory and redemptive purposes for mankind."

Robinson extends this to non-human manifestations in the physical world, e.g. miracles. For the Biblical writers, he says, the miracle is not a *violation* of nature's laws (they did not know of any such laws) but concrete manifestations of the special agency of God's power. This concept, Robinson argues, is still philosophically respectable, since the picture we obtain by correlating the data of various sciences (e.g. quantum physics, psychosomatic medicine, parasychology, etc.) is that the world is characterised by *flexibility* and *variability* in its *orderly* patterns of interrelation and interaction. In his simile, the world is not a very long-playing record whose grooves are all rigidly cut in advance! Thus the difficulty of God engaging, as it were, in large-scale suspensions of the natural order is obviated. A small event in history, e.g. a slight variation in a physical field, may induce a series of meteorological consequences culminating in a large-scale weather phenomenon, which, in turn, effects the whole course of human history: "say a 'strong east wind' arriving at just the right kairotic [sic] moment over the northern part of the Sea of Reeds". This results in a "field alteration".

Robinson[11] refers to Pollard's significant insights but feels that these do not finally "gell" into any clear picture. The same might be said of Robinson's own views.

10. Pp. 133–134.   11. P. 138.

Thus far we have obtained some indications of how we can grapple with the problem. But why is the whole concept of providence so little discussed today? Langdon B. Gilkey has made a number of interesting suggestions why this should be so.[12] Before the age of Darwin, says Gilkey, providence could be detected in design. When Darwinism put forward the view that it was adaptation which enabled organisms to survive, a fatal blow was given to the design argument. Liberal post-Darwin theology (read Christian theology) tended to see providence, therefore, in the process as a whole. But the opinion of the liberal theologians that providence could be interpreted in terms of divine guidance in the evolutionary process as a whole to ever great heights has obviously suffered a decline in an age in which the idea of progress itself is suspect. Hence Gilkey[13] poses the question: "Why has no *new* understanding of Providence followed upon the recent demise, or at least transformation, of liberal theology?"

Gilkey suggests that nowadays the whole idea of a divine *telos* is harder to accept because of the naked evil which has been uncovered in this century. The belief that life is a game in which the prize is to be the victors no longer rings a bell. It is, says Gilkey, as if the gentle-manly rugger-players had suddenly produced knives and guns, so that at the end of the game the field is littered with mangled corpses. The belief still obtains that God will heal us all at the end, but it is hard to see the idea of purpose in the here and now. Furthermore, we tend nowadays to deny that God *wills* evil, and yet we go on to affirm God's sovereignty over nature. Similarly, we accept the conclusions of modern science, e.g. that the plane disaster was caused by a broken strut, or that disease is caused by germs. Therefore, even if we say with Brunner that God is "free" over His natural laws, so that these are His servants which can be set aside, we still tend to feel that theo-logical statements about the role of God in and through "natural events" have an air of unreality about them. The result is that when we speak of trust in God we seem to be referring in fact to trust in ourselves. Gilkey argues that contemporary theology is particularly vulnerable to the accusation of linguistic analysis that its statements have no meaning. For at one and the same time it seems to accept both the claims of the Biblical world regarding God's complete sovereignty and the proximate causalities of modern science.

12. *The Concept of Providence in Contemporary Theology.*
13. P. 17.3

On the deeper level the existentialist emphasis, which has been so influential in contemporary theology, has meant that theology has come to be a matter of our knowing God and not about God. On this view talk about God's providence is "objective" and has nothing to do with the encounter that is revelation. In all these ways the dominent methodology for the discussion of theological questions seems to inhibit the consideration of providence.

Gilkey offers no solution but simply points to the unfortunate neglect of the subject. He sums up[14] "If our methodology prevents our achieving some comprehensible expression of the work of God in the natural and historical environment, it is, it seems to me, incumbent upon us not to remove God from that theatre of activity but to take a second look at the limitations of our methodology." (For "our methodology" read "Christian methodology". Jews are less affected, but, unfortunately, because, on the whole, there is little Jewish theological methodology at all nowadays.)

Gilkey is correct in pointing to the strong suspicion, nowadays, of an evolutionary interpretation of divine providence but, of course, in the work of Teilhard de Chardin there is the strongest evolutionary emphasis. Teilhard sees the evolutionary process in terms of simple elements building up into more complex ones. With the appearance of man and consciousness the evolutionary process becomes conscious of itself. The emergence of life added the "biosphere" to the earth and the emergence of man the "noosphere", man's thought and his works. Since, in Teilhard's reading of the situation, the simple is yielding always to the more complex, he envisages the continuation of the process to ever greater heights, reaching towards the "omega point" which is God drawing all perfection into Himself. It has not been sufficiently noted that some years previously Rabbi Abraham Kook, speaking not as a scientist but as a Kabbalist, developed a system which has a similar thrust to that of Teilhard's. The theory of evolution, according to Kook, is of all modern philosophies the one nearest to the Kabbalistic view of nature rising back towards God from whence it came. Kook goes so far as to suggest that man is progressing in an upward direction even in the moral sphere so that the ethical demands of the Torah are coming increasingly to be seen not as unpleasant duties imposed from without but as as aspirations fully in accord with man's own. For Rabbi Kook's view see his *Orot Ha-Kodesh*, Part V, 19–22. See Teilhard's *The Phenomenon of Man* with an *Introduction* by Julian Huxley.

14. P. 186.

A full-scale survey of the field we are examining is Ian G. Barbour's *God and Nature*.[15] Barbour[16] suggests that the "dominant viewpoint today combines a deistic representation of God and nature with an existentialist understanding of God's action in the sphere of personal selfhood". Barbour is particularly good in describing the three main contemporary attitudes to the problem—those of the traditionalists (the neo-Thomists and Barth), the existentialists, and the process philosophers. For the traditionalists God is *sovereign ruler of the created order*. For the existentialists God is *transformer of personal existence*. For the process philosophers God is *influence on the world's processes*.[17]

The traditionalists see God as active in nature. According to the neo-Thomists God can produce effects directly (miracles), but usually He works through natural causes. He is primary cause. Any act in the world is uncertain before it has taken place, but for God there is no "before". For Him every act has as it were, already taken place; He sees the future not as potential but as actualised.[18] For the religious existentialists God's providence does not consist in affecting the outcome of natural processes but in the way we relate to them. From the point of view of the description of natural processes there is indeed "no need for the hypothesis"; but the man of faith interprets the events as God speaking to him.[19] But it is far from easy to see how man can so "interpret" them if the transcendent is truly transcendent and not involved in the natural processes. The process philosophers, on the other hand, limit God's omnipotence in order to leave room for the organic processes of nature.

The Jew concerned with this question must examine all these views and decide which makes the most sense both of the Jewish tradition and our experience. But it seems to me that only something like the neo-Thomist approach (the Jew would call it the neo-Maimonidean approach) does justice here. We have argued earlier[20] against the limitation of God's omnipotence as suggested by the process philosophers. And Barbour is surely right in his critique of the existentialist position. How can man see with the eye of faith God's providence at work if it is not really at work? Naturally, as Hume pointed out long

15. In his *Issues in Science and Religion*, pp. 419–452.
16. P. 420.
17. P. 439.
18. Pp. 425–428.
19. Pp. 431–434.
20. *Supra*, pp. 75–77.

ago, the question of miracles is not that they cannot happen on *a priori grounds* but whether they did in fact happen. The question is one of evidence. The modern Jew will no doubt accept the argument that many of the Biblical accounts of miracles belong to *Heilsgeschichte* and occasionally even to simple myth or legend. But he need not deny the possibility of miracles occurring as the neo-Thomists rightly point out.

This leads to a consideration of a recent book relevant to the question: *Miracles—Cambridge Studies in Their Philosophy and History.*[21] The majority of the essays in this volume are historical, but Dr. Mary Hesse, an expert in the philosophy of science, writes on: *Miracles and the Laws of Nature.*[22] She observes that in the new situation created by the discrediting of the Newtonian in favour of quantum physics the notion of a miracle as a "violation" of a mechanical system no longer has meaning, and from this point of view it is easier nowadays to believe that miracles are possible. But she warns that contemporary science, despite its relativistic tendencies, continues to expect a certain stability and uniformity in nature and is suspicious of alleged events which seem to disturb the expected order. Can miracles be interpreted, she asks, in such a way that even violation in the weak sense is avoided? On the philosophical level, how are particular events, rather than all events, to be seen as the special acts of a transcendent God? "The offence of particularity is still with us, whether these special acts violate or confirm with the laws of nature. The fundamental problem is not about miracles, but about transcendence."

In the same symposium J. P. Ross writes[23] on: *Some Notes on Miracles in the Old Testament.* The ancient Hebrew, he notes, believed in the regularity of the natural order, but for him it is a moral regularity in God's consistently faithful character, not a mere physical regularity. The importance of the miracle for the Biblical writers consisted in the insight it provided into the character of God. This, says Ross, is what Y. Kaufmann is getting at when he writes (of the conquest of Canaan): "There never was a 'realistic' account of the events. The account of the events was 'idealistic', 'legendary', right from the start. Every warrior who came from the battle-line to the camp and told his story to the women and children related 'legendary'

21. Ed. C. F. D. Moule. 22. Pp. 33–42. 23. P. 43–60.

things, 'idealistic' history stamped with the mark of the miraculous sign." When Israel won a battle in a hailstorm the Israelites saw, heard and felt God fighting for them with hailstones from heaven. This, suggests Ross, can provide us with a kind of bilingual text, a key to translate more and more of our present experience into "Old Testament" terms. In this way Israel's insights come into the heart and reality of our life. Not that their point of view is the only, or altogether the best, way of looking at things. We are not likely to forget our twentieth-century outlook completely. But we may avoid the temptation to imagine that our way of thinking is complete and perfect, and that no improvement is possible to the framework within which we approach reality".

The editor of the symposium, Professor C. F. D. Moule, takes this up further.[24] If the ancient Hebrews were closer to reality when they looked for consistency in the power of God rather than in an impersonal system of causation, it seems reasonable to postulate that the ultimate and most inclusive field in which consistency is to be sought is the realm of the personal. It may be, then, he argues, that our notions of what is possible when a proper relationship with God is achieved is too narrow. "If the ultimate *locus* of consistency is in the realm of the personal—in the character of a God who 'cannot deny himself'—then what is (in our present conditions) unusual need not be ultimately an intervention or a dislocation or suspension of natural law." It need only be what "normally" happens when an individual achieves the right relationship with God. This takes us back with a vengeance to what Maimonides was saying so long ago.

24. Pp. 13f.

CHAPTER NINE

THE GOODNESS OF GOD

IT is noteworthy, and a suitable point to be emphasised at the beginning of a discussion of the doctrine of God's goodness, that, in the Bible, while God is described as "creating evil" (Is. 45: 7), in that He alone is responsible for everything that is, it is nowhere suggested that evil belongs in any way to His essential nature or that He is indifferent to evil. All the Biblical authors seem to have thought of goodness as intrinsic, as it were, to the character of God. By contrast, He creates evil, He tolerates its continued existence, He encourages man to fight it and destroy it if he can, but evil has no part in His being. Speculation of why in that case God does allow evil to exist is not, however, found in the Bible. Abstract speculations of this kind are foreign to ancient Hebraic thinking. The Biblical authors were concerned with man and the life he is to lead so that when the mystery of evil is discussed—in the books of Job and Ecclesiastes for example—the problem centres around why the righteous suffer not around the deeper problem of why there is suffering at all or evil of any kind. The same applies to a very large extent to the Rabbinic literature. It was not until the mediaeval period that the metaphysical problem regarding the very existence of evil was discussed by Jewish thinkers.

The word *tov*, "good", is used of God many times in the Bible. He sees that the things He has created are "good" (Gen. 1: 4, 10, 12, 18, 21, 25) and His creation as a whole as "very good" (Gen. 1: 31). He is good and upright (Ps. 25: 8); man can see that He is good)Ps. 34: 9); and His name is good (Ps. 52: 11; 54: 8). He is good and ready to pardon (Ps. 86: 5); and it is right to give thanks to Him for He is good (Ps. 100: 4-5; 106: 1; 107: 1; 118: 1; 29; 135: 3; 136: 1). He is good and does good (Ps. 118: 68) and is good to all (Ps. 145: 9).

As has been said, the Biblical and Rabbinic teaching is averse to speculation on the mystery of evil. But the philosophical mind has always been bothered by this most terrible of questions. Theistic faith, in its traditional version, always seems to assert three propositions: (1) God is wholly good; (2) Evil is real; (3) God is all-powerful. But the acceptance of all three propositions as true seems to involve us in contradiction. For if evil is real then either God wishes to remove it (or not to have brought it into being) and cannot do so in which case there are limits to His power, or He can remove it (or need not have brought it into being) but does not choose to do so, in which case He cannot be wholly good. The only way out of the dilemma is to deny (or at least qualify) one of these propositions.

No representative Jewish thinker has sought to deny the first proposition—that God is wholly good. (Even those thinkers who have hesitated to use attributes like "goodness" of God, because of the anthropomorphism involved, have gone on to say that in any event this can be said of God that He is not the opposite of good.)[1] And it is surely a sound religious instinct which refuses to ascribe any evil to the nature of God. A being who desired evil in any ultimate sense would not be an Object of worship. He would be less than the man he has created who would banish evil if he had the power to do so or, at least, men who do not wish to banish evil if they can do so are considered morally inferior.

The temptation for the religious mind is to deny any reality to evil: to reject, in other words, the second proposition. This is not the Biblical view. Indeed, the moral drama of the Biblical record consists precisely in this that a real fight is going on between good and evil with God at man's side to assist him in his struggle for the good. Nor is it at all philosophically helpful to attempt to solve the problem of evil by denying its existence. Even if evil is an illusion the illusion is itself evil, and in any event it is hard to see what meaning "illusion" can have in this context. Nor is it much use describing evil as "merely" the negation of the good. Even if this were true that negation is evil.

The only approach valid for the theist would seem to be that which qualifies God's omnipotence. This, we have argued earlier, should not go so far as to see God as finite[2] but to recognise that omnipotence cannot embrace a contradiction.[3] For the world to be an arena for the emergence of moral worth and value requires a world in which there

1. See *supra*, pp. 39–43.   2. See *supra*, pp. 75–77.
3. See *supra*, pp. 73–75.

is evil to overcome that this value might emerge. Thus, even God cannot create such a world without evil, not because there are limits to His powers but because a contradiction would be involved. We would, in fact, be asking God to create a world without evil in which there is evil. A nonsense statement does not make sense, it must be repeated, simply because the word "God" has been tagged on to it. This is the famous "free will defence", that is, that for man to be free, evil must be a real possibility, and we must examine its adequacy today. But first it might be helpful to see how some of the mediaeval Jewish thinkers tried to grapple with this most stubborn and burning problem for the man of faith. We begin with the inquiry of Abraham Ibn David.[4]

Abraham Ibn David declares that our reason tells us that God cannot produce evil and this is taught by Scripture and in the Jewish tradition generally. Reason tells us that this is so because for God, who is wholly good, to produce evil is a contradiction in terms. Human beings are both good and evil at the same time because the good stems from one part of their character, the evil from another. But since God is not composite it is logically impossible for His nature to embrace both good and evil. Why, then, do we find evil in the universe? The answer Abraham Ibn David gives is that most types of evil we can imagine are due to the absence of the good, e.g. poverty is the absence of wealth, darkness the absence of light, folly the absence of wisdom. It is not correct to say that God creates poverty or darkness or stupidity any more than it would be correct to say that God has made no elephants in Spain. The absence of elephants in Spain is not something positive which God has to make. The only logical way of stating the proposition is to say that while God did create elephants He did not create them in Spain, i.e. God is certainly responsible for the fact that there are no elephants in Spain but this is not by means of a no-elephant creating process but simply means that the scope of His elephant creating is not extended to Spain. By the same token God does not create evil (because there is no evil to be created, evil being simply the absence of the good). What can be said is rather that God does not create certain goods for certain persons, i.e. He does not give wisdom to the fool. But is not the absence of the good evil in itself? To this Abraham Ibn David replies that when we ask God to make the

<hr>

4. *Emunah Ramah*, VI, 2, ed. Weil, pp. 93f.

imperfect perfect we are asking for the world as we know it to be
abolished. For if plants are to be made more perfect by becoming
animals and animals more perfect by becoming humans and humans
like Moses and Moses like the angels, then there would be no grada-
tions in creation. Only God and perhaps a few of the highest angels
would exist. God in His goodness wishes to benefit a multitude of
creatures of various forms and this is only possible in a world in
which there are imperfections as well as perfections!

It cannot be said that Abraham Ibn David's attempted solution is
satisfactory. It overlooks entirely the many instances of extreme pain
which, if we are not to indulge in an abuse of language, can only be
described as evil. It helps not at all to say that a man suffering from a
cruel disease which torments his body and makes him cry out in
anguish is only being deprived by God of his health. But, for all that,
Abraham Ibn David does touch here on an important factor in any
consideration of this problem. A world without evil would be a
world without struggle for the good and would in fact not be a
world at all. This leads eventually to the free will defence but Abraham
Ibn David's formulation only serves to obscure the issue.

Maimonides[5] follows more or less the same line of argument as
Abraham Ibn David. All evils are privations. Therefore God does not
create evil but is responsible rather for the privation of the good, i.e.
He cannot be said to have created a blind man but rather to have
created a man to whom He has not given sight.

It is astonishing to us that these mediaeval thinkers should not have
seen that they were simply playing with words. How could they have
attached any significance to their distinction? How does it help the
problem if instead of saying that God created blind men He created
men without the gift of sight? Probably the need of the mediaeval
thinkers was psychological. They shrank at ascribing evil in a positive
sense to the All-good. What they were doing, in fact, consciously or
unconsciously, was to try to minimise in a number of ways the power
and force of evil. They were trying to say in various ways that while
we cannot deny the existence of evil in the universe it is all not quite
so bad as we imagine at first glance. But they seem to have been oddly
unaware that even a small amount of evil, even an evil minimised and
expressed negatively, is still a tremendous obstacle to a belief in God

5. *Guide*, III, 10–12.

as wholly good. Maimonides, it is true, is not entirely unaware of the difficulty. He argues that God cannot make a material universe without the properties of privation because, in his view, which goes back to Plato,[6] matter must have this property in order to be matter. To expect God to create matter which is not matter is to expect Him to do the logically impossible. Again we are back with the thought that the world as we know it must have the nature it does have if it is to be an imaginable world at all. But what of moral evil? Maimonides replies that this, too, is the result of ignorance. If men knew the truth there would be no wars or hatred or enmity. That is why the promise is held out that one day: "They shall not hurt nor destroy in all my holy mountain; for the earth shall be full of the knowledge of the Lord, as the waters cover the sea" (Is. 11:9). Maimonides denies that there is more evil in the world than good. Most of the evils which befall men are due to their wrong exercise of free will. From all Maimonides' analysis once again the valuable part is the idea that the kind of world we have is the only one that can serve as an arena for the emergence of moral worth and of this more must be said.

In the Kabbalah, on the other hand, evil is treated as something positive. Indeed, the Kabbalistic doctrine of the "Other Side" (*sitra ahara*), the demonic side of existence, comes very close to dualism, although the Kabbalists warn against this repeatedly. They give the illustration of a wild dog controlled by its master's chain even though appearing to enjoy a certain degree of freedom to bite. Particularly in the Lurianic Kabbalah the doctrine of evil is treated at length. We have noted earlier[7] the Lurianic doctrine of *Tzimtzum* in which God withdraws from Himself into Himself to make room for the world. The light which pours into the "empty space" results in the "breaking of the vessels" and even after the reconstruction of the Sefirotic realms some of the infinite light is spilled over, as it were, to form worlds in decreasing order until eventually the over-spill nourishes the denizens of the "Other Side"—the *kelipot*, "shells" or "husks" which surround the good, as the bark the tree or the rind the fruit, and which parasitically take nourishment from the good. Thus evil is the result of the cosmic catastrophe known as the "breaking of the vessels" which some of the bolder Kabbalists tend to see as a kind of purging

---

6. See Husik: *History of Mediaeval Jewish Philosophy.* p. 288.
7. See *supra*, pp. 32–34 and especially the fine treatment of I. Tishby: *Torat Ha-Ra Ve-Ha-Kelipah Be-Torat Ha-Ari.*

by God of the evil in Him.[8] This comes perilously close to the doctrine of a finite and limited God.[9] In any event the Kabbalists are grappling with the problem of how the Infinite can produce the finite. Since God has to have creatures, as it were, so that He can benefit them, He has to produce that which is not God as the environment in which alone they can exist and this not-God is bound to contain imperfections and evil. This is, in fact, another statement in mythical terms of the freewill defence. Man can only become God-like by making the good his own through the exercise of his free choice. For this he requires a world in which there is evil as well as good.

The statement of the Kabbalistic view on this matter is given by the later Kabbalist Moses Hayim Luzzatto (*K'lah Pithe Hokhmah*, 1–4, pp. 9–14) as follows: "The unification of *En Sof* means that only His will exists and no other will exists independently of Him. Consequently, He alone rules and no other will. The whole Kabbalistic edifice is constructed on the basis of this principle. The will of the Emanator is only good. Therefore, only His goodness alone can endure. Whatever is evil at the beginning does not proceed, God forfend, from any other domain so that it can endure in opposition to Him. In the end it will be good for certain and then it will be known that there is no other dominion than His. The purpose of creation is for Him to bestow of His goodness in accordance with His longing to bring goodness to others to the uttermost limits of goodness. *En Sof*, blessed be He, wished His goodness to be complete so that there should not be an element of shame among its recipients. He ordained, therefore, for His perfect unity to be revealed, namely, that nothing acts counter to Him and no imperfection. Consequently, He ordained the following order by which He governs the world: there should be realised the restoration of the evil to the good. This means that at first He permits the evil to do its worst but at the end all destructive forces will find their rectification and all evil will become real good. Then will the unification be revealed and this revelation itself is the delight of the souls". The meaning of Luzzatto's somewhat enigmatic statement is that just as a man cannot really enjoy the good things of life if they are given to him free (because man's independence of spirit refuses to allow him to eat unearned bread, "bread of shame" as the Kabbalists call it) so, too the spiritual delight of the soul is less than complete if unearned. Consequently, God places man in this world of evil and imperfection to make the good his own. He then becomes the creator, as it were, of his own good and thus becomes as close to resembling

8. See Tishby for this and for an attempt to apply this to current Jewish theological thought Byron L. Sherwin in *Judaism*, Winter, 1959.
9. See *supra*, pp. 75–77.

his Creator as man can come. The evil thus serves the good and eventually it is vanquished by becoming good. When that happens and the whole cosmic process is complete, God is seen in all His Unity. The recognition by the soul of this is the delight of the soul in which it enjoys God for all eternity.

So much for the discussions on this soul-rending problem in the mediaeval writers. With the exception of the Kabbalah, it is rather surprising that comparatively little sustained discussion is found among these writers on the real depths of the problem. We turn now to the work of modern religious thinkers.

It is generally acknowledged in contemporary theological discussion that while the terrible problem of how God, the All-Good and All-powerful, can tolerate evil in His creation, has always been the most difficult the theist has to face, the problem as it confronts twentieth-century man is so acute as to render banal most of the earlier attempts at a solution. This is for a number of reasons. First, there is the sheer nakedness of the evil our generation has witnessed. Babies have suffered cruel deaths in former ages, but it was left to the Nazis to hurl them alive into gas-chambers and burn their bodies in crematoria. The horrors of Hiroshima and the napalm bomb seem too monstrous for theodicy to cope with so that the more subtle the defence the greater appears to be the affront. Secondly, the colossal scale of evils embracing large areas of the earth's surface tends to weight the dice against the possibility of ever finding a satisfactory solution. It is much harder to believe, nowadays, with Maimonides that there is more good than evil in the universe. Thirdly, the emergence of such evils in this century, when men had been thought to have reached a high level of mature moral and intellectual development, has shattered the hopes of those thinkers who were groping for a solution in evolutionary terms.

For many sensitive Jews there is the strongest distaste for even considering this problem. Haunted by feelings of guilt at having been spared when the six million were foully destroyed, these Jews discover within themselves a psychological block which prevents them from contemplating any explanation of such insanity on a cosmic scale, and this reinforces the natural and commendable Jewish reticence which has ever frowned on *tzidduk ha-din* (justifying God's justice) when the suffering of others is at issue. Against every attempt at understanding with the mind, the heart cries out as at a desecration of the memory of the innocents who perished.

Yet a number of Jews have written on the holocaust and its theological implications. From such writings various attitudes emerge. There is considerable agreement among Jewish thinkers that any neat solution amounts to a callous unawareness of the magnitude of the disaster and that, for example, it would be an insufferable insult to the memory of the victims to dare even to try to see their torture within a tidy scheme of reward and punishment. The tit-for-tat solution is no help. Even in former ages such a solution had to contend with insuperable obstacles. How did it explain the suffering of those innocent of fault and the escape of the guilty? How did it understand the sufferings of little children? Some thoroughgoing tit-for-tat thinkers did not hesitate to suggest that these latter were being punished for offences they had committed in a previous existence! Jewish theology must, to be sure, build on the experience and insights of the past, but it commits suicide if it abdicates to them completely.

Among the majority of Jewish thinkers there is a consensus that God is not to be defended by laying any blame at the doors of European Jewry. With a kind of spontaneous religious insight, the Jewish people has given the slaughtered innocents the name *Kedoshim*, "martyrs". At the opposite end of the scale some thinkers have given up the struggle in despair and prefer to speak of Jewish values to be preserved in spite of all that has happened rather than of the One in whose name these values have been proclaimed. But this is a form of atheism and should be recognised as such even though it is wrenched from faithful hearts torn in agony. "Nothing" is still "not anything", even if it is spelled with a capital "N".

Most of the Jewish thinkers who have dared to write on the problem at all still affirm the truth of traditional theism, but many of them come close to suggesting at the same time that in the particular circumstances it is irreligious to probe too deeply. A text hallowed by tradition is: "And Aaron was silent" (Lev. 10: 3). For all that, and with the fullest appreciation of the overwhelming need for a theology of silence on the emotional, moral and pyschological levels, one can argue that the mind of the believer cannot find repose in faith unless it seeks to discover some glimpse of how apparent chaos can be the product of purposive Mind. From this point of view, and in spite of existentialist shudders, the quest for a theodicy is still valid if God is to continue to be worshipped. The sober fact is, however, that the only recent full-scale treatment of the problem is by the Christian writer John Hick in his *Evil and the God of Love*.

To the claim that the investigation of the problem of evil is religiously improper, that it is *ipso facto* irreligious for man to seek to justify God, Hick[10] retorts: "In this formulation of the difficulty the word 'justify' seems to cause the trouble. But suppose we use instead the more neutral term 'understand'. Is it impious to try to understand God's dealings with mankind? Surely, if theology is permissible at all, it would be arbitrary to disallow discussion of the topics that come under the heading of theodicy . . . By what authority must we insist upon maintaining an unrelieved mystery and darkness concerning God's permission of evil? Surely this would be a dogmatism of the least defensible kind. It is, of course, permissible to hold, on the basis of an investigation of the issues, that there is in fact no theodicy, no legitimate way of thinking about the problem of evil that satisfies both mind and conscience; but in view of the fallibility of human reasoning it would be unwise to hold this with absolute confidence, and quite unjustifiable to forbid others from making their own attempts. It may be that what the theodicist is searching for does not exist. But, on the other hand, even if no complete theodicy is attainable, certain approaches to it may be less adequate than others, and it may thus be possible to reach some modest degree of genuine illumination upon the subject and to discover helpful criteria by which to discriminate among speculations concerning it. If so, efforts in this direction need not be wasted."

Hick's own argument is to take sides with Irenaeus (second century) against St. Augustine who stresses the idea of the Fall of man and attributes the evil in the world to this. Irenaeus, on the other hand, sees the world with its hardships and challenges as the appropriate arena for the emergence of those values which make man God-like in his struggle for the good and thus equip him for his role of enjoying God for ever. In Keats's famous phrase this world is not a vale of tears but a vale of soul-making. The myth of Genesis represents the natural condition of man as a finite creature remote from God. But this state is natural to man and is not the result of a "Fall". Only in a world in which there has to be a struggle for the good can man freely choose God. Hick thus presents the classical free will defence, but he explores

10. P. 7.

it more acutely and more comprehensively than most other theistic thinkers have done. Basically, as we have noted earlier, the free will defence considers what meaning can be given to God's omnipotence. As the mediaeval thinkers said, God cannot do the absolutely or logically impossible because this involves a contradiction in terms. Even God cannot give man free will and the opportunity of exercising it, of choosing good and rejecting evil, if man is placed in a world in which there is no evil and therefore no possibility of choice.

The parallels to this in classical Jewish thought are numerous. We have seen that both Abraham Ibn David and Maimonides come very close to it and that the Kabbalistic doctrine implies it, at least in some interpretations.

A biting critique of Hick is that of Roland Puccetti.[11] Puccetti agrees that if the world is to be a vale of soul-making it cannot at the same time be a hedonistic paradise, but he cannot see why God should allow His creatures to suffer pain when this is not necessary for their moral development, e.g. the sufferings of children and animals and all physical evils which seem completely pointless. On this question of the amount of suffering, Hick admits that we do not know why it should be necessary but invokes the idea of a mystery: "The mystery of dysteleological sufferings is a real mystery, impenetrable to the rationalising human mind." But, argues Puccetti, if we are to fall back on the idea of a mystery, this only means that the problem is insoluble. What it results in is saying that God must have a morally sufficient reason for allowing instances of human suffering, but we do not know what these are. This is tantamount to saying that we do not know the answer to the problem of pain and that there is, therefore, no theodicy.

Hick leaps to the defence in his essay: "God, Evil and Mystery." Hick retorts that he has not invoked the principle of mystery as an unsupported hope that there is some explanation of the fact of evil even though we cannot see what it is. The apparent random element in nature is essential, for if it were always possible to discover the teleological necessity of each kind of suffering this would interfere with man's free choice. This does not mean that God sends the diseases, earthquakes and so on to provide opportunities for sympathy and help but only that an environment in which these are possible can serve as a vale of soul-making. Hick sums it up as follows: "The

11. *The Loving God—Some Observations on John Hick's Evil and the Love of God.*

contingencies of the world process are genuine; though the existence of the whole process, with its contingencies, represents a divine creative act, the purpose of which is to make it possible for finite creatures to inhabit an autonomous world in which their creator is not involuntarily evident and in which, accordingly, their moral and spiritual nature may freely develop. In and through and out of this religiously and morally ambiguous situation—which is human existence as we now experience it—and out of its continuation, variation and transformation beyond this present life, the infinite good symbolised by the Kingdom of God is finally to come. Within the context of this theory the positive contribution of mystery to the soul-making process consists in the fact that in a world in which rewards and punishments were justly apportioned to our deeds, our moral natures could never have occasion to develop; and that a world in which the ultimate constructive use of adversity was an established scientific fact would not function as a vale of soul-making".

From the Jewish side see G. N. Schlesinger: *Divine Benevolence* and the state-ment, with striking affinities to Hick's but without Hick's eloquence, of L. Carmel, based on the ideas of Rabbi E. Dessler: *The Problem of Evil: The Jewish Synthesis.* On the holocaust see: Richard Rubenstein: *After Auschwitz;* Ignaz Maybaum: *The Face of God After Auschwitz* and Ulrich Simon: *A Theology of Auschwitz.* Simon, of Jewish origin but now a Christian, lost his father and several other relatives in Auschwitz. His work is strongly Christological but he tries hard to be fair to Judaism. His statement on p. 79 that the Hebrew term for the holocaust *churban* is a "sacrificial term" evidently confuses the term with *korban.* The doctrine of Satan as responsible for the evil in the universe solves nothing, of course, since the problem remains of why Satan should have been created. On Satan see Kohler: Jewish Theology, Chapter XXXI, pp. 189–196.

All that has been said can afford at the most only a glimpse through the darkness. The man of faith does not deny that God hides himself, to use Biblical language. But he persists in his faith that hard though it is to believe in God it is even harder not to believe in Him. Or as the Hasidim were fond of saying when man knows that God is hidden God is hidden no longer.

CHAPTER TEN

EXCURSUS: THE NAMES OF GOD

THROUGHOUT Jewish history[1] various names have been given to God. These obviously reflect the particular concepts held by the people who used the names; they call attention to one or other aspect of the Deity as it made its special impact. An examination of the names given to God at various stages of Jewish thought is consequently essential in a work of Jewish theology if only for the light this throws on the history of the subject. We must note the chief names for God as they apear in the Bible, in the Rabbinic literature, among the mediaeval Jewish thinkers and in the Kabbalah.

The bibliography on the subject is immense but the following works are especially helpful: E. Landau: *Die den Raume entnommenon Synonyma für Gott*; A. Marmorstein: *The Old Rabbinic Doctrine of God*; Israel Konovitz: *Ha-Elohut*, Chapter 1, pp. 2–8; J. F. McLaughlin and J. D. Eisenstein in *Jewish Encyclopedia*, Vol. IX, pp. 160–165; Simon Cohen in *Universal Jewish Encyclopedia*, Vol. 5, pp. 6–8; James Barr: *Names of God in the Old Testament* in Hasting's *Dictionary of the Bible*, pp. 334–335; R. C. Dentan: *Digression: The Names of God* in his *The Knowledge of God in Ancient Israel*, pp. 187–196; Kohler: *Jewish Theology*, pp. 58–63; Solomon Goldman: *From Slavery to Freedom*, pp. 139–148: M.D. (U.) Cassuto: *Shemot Elohim Ba-Mikra* in *Encyclopedia Mikrait*, Vol. I, pp. 301–322 (to which a full bibliography for the Biblical period is appended); Edmond Jacob: *Theology of the Old Testament*, pp. 43–64 (with a bibliography of recent works on the subject).

THE NAMES OF GOD IN THE BIBLE

(i) *The Tetragrammaton*

The special four letter name JHVH (so, after the German spelling —the English form would be JHWH) is, as it were, the personal name for the God of Israel in the Bible. (This name occurs 6,823 times in the

1. In view of the detailed references on each of the divine names the notes in this chapter have been incorporated into the text.

present Hebrew text of the Bible). The usual English translation of this as "the Lord" (which follows the Greek translation as kyrios) is based on the fact that in Jewish practice this name was never pronounced as it is written but as *Adonai*, "the Lord". In printed texts the vowels of the latter word are placed under the letters of the Tetragrammaton. (Hence the name was read erroneously by Christian scholars as "Jehovah".) The original pronunciation of the Tetragrammaton has been lost owing to the strong Jewish disapproval of pronouncing this name. Consequently, we can only guess at the original pronunciation. The pronunciation *Yahweh* or *Yahveh* is based on that used by some of the Church Fathers but there is no certainty at all in this matter. Most scholars, nowadays, prefer to render it simply as YHWH or JHVH without the vowels.

What does this name mean? The most important Biblical passage in this connection is Exodus 3: 14–15 in which the name is associated with the idea of "being". Hence some have understood it to mean "He-Who-Is". This, however, has sometimes been seen as a later interpretation of the name. On this view various suggestions have been put forward as to the original meaning, e.g. that it was a primitive cult cry (*ya-hu*, "O He") or "He who brings into being".

(ii) *Ehyeh*

In Exodus 3: 14 we read that, in response to Moses' request to know what name to give God when he brings the message of redemption to the people, God replies: *"Ehyeh-Asher-Ehyeh"* and continues: "Thus shall you say to the Israelites, 'Ehyeh' sent me to you." In verse 15 the name is connected with the Tetragrammaton. There are thus two forms of the name, the longer one *Ehyeh-Asher-Ehyeh* and the shorter *Ehyeh*, both connected with a root meaning "to be". Various translations have been suggested, e.g. "I Am That I Am" for the longer name and "I Am" for the shorter; "I Am Who I Am" for the longer name and "I Will Be" for the shorter.

(iii) *Yah*

This is another name associated with the Tetragrammaton, of which it is in fact, a shortened version. It is found in a number of instances in the Bible (e.g. Ex. 15: 2) where it is usually translated in English by "the Lord". It is also found in a number of personal names, e.g. Azariah ("Yah has helped") and Jehoiakim (= *yeho-yakim*, "May Yah raise up") and in the term *Hallelujah* ("Praise ye Yah").

(iv) *Elohim*

This is the usual Hebrew name for God and is connected with the name *El*. The name Elohim is a plural form (but occasionally the singular *Eloah* is found, e.g. in Deut. 32: 15 and many times in the book of Job). It is also used of the gods as in the expression "other gods", ! *elohim aherim*. Generally when the reference is to God the verbs and adjectives used with it are in the singular. The plural form has long been a puzzle, the Rabbis being obliged to defend it against the "sectarians" who adduced from the plural form that there is more than one god. Many moderns explain the plural form on the basis of the idea that in God are to be found all the attributes of deity. The idea appears to be that all these are concentrated in God and in no other.

(v) *El*

Since we find a verse (Gen. 31: 29) which reads: "I have it in my power (*el*) to do you harm" the meaning of *El* is generally assumed to be "Power". (The root *el* is found in the generic name of God among all Semitic peoples but *El* can also be the Semitic name for a particular deity—the god *El*.) We know from the Ugaritic literature that *El* was the name of one of the Canaanite gods. It has been conjectured that Beth-el (= "house of *El*") was originally a site dedicated to the worship of this god which the narrative in Gen. 28: 10–22 transforms into a place at which God appeared in a dream to the patriarch Jacob. It has further been noted that in this narrative God does not come down to earth, as did the pagans deities, but is linked to earth by the ladder on which only the angels of God ascend and descend. *El* is also found in various compound names, e.g. *El Shaddai* (Gen. 17: 1); *El Elyon*, "Most High God" (Gen. 14: 18–20); and *El Roi*, "God of seeing" (Gen. 16: 13).

(vi) *Shaddai*

This name is found on its own in Job 5: 17 and together with *El* (see especially Ex. 6: 3). It is found in a number of personal names, e.g. Zurishaddai, "My rock is Shaddai" and Ammishaddai, "My people (or kinsman) is Shaddai" (see Num. 1: 5–15). This name, following the Septuagint "Pantocrator" and the Vulgate *deus omnipotens*, is generally translated in English as "Almighty". There have been various conjectures as to the origin of the name, e.g. from *shadod*, "to thunder" or from *shod*, "destruction" or as meaning "the mountain god".

(vii) *Adonai*

This is the word which was later used as a substitute whenever the Tetragrammaton is written. The name appears in a few Biblical passages (e.g. Ex. 4: 10 and 13). The name is clearly from *adon*, "lord", possibly with the pronominal suffix, "my Lord". But eventually it became a personal name for God. (The traditional way of writing this with a *kametz* as the final vowel may have been the original reading or may have been introduced to distinguish it from *adonai* with a *patah* where the meaning is "my lords", e.g. in Gen. 19: 2.)

(viii) *Tzevaot*

This name meaning "hosts" is only found in compounds such as "the Lord of hosts" (Is. 6: 3). The "hosts" referred to are understood either as the hosts of heaven or of all creatures or of the angels or of the people of Israel. In the Isaiah passage and elsewhere the term is not found in the construct but in apposition to another divine name, hence it would seem, as the Rabbis indeed declare, that it is a divine name. It has been suggested that as a special name for God *Tzevaot* means "He who is to be identified with all the hosts", i.e. with all the powers that were attributed to the gods.

(ix) *Elyon*

This name means "The Most High". It is found, as above, together with *El*, but also on its own (e.g. in Num. 24: 16; Deut. 32: 8).

(x) *Attributes*

Various attributes of God are found in the Bible but these are not names of God. However, there are indications that occasionally some of these are used as personal names. The most frequent are: *Kedosh Yisrael*, "The Holy One of Israel", particularly in the book of Isaiah, see e.g. Is. 5: 19 and cf. Ps. 111: 9; *Tzur*, "The Rock", e.g. in Deut. 32: 4 and in personal names as a compound; *Pahad Yitzhak*, "The

Fear of Isaac", Gen. 31: 42 and 54; *Avir Yaakov*, "The Mighty One of Jacob", e.g. Gen. 49: 24, and *Avir Yisrael*, "The Mighty One of Israel", Isaiah 1: 24. It has also been suggested that the pronoun *hu*, "he" is sometimes used as a name of God, e.g. in Deut. 32: 39: "See, then, that I, I am He" (*Hu*) i.e. "I am *Hu*". Reference should also be made to *Attik Yomin*, "Ancient of Days" in Dan. 7: 9 (*Attik Yommaya* in Dan. 7: 13 and 22). The book of Esther is the only book in the Bible which contains no divine name.

THE NAMES OF GOD IN THE RABBINIC LITERATURE

An inquiry into the names of God in the Rabbinic literature can be divided into two parts. The first concerns the interpretations given by the Rabbis to the divine names found in the Bible and the various rules governing the use of these. The second concerns the specific names used in post-Biblical times and found in the Rabbinic literature. We begin with the prior task. Jacob b. Asher in his *Baal Ha-Turim* to Num. 11: 16 gives a list of 70 names of God found in the Bible but these include the attributes which are not really names at all. The 70 divine names are mentioned in Num. R. 14 and in Targum to Cant. 2: 17.

The Tetragrammaton is known in the Rabbinic literature as *Ha-Shem*, "The Name" or *Shem Ha-Meforash* (meaning either the "special" name or the name stated explicitly, i.e. by the High Priest) or *Shem Ha-Meyuhad* ("special name") or "The Four Letter Name". There is evidence that even after the change over (between the fourth and second centuries B.C.E.) from the old Hebrew writing to the so-called "square" script now used, the Tetragrammaton was sometimes written in the old script. Although the Rabbis did not accept this procedure, it is attested to as late as the fifth century C.E. in a fragment of Aquilas' Greek translation of the Bible and is mentioned by Origen as well as being found in some of the Dea Sea manuscripts. (For details, see Wurthwein: *The Text of the Old Testament*, p. 5.)

From an early period the Tetragrammaton was not pronounced as written but as *Adonai*, "the Lord". The data regarding the prohibition of pronouncing the divine name are complicated but the following are the main details of this very complex question.

Philo (*Vita Mosis*, ii, 11) observes that on the front of the High Priest's mitre were incised the four letters of the divine name which it is lawful only for the priests to utter in the Temple (in the priestly benediction) and for no-one else to say anywhere. The Sifre (Num. 43) similarly states that in the Temple the priestly benediction was given with the pronunciation of the special name (*Shem Ha-Meforash*) but outside the Temple with the substitute name (*Adonai*). In the Mishnah (Sot. 7: 6 and Tam 7: 2) it is also stated that in the Temple the name was uttered as written but outside the Temple by its substitute. The Mishnah (Yoma 6: 2) notes that on the Day of Atonement when the High Priest uttered the *Shem Ha-Meforash* the people fell on their faces and proclaimed: "Blessed be the name of His glorious kingdom for ever." Even in the Temple, it is reported later, when there was an increase of unworthy persons the name was spoken softly, the High Priest uttering it in such a way as to be drowned by the singing of the other priests (Kidd. 71a). In the Mishnah (Sanh. 10: 1) it is said that Abba Saul declared that one who pronounced the divine name with its letters (i.e. as it is spelled) has no share in the World to Come. On the other hand, another Mishnah (Ber. 9: 5) states that, as a guard against the heretics (i.e. in order for the faithful to recognise one another) it was ordained that the divine name should be used for greeting, but this is treated as a special dispensation. The conclusion seems to be that at quite an early period the special divine name was not uttered as spelled. (On this subject see W. Bacher in *Jewish Encyclopedia*, Vol. XI, pp. 262–264; G. F. Moore: *Judaism*, Vol. I, pp. 423–429 and notes; and for the later Rabbinic views and post-talmudic rulings Encyclopedia Talmudit, Vol. VIII, *hogeh et ha-shem*, pp. 381–392.) The reason for the prohibition of pronouncing the divine name is not stated in the sources. Marmorstein (*The Old Rabbinic Doctrine of God*, pp. 17–40) detects the influence of Hellenistic ideas that God cannot be named. Actually the very opposite idea seems to be contained in the prohibition. The divine name was thought to be so descriptive of God that it was considered irreverent to use it. The use of this name for magical purposes may have been a further reason why its pronunciation was forbidden.

From the juxtaposition of the two verses in Deut. 12: 3–4 the Rabbis derive the rule that it is forbidden to erase God's name. ("Thou shalt destroy *their* names but thou shalt not do so to the Lord thy God.") For this purpose there are said to be (Shev. 35a) seven divine names which must not be erased. These are: *El*, *Elohim*, *Ehyeh Asher Ehyeh*, *Alef Dalet* (= *Adonai*), *Yod He* (= the Tetragrammaton), *Shaddai* and *Tzevaot*.

In the Rabbinic literature generally the Tetragrammaton is interpreted as referring to God in His attribute of mercy (*middat ha-rahamim*) and *Elohim* to God in His attribute of judgement (*middat ha-din*). Thus the change from *Elohim* in the first chapter of Genesis to the Tetragrammaton in the second is explained (Gen. R. 12: 15, cf. Sifre, 27) on the basis of the idea that God created the world with His attribute of judgement and added the attribute of mercy because both were necessary if the world were to endure. Similarly, Psalm 47 verse 6: "God (*Elohim*) is gone up amidst shouting, The Lord (the Tetragrammaton) amidst the sound of the horn" is interpreted (Midrash Psalms ad loc.) to mean that when the *shofar* is sounded God rises from His throne of judgement to sit on His throne of mercy. The name *Shaddai* is given, in the Rabbinic literature, a fanciful interpretation (Hag. 12a) "He who said to His world: 'Enough!'" (*she-amar le-olamo dai*) i.e. who imposed controls and limits on His creation.

When we turn to the new names used in post-biblical literature, the number expands substantially. Marmorstein (op. cit. pp. 54–107) lists over ninety names for God used in the Rabbinic literature. It is beyond the scope of this chapter to give all these but we must note the more important of the Rabbinic names for God. Marmorstein (p. 55) remarks apropos of the rich variety of names for God in the Rabbinic literature: "It is needless to emphasise the wealth of religious fervour and enthusiasm, deep thought and high intelligence, which lie behind these words. Many strenuous mental struggles, often lasting for centuries, phases of the conflicts between ignorance and culture, the growth of religious advancement from lower to higher stages, and the increasing war between light and darkness are concealed within these words. They bear eloquent witness to Israel's victory over gods and their temples. Products of Israel's gestation, these names fertilised in turn nations and people, doomed without them to decay and death".

(i) Ha-Makom

Ha-Makom, "The Place", is one of the earliest Rabbinic names for God. Its meaning is given as: "He is the place of the world but the world is not His place" (Gen. R. 68: 9, see Landau, pp. 30–45; Marmorstein, pp. 92–93). The term is more abstract than the names of God in the Bible and anthropomorphism is avoided. The term is generally used to denote God's immanence (hence the English rendering of this as "The Omnipresent") or, at least, His providential care. The name is found frequently, e.g. in the Mishnah: Taan. 3: 8; Ed. 5: 6; Avot 3: 3; in Tos.: Kidd. 5: 21; in Talmud: Ber. 16b; Sabb. 13b; Eruv. 19a; Yoma 38a; Sot. 9a. Cf. Ibn Ezra to Gen. 28: 11 and to Job 33: 24; 34: 14; 36: 3-4. Landau pp. 41-43 detects a Persian influence, e.g. the name is found in *Dadistani Dinik*, Chapter 26, p. 57 and Chapter 31, p. 70.

(ii) *Shamayim*

Shamayim, "Heaven", is similarly an early, more abstract name for God. It is found particularly in the term *yirat shamayim*, the "fear of Heaven", corresponding to the Biblical "fear of the Lord" (e.g. in Ber. 6b; 8a; 16b; 28b; Sabb. 31b; 63b; Yom. 72b; Sukk. 49b; Yev. 62b; Ket. 96a; Cf. Aramaic *emta di-shemaya*, Sabb. 156b). A well-known instance of its use is in the saying of the second century Palestinian teacher R. Hanina (Ber. 33b) "Everything is in the hands of Heaven (i.e. is divinely ordained) except the fear of Heaven".

On *Shamayim* see Landau, pp. 14-28; Marmorstein, pp. 105-107. The name is found in Aramaic in the (late) Biblical book of Daniel (4: 23). It is found in I. Macc. 3: 19; 50; 53; 4: 10; 24; 55; 11: 3; 12: 15; II Macc. 3: 15; 9: 20; 11: 10; 30; 15: 34; III Macc. 3: 21; 34; 5: 9; 50; 6: 33; 9: 4; in the New Testament in Matt. 21:25; Mark 11: 30; Luke 15: 18; 21; John 3: 27. Landau, pp. 25f detects a Persian influence—God is called "Heaven" in Herodotus I, 131. The following are some of the instances of the use of *Shamayim* as a divine name in the Rabbinic literature: act of consecration to S. Tos. Nidd. 5: 16; Tos. Zev. 11: 16-17; there is no doubt before S. Gitt. 6b; there must be no undue familiarity with S. Ber. 34a; B.B. 16a; a person can be banned to S. Pes. 113b; S. is an oath Ber. 53b; Naz. 66b; the name of God .. *shem S.* Yom. 86a; Avot 2: 12; death by S. Sanh. 89a; the Kingdom of S. Ber. 13b;14b; matters of S. Sabb. 113a; 114a; Ber. 7b; Meg. 6b; M.K. 17a; help of S. B.B. 55a.

(iii) *Ha-Kadosh Barukh Hu*

Ha-Kadosh Barukh Hu, "The Holy One, blessed be He", is one of the most frequently used names for God in the Rabbinic literature (e.g. Ber. 4a; 7a; and very freq.). It is evidently from the Aramaic form *Kudsha Berikh Hu* and the Hebrew form then displaced the earlier term *Makom* (see Marmorstein, pp. 90, 93 and 97). It is used only when God is spoken of in the third person, never when He is addressed in the second person (e.g. Ber. 4a: "David said to the Holy

One, blessed be He: Master of the universe."). The Aramaic equivalent of this name, *Kudsha Berikh Hu*, is found frequently.

(iv) *Ribbono Shel Olam*

Ribbono Shel Olam, "Master of the universe" is similarly a very frequent name of God in the Rabbinic literature (e.g. Ber. 4a; 7a; and very freq.). It is always used when God is addressed in the second person, never when He is spoken of in the third person (e.g. Ber. 4a: "David said to the Holy One, blessed be He: Master of the universe . . .").

(v) *Father*

The term *Av*, "Father" is generally used in the Rabbinic literature as a name of God with the pronominal suffix, "our Father", *avinu*. A frequent compound name is *Avinu She-Ba-Shamayim*, "Our Father in Heaven" (Mekhilta to Ex. 20: 25; Mishnah Yom. 8: 9; Sot. 9: 15; R.H. 3: 8 and very freq.). Landau, pp. 10–11 remarks that the tendency in Rabbinic literature is to make the divine name more abstract and impersonal so that instead of the Biblical *Avinu*, "our Father", the term used is *Avinu She-Ba-Shamayim:* instead of the Biblical "the Holy One of Israel", the term used is "the Holy One, blessed be He". Marmorstein quotes in support of the very early use of the name "Father" for God the story of Simon b. Shetach and Honi (Taan. 23a) but while the heroes of the story lived in the first century B.C.E. the story as told in the Talmud is centuries later and Marmorstein' conclusion is therefore unsupported. Cf. Midrash Prov. 10: 1.

(vi) *King*

"King", *Melekh*, as a name for God is found with the pronominal suffix, "our King", *Malkenu* (as in the prayer *Avinu Malkenu*, "our Father, our King", Taan. 25b) and in various compound names, e.g. *Melekh Ha-Olam* (as in the benedictions, and *Malko Shel Olam*, e.g. Meg. 16b; Gen. R. 42; 5), *Melekh Malkhe Ha-Melakhim*, "King of the kings of kings" (Tos. Sanh. 8: 5; Ber. 62b; generally together with "the Holy One, blessed be He"). Landau, p. 9 note 2 observes that the Persian rulers were called "The King of kings" hence God is: "The King of the king of kings".

(vii) *The Merciful*

The Hebrew form of "The Merciful", *Ha-Rahaman*, is found frequently in the Rabbinic literature (e.g. *Baal Ha-Rahamin*, Lev. R. 17: 4; Ruth R. 1: 5) but its Aramaic equivalent, *Rahamana* is very frequent, particularly in a legal context, i.e. as Giver of the law (Ber. 60b; Pes. 90a; B. K. 71b; Pes. 39a; Nidd. 44a and very freq.).

(viii) *Gevurah*

Gevurah, "Power" as a name for God is found not infrequently in the Rabbinic literature (e.g. Sabb. 87a; Meg. 31b). It is used together with the Hebrew word *peh*, "mouth", when the reference is to God's revelation in the term *mi-pi ha-gevurah*, "from the mouth of the *Gevurah*" (Makk. 24a; Sot. 37a; Ex. R. 50: 2).

(ix) *Shekhinah*

The term *Shekhinah*, "The Divine Presence", has been discussed earlier in the section on God's immanence, cf. Landau, pp. 47–60; Marmorstein, pp. 103–104. According to Landau, p. 47, this is the latest of the three names: *Shamayim*, *Makom*, *Shekhinah* and is, in fact, a representation of the connecting idea between *Shamayin* = transcendence and *Makom* = immanence. Unlike the other two there is no Persian influence in the use of this name. But Marmorstein suggests that the terms *Makom* and *Shekhinah* may originally have given expression to the same idea. Urbach (quoted by Werblowsky in his Preface to the Ktav ed. of Marmorstein, 1968, pp. xiii–xiv) thinks that the Amoraic explanation of *Makom* as "He is the place of the world" (Gen. R. 68: 9) is not the original meaning of the name, which was rather "the One who dwells in the place he has chosen".

(x) *Gavoah*

Gavoah, "The One on High", is used especially in contexts in which the property of the Temple is referred to and especially when this is contrasted with property belonging to mortals (e.g. Mishnah Kidd. 1: 6; Sifre 104; Num. R. 8: 4).

(xi) *Maalah*

Maalah, "The One Above", is found in the Rabbinic literature as a divine name. (Ber. 31b; Hull. 7b; Lev. R. 26: 1; Num. 19: 2).

(xii) *Shalom*

Shalom, "Peace", is said to be one of the divine names hence, for instance, it is forbidden to use this word in greeting in a bath-house (Ber. 55b; Sabb. 10b; cf. Maimonides' Commentary to the Mishnah Ber. 9: 5).

(xiii) *The Creator*

Ha-Boré, "The Creator", is found as a divine name in the Rabbinic literature, especially in contexts in which the idea of creation is discussed (Avot 4: 22; Gen. R. 30: 8; 64: 64; 68: 2; 98: 4; Lev. R. 5: 8; Pes. 113a; Jer. T. 5: 1).

(xiv) *Ani and Ho*

Ani, "I" and *Ho* (or *Hu*) are *possibly* found as divine names, the former in Sukk. 45a; 53a; and the latter in Sukk. 45a and Sabb. 104a. If these are divine names the meaning of the first would be the absolute "I" of the universe and of the second either as meaning "He" or a shortened version of the Tetragrammaton. According to Landau, p. 8, *Ani* as a divine name is also found in Avot 1: 14 but this is extremely doubtful. Landau, p. 8 note 1, connects *Ani* with Akkadian *Ana*, Babylonian *Anu*, for "Heaven". But there is no real proof that *Ani* is, in fact, ever used as a divine name (*Ho* is much more probable in the context mentioned above as a divine name) and the references in Sukk. may refer not to God but to Hillel. Marmorstein, p. 73 is more cautious: "Some see this name in Hillel's saying . . ."

THE NAMES OF GOD IN MEDIAEVAL JEWISH PHILOSOPHY

In the writings of the mediaeval Jewish philosophers a number of new names for God are found, coined, of course, under the influence of Greek philosophy in its Arabic garb. The more important of these are: *illat ha-illot*, "Cause of causes" (Bahya: *Duties of the Heart, Shaar Ha-Yihud*, 2: 7; Ha-Levi: *Kuzari*, I, 1); *illah ha-rishonah*, "First Cause" (*Kuzari*, IV, 14; Maimonides: *Guide*, I, 69); *sibbah rishonah*, "First Cause" (Kuzari I, 1; Maimonides *Guide*, I, 69); *matzui rishon*, "The Prime Being" (Maimonides *Yad, Yesode Ha-Torah*, 1: 1); *ha-boré*, "The Creator" (Bahya: *Shaar Ha-Yihud*, 2, and freq.); *ha-shem yitbarakh*, "The Name, Blessed be He" (Maimonides: *Guide*, I, 50,

60); *tehilat ha-hathalot*, "The Beginnings of beginnings" (Bahya: *Shaar Ha-Yihud*, 2); *maatzil*, "The One who produces emanations" (Herrera: *Shaar Ha-Shamayim*, 5: 7).

In addition, the writings of the mediaeval Jewish philosophers contain interpretations in the philosophic vein of the Biblical names, especially of the Tetragrammaton. The three main discussions in the mediaeval literature of the significance of the divine names are: Judah Ha-Levi (*Kuzari*, IV, 1–17); Maimonides (*Guide*, I, 61) and Albo (*Ikkarim*, II, 28).

For Ha-Levi, *Elohim* expresses the idea of divinity but does not necessarily refer to God. Sometimes in Scripture the term refers to the gods of polytheistic religion. *Elohim* is God arrived at by the use of the speculative reason and by means of rational demonstration. The Tetragrammaton is, on the other hand, God's personal name. (Only the prophet can "know" God intuitively but the people of Israel can also "know" Him in this sense since He works among them.) Man, says Ha-Levi, can know *Elohim* by his own unaided reason, i.e. he can know by these means that divinity exists but this, the result of ratiocination, is cold and remote, the distant God of the philosophers who issues no commands and cannot be worshipped. Israel alone knows God as implied by the Tetragrammaton because He has revealed Himself to them. The substitute for the Tetragrammaton, *Adonai*, similarly implies something which stands at such an immeasurable distance that a real designation is impossible. We can only point to things created by Him by means of which He becomes manifest. The meaning of *Elohim* can be grasped by speculation since reason postulates that there is a Governor of the world. The meaning of *Adonai* cannot be grasped by speculation, only by the special kind of prophetic vision by means of which certain men are, as it were, separated from other humans and brought into contact with angelic beings. The King of the Khazars, the other person beside the Rabbi in Ha-Levi's dialogue, after having been convinced by the Rabbi's presentation of all this, remarks: "Now I understand the difference between *Elohim* and *Adonai*, and I see how far the God of Abraham is different from that of Aristotle. Man yearns for *Adonai* as a matter of love, taste and conviction; while attachment to *Elohim* is the result of speculation. A feeling of the former kind invites its adherents to give their life for His sake, and to prefer death to His absence. Speculation, however, makes veneration only a necessity as long as it entails no harm, but bears no pain for its sake. I would, therefore, excuse Aristotle for thinking lightly about the observance of the law, since he doubts whether God has any cognizance of it".

In Maimonides' view all the divine names are simply descriptions of God's actions. This includes the name *Adonai* which simply expresses the lordship of God (and similar terms can be used of humans). The sole exception is the Tetragrammaton. This is called *Shem Ha-Meforash*, "the articulated name", because, unlike the others, it gives a clear, unequivocal indication of God's essence. This name has no derivation. The prohibition of pronouncing the name is due to its being indicative of God's essence in a way that no created thing is associated with Him in this indication. When the Rabbis declare that before the world was created there was only God and His name they call attention to the special nature of this name and how it differs from all other names of God. All the other names are derived from God's action in the world and therefore could only have come into being *after* the world had been created. But the special name indicates God's essence and was therefore in being *before* the world was created. Maimonides takes issue with the whole doctrine of the magical powers of the *Shem Ha-Meforash* or that there are a number of mystical divine names by which magical influences can be brought to bear on the world. The *Shem Ha-Meforash* is nothing else than the four letter name and distinguished from all others solely because it is indicative of God's essence.

Albo understands the term *Shem Ha-Meforash* to mean "the separate name", i.e. the name distinct from all others. Following Maimonides, Albo declares that all the other divine names refer to some aspect of God's actions and can be used of human beings. The Tetragrammaton alone refers to God's essence.

THE NAMES OF GOD IN THE KABBALAH

The subject of the divine names in the Kabbalah is so vast and complicated that it is quite impossible to do more here than to point to one or two of the more typical Kabbalistic ideas on this topic.

For the Kabbalists there are innumerable divine names, each with power of its own. These are the instruments which God used in creating the world. A corollary is that man can use these names in order to perform white magic, though, generally speaking, resort to "practical Kabbalah" was severely discouraged. As late as the

18th century, however, there were to be found miracle workers known as *baale shem*, 'masters of the Name' who were reputed to possess the secret of working magic by means of the divine Name. The best-known of these is the founder of the Hasidic movement, Israel Baal Shem Tov ("master of the good name"). On one level of interpretation, for the Kabbalists, the whole of the Torah is nothing other than a combination of divine names (see e.g. Nahmanides' Introduction to his Commentary on Genesis, ed. Chavel, Vol. I, pp. 6–7. Chavel points to the source of this idea in the Zohar II, 87a).

According to the Kabbalists the divine names in the Bible represent the *Sefirot* (see *supra*, pp. 28–29). In the Zohar (see I. Tishby; *Mishnat Ha-Zohar*, Vol. I, pp. 152–155) there are ten different divine names in the Bible. Each of these represents one of the *Sefirot*. The resulting scheme is:

1. *Ehyeh* = *Keter*
2. *Yah* = *Hokhmah*
3. *YHWH* (pointed as *Elohim*) = *Binah*
4. *El* = *Hesed*
5. *Elohim* = *Gevurah*
6. *YHWH* = *Tiferet*
7. *YHWH Tzevaot* = *Netzah*
8. *Elohim Tzevaot* = *Hod*
9. *Shaddai* = *Yesod*
10. *Adonai* = *Malkhut*

The new name for God in the Kabbalah is *En Sof*, "The limitless" (see *supra*, pp. 28–30). This represents God as He is in Himself and is not referred to in the Bible except by hint. The Bible speaks only of God in manifestation, i.e. as revealed by the *Sefirot*. Hence the divine names in the Bible all represent God in manifestation, not as He is in Himself, and are therefore references to the Sefirotic realm in its various aspects.

For the use of divine names for magical purposes see J. Trachtenberg: *Jewish Magic and Superstition*, pp. 78–103. Of the mystical names mentioned in the sources three are especially prominent, the 22 letter name, the 42 letter name, and the 72 letter name. The name of 22 letters (*Shem Kaf Bet*) is built up by a series of alphabetical computations from the 22 letters in the first part of the priestly benediction in Num. 22: 24–25a (see Cordovero: *Pardes Rimmonium*, 21: 14, p. 113a). There are of course, 22 letters in the

Hebrew alphabet. The name of 42 letters (*Shem Mem Bet*) is referred to in
the Talmud (Kidd. 71a) and by R. Hai Gaon (Levin: *Otzar Ha-Geonim*
to Hag. pp. 20f. Cf. Rabbenu Tam in Tos. Hag. 11b s.v. *ein doreshin* and
Cordovero: *Pardes*, 21: 13, p. 112b). In the Kabbalistic scheme this name
is formed from the rearranged 42 letters which appear first in the Bible
(i.e. the first 42 letters of Genesis). The letters of this name are used in the
mystical prayer of "R. Nehuniah b. Ha-Kanah" (see Singer's Prayer Book,
p. 371). The number 42 is the total of the letters of the *Ten Sefirot*. The name
of 72 letters (*Shem Ayin Bet*) is not made up of 72 letters but of 72 syllables
taken from the three verses Exodus 14: 19–21. The method is to take
the first letter of verse 1, the last letter of verse 2, and the first letter of verse 3;
then the second letter of verse 1, the penultimate letter of verse 2, and
the second letter of verse 3, and so on. (See Rashi to Sukk. 45a and
Jewish Encyclopedia, Vol. IX, p. 164. Cf. Zohar II, 52a and Appendix in Vilna
ed. p. 270a. There is a reference to a name of 72 letters in Gen. R. 44: 19).
In the Lurianic Kabbalah (based on Zohar II, 79a) there are four divine
names of great significance for the whole Lurianic scheme (see *supra*,
pp. 32–34) formed by spelling out in full the letters of the Tetragrammaton. Thus, if the Tetragrammaton is spelled out in full as *yod* (= yod,
10, *vav* = 6, *dalet* = 4) *he* (= *he* = 5, *yod* = 10) *vav* (= *vav* = 6, *yod* = 10,
vav = 6) *he* (= *he* = 5, *yod* = 10) we have a total of 72 and this is the 72
letter name (*Shem Av* = *Ayin Bet* = 72). If the Tetragrammaton is spelled
in the same way but with an *alef* as the middle letter of the *vav* instead of
yod we have nine less (*alef* = 1, *yod* = 10). This is the 63 letter name
(*Shem Sag* = *Samekh Gimmel* = 63). In the spelling *yod* (= *yod* = 10, *vav* = 6,
dalet = 4) *he* (= *he* = 5, *alef* = 1) *vav* (= *vav* = 6, *alef* = 1, *vav* = 6)
he (= *he* = 5, *alef* = 1) we have a total of 45 and this is the 45 letter
name (*Shem Mah* = *Mem He* = 45). Finally, if we spell the name as *yod*
(= *yod* = 10, *vav* = 6, *dalet* = 4) *he* (= *he* = 5, *he* = 5) *vav* (= *vav* = 6,
vav = 6) *he* (= *he* = 5, *he* = 5) we have a total of 52 and this is the 52
letter name (*Shem Ben* = *Nun Bet* = 52). Each of these represents part of
God's creative processes. The names *Mah* and *Ben*, for instance, represent,
respectively the male and female principles. The total of the four names—72,
63, 45, and 52 is 232 and this is the numerical value of the Hebrew letters
yehi or, "let there be light". The 72 letter name also represents the world
of emanation; the 63 letter name the world of creation, the 45 letter
name the world of formation and the 52 letter name the world of action.

The history of the naming of God demonstrates very clearly that
men have given names to the Deity in accordance with the particular
ideas they wished to emphasise in their approach to the great mystery.
In the Bible, for example, *Elohim* generally denotes the distance of
God, the Tetragrammaton His nearness. Maimonides, without being
aware of it, reverses the procedure in obedience to his philosophical
viewpoint that God can only be described in manifestation, not in

essence. For Maimonides *Elohim* and the other names denote God's acts; the Tetragrammaton alone denotes His essence. Among the Rabbis names like *Shamayim* and *Makom* suggest abstraction while names like *Ribbono Shel Olam* and *Avinu* express a homely familiarity. (It might be noted that the father–son relationship is a paradigm for the God–Israel relationship but Israel is also frequently spoken of as "daughter" not "son", see e.g. Ber. 32b; Taan. 4a). The Kabbalists use the term *En Sof* to denote complete otherness on the part of the impersonal Godhead while utilizing all the divine names, including the Tetragrammaton, to denote the *Sefirot*!

CHAPTER ELEVEN

THE LOVE OF GOD

THUS far we have been considering some of the things a Jewish theology might say on the understanding of what God means in His relation to man. But Jewish teaching places great emphasis on man in his relation to God. In this relationship Judaism speaks of the love of God as a prime factor. For all the difficulties in the whole concept of the love of God—to be examined in this chapter—the concept takes us to the vital heart of religion, "heart" being the appropriate word here. Judaism is profoundly concerned with the inner life of man. It is this which provides the driving power to do God's will as reflected in the deeds Judaism expects of its adherents. In Bahya Ibn Pakudah's terminology, the love of God belongs to the "duties of the heart" while the practical precepts belong to the "duties of the limbs".[1]

The great Biblical text for the love of God is: "You shall love the Lord your God with all your heart and with all your soul and with all your might" (Deut. 6: 5). "All your heart" in this context refers less to the emotions than to the mind; in the Biblical idiom the intellect is located in the heart. "With all your soul" means "with the whole of your being"; the Hebrew word *nefesh* generally refers in the Bible to what we would call the person rather than the soul. The meaning of the verse is attachment to God without reservation. It speaks of what Tillich calls "ultimate concern". Tillich, in fact, quotes this verse as the most powerful expression in the Bible of "ultimate concern".[2]

In the Mishnah[3] the verse is quoted as proof that man has to give thanks to God not alone for the good which comes to him but also

---

1. Bahya: *Duties of the Heart*, Introduction. The indispensible work on this theme is Georges Vajda: *L'amour De Dieu Dans La Theologie Juive Du Moyen Age*.
2. See Tillich: *Dynamics of Faith*. beg.
3. Ber. 9: 5.

for the evils which befall him. This is adduced by a Midrashic interpretation of the three clauses. "With all your heart" means, according
to the Mishnah, "with both your hearts" (*levavekha*, with the letter
bet doubled): love Him with the evil inclination as well as the good,
i.e. subdue the evil inclination in God's service (or, as it has been
interpreted, discover ways of serving God even with the baser
elements in your makeup). "With all your soul" means "even if He
takes away your soul" (= your life) i.e. that, if necessary, martyrdom
is demanded for the sake of God. "And with all your might" means
"with all your wealth". Another explanation of "and with all your
might" is "for every measure (*middah*) that He measures out to you,
praise (*modeh*) Him exceedingly" (*meod*), i.e. give thanks to Him for
the evil as well as for the good. (The word *meodekha*, "might", is
played upon, *meod-middah-modeh*, *meod*). The Mishnah, then, understands the injunction to love God less as an attitude of mind, of
emotional response, as advocating a course of action. In the Mishnaic
understanding of the verse, the Jew is commanded to be faithful to
God by serving Him, by suffering martyrdom if need be, by giving
of his wealth, and by giving thanks to God whatever happens.

The Sifre[4] gives the same explanation as the Mishnah of the three
clauses. On the beginning of the verse: "You shall love the Lord your
God" the Sifre comments: "Do it out of love. Scripture distinguishes
between one who does it out of love and one who does it out of fear.
Out of love, his reward is doubled and again doubled. Scripture says:
'Fear the Lord your God: only Him shall you worship, to Him shall
you hold fast' (Deut. 10: 20). A man who fears his neighbour will
leave him when his demands become too troublesome but you do it
out of love. For love and fear are never found together except in
relation to God". "Doing it" means, of course, the practice of the
precepts of the Torah. The command to love God is seen as a command
to carry out His laws willingly and not to leave them undone even
when this is difficult as one would do where the motive is fear alone.
The Sifre suggests that love and fear are incompatible so far as human
relations are concerned but it is possible both to love and fear God.
The Sifre continues with another explanation of "You shall love the
Lord your God". This is taken to mean that a man should cause others
to love God as did Abraham who converted people to monotheism
and "brought them under the wings of the *Shekhinah*". Loving God,

4. Deut. 32.

according to this explanation, means causing others to acknowledge
Him.

In a comment on the verse which follows the command to love:
"Take to heart these instructions with which I charge you this day"
(Deut. 6: 6) the Sifre observes: "Why is this said? Because it is said:
'You shall love the Lord your God with all your heart' and I do not
know in what way God is to be loved, therefore it says: 'Take to
heart these instructions with which I charge you this day'. Take these
to heart and in this way you will come to recognise God and cleave
to His ways." Here again love is interpreted to mean the practice of
the precepts and the study of the Torah. This leads to the "recognition"
of God and attachment to His laws.

It would be a mistake to conclude from these quotations from the
Mishnah and the Sifre that Rabbinic Judaism knows nothing of the
love of God as an emotion of the heart. There are passages in the
Rabbinic literature which clearly think of the love of God as an
intense longing for God's nearness. For instance, the Midrash[5] comments that the righteous are compared to a palm tree (Ps. 92: 13)
because just as the palm tree longs to be grafted with another palm
the righteous long for God. But it is true to say that the main emphasis
in the Rabbinic literature is on love as expressed in the deed. It is as
if the Mishnah and the Sifre were bothered by the command to love
God. How can love be commanded? Is it possible for man to love
God? If it is possible for some, how can this be enjoined on all men?
Consequently, love is identified in these sources with the carrying
out of God's will. The stress is on living by God's law. This is the
significance of the command to love. It is a call to heroic behaviour
and of a kind that is attainable by all men. Vajda[6] is correct in summing
up the Rabbinic view that while the mystical love of God is not
entirely absent from Rabbinic theology it is not at the centre of
Rabbinic thought.

For the mediaeval thinkers, on the other hand, it is precisely the
mystical love of God that is stressed. For them the love of God is an
attitude of mind and heart. Care must be taken against drawing too
neat a distinction. The Rabbis know of the love of God and the
mediaeval thinkers of love expressed in the deed. Nonetheless, it is
near to the truth to observe that while for the Rabbis love was

5. Num. R. 3: 1.   6. Op. cit., p. 67.

chiefly a matter of conduct with the mystical love as its background, for the mediaeval thinkers the mystical love of God was in the foreground with good conduct as its fruit.

Saadia has a complete analysis of the meaning of the love of God.[7] Saadia begins with a question: how is it possible to have a concept of God at all, to say nothing of loving Him, when none of our senses have ever perceived Him? His reply is that certain propositions are acknowledged as true even though they are not subject to sense perception, e.g. that it is good to tell the truth and wrong to lie or that a thing cannot be both existent and non-existent at the same time. Saadia acknowledges here that love must have an object it knows and God by definition is unknowable.[8] But the truth is that, in a sense, He *is* knowable, once a man has acquired this knowledge through rational speculation and the proofs afforded by the marvels and miracles recounted in Scripture, this truth becomes part of himself. It "mingles with his spirit", in Saadia's words. This truth is then with the soul at all times. Hence the prophet declares: "With my soul have I desired Thee in the night: yea, with my spirit within me have I sought thee earnestly" (Is. 26: 9). The result of this is that the soul is filled with a sincere love of God, for which Saadia quotes: "You shall love the Lord your God with all your heart" (Deut. 6: 5). Here the same text used by the Sifre with regard to action is used by Saadia for the idea of mystical love. The soul of God's servant, continues Saadia, will become accustomed to remembering God at all times. It will be lovesick for Him. The very mention of God will nourish the soul more than food. Such a man will have complete faith and trust in God. He will be grateful for all the good he receives and endure patiently and with love the pain he suffers. He will love those who love God and hate those who hate Him. He will seek to use his reason to further God's cause and employ rational arguments to refute all objections raised against God.

Bahya Ibn Pakudah[9] devotes the final chapter of his "Duties of the Heart" (Gate 10) to the love of God, which, he remarks, is the goal

7. *Beliefs and Opinions*, II, 3.1
8. Cf. Abraham Ibn David: *Emunah Ramah*, III, ed. Weil, p. 100, who remarks that the command to love God embraces the command to know God since it is impossible for man to experience love of the most intense kind without any knowledge of the object to which that love is directed.
9. See Vajda, op. cit., pp. 92–98; S. B. Urbach: *Pillars of Jewish Thought*, pp. 193–196.

towards which the rest of the book leads. All virtues lead eventually
to the love of God. This is their ultimate aim than which there is none
higher. But the only way to the love of God is through the fear of
Him. This fear of God involves for Bahya abstinence from worldly
things. "For it is impossible for the love of God to find a place in our
hearts together with love of the world. But when because of his
discernment and comprehension the heart of the believer is emptied
of the love of the world and free of its desires, then the love of God
will find lodgement in his heart and become fixed there in direct
proportion to his desire for it."[10]

Bahya's definition of the love of God is:[11] "the soul's longing of
her own accord for her Creator, to cleave to His supernal light".
When man reflects on God's power and greatness he bows in dread
before His sublime majesty until God stills the soul's dread so that
the fear and love of God are awakened in the soul. Such a God-lover
has no interest in anything other than God's service and gives no
thought to it. No limb of his body moves unless it be for the purposes
of worship or to do God's will. He has complete faith and trust in
God and accepts all his sufferings patiently and with love. Bahya
quotes the saint who used to rise at night to proclaim: "My God!
Thou hast made me hungry and left me naked. Thou hast caused me
to dwell in night's darkness and hast shown me Thy power and might.
Yet even if Thou wouldst burn me in fire I would continue only to
love Thee and rejoice in Thee."

Bahya[12] acknowledges that the way to the pure love of God is
long and arduous. The detailed spiritual exercises described in his book
are all essential preliminaries, especially those connected with the fear
of God. When man recognises God's majesty and bows in dread at
His presence, then and then only, will the love of God bestir itself in
his heart.

Bahya, having described the extent of the pure love of God, goes
on to ask[13] whether this is really possible for humans. Can man really
rise to these heights? Bahya's reply is that it is indeed only possible
in its purest form for a very few individuals. To sacrifice wealth for
God's sake and even to suffer for His sake is, for Bahya, within the
capacity of every man if he is prepared to make the effort, i.e. if he

10. Gate 10, Introduction.   12. Gate 10, Chapter 3.
11. Gate 10, Chapter 1.   13. Gate 10, Chapter 4.

follows the path Bahya has mapped out in his book. But to be capable
of so intense a love of God as to be prepared to offer life itself for Him
this is only possible for the chosen few, the prophets and martyrs, and
that not by their own efforts but solely by God's grace. To love God
because He benefits man and to love Him as a result of fear, these are
within the capacity of most men. But that pure love, completely
devoid of self-interest, which is ready to offer up life itself for God,
this is the fruit of divine aid which is given only after much effort has
been made to acquire the lower types of love.

The true God-lovers[14] have given up all bodily thoughts, attending
to the basic bodily needs only by instinct. They are world-losers,
their thoughts solely on God and His service. Their bodies are in this
world but their souls soar in the realms of the spirit. They are like the
angels in Heaven, all worldly longing driven from their hearts by their
powerful longing for God.

Bahya's idea that the highest love of God is a gift of God and that it can
only come after severe effort at attaining the lower kind of love is mirrored
in later Jewish thought. In Hasidic thought we find the following parable,
attributed by some to the Baal Shem (see Nahman of Tcherin: *Leshon
Hasidim*, s.v. *devekut*, p. 51 in name of R. Joseph Yossel author of *Sefer
Rav Yeve, Bemidbar*): When a man goes for the first time into a shop
selling confectionary he is given a little to taste free of charge but he
cannot expect to have a large amount without paying for it. God sometimes sends a little of the love for Him into man's heart in order to enable
him to see how sweet it is but then it depends on man whether he is to earn
further manifestations of the divine grace. This passage in Bahya and
similar ones in the writings of the mediaeval thinkers, especially the views
of Maimonides, to be considered shortly, form the ideal of *devekut*, "cleaving
to God". This involves being with Him in thought at all times and in
constant communion with Him. The Neo-platonic element in the idea is
obvious. The Talmudic Rabbis (see e.g. Ket. 111b) interpret the Biblical
references to "cleaving to God" as referring to attachment to scholars and
the like, who can teach men how to behave but they expressly deny that
it is possible for man to "cleave" to the *Shekhinah*, as they put it. On the
whole subject see Scholem's analysis: "Deveukut or Communion With God."
Nahmanides (Commentary to Deut. 11: 22) writes: "It is possible that included in the idea of 'attachment' is that you should always keep God
and His love in mind, never separating your thoughts from Him when
you walk in the way, when you lie down and when you rise up, to the extent
that a man's conversation with others should only be verbal, his heart not

14. Gate 10, Chapter 6.

being with them but with God." Such a man, remarks Nahmanides (without quoting Bahya) is in Heaven even while walking this earth and he refers to Judah Ha-Levi: *Kuzari*, III, 1, who quotes in this connection: And Enoch walked with God" (Gen. 5: 24).

Maimonides, in his great Code of Law, devotes the first section[15] of the work to a description of the physical universe in the light of the science of his day. The reason why this kind of excursus should have been included in a survey of Judaism is, observes Maimonides, because only by means of deep contemplation on God's marvellous creation can man attain to a profound sense of awe and wonder and thus come to love the Creator. Maimonides' formulation deserves to be quoted in full:[16] "It is a religious obligation (*mitzvah*) to love and fear this glorious and tremendous God, as it is said: 'You shall love the Lord your God' (Deut. 6: 5); and it is said: 'Fear the Lord your God' (Deut. 6: 13). How does man come to love and fear God? No sooner does man reflect on His deeds and on His great and marvellous creatures, seeing in them His incomparable and limitless wisdom, than he is moved to love and to praise and to glorify and he has an intense desire to know the great Name, as David said: 'My soul thirsteth for God, for the living God' (Ps. 42: 3). When man reflects on these very things he immediately recoils in fear and dread, aware that he is only a puny creature, dark and lowly, standing with his minute fraction of unstable thought, in the presence of the Perfect in Knowledge. As David said: 'When I behold Thy heavens, the work of Thy fingers . . . What is man, that Thou art mindful of him?' (Ps. 8: 4–5) This reminds us of Pascal's "The eternal silence of these infinite spaces terrifies me". At the end of his account of the majestic universe, Maimonides[17] concludes: "When man reflects on these matters and recognises all creatures—angels, the spheres and other humans— and when he observes the wisdom of the Holy One, Blessed be He, as manifested in all creatures, his love for God increases so that his soul thirsts and his flesh longs to love God, Blessed be He. He is in a state of awe and dread at his own lowliness, poverty and instability when he compares himself to one of the great holy bodies (i.e. the planets which Maimonides, together with other mediaeval

15. *Yad, Yesode Ha-Torah*, Chapters 2–4.
16. Chapter 2: 1–2.
17. Chapter 4: 12.

thinkers, considered to be sentient beings who sing their praises of
God as they revolve), and how much more when he compares himself
to one of the pure disembodied spirits, and finds himself to be a vessel
filled with shame and confusion, empty and lacking."

We have noted earlier that in the Rabbinic interpretation the love
of God is understood chiefly in terms of the practical life of religion
while for the mediaeval thinkers the stress is on love as an attitude of
mind and soul. Maimonides' most famous statement[18] of what is
involved in the love of God contains a remarkable blending of both
views. The great lawyer and philosopher writes as follows in accord
with both his aptitudes: "A man should not say: I shall carry out the
precepts of the Torah and study her wisdom in order to receive all
the blessings written therein or in order to merit the life of the World
to Come and I shall keep away from the sins forbidden by the Torah
in order to be spared the curses mentioned in the Torah or in order
not to be cut off from the life of the World to Come. It is not proper
to serve God in this fashion. For one who serves thus serves out of fear.
Such a way is not that of the prophets and sages. Only the ignorant,
and the women and children serve God in this way. These are trained
to serve out of fear until they obtain sufficient knowledge to serve out
of love. One who serves God out of love studies the Torah and
practices the precepts and walks in the way of wisdom for no ulterior
motive at all, neither out of fear of evil nor in order to acquire the
good, but follows the truth because it is true and the good will follow
in its wake. This stage is a most elevated one, not every sage having
the merit of attaining to it. It is the stage of Abraham our father whom
the Holy One, blessed be He, called 'My friend' (Is. 41: 8—*ohavi* =
'the one who loves Me') because he served out of love alone. It is
regarding this stage that the Holy One, Blessed be He, commanded
us through Moses, as it is said: 'You shall love the Lord your God'
(Deut. 6: 5). When man loves God with a love that is fitting he automatically carries out all the precepts of love. What is the love that is
fitting? It is that man should love God with an extraordinary powerful
love to the extent that his soul becomes tied to the love of God so
that he pines for it constantly. It should be as if he were lovesick,
unable to get the woman he loves out of his mind, pining for her
constantly when he sits or stands, when he eats or drinks, even more

than this should the love of God be in the hearts of those who love Him and yearn constantly for Him, as He has commanded us: 'With all your heart and with all your soul' (Deut. 6: 5). Solomon expresses it in the form of a parable: 'For I am love-sick' (Cant. 2: 5). The whole of the Song of Songs is a parable to illustrate this topic. The Sages of old said:[19] Perhaps you might say: I shall study the Torah that I might be wealthy; that I might be called 'Rabbi'; that I might receive my reward in the World to Come, therefore Scripture says: 'Loving the Lord' (Deut. 11: 13), whatever you do only do it out of love. The Sages said further:[20] 'That delighteth greatly in His commandments' (Ps. 112: 1)—and not in the reward for His commandments. The Great Sages used to urge, especially the most intelligent of their disciples, Be not as slaves who serve their master in order to receive reward[21]—but because He is their master whom it is right to serve, that is to say, serve God out of love. Whoever studies the Torah in order to receive reward or that sufferings should not befall him, such a man studies not for its own sake. But whoever studies the Torah neither in order to receive reward nor in order to avoid suffering but out of his love for the Lord of all the earth who commanded him to do so, such a man studies for its own sake. The Sages say:[22] A man should always study the Torah even not for its own sake for by studying it not for its own sake he will eventually come to study it for its own sake. Consequently, when one teaches little children and women and the ignorant in general one teaches them only to serve out of fear and in order to receive reward, until their knowledge increases and they acquire greater wisdom. This secret is imparted to them little by little and they are to be trained gently and gradually to appreciate the matter until they come to comprehend Him and know Him and serve Him out of love. It is clear and obvious that the love of the Holy One, blessed be He, cannot become bound to man's heart unless he meditates on it constantly in a proper manner, leaving aside everything in the world except this love, as He commanded saying: 'With all your heart and with all your soul' (Deut. 6: 5). God can only be loved in proportion to the knowledge one has of Him. Where there is little knowledge there is little love; where there is much knowledge there is much love.

19. *Sifre* Deut. 48; Ned. 62a.   21. Avot 1: 3.
20. A.Z. 91a.   22. Pes. 50b.

Consequently, a man must devote himself to the understanding and comprehension of those sciences and arts which make God known to him in accordance with his capacity to understand and to comprehend."

In his *Guide*[23] Maimonides is more explicit. Here Maimonides draws a distinction between the ordinary love of God (from root *ahav*) and the passionate love of God (from root *hashak*) referred to in Psalm 91 verse 14. The latter refers to the man whose thought is directed to no other thing than the Beloved. This stage is only for the very few such as Moses and the Patriarchs . . . Like Bahya, Maimonides believes that the bodily faculties impede the ascent of the soul. Since the knowledge of God is the essential condition for love and, indeed, the greater part of its content and since the body acts as a barrier to this knowledge, it follows that young men, in whom the bodily faculties are strong, cannot possibly attain to that pure mode of thought required to lead to the passionate love of God. Only when the bodily faculties become weak, when the perfect man is stricken in years and approaches death, does the power become refined of intellectual perception of these tremendous matters. Such a man departs this life in the state of delight that attends pure comprehension of God and pure, passionate love for Him. This, according to Maimonides, is the meaning of "the kiss of death" of which the Rabbis speak.[24] God "kisses" the soul as it leaves the body. This stage was only attained by Moses, Aaron and Miriam. The other prophets and sages did not reach this elevated stage but of all of them it was true, and is still true of such men, that their intellectual perception became stronger at the moment of death. This death is no death but the state in which the intellect enters into its own to enjoy God for ever. For Maimonides, the philosopher, the highest love of God is the purest sort of thinking about Him.

Naturally the idea of the love of God occupies a prominent place in the Kabbalah. An acute analysis of the theme of the fear and love of God as it appears in the Zoharic literature has been made by I. Tishby,[25] on which the following relies.

We noticed earlier, in connection with Maimonides' views, that man's love for God is expressed by Maimonides on the analogy of

23. III, 51.
24. B.B. 17a.
25. *Mishmat Ha-Zohar*, Vol. II, pp. 280–301.

erotic human love. Scholem[26] has argued that the Zohar, while it uses the strongest erotic imagery to depict the relationship between the *Sefirot* (especially between *Tiferet* and *Malkhut*, "The Holy One, blessed be He" and the *Shekhinah*), hardly ever uses this type of imagery in describing the relationship between God and man. Scholem makes the interesting observation that the older Kabbalists never interpreted the Song of Songs as a dialogue between God and the soul. This was left to the later Kabbalists of 16th century Safed. (It should be noted in passing that, as we have seen, Maimonides does use the Song of Songs to describe the individual soul's love-sickness for God.) Only of Moses, and according to Scholem this is the sole exception, does the Zohar speak of in terms of sexual symbolism. Of Moses, the man of God, it is said that he had intercourse with the Shekhinah![27] Tishby has, however, shown that there are, in fact, many passages in the Zohar in which erotic symbolism is used for man's relationship to God and not only with regard to Moses.[28] The male and female elements in the world of the *Sefirot* are mirrored on earth in the marriage of the mystical adept and his wife. When a man cannot be with his wife, for example, when he is away from home, or when he is studying the Torah, or when his wife has her periods, the *Shekhinah* is then with him so that there can be "male and female".[29]

But it would be a mistake to imagine that the Zoharic doctrine of the love of God relies exclusively, or even generally, on erotic symbolism. On the verse: "You shall love the Lord your God" the Zohar[30] comments: "It is necessary for man to be attached to God with a most elevated love, that all man's worship of the Holy One, blessed be He, should be with love; for no form of worship can be compared to the love of the Holy One, blessed be He . . . Come and see, nothing is so precious to the Holy One, blessed be He, as the one who loves Him with a pure love . . . The man who loves the Holy One, blessed be He, is surrounded by Lovingkindness from every side and he performs acts of Lovingkindness to all, having no regard for his own person and property. We know this from Abraham who,

26. *Major Trends*, pp. 226–227.
27. Zohar I, 21b–22a, cf. the special role of Moses in this connection in Maimonides' thought, as above.
28. Op. cit., pp. 288f.
29. Zohar I, 49b–50a and 230a.
30. III, 267a.

in his love for the Holy One, blessed be He, had no regard for his own heart, his own soul and his own wealth."

The theme of the love of God naturally features prominently in the writings of the later Kabbalists. The sixteenth century author Elijah de Vidas devotes a whole section, containing 12 chapters, of his book *Reshit Hokhmah* (*Shaar Ha-Ahavah*) to the theme. We have noted that the Zohar speaks of the love of man for the *Shekhinah*. This whole doctrine of a female element in the Godhead has, of course, been a source of offence to many, the critics of the Kabbalah seizing on it as evidence of paganism and mythology. S. Rubin (*Heidenthum and Kabbala*) is an especially severe critic of this aspect of Kabbalism. This *motif* is particularly prominent in the *Reshit Hokhmah*. In a very strange and remarkable passage (*Shaar Ha-Ahavah*, Chapter 1) de Vidas states that it is impossible for man to love disembodied spirit and that, therefore, the love man has for God must refer to something that is not disembodied. There is no "body" (God forfend, says Vidas) "up there" but the meaning is that man cannot love God in His *En Sof* aspect but only as He is manifested in the *Sefirot*. Thus de Vidas is led to the emphasis in the idea of the love of God on its application as "love of the *Shekhinah*" (*Shaar Ha-Ahavah*, Chapter 4, from which the following is taken). The mythological element in de Vidas' thought is here especially pronounced. Schechem son of Hamor the Hivite who took Dinah, the daughter whom Leah had borne to Jacob (Gen. 34), represents the serpent who had intercourse with Eve (Sabb. 146a). Dinah represents the *Shekhinah* whom the serpent, the symbol of the *sitra ahara*, the "other side", the demonic side of existence, seeks to defile. Now since of Schechem it is said that he "cleaved" to Dinah (verse 3), that he "longed" for her (verse 8) and that he "wanted" her (verse 19), it follows that in order to counteract the power of the demonic side in the cosmic struggle man must love the *Shekhinah* by "cleaving" to Her (*devekut*), by "longing" for Her (*hashikah*) and by "wanting" Her (*hafitzah*). When a man wishes his wife to love him he must show her that she has no rival for his affections. By the same token the *Shekhinah* cannot love the man who loves worldly things. "Consequently, the chief meaning of the love of God is that a man should not love anything at all more than he loves God. His love for God should be greater than the love he bears for wife and children and all other things of the world." De Vidas makes it clear, of course, that he is not thinking of the *Shekhinah* as in any way apart from God. This is to commit the great heresy, against which the Kabbalists are ever warning, of a dualistic understanding of the Sefirotic doctrine. Man's attachment in love is to God but the stress on the *Shekhinah* aspect is to provide man with something he can grasp so as to enable him to rise above worldly desires. Especially when man studies the Torah should this complete attachment to God and rejection of the world be strong. De Vidas remarks that he has heard many tales of how sages of recent times would have no physical sensations at all while they studied the Torah so lost were they to the world and absorbed in divine contemplation. The illustration he gives (this illustration was given by Maimonides as above) is of a man so in love with a woman that all his thoughts are directed towards her and he is completely insensitive to anything else. Very curious is the story De Vidas tells in the name of Isaac of Acre (13th–14th cent.). A loose man, sitting near the bath-house, noticed the princess emerging from her ablutions and was struck with her great beauty. When the princess overheard him sighing deeply in anguish, she said to him: "This can only be in the cemetery, not here," her intention being that only in death are class distinctions abolished. But the man took her to mean that she would come to him in the cemetery and so he made his home there, longing each day for her to come to him, with all his thoughts on the princess with whom he had fallen in love. Eventually, as a result of his powerful concentration on this one thing he desired, his soul lost all feeling for anything else. So in love was he with an idea, that eventually only ideas came to matter for him. The princess herself no longer attracted him. He became a holy hermit whose prayers on behalf of wayfarers brought blessing to them. De Vidas continues that Isaac of Acre only admires this kind of hermit who once loved a woman, but one who had never desired a woman was inferior to a donkey! De Vidas understands this to mean that only on the analogy of man's longing for a woman can he know what it means to love God passionately and with utter negation of all else. "From this tale we can learn that the man who loves the Torah so passionately that he thinks of nothing else in the world by day and by night will undoubtedly attain to a most marvellous degree of soul without him requiring any mortification of the flesh or fasting. For attachment to God depends on nothing other than the love of the Torah to the extent that he loves the Torah as a man loves the woman he passionately desires."

The love of God was expressed for many Jews in the form of martyrdom, when they gave their lives for their faith. But some writers urge that man should depict to himself daily that he suffers martyrdom because of his burning love for God. Alexander Süsskind b. Moses of Grodno (d. 1794), for example, in his devotional commentary to the Prayer Book: *Yesod Ve-Shoresh Ha-Avodah*,[31] gives the illustration of a mother who puts all of herself into the kiss she gives her babe. While reciting each day the verse: "You shall love the Lord your God" man should similarly give himself completely to God's love. He should depict to himself various torments that may be devised by heathens in order to compel him to be unfaithful to God but he should imagine himself enduring them all and even suffering death rather than be faithless, and it should all be done out of

31. Chapter 5, pp. 96–101.

love. This idea of imaginative martyrdom is referred to by many writers. The Hasidic master Elimelech of Lizensk writes:[32] "Whenever a man has leisure from his studies he should imagine a terrible fire burning in front of him into which he is ready to allow himself to be cast rather than be false to Israel's God, 'breaking his nature' for God's sake. He should have in mind this thought of readiness to suffer martyrdom when reading the *Shema* and the first benediction of the *Shemoneh Esrah* and he should imagine that he is cruelly tortured without yielding. This thought should also be in his mind during eating, drinking and the marital act. He should say to himself, in fact, as soon as he experiences the physical pleasure, that he would take far greater delight in being tortured to death for God's sake and he would joyfully give up the physical pleasure for this purpose. But he should really mean it and not fool God or himself."

The longing for martyrdom is expressed in the Talmudic tale (Ber. 61b) of R. Akiba who declared, as he was suffering torture: "All my life I said: When will I have the opportunity of suffering martyrdom that I might fulfil it, and now that it has come shall I not fulfil it in joy?" R. Joseph Karo, in the sixteenth century, had a similar longing for martyrdom, see Werblowsky: *Joseph Karo*, pp. 152f, but Werblowsky thinks that this is "alien to even the most fervent type of Jewish piety". The sources behind Alexander Süsskind and Elimelech of Lizensk are those quoted by Werblowsky on p. 152, note 4, namely Eleazar Azikri: *Sefer Haredim*, Part I, Chapter 1, par. 16, pp. 55–56 and Hayim Vital: *Shaare Kedushah*, Part I (not Part II as in Werblowsky) Gate 4, 5. The idea of reflecting on the thought of martyrdom if need be while reading the *Shema* is found in Zohar III, 195b: "To place himself among those who give their lives for the sanctification of God's name, at the time of unification when the *Shema* is recited. For whoever has this intention while reciting this verse it is accounted to him as if he had given his life for the sanctification of the Name". Cf. Isaiah Horowitz: *Shene Luhot Ha-Berit, Shaar Ha-Otiot*, 1, and notes to *Sidra, Reah* and *Inyane Tefillah* where the following prayer is quoted: "Thou art holy and Thy name is holy and the holy ones of Thy people Israel have sanctified Thy name and will sanctify it, to suffer stoning, burning, decapitation, strangling, and all bitter and severe tortures for the sake of the sanctification of Thy name and for the sake of the salvation of Israel. O Holy God! If it will be Thy will to bring me to this test, sanctify me and purify me and put it into my thoughts and my mouth to sanctify Thy name in public, as did the ten holy martyrs and myriads and thousands of Israel's saints. For Thou Lord my God knowest the secrets of my heart and that I am ready and prepared to offer up myself, my flesh and sinews, my blood and my

32. *Tzetil Katan* in *Noam Elimelekh*, end.

fat, to the four types of execution and to all the severe and bitter tortures
in the world for the sake of Thy unity, for Thou O Lord our God art One,
truly One, and for the sake of Thy holy Torah, the true Torah, one and
eternal, and for the sake of Thy people Israel, a unique nation upon earth,
a holy and pure nation. Answer me O Lord, answer me, and let holiness
be released by the true and righteous judge. Our Sages have taught us that
whoever offers himself as a martyr for the sake of the sanctification of Thy
name feels nothing of the great pain inflicted upon him. However, it is
impossible to rely in these words of the sages. But come what may, be Thou
with me that the torment should not prevent me having my thoughts on
Thee and let me rejoice in my heart at the very moment of torture. Give
power to my mouth to speak and to sanctify Thy name with wisdom,
understanding and knowledge in public and in the sight of all. Cleanse me
from my sins, my iniquities and my transgressions and let my portion be
with the martyrs who cleave to Thy holiness. May the words of my mouth
and the meditation of my heart be acceptable before Thee O Lord". On
the whole subject see Katz: "Martyrdom in the Middle Ages", pp. 322–327.

As for Hasidism the love of God receives the greatest possible
emphasis in all writings of the movement.[33] R. Jacob Joseph of
Pulnoy, the first of the Hasidic authors, writes[34] that he had heard the
following question and answer in the name of his teacher, the Baal
Shem Tov. What can it matter to God whether or not we love Him,
of what value is it to a great king if a tiny, insignificant insect loves
him? But the verse says: "You shall love the Lord your God" (Deut.
6: 5). The Lord (the Tetragrammaton) represents God's love, "your
God" (Elohim) represents God's judgements. Now the finite world
can only have come into being through the withdrawal of God—
Tzimtzum,[35] since the finite cannot endure in the full splendour of the
Infinite. This is the source of all judgement. Evil and sufferings are
the price we have to pay for our very existence since without a finite,
imperfect world there could be no creatures to benefit from God's
goodness. Consequently, God's judgement and sternness are themselves the products of God's love. When man acknowledges this and
accepts his sufferings in love He makes, as it were, Elohim "the Lord",
the God of mercy. By so doing man brings his body and its needs in
touch with the spiritual vitality which sustains all things and this, in

33. See e.g. the numerous teachings in the two anthologies by Nahman of Tcherin:
Leshon Hasidim, pp. 70–165 (listing no fewer than 416 items), and Derekh Hasidim,
pp. 107–256 (listing 540 items).
34. Toledot to Deut. 6: 5, p. 180b.
35. See supra, pp. 32–34.

turn, causes the judgements to be nullified. Thus the command to love is for man's sake, not for God's. By loving God (= accepting his sufferings in love) man causes the divine grace to flow, a typical Hasidic and Kabbalistic idea. Of the Baal Shem Tov himself and of other Hasidic saints it is said that on occasion they felt that they had forfeited their right to heavenly bliss but declared: "I love God even if I will never go to Heaven."[36] In particular Hasidism stresses joy in God's service as an integral part of the love of God.

A discussion of the love of God in Judaism would be incomplete without an examination of the great Rabbinic doctrine that all man's deeds should be for the sake of Heaven.

R. Jose Ha-Kohen (1st–2nd cent.), one of the five special disciples of Rabban Johanan b. Zakkai and described by his master as a saint chasid) is said to have declared:[37] "Let all thy deeds be for the sake of Heaven" (le-shem shamayim). An early Rabbinic comment on this[38] is: "For the sake of the Torah, as it is said: 'In all thy ways acknowledge Him and He will direct thy paths'" (Prov. 3: 6). The early third century teacher Bar Kappara further expounded[39] "Which is a small portion upon which all the main principles of the Torah depend? 'In all thy ways acknowledge Him and He will direct thy paths'." The later Babylonian teacher Raba comments on this: "Even when he sins a man should have God in mind." In the Ein Yaakov version of the passage R. Pappa adds: "This is why people say: The thief calls on God to help him even while he is engaged in breaking into the house he intends to rob." Finally in Midrash Psalms[40] the verse in Proverbs is quoted and explained: "If you acknowledge Him in everything (be-khol davar ve-davar) He will direct thy paths".

Relevant to the doctrine of le-shem shamayim is the discussion in Nazir 23b. R. Nahman B. Isaac said: A sin with a good motive (lishmah) is greater than a good deed (mitzvah) with a bad motive (she-lo lishmah). The Gemara objects that R. Judah said in the name of Rab that a man should study the Torah and practise the precepts even if his motives are unworthy (she-lo lishmah) because from the bad motive the good will eventually result, i.e. and therefore a good deed is of great value even with

36. Sefer Baal Shem Tov to Deut. 6: 5, pp. 182–183.
37. Avot 2: 12.
38. ARN. Chapter 17.
39. Ber. 63a.
40. To 119: 5, ed. Buber, p. 492.

an ulterior motive. To this the reply is given that a sin committed with a
good motive is not *greater* than a good deed performed with an ulterior
motive but both are of equal value, i.e. in the one case the motive is sound
but not the deed, in the other the deed but not the motive. An example
of the good deed performed with an ulterior motive is given as that of the
Matriarchs who urged their husbands to take their maidservants to wife and
an example of the sin with a good motive is given as that of Jael (Judges,
Chapter 4). The idea of committing a sin for the sake of Heaven was
puzzling to a classical Talmudist like R. Hayim of Volozhyn, disciple of the
Gaon of Vilna, see *Keter Rosh* (notes by Asher Ha-Kohen, pupil of R.
Hayim on matters which R. Hayim either suggested himself or had heard
in the name of his master), Volozhyn, 1819, printed at the end of the
Siddur Ishe Yisrael, Tel-Aviv, 1968, No. 132, p. 539. R. Hayim objects that
if this is the case why have the *mitzvot*, that which is *lishmah* should be done
and that which is *she-lo lishmah* rejected? His solution is that a sin for the
sake of Heaven is not permitted once the Torah has been given. The Rabbis
refer to Jael and she had the soul of someone who lived before the Torah
was given (*gilgul*) as Luria says or else she did it to save all Israel and so is a
special case. Nowadays, certainly, we dare not rely on this because we
are incapable of knowing right from wrong without the Torah. R. Hayim
also makes the interesting observation that a Gentile may serve the Lord as
he pleases (i.e. provided it is *lishmah*) if this does not involve him in an offence
against one of the seven precepts of the sons of Noah. All this is undoubtedly
in reaction to the Hasidic stress on *lishmah* against which, incidentally,
R. Hayim wrote his book *Nefesh Ha-Hayim*.

Maimonides devotes the fifth of his *Eight Chapters*, his Introduction
to *Ethics of the Fathers*, to the doctrine of *le-shem shamayim*. Maimonides understands the doctrine to mean that man's *ultimate* purpose
should be the apprehension of God to the utmost of his intellectual
capacity. For this to be possible, man must have a healthy body and,
consequently, as a means towards the achievement of his ultimate aim,
he must have the secondary aim of keeping healthy. His bodily
appetites, far from being unworthy, are essential and must not be
denied. But they should not be indulged in in such a way as to thwart
his ultimate aim. None of man's acts should be carried out without
purpose. They should all be directed in the first instance to the
improvement of his bodily health which in turn will help to endow
him with the capacity to engage in contemplation of God. Physical
fitness is thus the means to the fulfilment of the ultimate goal of
contemplation. Physical pleasure is frequently associated with these
means but where it is in conflict with them, e.g. when a pleasurable act
is detrimental to health it must be rejected. Food beneficial to the

body should be eaten whether it is pleasurable or not but food that is tasty but unhealthy must not be eaten. The enjoyment of tasty food when ordered by the doctor for the purpose of increasing the appetite is similarly good since this, too, is conducive to health. Similarly, recreational puruits have their place in life but never as an end in themselves, always as a means to physical fitness and ultimately to serve the aim of contemplation.

The man who pursues pleasure whether it is beneficial to health or not is like the beasts. To be fully human man has to use his mind to discern between the truly beneficial and the merely pleasurable. But even such a person is not a saint (*hasid*). In a sense he is not very different from the gourmet or libertine. Their aim is the enjoyment of food or sex while his is the enjoyment of health. Unless the ultimate aim of contemplation is kept in mind the ideal has been overlooked.

Maimonides thus has a realistic, though very austere, understanding of the doctrine. It does not mean that physical pleasures are outlawed or that man should engage in pleasurable acts without enjoying them. Maimonides is realistic, too, in recognising how very difficult the doctrine is of attainment. He writes: "Know that this stage is an exceedingly elevated and difficult one, only to be attained by the very few and then only after great training. If a man does manage to reach this stage I would not say that he is inferior to the prophets. The stage I am thinking of is that all man's psychological motivation and all his final aim is only for the knowledge of God. Such a man performs no act, whether great or small, and speaks no word, unless it brings him directly or indirectly to his ideal. He examines every one of his acts to see whether it leads him towards his aim or away from it . . . Our Sages of blessed memory have summed up this whole topic in a few short words which describe adequately the whole idea, and they have done it so effectively that if you note the way they have formulated this tremendous idea—one about which whole books have been written without exhausting the topic—you will appreciate that their words were undoubtedly uttered under the influence of a divine power. I refer to their injunction: 'Let all thy deeds be done for the sake of Heaven.' This is the idea we have developed in this chapter."[41]

In his Code[42] Maimonides takes up the matter again. Here he refers to man in his business dealings, in his marital relations and even in his

41. *Eight Chapters*, Chapter 5, end.   42. *Yad, Deot*, 3:2–3.

sleep. All that he does should be for the sake of the ultimate aim of contemplation.

On the passage: "Let all thy deeds be for the sake of Heaven" the commentary of R. Jonah b. Abraham Gerondi (d. 1263)[43] goes much further than Maimonides. Maimonides, as we have seen, states that the ideal is for the deed to be done for the sake of Heaven and not *solely* for pleasure. R. Jonah states that the deed should be done for the sake of Heaven and *not* for pleasure. For Maimonides the doctrine "for the sake of Heaven" refers to the ultimate aim; for R. Johan it refers to the immediate aim. This is R. Jonah's comment: "Let all thy deeds be for the sake of Heaven.' Even permitted things such as eating, drinking, sitting, rising, walking, lying down, sexual intercourse, speech and all the needs of your body should all be for the worship of God or for that which brings about His worship. How so with regard to eating and drinking? Needless to say man should not eat forbidden things. But even if he ate permitted things and was hungry and thirsty it is not praiseworthy if he did it for bodily pleasure unless he intended to satisfy his bodily needs and ate only enough to keep him alive to serve God . . . Sitting, rising and walking how so? Needless to say, he should not sit in the seat of the scoffers . . . But even to sit in the secret counsel of the upright . . . it is not praiseworthy if he does it for his own pleasure and to satisfy his bodily desires and appetites unless he does it for the sake of Heaven. Lying down how so? Needless to say, it is improper to take delight in sleep at a time when he could be studying the Torah or doing good deeds but even when he is weary and needs to sleep it is not praiseworthy if he does it for his own pleasure unless he has the intention to attend to his bodily needs in order to serve his Maker and he should give sleep to his eyes and rest his body for the sake of health and so that his mind should not be confused through tiredness when studying the Torah. With regard to sexual intercourse, needless to say he should commit no sin. But even in connection with the payment of the marital debt as enjoined in the Torah it is disgraceful if he does it for his pleasure or in order to slake his lust. And it is not praiseworthy even if he had the intention of giving birth to sons who will serve him and take his place but he should intend to have sons who will serve God, or he should intend to have intercourse in order to carry out the duty the Torah places upon him just as a man pays his debt to his creditor. Speech

43. Commentary to Avot 2: 12.

how so? Needless to say he should not slander others or speak unclean words and so forth. But even when he speaks words of wisdom it is necessary for his intention to be for the worship of his Maker or for that which results in His worship. To sum it all up. A man is obliged to give thought to his actions and to weigh his deeds in the balance of reason. And when he sees that something will lead to God's service he should do it, otherwise he should keep away from it."

The Tur[44] quotes R. Jonah *verbatim* but adds the following, which is not found in our versions of R. Jonah's commentary: "One who has these qualities serves his Maker all his days even when he sits down, when he rises up, when he walks, when he does business, and even when he eats and drinks, and even when he has intercourse and in whatever he does. It is in this connection that our holy master[45] lifted his fingers heavenwards at the time of his death and said: 'It is revealed and known to Thee that I have had no benefit from them,' but only for the sake of Heaven." Before quoting from R. Jonah, the Tur remarks: "Whatever benefit a man has from the world he should not have the intention of having pleasure but for the worship of his Creator, as it is written: 'In all thy ways acknowledge Him.' And our Sages of blessed memory said: 'Let all thy deeds be for the sake of Heaven'." The Shulhan Arukh[46] quotes the Tur. Thus what was originally the pious saying of R. Jose Ha-Kohen and the elaboration of Bar Kappara becomes in Maimonides an ideal for all. But in Maimonides it is still qualified so as not to rule pleasure out entirely and, moreover, the full attainment of the ideal is, for Maimonides, only possible for the greatest of saints. In R. Jonah these qualifications are omitted but his statement is still only in the form of a comment to the Mishnah not in the form of a general rule. Through being recorded in the Tur and the Shulhan Arukh, which are Codes of Jewish law for the general run of Jews, and being recorded moreover in its most extreme form (that of R. Jonah) a rule for the greatest of saints becomes a rule for all Jews!

Strangely enough one of the very few attempts to qualify the rigour of these formulations is that of the Hasidic master Zevi Elimelech

44. *Orah Hayim*, 231. Bertinoro in his Commentary to Avot 2: 12 says: "Let all thy deeds be for the sake of Heaven—even when you are engaged in eating and drinking and in business do not have the intention of giving your body pleasure but that you should be healthy so as to do the will of your Maker".
45. Ket. 104a.
46. *Orah Hayim*, 231.

Spira (d. 1841) in his *Derekh Pikkudekha*.[47] Zevi Elimelech first states that a man should sanctify himself before the marital act. He then quotes a saying of an earlier teacher that the injunction regarding this sanctification (i.e. that the act be done for the sake of Heaven and not for pleasure) only applies before the act but during the act it is impossible for there to be no pleasure in it. In proof the Midrash is quoted on the verse: "Behold I was brought forth in iniquity: in sin did my mother conceive me" (Ps. 51: 7). On this the Midrash[48] comments: "David said: 'Did Jesse have the intention of producing me? His intention was for his own needs.'" Now in the Rabbinic tradition Jesse the father of David was one of the four men who died without sin,[49] and yet the Midrash states that he intended the act for his own pleasure. From which this teacher concludes that during the act itself it is quite impossible for no pleasure to be experienced. Zevi Elimelech concludes, therefore, that it is no obstacle to the performance of the *mitzvah* (the precept to be fruitful and multiply) if a man has pleasure in the act.

Zevi Elimelech continues by quoting his great-uncle R. Elimelech of Lizensk who, in his *Noam Elimelekh*,[50] observes in the name of the Codes that the reason why no benediction is recited before the performance of the marital act (as it is prior to the performance of other precepts) is because this *mitzvah* cannot be performed without an admixture of the "evil inclination". R. Zevi Elimelech notes that he has not discovered this in any of the Codes but relies on his great-uncle that it is found somewhere. However, he concludes, in the name of his father-in-law, that since a man does have pleasure in the act whether or not he wills it he should give thanks to God for it!

From our survey in this chapter of the love of God in Jewish teaching it is evident both that the Jewish teachers did not overlook the difficulties in the concept and that there is no single Jewish approach to what, at any reading of the situation, is a religious concept of the greatest profundity. On the whole, two distinct tendencies emerge. On the one hand, there are those teachers, represented particularly in the classical Rabbinic tradition, who prefer to speak of the love of God in terms of the practical details of the religious life. To study the Torah and observe the precepts this *is* the love of God. On the other hand, there are those who understand the love of God

47. *Mitzvah*, I *Helek ha-dibbur*, 5, p. 34.   49. Sabb. 55b.
48. *Yalkut*, Psalms, 765.   50. *Va-Yishlah* on Gen. 32: 26.

in its mystical sense of intense longing for the nearness of God and for communion with Him. But even this latter group of teachers emphasise the great difficulties in the way of attainment of their ideal and teach that in its highest reaches it is only for a very few rare souls. The contemporary Jew will hardly wish to eliminate this mystical approach from his own religious strivings and he will have some appreciation of its tremendous power. The late Rabbi Kook used to say that man is by nature a mystic. But the contemporary Jew, the heir to both trends, will rightly be more than a little suspicious of the more bizarre, and especially erotic, fancies with which the concept is at times attended. If he is wise he will avoid self-delusion and he will not aim too high. He will fall back on the moral force of the first tendency in which to love God is to do His will.

CHAPTER TWELVE

THE FEAR OF GOD

IN the Bible there are many references both to the love of God and the fear of God but nowhere is a clear distinction made between the two. They both seem to express an especially intense relationship with God, especially as realised in terms of high ethical conduct. The fear of God in the Bible frequently refers to an extraordinary degree of piety and moral worth. Job, for instance, is described as "whole-hearted and upright, and one that feared God, and shunned evil" (Job 1: 1). The Rabbis generally use the term *yirat shamayim*, "the fear of Heaven", for "the fear of God".

In mediaeval thought a distinction is made between two types of fear. The first is *yirat ha-onesh*, "fear of punishment", fear of the consequences of wrong-doing. The second and more elevated is *yirat ha-romemut*, "fear in the presence of the exalted majesty of God", the dread and awe the creature feels when confronted with the splendour of the Creator.

One of the earliest authors who refers explicitly to these two types of fear is Abraham Ibn David,[1] who writes: "Scripture enjoins us to fear God, as it is said: 'Fear the Lord your God' (Deut. 10: 20). However, the reference is to the fear produced by His greatness not the fear of harm. There is a difference between these two types of fear. A man may be afraid of an honourable prophet who would certainly not harm him and he may be afraid of a hyena and a snake. The first type is fear at the greatness of the one feared, shame in his presence, and recognition on the part of the one who fears of his imperfections in relation to the one feared. As Job said: 'Behold, I am of small account; what shall I answer Thee?' (Job 40: 4). And Ezra said: 'O my God, I am ashamed and blush to lift up my face to Thee' (Ezra 9: 6). And Daniel said: 'Unto Thee, O Lord, belongeth

---

1. *Emunah Ramah*, III, ed. Weil p. 100.

righteousness, but unto us confusion of face' (Dan. 9: 7) and David, on whom be peace, said: 'But I am brutish and ignorant; I am as a beast before Thee' (Ps. 73: 22). Fear of God should be of this kind not of the kind of fear we have for kings whom we are afraid will do harm to us".

Bahya Ibn Pakudah[2] makes the same distinction. Only the second kind of fear, *yirat ha-romemut*, says Bahya, can lead to the pure love of God and is a necessary condition to it. One who attains to this degree will neither fear nor love other than the Creator. Bahya relates of a certain saint that he discovered a God-fearing man sleeping in the desert and said to him: "Are you not afraid of lions that you sleep in such a place?" The God-fearer replied: "I am ashamed that God should see that I am afraid of anything apart from Him." It is all the same to such God-fearing men if men praise them or blame them when they rebuke men to do good and refrain from evil.

It should not be concluded from the above that the mediaeval thinkers reject the doctrine of reward and punishment. They all believe in it since it is mentioned frequently in the Bible. But fear of punishment is for them a far lower degree and their ideal is the second type of fear.

The distinction between the two types of fear is found, too, in the mystic classic Zohar. The Zoharic turn given to the first words of Genesis is: "For the sake of 'the beginning' God created the heavens and the earth." That is, for the sake of the fear of God which is called "the beginning", *reshit*: "The fear of the Lord is the beginning (*reshit*) of wisdom" (Ps. 111: 10); and "The fear of the Lord is the beginning (*reshit*) of knowledge" (Prov. 1: 7). The Zohar[3] continues: "The whole world endures by virtue of this precept (to fear God). There are three types of fear; two of these have no proper foundation but the third is the main foundation of fear. A man may fear God in order that his sons may live and not die or because he is afraid of some punishment to be visited on his person or his wealth and because of it he is in constant fear. But it follows that such a man's fear has no proper foundation. There is another man who fears God because he is terrified of punishment in the next world, in dread of Hell. Both these types of fear do not belong to the main foundation of fear and

2. *Duties of the Heart*, Gate 10, Chapter 10.
3. I, 11b.

to its root meaning. But the fear which does have a proper foundation is when a man fears his Master because He is the great and mighty Ruler, the Foundation and Root of all worlds and all before Him are accounted as naught, as it is said: 'And all the inhabitants of the earth are reputed as nothing'" (Dan. 4: 32). The meaning of this passage is that fear of punishment is in reality only fear for oneself. Whatever fear of God there is in it is only secondary. Thus, it has no "foundation" or "root". The highest type of fear is fear of God Himself for this has its "foundation" in Him and not in anything apart from Him.

Albo follows the same line of thought in the chapter of his *Ikkarim* that he devotes to an analysis of the whole concept of the fear of God.[4] Albo's definition of fear is "the receding of the soul and the gathering of all her powers into herself, when she imagines some fear-inspiring thing". This may be because of a harmful thing, which the soul fears because of the harm it may do. But there is another kind of fear in which the soul recoils, not because of any fear of harm, but because of her own unworthiness when confronted with something very great, elevated and high. Fear of God which stems from fear of punishment is not to be condemned but it is only the first step towards the higher fear. In a passage strongly reminiscent of Abraham Ibn David's remarks in the same connection Albo describes the higher type of fear: "For if a man reflects and considers that God sees his open and as well as his hidden acts, and compares his imperfection and poverty of understanding with the sublimity and dignity of God, he will stand in awe before Him and will be ashamed to transgress His commandments and not to do His will, as a person is ashamed to do an unbecoming thing in the presence of an honourable prince, a respected and wise old man, who has a reputation for learning, character and dignity. Though he may not contemplate that any harm will come to him from a violation of his command, nevertheless he will without doubt feel ashamed and abashed and hesitate very much to offend his honour in his presence." The high and nobler type of fear is natural to man. The soul is attracted to God as like is attracted to like. But man's physical nature prevents him from acknowledging the truth that is within him.

Consequently, the Torah lays down punishments for the purpose of coercing man's physical nature to yield. Both types of fear are

<hr>

4. *Ikkarim*, III, 32, ed. Husik, pp. 298–303.

therefore necessary: the lower fear to subdue the stubborn physical nature of man and the higher fear as reason's natural response to the truth man knows deep within him. This is Albo's attempted solution of why there are so many appeals to the lower fear in the Jewish teachings.

Probably the most comprehensive analysis in Jewish literature of the fear of God is to be found in Elijah de Vidas's *Reshit Hokhmah*. The whole of its first "Gate", containing 15 chapters, is devoted to this theme, with the title: *Shaar Ha-Yirah*, "The Gate of Fear". The fear of God, notes de Vidas, is the gate through which every servant of God must pass. Without it there can be no true worship of God and it is the necessary condition for the love of God.[5] De Vidas quotes the passage from the Zohar which speaks of the two kinds of fear. The higher type of fear is the fruit of deep contemplation on the way in which the divine power sustains all things, on the marvellous creatures God has brought into being, and on the sheer wondrousness of the world we inhabit.[6] In addition to the fear of God there is the fear of sin. The soul of man is pure and must be protected against the filth of sin. Even an unintentional sin stains the soul just as ink soils a pure, white, clean robe even when spilled accidently.[7] De Vidas develops the Kabbalistic idea that since man is fashioned after the pattern of the upper worlds his deeds have a cosmic effect. His good deeds cause the divine grace to flow through all worlds whereas his evil deeds arrest the flow and cause a flaw (*pegam*) in the world of the *Sefirot*. In this typical Kabbalistic scheme the role of man is of the utmost significance, the harmony of the *Sefirot* depending on him. The fear of sin therefore assumes cosmic proportions. Man's sins weaken the power of the *Shekhinah* and cause her to be delivered into the greedy hands of the demonic forces.[8] Man should also be in constant dread of his soul being rejected when, after the death of the body, she ascends Heavenwards.[9] Man's sins envelop his soul like a garment and prevent his entry into Paradise. Even David feared this, how much more ordinary mortals. Man should therefore fear death and be apprehensive about the fate that might be in store for him in the Hereafter.[10] This leads De Vidas to treat of the terrors of Hell and he transmits a manuscript on Hell (*Massekhet Gehinnom*, "Tractate

5. *Shaar Ha-Yirah*, Introduction.
6. *Shaar Ha-Yirah*, Chapter 2.
7. *Shaar Ha-Yirah*, Chapter 4.
8. *Shaar Ha-Yirah*, Chapter 5.
9. *Shaar Ha-Yirah*, Chapter 8.
10. *Shaar Ha-Yirah*, Chapter 12.

Hell") which contains the usual mediaeval descriptions of the torments of the damned.[11] Even more than Hell man should be afraid
lest his soul be sent back to earth to put right something he has left
undone. De Vidas says that many have rejected the whole doctrine
of the transmigration of souls (which the Jewish mystic tradition
affirmed) but the Rabbis accept the doctrine "and Pythagoras agrees
with them".

All this is certainly a far cry from the statement in the Zohar that
fear of punishment in this world or the next is a lower type of fear.
De Vidas[12] is aware of the difficulty. The Zohar, he says, appears to
contradict itself since it does contain detailed descriptions of the
fate of the wicked in Hell. De Vidas obviously finds himself in
great difficulty here so he falls back on the idea that man needs
the less worthy type of fear as a spur. The coarser the man the more
he needs this spur, the higher fear being reserved for the wise in
heart.

The by now familiar distinction between the two types of fear was
elaborated on by the 18th century Italian Kabbalist, R. Moses Hayim
Luzzatto, in his famous moralistic work: Mesillat Yesharim, "The
Path of the Upright".[13] The Path of the Upright, as its name implies, is a
detailed description of the road to spiritual perfection. Various
stages in the spiritual life are described, one leading on to the other.
In this scheme "The Fear of Sin" comes near the end of the road.
Luzzatto holds that this virtue is very difficult of attainment and can
only be reached by one who has made all the other virtues, treated in
the earlier chapters, his own. "Fear of Sin" is to be identified with the
higher type of fear (yirat ha-romemut) not with the fear of punishment which it is extremely easy to acquire.[14] Fear of punishment
means to fear transgressing a divine precept because of the punishment, physical or spiritual, which is sure to follow. The capacity for
this type of fear is easy to acquire, since every man loves himself
and fears for his soul. This type of fear is only suitable "for the ignorant and for women who are frivolous" but not for men of learning.
The higher type of fear consists in refraining from sin out of regard
for God's glory. Such fear is far from easy to attain since it involves

11. *Shaar Ha-Yirah*, Chapter 13.
12. *Shaar Ha-Yirah*, Chapter 14.
13. Chapters 24 and 25, ed. Kaplan, pp. 211–221.
14. Chapter 24, beg. p. 211.

knowledge of the exalted nature of God and the worthlessness of the human being. It is the fruit of deep contemplation. "Fear of sin" is a part of the sense of awe that is known as the higher fear of God. But while the sense of awe is not constant, man can only be moved to awe in certain circumstances, he can always have the fear of sin, always be apprehensive that he offends against God's majesty and glory.[15] Only Moses was able to attain with ease to the fear of sin because he was devotedly attached to God but other human beings find their physical nature a great hindrance to them. Nevertheless every saintly man must try to attain as much of the fear of sin as he can. The true and higher fear of God is only possible through profound and sustained contemplation on the theme of God's omnipresence.[16] The matter is so remote from our senses that the intellect can only grasp it after much reflection and it tends to recede unless efforts are made to keep it constantly in mind. Luzzatto sums it up:[17] "When a man sits, walks, lies down, or rises up, he should ponder on God's omnipresence, and upon our confronting God at all times, until these truths become deeply rooted in his mind. Then will he fear God in truth. Thus David prayed, 'Teach me, O Lord, Thy way, that I may walk in Thy truth; make one my heart to fear Thy name' " (Ps. 86: 11).

In Hasidic teaching the fear of God is generally discussed as parallel and complimentary to the love of God. Fear of punishment in Hell is entirely absent from Hasidic thought. R. Zevi Elinelech Spira writes in his *Bene Yisakhar* (*Tishri, Mammar* IV, No. 14, Part II, p. 14b). "The disciples of the Baal Shem Tov write in the name of their master that human effort is only required in order to attain to the stage of worship out of fear whereas God Himself sends man the love of Him since the male pursues the female and you know that fear is the category of the female and love that of the male." That is, in the Kabbalah "fear" belongs to *Gevurah*, which is the female element, while love belongs to *Hesed*, the male element. The love of God is given to man by divine grace if he strives first to acquire the fear of God. God woos man to love Him when he strives to fear Him. In typical Hasidic vein R. Levi Yitzhak of Berditchev (*Kedushat Levi, Ekev*, pp. 257–258) distinguishes between the "lower fear" which is fear of sin and the "higher fear". In the former state a man is fully aware of his unworthiness because of his reflection on the greatness of God and his own sinfulness. But in the stage of the "higher fear" he is so overawed by God's majesty that he has no self-awareness at all, not even a sense of his own unworthiness. But the "higher fear" can only be attained as a product of the "lower fear".

15. Chapter 24, p. 214.   16. Chapter 25, p. 220.   17. Chapter 25, p. 221.

When a man is distant from the king he reflects on how unworthy he is to
be admitted into the king's presence but once he has been admitted and is
in the king's presence he is lost to himself completely. Cf. the lengthy
analysis of the love and fear of God in Jacob Joseph of Pulnoy: *Toledot*
(*Ekev*, pp. 360–363). The higher fear belongs to the innermost part of man's
soul and is not external, unlike the lower fear. Consequently, at this level of
inwardness fear and love meet and are in fact one and the same thing!
For further teachings of the *Hasidim* on the fear of God see the anthologies
of Nahman of Tcherin: *Leshon Hasidim*, pp. 70–165; *Derekh Hasidim*,
pp. 107–256; *Sefer Baal Shem Tov*, *Ekev*, 12–30, pp. 205–216; Nahman of
Bratzlav: *Sefer Ha-Middot*, s.v. *yirah*, pp. 73–74.

Very different from the Hasidic approach is that of the Lithuanian Musar
movement, which arose in the nineteenth century and was founded by R. Israel
Salanter. Here the fear of punishment occupies a significant place and is
considered essential if man is to strive for perfection. See e.g. the views of a
leading figure of the movement R. Isaac Blazer as described in Dov Katz:
Tenuat Ha-Musar, Vol. II, pp. 259–273. This teacher agrees that the "higher
fear" is the ultimate aim but observes that it is impossible for man to begin
to attain to it without serious reflection of the lower fear, the fear of punishment. The philosophical appeals to the attainment of the fear of God are no
longer suitable for us so far removed are we from the truth. Only simple
reflection on the severe punishment in store for the transgressor can penetrate
our stony heart. Hence R. Isaac Blazer's saying (Katz, p. 264) that the
best kind of rebuke for us is of the type favoured by women! Although this
attitude was common to the whole Musar School it is only right to observe
as Katz (p. 265) points out that other prominent leaders of the movement
placed greater stress on the unemotional approach.

Modern Jewish thinkers have tended to ignore completely this whole topic
of the fear of God. Kohler is typical, devoting no more than a line or two
(*Jewish Theology*, p. 29) to the "fear of God" as it appears in the Bible and
virtually leaving it at that.

One cannot read all the references in the writings of the Jewish
thinkers to the "higher fear" without a sense that this is what the
modern scholar Rudolf Otto has called the "numinous". Otto's
book[18] in which this phenomenon is described is justly considered to
be one of the seminal works on religion published in modern times.
The states he describes, as he would have been the first to admit, have
long been recognised. Otto's famous definition of the Object of
religious experience—the *numinous* (from the Latin *numen*, "spirit")
—is *mysterium tremendum et fascinans*, i.e. awareness of the numinous
is the apprehension of a mystery that is awe-inspiring and fascinating.

18. *The Idea of the Holy*. Cf. Robert E. Davidson: *Rudolf Otto's Interpretation of
Religion*; Ninian Smart: *Philosophers and Religious Truth*, pp. 130–166.

Experience of this is non-rational, that is to say it is *sui generis*, only to be understood on its own terms in the way in which, for instance, the appreciation of music is non-rational. The English sub-title of Otto's book (*Das Heilige* = *The Idea of the Holy*) is: *An Inquiry into the non-rational factor in the idea of the divine and its relation to the rational.*

In addition to the thinkers we have mentioned, the numinous is evident in all the classics of Judaism. Otto has a chapter on: *The Numinous in the Old Testament*[19] and the Jewish liturgy is rich in numinous associations. It is said that, in fact, the idea of the numinous came to Otto when he witnessed a Day of Atonement service in a little synagogue in North Africa. There he saw the worshippers wrapped in large, white prayer-shawls, expressing their sense of God's tremendous majesty during a day on which they rejected all food and drink. Otto[21] quotes from the Rosh Ha-Shanah and Yom Kippur prayer:[21] "So then, let Thy fear, O Lord our God, come over all Thy creatures, and reverent dread of Thee upon all that Thou hast made, that all Thy creatures may fear Thee and every being bow before Thee and that they may all become banded together to do Thy will with all their heart, even as we know, O Lord our God, that Thine is the lordship, that might is in Thy hand and power in Thy right hand and Thy name is exalted above all that Thou has created."

The analysis undertaken above of the meaning of the fear of God in Jewish thought is relevant to a contemporary Jewish theology. Blithely indifferent to the whole of this tradition there are some who are acutely embarrassed by the idea of fear in religion. To be sure, it is easy to point out, the primitive notions associated with fear in religion and the lurid descriptions of Hell-fire as well as the cruder details of a tit-for-tat scheme of punishment are not to our taste. These, indeed, raised difficulties even in ages of greater credulity. But a religious outlook which abandons the fear of God dooms itself to banality. All the Jewish teachers are unanimous in seeing the fear of God as an essential preliminary for the love of God. These teachers think of both love and fear in the most exalted terms, as the aim of the great mystics in their quest for the Infinite. Love without fear, moreover, always totters on the brink of sentimentality. The God who is loved without being feared is, in C. S. Lewis's phrase, a Grandfather

19. *The Idea of the Holy*, X. pp. 72–81.
20. *The Idea of the Holy*, p. 190.
21. *New Year Prayer Book*, ed. Routledge, 1955, p. 15.

in Heaven, a senile deity without power to evoke the feelings of awe which appear to be inseparable from religious experience in its most intense form. The fear of God is now as ever basic to a sound theological approach to Judaism.

CHAPTER THIRTEEN

WORSHIP AND PRAYER

THE Jewish term for "worship" is *avodah* or *avodat Ha-Boré* ("Service of the Creator"). It embraces the whole range of the precepts of the Torah as well as the act of prayer.

A discussion of the Jewish understanding of the significance of divine worship cannot do better than begin with Nahmanides' analysis in his Commentary to the Pentateuch.[1]

Nahmanides quotes the Midrash[2] to the verse (Ps. 18: 31): "The word of the Lord is tried (*tzerufah*)." The Babylonian teacher Rab takes the word *tzerufah* to mean "refining"; the word of God refines man, it has a purifying effect on his soul. Hence Rab's saying: "The precepts were given for no other purpose than to refine people (*le-tzaref bahen et ha-beriot*). For what difference does it make to God whether the act of slaughtering animals for food is done at the neck or at the back of the neck? But the precepts were given for no other purpose than to refine people." (The meaning of this Midrashic passage would seem to be that the deed in itself can have no significance so far as God is concerned but it is the effect of the deed on the human character that He wants. The command to slaughter animals in this way rather than that, at the neck rather than at the back of the neck, has as its aim the inculcation of kindness and compassion. By slaughtering animals in the most painless way rather than by cruel methods man's character becomes refined.)

Nahmanides sees in this Midrash the key to the understanding of the aim of worship. By worshipping God, by obeying His laws, all of which have the effect of inculcating virtue and wholesome character traits, man becomes more perfect, more God-like. God does, as it were, want us to worship Him but it is not the bare act of worship that He requires but the effect it has on the human character. In

1. To Deut. 22: 6, ed. Chavel, Vol. II, pp. 448–451.
2. Gen. R. 44: 1.

Nahmanides' own words: "The advantage which results from the observance of the precepts is not to God Himself, may He be exalted, but the advantage is to man himself, to keep him far from harm or from evil beliefs or from ugly character traits or to remind him of the wonders of the Creator, blessed be He, so that man might know God. This is the meaning of 'to refine people', that they should be as refined silver. For the refiner of silver does not carry out his task without reason but does it in order to remove all dross from the silver. So it is with regard to the precepts. Their aim is to eradicate every evil belief from our hearts, to make the truth known to us and to remind us of it all the time." It goes without saying, continues Nahmanides, that God does not need for Himself such things as the light of the Menorah, the meat of sacrifices and the fragrance of incense but even when He commands us to remember the wonders He wrought in Egypt and that He created the world it is not for His advantage, only that we should know the truth, for our words and our recalling these things are as nothing to Him.

Nahmanides was an early Kabbalist but the idea which became prominent in the Kabbalah, that, in a sense, worship is for God not for man, is not mentioned here by him. It is not that the Kabbalists believe that of God as He is in Himself it can be said that He needs man's worship. Of God as He is in Himself—En Sof—nothing can be said at all and no thought can reach there. As manifested in the Sefirot, however, God needs human worship in that His desire is to benefit His creatures and He has consequently given into their hands the cosmic task of causing the divine grace to flow through all creation. For the Kabbalists it is not alone the effect on the human character produced by the deed that is significant. The deed itself has a semi-magical aim. The details of the divine precepts all mirror the divine mysteries in the "upper worlds", i.e. they are the lowest stage in this material world of various combinations and associations in the Sefirotic realm. For instance, to refer to the example quoted by Nahmanides, to slaughter an animal from the back of the neck is not only a cruel act which harms the character of its perpertrator. It sets in motion, too, an adverse process in the upper worlds. Conversely, a good deed is not only of value because of its effect on the human psyche. It, too, sets in motion benevolent forces "on high" and helps to promote cosmic grace and harmony. God wants this effect since this is the closest a man can come to Him, to resemble Him in bringing love and grace to all creation, and since it is God's will to benefit His creatures there is no greater goodness that He can bestow on them than this, to resemble Him, to be God-like, to share in His goodness.

The Kabbalistic view is described at length in Isaiah Horowitz's (c. 1555–1628) great compendium *The Two Tablets of Stone, Shene Luhot Ha-Berit* or the *Shelah*, as it is called after the initial letters of the title.[3] The *Shelah* defines the Kabbalistic view as: "worship for the needs of the Most High" (*avodah le-tzorekh gavaoh*), i.e. that in a sense God *needs* man's worship, and continues:[4] "It is not enough for man to carry out the precepts and serve God in all that He has commanded with joy and a good heart. In addition he should become a 'chariot' for God that from his worship the needs of the Most High should be satisfied, the Name perfected, and the King united with His Glory, according to the mystery of the unification of *Tiferet* and *Malkhut*,[5] as I have explained at length earlier. This is the ultimate purpose of worship, for the needs of the Most High. For man undoubtedly has the capacity of bringing about this perfection. Consequently, when man attaches himself to God with passionate desire and longing he attains to this stage of perfecting the Name. He then adds to his fear of God to become a sin-fearing man. Before I expound the meaning of 'sin-fearing' I must state the following. I have explained at length earlier that by means of true worship the worshipper perfects the Name in its Glory. When the Name is perfect then all worlds are in a state of perfection and all is well and full of blessing as God desires. For then the Lord rejoices in His works since He created them all for His glory and He brought His creatures into existence that they might recognise His glory and thus be blessed with ultimate blessing, for this is His will in His great goodness and love. But the sinner cuts down and destroys and produces flaws in all the worlds."

Unless we believe in the reality of the Kabbalistic scheme, and very few of us do, the Kabbalistic view as it stands will have no appeal for us. But may it not serve as a reminder that worship invokes a reaching out for the Infinite, that it does not deserve the name if it is directed solely towards the immediate satisfaction of human needs? To put this in other words, perhaps the deepest human need is the worship of

3. Part I, *Asarah Maamarot, Maamar* 3 and 4, pp. 34a–38b.
4. P. 36b.
5. See *supra*, pp. 29–30.

the Highest so that human fulfilment demands that the self be brought into relationship with the Creator. In modern times there is to be observed a definite tendency in Jewish thought to preserve the forms of worship without any significant appreciation of the Object of worship. There is brave talk about the value of the "Jewish way of life". To be sure the Jewish "way" has its great values. The individual Jew, the Jewish community, and, one might add, the world needs these. But if there is an urge to worship in the human breast, and experience suggests that there is, it cannot be satisfied with utilitarianism even of the loftiest variety.

Eugene Borowitz[6] has well said in this connection: "We are that group who, having stampeded from Jewish tradition into general culture, now find it a higher wisdom to reclaim our stake in our traditional faith. Having gone as far into contemporary intellectuality as we have, we now realise that we cannot base our Jewish theology on science, philosophy, or the mood of the times even as we still cannot found it on verbal revelation. Contemporary Christianity may be agog over secularity. Since we were in it up to our nostrils for several decades, we know we are men of faith precisely because we must move beyond it. We obviously do not believe as much as our grandfathers did, but we have discovered painfully that we believe far more than our society does." Sensitive religious folk have always grasped the sense of paradox in this matter of divine worship. From one point of view, as the Kabbalists affirmed, it is absurd to speak of God *needing* us. Yet, if we are to speak of God at all and if we are to be true to what is, after all, a not uncommon human experience, our religion cannot be *for us*, in the utilitarian sense, but for God or, better, by being for God it is for us in the only manner this can be without religious Philistinism. In her fine book on worship Evelyn Underhill[7] has put it convincingly: "It is true that from first to last self-regarding elements are mixed with human worship; but these are no real part of it. Not man's needs and wishes, but God's presence and incitement, first invoke it. As it rises towards purity and leaves egotistic piety behind, He becomes more and more the only Fact of experience, the one Reality; and the very meaning of Creation is seen to be an act of worship, a devoted proclamation of the splendour, the wonder, and the beauty of God. In this great *Sanctus*, all things

6. *A New Jewish Theology in the Making*, p. 8.   7. *Worship*, p. 5.

justify their being and have their place. God alone matters, alone Is—creation only matters because of Him."

Worship in Judaism is by no means limited to prayer. It embraces the whole range of Jewish religious experience—the study of the Torah, the observance of the precepts, as well as man's ethical conduct and his character formation. But prayer is certainly an important aspect of divine worship. No apology is required for considering in some detail in this chapter Jewish attitudes towards prayer. Prayer is spoken of by the Rabbis[8] as "standing in the highest point of the world", i.e. of supreme importance.

There are four types of prayer (though this precise classification is not found in the Jewish sources); (1) The prayer of petition (the usual form in the Bible); (2) The prayer of adoration; (3) The prayer of thanksgiving; (4) the penitential prayer, The Jewish liturgy contains all four types. The word used for "prayer" is *tefillah*, from the root *palal*, meaning either "to judge", "to intercede", or, possibly, "to cut oneself" as in the Arabic *fella*,[9] in which case the original meaning comes from pagan times before the Bible when worshippers still gashed their bodies. But it must be remarked that whatever the derivation of the word it is extremely precarious to build on etymology theories as to the nature of Biblical prayer. The popular suggestion that *tefillah* means "to judge oneself" is incorrect. There were Jewish teachers who would use their prayers as an exercise in severe self-scrutiny, e.g. if I pray for wisdom am I doing all I can to attain it, if I pray for mercy do I try to show it in my dealings with others, and so forth. But this is a much later elaboration and was not part of the meaning of prayer in any of the classical Jewish sources. It should also be noted that communal prayer as found in the synagogue is not mentioned in the Bible. Most of the Biblical instances of prayer refer to the prayers of private individuals.

An important aspect of the life of prayer is what the Rabbis called *kavvanah*, "intention". This term has had an interesting history. In Rabbinic times *kavvanah* had the meaning of awareness of what one was doing and, with regard to prayer, reflection on the meaning of the words of prayers. While there is no doubt that *kavvanah* in prayer was the ideal for the Rabbis, it was not until the middle ages that it

---

8. Ber. 6b.
9. See E. Ullendorf in: Studies in *Rationalism, Judaism and Universalism*, ed, R. Loewe, pp. 278–281.

became the most important aspect of prayer. Bahya Ibn Pakudah's famous saying[10] is typical of the mediaeval struggle for greater inwardness in the religious life: "Prayer without *kavvanah* is like a body without a soul or a husk without a kernal". Maimonides[11] definition of *kavvanah* is: "*Kavvanah* means that a man should empty his mind of all other thoughts and regard himself as if he were standing before the Divine Presence."

The Kabbalists gave a completely new turn to the idea of *kavvanah*. Particularly among the adherents of the Lurianic school, *kavvanah* in prayer refers to what became known as *kavvanot*, "intentions", in the plural. These "intentions" were on the *Sefirot*. For the Kabbalists the words of the prayers in the standard liturgy did not have their obvious plain meaning but were all combinations of the letters of various divine names, each referring to some association or balance in the Sefirotic realm. By having these in mind when he prayed the Kabbalist was able to "assist" the *Sefirot*, to "put them right" (*tikkun*) and thus promote the flow of grace through all worlds.

The *Hasidim* gave up this Kabbalistic type of *kavvanah*. For the *Hasidim* prayer with *kavvanah* means with powerful attachment to God (*devekut*).[12] As J. G. Weiss put it:[13] "The metamorphosis which took place in the meaning of *Kavvanot* at the advent of Hasidism, and more explicitly after the Great Maggid, consists in this—than an originally intellectual effort of meditation and contemplation has become an intensely emotional and highly enthusiastic act." But "intensely emotional" though Hasidic prayer is it is, at least among many adherents of the movement, a contemplative exercise in which man pushes through in his thought, as it were, to meet in communion the God whose presence is felt everywhere in the universe. Rivkah Schatz, speaking particularly of the Great Maggid and his school, writes:[14] "Contemplative prayer became the spiritual message *par excellence* of Hasidism. A Hasid who did not pray with the aim of divesting himself of corporeality, detaching himself from this world, and rising above nature and time in order to attain complete union with the divine 'Nothing', had not really achieved anything of

---

10. *Duties of the Heart*, Gate 8, 3: 9. On the subject of *Kavannah* see the important article by H. G. Enelow: *Kawwanah: the Struggle for Inwardness in Judaism*.
11. *Yad, Tefillah* 6: 16.
12. See *supra*, pp. 157–158.
13. *The Kavvanot of Prayer in Early Hasidism*, p. 178.
14. *Contemplative Prayer in Hasidism*, pp. 209.

spiritual value. The intensity with which these doctrines were taught points to the nature of the longing they express: prayer is a guide for breaking out of nature towards the spirit. From this point of view prayer is essentially spiritual; its means are meditation and intellectual concentration on the spiritual element which is embedded in the natural world. The breakthrough to the spiritual is possible according to both the transcendent and the immanentist view of God. According to the former it is the transcendent 'Nothing' which is the ultimate aim; according to the latter it is the 'Nothing' immanent in man which is the goal of this breakthrough. Both formulas are used concurrently in Hasidic doctrine, and both share the basic assumption that prayer is essentially a supernatural act in which man seeks to break down the limitations of his natural existence in order to reach the divine. Man's natural existence, subject as it is to pride and to the desire for personal advantage and honour blocks the path to unification. The life of individuality is in fact a life of plurality, for it derives from nature, whereas the life of the spirit springs from the encounter with the one and only reality, which is the unity of all contradictions and the effacement of all individuality, and as such included, paradoxically, in the divine 'Nothing'."

For all its recognition of the value of *kavvanah* classical Rabbinism saw prayer as a religious obligation which was valid in itself and binding on all Jews. It saw danger in the Hasidic emphasis on *kavvanah* as the sole criterion of prayer's value. Very revealing is the Hasidic legend (see Dubnow: *Toledot Ha-Hasidut*, Chapter 12, pp. 64–65) that the Rabbis wishing to expose the Baal Shem Tov as an ignoramus asked him what the law has to say in the event of a man forgetting to recite the special prayer (*yaaleh ve-yavo*) on the New Moon. The Baal Shem Tov is reported to have replied that this law was intended neither for the inquisitors nor for himself since they would forget the prayer no matter how severe the law that it be recited whereas he would not forget the prayer no matter what happened! No doubt in opposition to the emphasis in Hasidism R. Hayim of Volozhyn is said to have commented on Bahya's "prayer with *kavvanah* is like a body without a soul", that if such a prayer cannot be accepted like an animal sacrifice on the altar there were in Temple times "lifeless" sacrifices of meal and even such a prayer would be acceptable before God like a meal-offering, see *Keter Rosh*, end of *Siddur Ishe Yisrael*, No. 22, p. 527. Cf. No. 28 on the same page where, contrary to the Hasidic ideal of *hitlahavut*, "burning enthusiasm", in prayer R. Hayim is reported as saying: "Prayer must come from the depths of the heart. It is better to pray gently and in the language of supplication rather than with tumultuous enthusiasm (*hitlahavut be-raash*).

Man's main intention in his prayers, even when he prays for his material needs, should be that God should derive satisfaction since when man suffers the *Shekhinah* suffers with him. He should, therefore, associate the name of Heaven with his sufferings." An important anthology of Hasidic views on *kavvanah* in prayer is to be found in the *Sefer Baal Shem Tov* (Vol. I, pp. 118–195) from which the following is taken: "The Baal Shem Tov revealed that although a man should pray with great attachment to God and with love and fear he should nevertheless be humble too before God. For it once happened that he prayed together with his disciples with great attachment to God but without humility, and a great prosecution was instituted in Heaven. Only one member of the company prayed with humility and through him they were spared. A man should think to himself before he recites his prayers that he is ready to die through powerful concentration during the prayers. There are some men who have so intense a concentration in their prayers that if nature were left to itself they would expire as soon as they uttered two or three words in God's presence. If a man reflects on this he will say to himself: 'Why should I have some ulterior motive or any pride when reciting this prayer?' since he is ready to die after reciting two or three words. And in truth it is a kindness of God that he is given the strength to complete his devotions and stay alive. When a man is at a low spiritual stage it is better if he prays from the prayer-book. As a result of seeing the words in print he will be able to pray with greater concentration. But when a man becomes attached to the world above he is then better advised to close his eyes so that nothing he may see might distract him from his attachment to the world above. It is essential that man progresses from stage to stage in his prayers. He should not spend all his strength at the beginning but should proceed gradually until, in the middle of his prayers, he attains the stage of profound attachment to God. When this happens man can utter the words of the prayers very speedily. Even if a man is unable to pray to God with great attachment at the beginning, he should nevertheless utter the words with powerful concentration and should try to strengthen himself little by little until God helps him to pray with great attachment. Similarly, when a man falls from his elevated stage while praying, he should still say the words with as much concentration as he can muster and he can then try hard to return to his earlier lofty stage. This can happen frequently. At first a man should attach himself to the words themselves and later he can put his soul into the words. At first he should move his body with all his might that the soul might shine forth. As the Zohar says: 'When an ember in the fire does not burn one must poke it and it will then come alight'. After this he will be able to worship in thought alone without any bodily movements."

In the Habad branch of Hasidism particular stress is placed on contemplation. Emotion for *Habad* is the fruit of contemplation. The task of man in prayer is to dwell long in reflection on the way in

which the light of *En Sof* sustains all things. His soul should move
from world to world, linking all worlds to the hidden power of
En Sof, stripping away all veils until the material universe dissolves
and only the light of *En Sof* is seen. There are two methods of contemplation: from above to below and from below to above. In the first,
man begins with *En Sof* and traces in his mind the descent of the
infinite light until it emerges in the material garments of this world.
In the second he begins with this world and traces back the light in its
ascent through all worlds until it reaches *En Sof*. The heart then moves
in rapture, the divine in the soul meeting the divine power by which
all things are sustained and which alone enjoys ultimate reality. In the
Habad literature there is much detailed examination of these weighty
matters, including the methods for distinguishing between true and
sham ecstasy.[15]

Special gestures in prayer are mentioned in the Bible, e.g. bending the
knee (1 Kings 8: 54; Is. 45: 23); prostration on the face (Exodus 34: 8;
Ps. 29: 2); the spreading of the hands heavenwards (1 Kings 8: 23; Is. 1: 15);
and, possibly, the placing of the face between the knees (1 Kings 18: 42).
In the Rabbinic period the practice was introduced, and is still followed, of
bowing the head and body at the beginning and the end of the statutory
prayers. Interesting is the observation that an ordinary person bows only
at the beginning and end of the prayer, the High Priest at the beginning and
end of each separate benediction, and the King remains bowed all through
the prayer (Ber. 34b). This is evidently based on the idea, as Rashi suggests,
that the greater a man's rank the greater the need for him to show abasement
before God. Swaying the body in prayer is mentioned in a number of works
and the practice was widely followed. Both the Zohar (III, 218b–219a)
and Judah Ha-Levi (*Kuzari*, II, 79–80) refer to the custom of swaying during
the study of the Torah but do not mention prayer. The *Shulhan Arukh*
(*Orah Hayim* 48: 1) refers to the practice of swaying in prayer but some
authorities frown on it (see *Magen Avraham ad loc.* and *Shelah*, Part II,
Inyane Tefillah, p. 79a). The Hasidim, in particular, were fond of powerful
body movements and gestures during prayer (see the illustration of the
ember in the previous quotation from the *Sefer Baal Shem Tov*), a favourite
text being: "All my bones shall say: 'Lord, who is like unto Thee'."
(See Wertheim: *Halakhot va-Halikhot Ba-Hasidut*, pp. 103–104). R. Hayim
of Volozhyn, on the other hand, is said to have remarked laconically that
swaying during prayer is solely for the purpose of keeping awake (!) but

15. On this topic see my translation of Dov Baer of Lübavitch: *Tract on Ecstasy* and
    my study of the rival *Habad* thinker R. Aaron of Starosselje: *Seeker of Unity*.

that when one sways of his own accord with great longing of the heart it is commendable, otherwise it is preferable to express one's feelings in the words (see *Keter Rosh*, end of *Siddur Ishe Yisrael*, No. 29, p. 527). Very curious is the idea found in Hasidic literature that swaying during prayer is on the analogy of movement during the sexual act since in prayer the soul "marries" the *Shekhinah*, see *Tzavaot Ha-Ribash*, p. 7b; Segal: *Likkute Yekarim*, p. 1b; *Sefer Baal Shem Tov*, Vol. I, p. 145, note 65. This and similar sexual illustrations were naturally the targets of the opponents of Hasidism, see e.g. Perl: *Megalle Temirin*, p. 40a (wrongly printed as "50") note 7. Cf. Nahman of Tcherin's anthology: *Derekh Hasidim*, p. 411, who quotes a bowlderised version of the *Likkute Yekarim*, contenting himself by advising the reader to consult the work itself.

One of the most effective discussions in modern times on prayer from the Jewish point of view is to be found in *Proceedings of the Rabbinical Assembly of America*.[16] The essay: *The Spirit of Prayer* by A. J. Heschel represents the supernaturalistic approach, *Prayer and the Modern Jew* by Eugene Kohn the naturalistic approach. Religious naturalism seeks to explore the possibility of retaining the act of prayer even after the idea of a personal God has been abandoned.[17] Prayer is seen as a kind of reaching out by the self towards its highest fulfilment and as a means of tapping those sources in the universe "which make for righteousness'. Religious supernaturalism seeks to retain the traditional theistic position in which the second half of the "I–Thou" (to use Buber's terminology) is a real "Thou" to be addressed, confronted and adored.

Heschel comments on the Rabbinic saying:[18] "When you pray know before Whom you stand." *"Before Whom.* To have said before *what* would have contradicted the spirit of Jewish prayer. *What* is the most indefinite pronoun. In asking *what*, one is totally uncommitted, uninitiated, bare of any anticipation of an answer: any answer may be acceptable. But he who is totally uncommitted, who does not even have the inkling of an answer, has not learned the meaning of the ultimate question, and is not ready to engage in prayer. If God is a *what*, a power, the sum total of values, how could one pray to it? An 'I' does not pray to an 'it'. Unless, therefore, God is at least as real as my own self; unless I am sure that God has at least as much life as I do, how could I pray?"

16. Vol. XVII, 1953, pp. 151–238.   17. See *supra*, pp. 50–51.   18. Ber. 28b.

Kohn replies in defence of the naturalistic approach: "Many people find prayer difficult because, having rejected the idea that God is a transcendent person, they feel that prayer cannot be addressed to God, that at best it is a form of talking to oneself. But the term *self* has more than one meaning. It may be used in the sense of the *ego*, the source of egoism and selfishness, or in the sense of the *soul*, the transcendent aspect of the Divine Nature. When we seek communion with God, it is not important whether we address God in the second person as Thou, or think of God in the third person. What is important is that we keep our conception of God before us, and that we endeavour to bring our thoughts and our desires into harmony with our idea of God."

On the psychological difficulty in praying to a "process" Kohn replies: "I know that it is very hard for people who have been in the habit of thinking of God as a person, to understand how one can address God if one regards God as a cosmic process. I don't think that it is so difficult if you understand that as being really is—I am talking to you, are you just static entities? Isn't everyone of you a life, and isn't life a process? Are you to whom I am talking the same being that you were on the day you were born? Are you not constantly becoming something different? You are a process and I am talking to you. I can talk in the same way and with the same freedom with that cosmic process which I regard as the very source and fountain of my own being."

The linguistic philosopher would demand greater clarity from both sides of the debate, and he would be right to do so. The concept of God as a person requires more detailed examination as to its meaning than is provided by the bare Pascalian distinction between the "God of the philosophers" and the "God of Abraham, Isaac and Jacob". The Jewish Neoplatonists, even those who tended to speak of *En Sof* as "It", were not religious naturalists, but they devoted a good deal of thought to a consideration of what "personality" (a term which, of course, they never used) can mean when applied to God. On the other hand, the naturalist would find it hard to explain, among other things, what meaning can, on his showing, be given to "atheism" or, rather, in what way precisely the atheist differs from the theist. More recent studies of prayer have been very much concerned with this kind of question. This book unashamedly adopts the religious super-naturalistic position and believes it to be the only one true to the

Jewish attitude. But non-Jewish religious thinkers have also had helpful things to say in this connection and their ideas should be investigated.

P. R. Baelz in his book *Prayer and Providence* discusses this central issue of supernaturalism versus naturalism as applied to prayer. He suggests that the dilemma modern man faces is that prayer either seems to be a vestigial survival from primitive magic or it is a form of interior reflection and meditation, however elaborately it may be dressed up in the mythological robing of a dialogue between man and God. The naturalist prefers to seize the second horn of the dilemma. But, as Baelz goes on to say, prayer is so central to theistic faith that it seems a part of what is understood as "belief-in-God"; thus the idea of real dialogue cannot be rejected if faith itself is to be retained. For all that, the problems are so acute that it is notorious that every book on prayer has a chapter on its difficulties. The most serious of these difficulties is with regard to petitionary prayer, and it has to do with the whole question of providence.[19] "If it is theologically and scientifically preposterous to imagine that one can persuade God to change His mind and intervene in the ordinary course of events, what room is left for intercession, except perhaps as an *aide-memoire* for one's own future actions?"

In reply Baelz proceeds to investigate the meaning of God's transcendence. In prayer man can be said to have communion with the transcendent God, and in his petitionary prayers man tries to bring his desires in accord with God's will. But what meaning is there to the statement that God's will is reflected in some states of affairs and not in others? Once such personalistic ideas are introduced, does this not run counter to the whole notion of God's transcendence? We are obliged to fall back on the idea, which, as Baelz observes, appears to be the Biblical insight, that some states of affairs reflect the mind and will of God *more* than others. This is because the created world, being what it is, imposes limitations, as it were, on God's creative activity. Hence prayer is to be seen as a real dialogue between man and God, an attempt by man to bring his being more into accord with God's will. Baelz sums it up (with, however, a trace of Christological thought) as follows: "His activity meets with the creaturely response which it seeks and towards which it is directed. It is fulfilled in the response which it evokes. It penetrates and enables the relatively

19. See *supra*, pp. 115-123.

independent activity of the creature. It supernaturalizes the natural. In such providential and redemptive [sic] activity we come to discern a deeper aspect of God's being. There is 'more' of God to be apprehended here than elsewhere."

A refreshing, though not entirely successful, essay in linguistic analysis of what it is that people are doing when they pray is *The Concept of Prayer* by D. I. Phillips. Prayer is said to be "talking to God" but obviously this is very different from what is generally understood as dialogue. The prayer of confession, for instance, is not to provide God with information He does not already possess, nor is it simply talking to oneself. "One has to learn to talk to God. But what kind of ability is this? What does it mean to talk to God whom one does not understand? One can begin to answer these questions by noting that, although God does not come to know anything when one tells one's sins to Him, the person who confesses comes to know something about himself which he did not know before." In this connection the famous definition of Maimonides[20] is relevant: "What is repentance? It is that the sinner should abandon his sin and remove it from his thoughts, resolving never to do it again . . . And he should regret his past mistakes . . . so that God who knows all secrets can testify that he will never again commit this sin . . . It is necessary for the confession to be expressed with the lips, so that verbal form is given to those matters upon which the heart has resolved."

Similarly, with regard to petitionary prayer, this differs from the magic spell in that the worshipper does not hold that the anticipated result follows automatically on the words. What he is really doing is to bring his desires to God. "When deep religious believers pray *for* something, they are not so much asking God to bring this about, but in a way telling Him of the strength of their desires. They realise that things may not go as they wish, but they are asking to go on living whatever happens. In prayers of confession and in prayers of petition, the believer is trying to find a meaning and a hope that will deliver him from the elements in his life which threaten to destroy it: in the first case, his guilt, and in the second place, his desires."

To return to a Jewish author, Jacob J. Petuchowski deals with our topic in his essay: "Can Modern Man Pray?" On the central problem of whether modern man can conceive of God in personal terms and so be capable of engaging in the dialogue of prayer with Him,

20. *Yad, Teshuvah* 2: 2.

Petuchowski rightly points to the danger of lumping all "modern" men together. There are still to be found many highly educated, sophisticated men who find no fatal objections to prayer as tradition- ally conceived. Moreover—and it is to this author's credit that he calls attention to it—the theological difficulty of prayer as asking for God to change His mind was frankly formulated by the mediaeval thinkers and is not a particularly modern problem at all. He quotes Albo's formulation[21] as an example. Petuchowki concludes—and it is a conclusion in line with the approach of this book—"We have been trying to provide some perspective and background for the question, 'Can modern man pray?' We have seen that some of the problems which trouble us are problems which have equally troubled our predecessors. We have also noted that one's ability to pray depends in the final analysis, upon the ability to see himself as a creature of God. There are those who have this ability, and there are those who do not. But this 'creature feeling' is something far too personal to be amenable to debate. That is why we have to end our answer as we have begun it. Can modern man pray? Some can, some cannot."

It is very surprising that, apart from Albo, there are very few discussions among the mediaeval Jewish thinkers of the theological difficulties of prayer or, for that matter, of prayer itself as a theological concept, though there are, of course, numerous works on the laws of prayer. A strangely neglected discussion of prayer is Moses b. Joseph di Trani's (the *Mabit*) *Bet Elohim*, Part I, *Shaar Ha-Tefillah*. In Chapter 14, pp. 18–19, the *Mabit* understands petitionary prayer to be necessary even though God can provide without it, because when he prays man is moved to repent and this renders him worthy to have his request granted. The same author (Chapter 1, pp. 4–5) gives this definition of prayer: "The act in which man asks of God for something he needs which he cannot achieve by his own efforts." This is explained as: *Man* and not an Angel. Angels do not offer prayers since God attends to their needs without it. *Asks*—and not demands. Prayer is an appeal to God to exercise His mercy. It is by God's grace that prayer is answered not as of right. *Of God*—and not of the angels. It is forbidden to pray to any creature. *For something he needs*—and not for luxuries. *Which he cannot achieve by his own efforts*—man should only pray for those things where his efforts are futile. But he should not rely on prayer to earn him a living, for example. God helps those who help themselves. It is not out of place in a chapter on Jewish worship to refer to lists of moral and religious rules of special piety (*hanhagot*) which saintly men drew up as guides for themselves over and above the minimum requirements of the law. More

21. *Ikkarim*, IV, 18, ed. Husik, Vol. IV, p. 160.

than the more formal works of piety these demonstrate how profoundly
religious men sought to be conscious of God at all times and to worship
Him with complete and utter devotion. This should be admired even if we
admit that some of these rules are not to our taste in that they are based on
on beliefs we no longer entertain.

As illustrations we can quote some of the 82 items in the list attributed to
the Hasidic master R. Jacob Isaac, the "Seer" of Lublin (d. 1815) printed
at the beginning of *Divre Emet.* pp. 5–9 in *Sheloshah Sefarim Niftahim:*

1. To remember God, as it is written: "And thou shalt remember the
Lord thy God" (Deut. 8: 18).
2. To love God constantly, as it is written: "And you shall love . . ."
(Deut. 6: 5).
3. To offer oneself as a sacrifice to God by imagining that one suffers
martyrdom for His sake. This applies at all times.
4. To fulfil: "Thou shalt fear the Lord thy God" (Deut. 10: 20). This also
applies at all times.
5. And so, too, "And to Him shalt thou cleave" (Deut. 10: 20).
6. Never to be angry.
7. To take care never to take offence for all that happens is for the best.
8. And so, too, never to hate.
9. And never to be too lazy to study the Torah for its own sake and to be
attached to God.
10. To try hard, if possible, to be attached to God through all worlds as
far as one can.
11. And to take care not to engage in too much gossip with women, not even
with one's own wife when she is ritually pure.
12. And to be very careful not to reveal any of the divine mysteries unless
it is necessary so to do and not to treat this matter leniently, since on many
occasions it seemed right to reveal them but later on it was regretted.
13. And not to speak differently from the way men normally speak,
namely, not to converse in saintly language or in marvellous great humility
. . . for this is a form of pride.
64. To take care never to be angry or to take any offence especially with
regard to one's wife.
66. To study Talmud each day.
67. To have the Tetragrammaton before one's eyes whenever possible.
70. To take great care never to be indifferent to the sufferings of any Jewish
soul, to say nothing of the sufferings of a scholar.
80. To take care never to be in a state of misery for this pushes away the
feet of the *Shekhinah*, God forfend.
82. To remember the need to feel lowly, abased and humble in God's presence. In contrast some of the items may be quoted from the list of 44 drawn
up by the non-Hasidic teacher Rabbi Jonathan of Lubtsh: (*Margenita Tava*,
printed at end of Israel Meir Kagan's (the *Hafetz Hayim*) *Ahavat Hesed*,
pp. 55–56).
90. To speak gently to others and to take care never to lose one's temper

even in a good cause. Even when rebuking another it should be done
gently and with tender words as if he were rebuking his teacher. For men's
deeds are unknown and it is possible that the recipient of the rebuke is
the greater man, especially if he is a scholar.

11. To remember the day of death, as the Rabbis say: "Repent one day
before your death." One should carry out the precepts with the utmost
energy and delight as if one had no more than a single day to serve the
Creator. One should imagine that one has been born this very day and has
not yet had an opportunity of serving the Creator.

16. To take care that just as one experiences dread, distress and humility
when in trouble or danger, God forfend, so, too, one should train oneself
to feel humble and in a state of dread even in tranquil times. He should
loathe worldly pleasures and these should have no value at all in his eyes.
He should also be in a state of constant dread of the enticements of the
evil inclination. He should not imagine that the evil inclination is no
enemy of his and will not bring him to sin but he should rather know that
the evil inclination can lead him very easily to sin and he should struggle
against it all the time, as the Rabbis say: "Do not trust yourself."
Consequently, he should construct fences and abstain constantly.

20. To reflect constantly on the duty of believing in God's Providence and
the love and fear of Him and to express this verbally: "Behold I accept
upon myself the obligation to believe in Providence and to love and fear."

23. While praying he should have in mind before reciting any of the benedictions the idea behind that benediction and its secret meaning. His
intention in his prayers should be for the sake of Heaven and not for his own
needs and his whole being should tremble whenever he utters God's name.

29. He should never cause any harm to any creature or pain to any man.
He should never raise his hand against another even when rebuking the
wicked for he may not be the saint who alone is permitted to do this.

40. Never to be haughty in his heart and to cleave to the quality of
humility. He should behave like a man recently arrived from a distant land
to the place of sages and scholars. He should look upon himself as wicked
and his neighbours as righteous men. Whenever he discovers some virtue
in himself he should give thanks to God for enabling him to attain it and
should claim no credit for himself. But if, God forfend, he discovers
some bad trait in himself he should blame no one but himself. Solomon
Schechter has published from manuscripts four of these lists produced among
the mystics of sixteenth century Safed, see his *Studies in Judaism*, Second Series,
Appendix A, pp. 289–301. Among others of this nature are: Elimelech of
Lizensk's *Tzetil Katan* (see *supra*, p. 165) and *Hanhaggot Adam*, printed at
end of his *Noam Elimelekh; Kunteros Tzav Ve-Ziruz* by Kalonymous Kalman
Schapiro of Pietzena, printed at the end of his: *Hakhsharat Ha-Avrekhim*;
the list in code of R. Nathan Hirsch of Slabodka (the "Old Man of
Slabodka") in Dov Katz: *Tenuat Ha-musar*, Vol. III, pp. 220–229; R. Zevi
Elimelech Spira, printed at the end of his *Derekh Pikkudekha*, Jer. ed.,
pp. 213–216.

CHAPTER FOURTEEN

REVELATION

THE traditional Jewish view of revelation is that the whole of the Bible was conveyed by God to man. A term like "conveyed" is, of course, vague. In the middle ages and even earlier the difficulty of ascribing vocal organs to God was acknowledged so that expressions such as "And the Lord spoke to Moses" were not taken literally. Maimonides' formulation, for example,[1] is: "The whole Torah came unto him (Moses) from before God in a manner which is metaphorically called 'speaking'; but the real nature of that communication is unknown to everybody except by Moses (peace to him!) to whom it came." The Rabbis recognised various degrees of inspiration, i.e. the inspiration of the Torah (the Pentateuch) is of a higher and more direct nature than that of the prophetic books. This is sometimes expressed by saying that the Torah was given by God Himself in direct fashion[2] whereas the prophetic books were given by means of "prophecy" (*nevuah*).[3] The books of the Hagiographa were of a lesser order still and were thought of as being conveyed not by means of prophecy but by the "holy spirit" (*ruah hakodesh*).[4] But in the Rabbinic view, once the canon of sacred Scripture had been fixed (albeit that the term "canon" is never used in the classical Jewish sources) it embraced all three divisions of the Bible —the Torah, the *Neviim* (the Prophets) and the *Ketuvim* (the Hagiographa), hence the term *Tanakh* = Torah, Neviim, Ketuvim. All

1. Commentary to the Mishnah, Sanhedrin X, 1.
2. For the subject of this chapter see in greater detail my *Principles of the Jewish Faith*, Chapter 9, pp. 216–301.
3. See e.g. Mishnah Megillah 4: 1 and the discussion on it in Meg. 27a that it is permissible to sell prophetic books in order to buy a Scroll of the Torah but not the other way round because the degree of sanctity of the Scroll is higher than that of the prophetic books.
4. See e.g. the discussion in Meg. 7a on whether the book of Esther was written by means of the holy spirit.

these belong to what the Rabbis call "the Written Torah" (*Torah She-Bi-Ketav*). In addition the expositions and derivations from Scripture found in the Rabbinic literature were thought of as revealed. They were given verbally in the first instance to Moses and then handed down from generation to generation, with provision for various additions and adaptations to new circumstances as they arose. This process is called by the Rabbis "the Oral Torah" (*Torah She-Be-Al Peh*). Both these *torot* are thought of as one complete Torah so that the term *Torah* means: (1) The Pentateuch; (2) The whole of Jewish teaching as revealed by God in the Written and in the Oral Torah; (3) the later applications and deeper understanding of the content of these down to the present day. The traditional view of revelation is thus essentially a static one. The Torah is the same always. It is the will of God for man. So he is obliged to study, to practice, to cherish and to follow it as his complete infallible guide to life's conduct. It is his link with God in a manner provided by no other means. In the words of the synagogue prayer:[5] "O our Father, merciful Father, ever compassionate, have mercy upon us; O put it into our hearts to understand and to discern, to mark, learn and teach, to heed, to do and to fulfil in love all the words of instruction in Thy Torah. Enlighten our eyes in Thy Torah, and let our hearts cling to Thy commandments, and make us single-hearted to love and fear Thy name, so that we be never put to shame."

Typical of the traditional understanding of the doctrine that the "Torah is from Heaven" is the discussion of this, the eighth principle of the Jewish faith as formulated by Maimonides (Commentary to the Mishnah, Sanhedrin X, 1), in Moses b. Joseph di Trani's (the *Mabit Bet Elohim*, Gate 3, Chapter 23, pp. 93–97). This sixteenth century author takes what was clearly the traditional view throughout the middle ages that the words of the Pentateuch are the very words of God. After having repeated that every word of the Torah from the first word of Genesis to the last word of Deuteronomy is from God, di Trani asks why, in that case, is the Torah not recorded in the first person, e.g. "In the beginning I created with My name *Elohim* the heavens and the earth . . . And I said with My name *Elohim*: 'Let there be light' . . . And I called the firmament heaven and I divided the light from the darkness . . ." Di Trani's answer embraces the idea that the Torah is the blueprint of "all worlds" and it cannot therefore be expressed too directly as if its concern were with this world and its events alone. Also, adds di Trani, this was done to teach God's humility in that He scrupled to speak of

5. Singer's Prayer Book, p. 41.

Himself in the first person! With regard to the Rabbinic view, there is
undoubtedly an element of hyperbole in the following statement, but
it is not untypical of how the Rabbis understood the doctrine of "Torah
from Heaven" (*Torah Min Ha-Shamayim*). "R. Levi b. Hama said in the
name of R. Simeon b. Lakish: The verse: 'And I will give thee the tables
of stone, and the law and the commandment, which I have written that
thou mayest teach them' (Ex. 24: 12) means as follows: "The tables of
stone" are the ten commandments, "the law" is the Pentateuch, "the commandment" is the Mishnah, "which I have written" are the Prophets and the
Hagiographa, "that thou mayest teach them" is the Gemara (the Talmud).
This teaches that all these things were given on Sinai" (Ber. 5a). As for the
idea that the interpretation of the Torah down to the present day is also
part of the Torah, Solomon Schechter (*Some Aspects of Rabbinic Theology*,
pp. 125–126) has put it as follows: "When certain Jewish Boswells apologised
for observing the private life of their masters too closely, they said: 'It
is a Torah, which we are desired of learning' (Ber. 62a). In this sense it is
used by another Rabbi, who maintained that even the everyday talk of the
people in the Holy Land is a Torah (that is, conveys an object lesson). For
the poor man in Palestine, when applying to his neighbour for relief, was
wont to say, 'Acquire for thyself merit, or strengthen and purify thyself'
(by helping me—Lev. R. 34: 7); thus implying the adage—that the man in
want is just as much performing an act of charity in receiving as his bene-
factor in giving . In the east of Europe we can, even today, hear a member
of the congregation addressing his minister, 'Pray, tell me some Torah'.
The Rabbi would never answer him by reciting verses from the Bible, but
would feel it incumbent upon him to give some spiritual or allegorical
explanation of a verse from the Scriptures, or would treat him to some
general remarks bearing upon morals and conduct."

For all the grandeur of the traditional view it has been heavily
assailed in modern times. Historical investigation into the Jewish
past has shown Judaism to be a developing faith. The very concept of
the Torah itself, for instance, has had a long history. In the Pentateuch
the term *torah* refers to a specific law or rule not to the Pentateuch
itself. For example the verse recited when the Torah is lifted up for
congregation to behold in the synagogue—"And this is the Torah
which Moses set before the children of Israel" (Deut. 4: 44)—refers
in its original context only to the particular law mentioned there and
not, as it was much later understood, to the Pentateuch as a whole.
Furthermore modern Biblical scholarship has detected, to the satisfaction of the vast majority of the experts in this field, diverse codes
of law, clearly reflecting different social conditions. This will be considered later in this chapter. Here it is sufficient to point out that,

particularly in the Reform movement, revelation has been interpreted in progressive terms. God is thought of as conveying enough of His truth, as it were, to satisfy the spiritual needs of each generation but as man has grown in understanding he has come to revise and re-interpret and, at times, to reject earlier teachings even if these are found in the Bible and in the Rabbinic literature. This process itself is seen as a mode of divine revelation, hence the term "progressive revelation".

The statement on "Torah" in the "Columbus Platform" of the American Reform Movement in 1937 reads:[6] "God reveals Himself not only in the majesty, beauty and orderliness of nature, but also in the vision and moral striving of the human spirit. Revelation is a continuous process, confined to no one group and to no one age. Yet the people of Israel, through its prophets and sages, achieved unique insight in the realm of religious truth. The Torah, both written and oral, enshrines Israel's ever-growing consciousness of God and the moral law. It preserves the historical precedents, sanctions and norms of Jewish life and, seeks to mould it in the patterns of goodness and of holiness. Being products of historical processes, certain of its laws have lost their binding force with the passing of the conditions that called them forth. But as a depository of permanent spiritual ideals, the Torah remains the dynamic source of the life of Israel. Each age has the obligation to adapt the teachings of the Torah to its basic needs in consonance with the genius of Judaism."

The doctrine of "progressive revelation", however, presents difficulties of its own no less severe than those presented by the traditional doctrine. It is clearly influenced by an evolutionary view of religious ideas in which the later is always the higher. Few today would accept such a view. The doctrine seems to imply that God has kept former generations in ignorance of the truth in its fullness until the spiritual supermen of the nineteenth and twentieth centuries came on the scene. It hints that in many ways we are spiritually superior to Amos, Isaiah, Akiba and Maimonides. It tends to set up the *Zeitgeist* as the final arbiter in religious and moral affairs. It leaves the content of revelation vague and undefined. It comes perilously close to a belief in a God who is constantly changing His mind.

Both doctrines—that of tradition and that of "progressive revelation"—see revelation in propositional terms. According to the

6. See W. Gunther Plaut: *The Growth of Reform Judaism*, p. 97.

traditional view God revealed certain propositions all at once whereas according to "progressive revelation" theory He revealed them gradually. In more recent times a very different (and to many minds far more satisfactory) view of revelation has gained ground. On this view revelation does not mean that God conveys to man detailed propositions at all but rather that He enables men to have an encounter with Him of a specially intense form. It is God Himself who is disclosed in revelation. Revelation is an event not a series of propositions about God and His demands.

The Bible is the *record* of how men were confronted with God. The actual words of the book of Isaiah, for instance, are the human retelling of what it meant to the prophet to be met by God in the specially intense way possible only for the prophet.[7] But, if this is the case, and it applies to the Pentateuch as well as to the prophetic books, what is the binding force of the Biblical (and Rabbinic) rules and regulations? If it is men who *recorded* the ten commandments, for example, does this mean that they can no longer be considered to be "the word of God"? The rest of this chapter is concerned with this theme.

First, it is necessary to examine the Biblical record itself in the light of modern scholarship. We begin with the stories in the book of Genesis.[4]

The new picture of these stories—attained after a century and a half and more of gigantic research on the part of a host of dedicated Bible scholars—is highly complex. The stories themselves still stand as marvellous descriptions of human motivation, of the workings of the human mind in temptation, success and failure, of the stresses of the moral life and the response to God's will, but the claim that they are factual accounts of what actually happened in those far-off days has been generally abandoned except in fundamentalistic circles. For one thing, whether we accept the Documentary Hypothesis or modify it or even reject it completely, it is very difficult to read these

---

7. The problem of how the prophetic books came to be written, e.g. by the prophets themselves or their disciples and whether the original sayings of the prophets were recorded exactly as they were uttered or whether their present literary form is a later adaptation, has much exercised modern Biblical scholarship, see, for example, J. Muilenburg's survey in *Peake's Commentary*, ed. Black and Rowley, pp. 477–479.

8. See the modern commentaries to Genesis, e.g. Driver, Skinner, and Speiser, and Nahum M. Sarna: *Understanding Genesis*.

stories now without seeing in them a composite account put together from different traditions. Then again, the names of persons and tribes are indistinguishable so that, for example, the Joseph saga reflects the later division between the Northern and Southern Kingdoms. It is very hard to believe, nowadays, that the struggle between Judah and Joseph, for instance, is a purely coincidental anticipation of the later struggles between the *Kingdom* of Judah in the South and that of Ephraim (the name of Joseph's son) in the North. Again, if we follow the archaeological evidence, it is clear that the Genesis narratives frequently reflect ancient myths and the like. The story of Noah's ark, for instance, clearly belongs to the cycle of Mesopotamian myths which produced the Utnapishtim story in the Gilgamesh Epic.[9]

To reconstruct the development of the Genesis narratives is probably impossible now and a strong element of guesswork is involved in any attempted reconstruction. But something of the following would appear to be not too far from the truth. Out of the early myths, tribal movements and ancient traditions, the Genesis narratives were woven and told originally in the form of saga. These traditional stories were eventually put together to form the more or less continuous narrative we have in Genesis as part of the *Heilsgeschichte*, the sacred history in which God makes His covenant with the Patriarchs and their descendants.

In what sense can this be said to be revelation? The Genesis narrative as a whole is about the covenant, about God and Israel, about God finding Israel and Israel finding God and bringing Him to mankind. For all the human colouring of the story, for all that Genesis is a book like other books and so amenable to literary and historical analysis, it is in this book that God is revealed. If God is then He is to be found in the Biblical record; nowhere else in human literature is He told of so clearly. What applies to the Genesis narrative applies to the rest of the Bible. It is all the record of a people's tremendous attempt— the believer declares a successful attempt—to meet God. The various propositions are, then, not themselves revelation but are the by-product of revelation. In this connection Mowinckel[10] has called

9. See e.g. the conservative examination of the parallels and differences between the Biblical narrative and the Mesopotamian myths in Cassuto: *From Noah to Abraham*, pp. 19–23 and in Alexander Heidel: *The Gilgamesh Epic and Old Testament Parallels*.

10. *The Old Testament and the Word of God*.

attention to the expression: "the word (*davar*) of God". Davar is Hebrew means "thing" as well as "word". The believer in verbal inspiration believes that he has in the Bible (for the Jew, the Bible as interpreted in the subsequent teachings of the Rabbis) the *ipsissima verba* of the prophets, indeed, of God Himself. The more sophisticated believer, nowadays, cannot accept this for the soundest reasons. But he, too, can find himself gripped by the "divine thing", by the existentialist situation in which he tries hard to discover what it is that God would have him do. He relives the experience of the prophets who were seized with an overwhelming conviction of complete commitment to the divine.

To make this clearer we can study the Biblical laws against theft. Now there can be no doubt that in all societies there are laws against theft but these acquire in the Bible a special dimension of their own because of their association with the Biblical divine–human encounter. These "natural" laws thus become part of the Torah, part of God's will for mankind. In all probability the ancient Israelites arrived at these laws in the same way as other ancient peoples arrived at similar laws. But in Israel they were eventually seen as God's will, as part of the life that man has to lead if the covenant between him and God is to be realised, as a reaching out for God in the process of understanding the claims of his neighbour.

Revelation can thus be seen as the disclosure of God Himself. The rules and regulations, the Torah and precepts, provide the vocabulary by which the God who is disclosed is to be worshipped, in the broad sense of the term. They are a repertoire which has evolved in response to the impact of the original disclosure. This idea of a vocabulary of worship can perhaps be understood more effectively on the analogy of the Hebrew language. This language did not drop down from Heaven. From one point of view it is simply one of the ancient Semitic tongues, used, in fact, by the Moabites as well as the Israelites. (The famous "Moabite Stone" is inscribed in a dialect of Hebrew). But, whatever its origins, it was this language in which the record of revelation was expressed and therefore the re-living of the original revelational experiences demands the use of this language. By the same token the whole range of Jewish observances is part of the language of worship, the way in which the people of the covenant relives and reaffirms the covenant.

Since the prophets do not hesitate to describe the relationship

between God and Israel on the analogy of the marriage relationship
it is perhaps permissible to give the further illustration taken from
this relationship.[11] A husband and wife, deeply in love with one
another, have a meal at a restaurant and hear the band playing the
song popular at the time they were courting. "Listen, darling, they
are playing our song" is Hollywood pure and simple but in this
instance Hollywood is true to life. The song in itself may be trivial but
it is not the song itself which matters for them but its associations with
their original meeting and the power of association it has for reinforc-
ing their love for one another.

The precepts of the Torah are binding because they provide the
vocabulary of worship—always understanding worship in its widest
sense. God did "command" them but not by direct communication—
as in the traditional view—but through the historical experiences of
the people of Israel. Of course, once one accepts the dynamic principle
it cannot be left simply at that. The problem of the nature of this
dynamism and the way it should be grasped is discussed in the next
chapter. But the idea of a "command" through the experiences of
Israel is basically sound and is not too radical a departure from the
traditional view. The following two passages from the Rabbinic
literature have often been quoted by those who favour the kind of
approach we are suggesting, though it would undoubtedly be
historically incorrect to pretend that the Rabbis anticipated the
modern problem. The Rabbis had what we would today call the
"fundamentalist" view. They believed in the doctrine of "verbal
inspiration".[12] The point in quoting these two passages is to show that
the idea of a "command" through man—of God, as it were, giving
the Torah not so much *to* Israel as *through* Israel—is not entirely
foreign to Rabbinic Judaism so that a creative Jewish theology can
build on it.

(1) The benediction before kindling the Hanukkah lights is:
"Blessed art Thou, Oh Lord our God, who has sanctified us with His
commandments and has commanded us to kindle the Hanukkah

---

11. J. J. Petuchowski's *Ever Since Sinai* is an excellent treatment of this theme.
12. R. Ishmael's famous dictum "the Torah speaks in the language of men" (*Sifre,
Shelah,* 112) only means that the *language* of verbal inspiration is human language.
i.e. God inspired Moses to write the Torah in ordinary human language. On
R. Akiba and R. Ishmael in this matter see the comprehensive study by A. J.
Heschel: *Torah Min Ha-Shamayim.*

lights." The Talmud asks:[13] "Where did He command us?", i.e. since the whole institution of Hanukkah is post-Biblical. The reply is that He commanded us either in the verse: "Thou shalt not turn aside..." (Deut. 17: 11) or in the verse: "Ask thy father, and he will shew thee; Thine elders, and they will tell thee" (Deut. 32: 7). The Rabbis thus discover Scriptural warrant for Rabbinic institutions. Whether the Rabbis really considered the Scriptural verses to be the sanction for Rabbinic innovation or whether they used these as a peg on which to hang their innovations is a moot point and was, in fact, discussed even in the middle ages.[14] In any event we have here the germ of the idea that indirect commands through the experiences of Israel and the institutions of its sages are also divine commands.

(2) One of the most remarkable poetic passages in the Talmudic literature tells[15] of Moses being transported in time to the school of R. Akiba. Moses sat at the back of the hall in which R. Akiba's lecture was being held and discovered to his horror that he was unable to understand what Akiba was teaching. But Moses' mind was set at ease when he heard Akiba reply to a question: "Master, how do you know this?" that it was a rule given to Moses at Sinai! The implication of the story is that the Torah that Akiba was teaching was so different from that which Moses had received that Moses could not understand it at all. Naturally this must have been so since conditions—social, economic, political and religious—were so different in Akiba's day from those which obtained in the days of Moses. But what Akiba was doing was not to invent a new Torah but to draw out the implications of the Torah of Moses. From the historical angle this process began, in fact, in the Pentateuch itself. It is widely acknowledged today that the frequently occurring formula: "And the Lord spoke to Moses saying" is often an attempt to read back later laws into the days of Moses, the first law-giver.[16] From the beginning the Mosaic Legislation is seen, then, in dynamic terms, attracting itself to much later legislation as part of the process in which Israel, the covenant people, tries to discover God's will in order to obey it.

13. Sabb. 23a.
14. See Maimonides: *Sefer Ha-Mitzvot, Shoresh Ha-Rishon*, ed. Warsaw, pp. 1–28 and commentaries.
15. Men. 29b.
16. See the fine treatment of this idea by H. Wheeler Robinson: *Inspiration and Revelation in the Old Testament*.

The argument we have presented obviously leans heavily on the existentialist idea of encounter, especially as developed by Buber. The great difficulty, as we have noted, for upholders of the binding character of Jewish laws, is the leap from the intensely personal meeting with God, of which the Bible is the record, to the full acceptance of the detailed laws. These belong not to the actual revelation but to its fallible human recording. Why, then, should they be held to be binding? Buber, indeed, draws the conclusion that the laws are not, in fact, binding in any traditional sense.

Franz Rosenzweig, similarly existentialist in approach, is more helpful to the traditionalist view—the view we are adopting. In a famous letter,[17] dated 21 April 1927, Rosenzweig writes to Jacob Rosenheim, leader of Orthodoxy in Germany: "Where we differ from Orthodoxy is our reluctance to draw from our belief in the holiness or uniqueness of the Torah, and in its character of revelation, any conclusions as to its literary genesis and the philological value of the text as it has come down to us. If all of Wellhousen's theories were correct and the Samaritans really had the better text, our faith would not be shaken in the least. This is the profound difference between you and us—a difference which, it seems to me, may be bridged by mutual esteem but not by understanding. I, at least, fail to understand the religious basis of Hirsch's commentary or Breuer's writings. Still, how does it happen then that our translation is more closely akin to that of Hirsch than to any other? We too translate the Torah as a single book. For us, too, it is the work of one spirit. Among ourselves we call him by the symbol which critical science is accustomed to use to designate its assumed redactor: R. But this symbol R we expand not into Redactor but into *Rabbenu*. For he is our teacher; his theology is our teaching."

The translation of the Bible, to which Rosenzweig alludes, was one undertaken by him and Buber. The Wellhausen thesis that there are four main, distinct documents in the Pentateuch ("J", "E", "D" and "P") combined eventually by a Redactor or Redactors ("R"), and the possibility that our present text is not always correct, pose problems for Rosenzweig who believes nonetheless in the sanctity and uniqueness of the Torah. Hirsch, the great Orthodox thinker, and his grandson Breuer, because of this, feel bound to reject both the

17. This letter has been frequently quoted, e.g. in Franz Rosenzweig: *His Life and Thought*, ed. Glatzer, p. 158.

Higher Criticism, as taught by Wellhausen, and the Lower Criticism,
i.e. textual criticism. Many more recent Biblical scholars, it should be
noted, either reject the theories of Wellhausen or modify them considerably but the vast majority agree that the Pentateuch is a composite work so that the theological problem considered by Rosenzweig
is still acute.

Rosenzweig's position is that even if Wellhausen is right and even
if the Samaritans had the better text (he does not say this is, in fact, so
but that we must be prepared to face the possibility) our present text
was put together under God's guidance. The "Redactor" was
inspired by God to put the whole together in this way rather than in
any other and this book in this form became Israel's Torah. Therefore,
says Rosenzweig, we continue to use the symbol "R" but for us it
does not stand for "Redactor" but for "Rabbenu", which means
"our teacher". He is our teacher who has conveyed to us the book
that has been most instrumental in the formation of the Jewish spirit.
This is a neat play on words. Moses is often called *Moshe Rabbenu*
"Moses our teacher". So even if the Torah is not by Moses, it is still by
Rabbenu.

What Rosenzweig is saying is that if we wish to know how the
various parts of the Torah came to be we must go to Biblical scholarship, and here we must be prepared to examine all the evidence with
complete honesty. If we come to the conclusion that Wellhausen is
right, we must accept his findings. But the process as a whole has to
be understood. The Jew who has faith will not fail to see the hand of
God in the process as a whole, i.e. through the work of people like the
Redactor—*Rabbenu.*

This view of Rosenzweig has been very influential. But it is not
without difficulties of its own. For one thing it comes close to the
propositional theory of revelation and therefore fails to account for
the existence of error as well as truth in the record. Furthermore, it is
hard to see how the process of editing can be said to produce the Torah
since the sources on which the editors drew are not only various but
are in some respects contradictory. It may be that Rosenzweig
himself, if questioned, would have elaborated on his thesis as follows
but in any event the elaboration is permissible. The key notion to be
stressed is that of *Rabbenu.* This is to be understood not as representing
an infallible guide but a "teacher" in the more mundane sense. The
final work, with its contradictions and errors, is the result of a teaching

process, frequently unconscious, in which the record was drawn up of Israel's quest for God and of God allowing Himself to be found. Such an understanding preserves the dynamic quality of the process. Revelation is still to be seen as God self-disclosure but what we have called the "vocabulary of worship" is as much a significant factor in the process as the original disclosure.

It need hardly be said that the view we have adopted is certainly not the traditional one. But it does preserve the idea—of the utmost significance for the Jewish religion—that to lead the good life is to obey God's will. The idea of the *mitzvah*, the divine command, can and should be maintained even though intellectual honesty compels us to interpret revelation in non-propositional terms. In the next chapter we must examine in greater detail how such an approach to Jewish observance can work in practice.

CHAPTER FIFTEEN

TORAH AND MITZVAH

THE two key words in the traditional scheme of Jewish practice are Torah and *mitzvah* (plural *mitzvot*) The Torah is the sum-total of Jewish teaching. Its study is enjoined as a sublime religious obligation. The *mitzvot* ("precepts", "commandments") are the practical injunctions of the Torah; alms-giving, honouring parents, sabbath observance, the marriage laws, ethical conduct, and, indeed, the whole range of Jewish practice. A typical Rabbinic saying regarding the significance of the *mitzvot* and the relatively greater significance of the study of the Torah is:[1] "These are the things whose fruit a man enjoys in this world while the capital is stored up for him in the World to Come; honouring parents, deeds of lovingkindness, making peace between a man and his fellow; but the study of the Torah is equal to them all."

The *mitzvot* are divided by the Rabbis into two groups: positive precepts (*mitzvot aseh*), things one must do, and negative precepts (*mitzvot lo taaseh*), things one must refrain from doing. Another Rabbinic grouping is of precepts between man and God (*ben adam la-Makom*) and precepts between man and his neighbour (*ben adam la-havero*).

In the traditional scheme the *mitzvot* are eternally binding upon the Jew because God has so commanded. In the previous chapter we have examined the difficulties in accepting the idea of a direct divine command of the detailed *mitzvot* and have argued for a different approach for the modern Jew. In this chapter we must try to spell out in greater detail what is really involved in practice if the different view of revelation is accepted.

During the middle ages, Jewish thinkers devoted a good deal of thought to discovering, or attempting to discover, the "reasons for the *mitzvot*" (*taame ha-mitzvot*). The situation with which they were

1. *Peah* 1: 1.

faced was this. They knew that Judaism taught many things which seemed most reasonable, appealing to every rational man: "Thou shalt not steal'; "Thou shalt not kill"; "Thou shalt not commit adultery"; "Love thy neighbour"; "Honor Thy father and thy mother"; "To do justly, to love mercy, and to walk humbly with thy God". They also knew that Judaism contains a number of rules and regulations by which the Jew is expected to live, which, on the face of it, seemed anything but reasonable. The dietary laws are an obvious example. But these thinkers were convinced that God does not impose arbitrary rules on His worshippers and therefore they tried to suggest what God's reasons may have been in commanding the *mitzvot*. Thus, they argued, the dietary laws have hygienic value or they help the Jewish people to survive or they provide a discipline through which holiness may be attained or they are a reaction to idolatrous practices.

The Jewish mystics went further. As we have seen earlier, they suggested that man's deeds on earth have an influence in the heavenly realms. Each of the details of the *mitzvot* corresponds with some sublime mystery in the "upper worlds". The performance of the *mitzvot* has a cosmic effect, awakening the divine grace and enabling it to flow through all creation. A favourite illustration of some of the latter-day Kabbalists is that of a blue-print drawn up by a skilled architect. A mere line on the print represents a corridor; a point might signify a door; a small square might be the sign for a large room in the finished building. Similarly, the Torah is God's blue-print for the cosmos. Although we cannot grasp these wondrous matters, it was argued, it is nonetheless true that if the Jew keeps the dietary laws, for instance, he protects himself and the whole universe from spiritual contamination. If the Jew wears *tzitzit* ("fringes", Num. 15: 37–41) he prepared in the special way the Torah ordains he brings down from Heaven certain divine illuminations the world requires for its continued existence.

I. Heinemann: *Taame Ha-Mitzvot* gives three reasons why the Jewish rationalistic thinker in the middle ages felt obliged to search for "reasons for the *mitzvot*": (1) As a defence of Judaism against Gentile ridicule. (2) As a means of understanding the purpose of the *mitzvot* with a resulting greater enthusiasm for their observance. (3) In the belief that God is no tyrant imposing arbitrary rules on His creature simply in order to test their obedience. While the mystics saw meaning, in terms of the supernal

mysteries, of even the details of the *mitzvot*, Maimonides (Guide, III, 26)
states that some of the details are arbitrary and that the search for reasons
should be confined to the general purpose of the commandments. Cf.
for the rationalist point of view: Leon Roth: *The Guide for the Perplexed:
Moses Maimonides*, pp. 72–80, and for the mystical point of view: Scholem:
Major Trends, pp. 28–30. For the Hasidic view of the function of the *mitzvot*,
based on the Kabbalah see R. Schneor Zalman of Liady: *Tanya, Iggeret
Ha-Kodesh*, 7, pp. 221–223 and for the view, based on the Kabbalah, too, of
their opponents (basically the two views here are identical) see R. Hayim
of Volozhyn: *Nefesh Ha-Hayim, Shaar I*, Chapters 2–6. See R. Hayim's
interpretation (Chapter 4, note) of Avot 2: 1: "Know what is above thee"
(*da mah le-maalah mimmekha*) as: "Know that what is above—(i.e. what
happens above) is from thee" (i.e. the result of your deeds on earth).

Whether rationalist or mystic, however, the Jewish thinker in the
middle ages was concerned only to answer the question: "Why did
God?" (There were not lacking thinkers who declared that even this
question bordered on the blasphemous. God so commanded because
He willed it so and it is not for man even to attempt to fathom the
divine will.)

In modern times the question the Jew asks is very different. For him
the question is not: "*Why* did God tell us to keep certain *mitzvot*?"
but: "*Did* God tell us to keep certain mitzvot?" That this very different kind of question is put by the modern Jew can be attributed to a
number of factors. Not the least of these is the abandonment of the
older doctrine which has it that every word and every letter of the
Pentateuch was dictated by God to Moses, together with the interpretations found in Rabbinic literature. There is no need to repeat
at length the arguments which have compelled moderns to depart
from this conception. Suffice it to say that as a result of the devoted
researches of a host of distinguished scholars and thinkers over the
past hundred and fifty years a new picture has emerged, as we have
noted in the previous chapter, concerning the nature of the Biblical
record and the Rabbinic interpretation of it. According to this
picture the Bible is still for the believing Jew the source of his faith
and his religion. It is still seen by him as the world-transforming
"word" or "thing" of God. But it is now seen that the Bible is not, as
the mediaeval Jew thought it was, a book *dictated* by God but a
collection of books which grew gradually over the centuries and that
it contains a human as well as a divine element.

This applies to the Pentateuch as well as to the rest of the Bible. It is impossible to follow the argument that the scientific study of the sacred texts is valid and commendable but must stop short of the Pentateuch. Either the new methods are sound or they are not. If they are not sound, if they must be rejected in the name of dogma, faith or tradition, then they cannot be applied to the book of Isaiah or, for that matter, to the Zohar. If they are sound and if elementary honesty demands their use then they must be applied to the Pentateuch. There is no middle way. Scholars all over the world have come to this conclusion. Christians have been compelled to apply these methods even to the Gospels, Muslims even to the Koran, and, by the same token, Jews even to the Pentateuch. The result has been that thinking men have tried valiantly to reinterpret a faith based on the idea of revelation so that it is in accord with the new facts.

As good an illustration as any of what the new picture means is Brunner's illustration of a gramophone record. We cannot now hear Caruso sing but we can do the next best thing. We buy a Caruso record and when we play it we hear the master's voice. But, of course, it is far from perfect. It is a reproduction. There is inevitable distortion. Similarly the new view of revelation is of a meeting or series of meetings with God Himself. Revelation is an event. It has been translated into words by the human beings who experienced it and their words are found in the record we know as the Bible. From out of its pages we, too, can hear the voice of God speaking to us, but it is the voice of God speaking through the distortions of the fallible human record. Unless we ourselves are prophets how else could we hear God's voice? There is nothing in this view basically opposed to the Jewish idea, though it does involve, of course, a thorough reinterpretation of what revelation means. We Jews have been taught to worship God, not any of His creatures, not even the Torah. The Torah is to be studied and the *mitzvot* practised because they lead to God.

On this view it is better to speak of the *sanction* for the *mitzvot* rather than the *reasons* for the *mitzvot*. It is precisely here that we differ from the mediaeval Jew. He had one cogent answer to the question why he should keep the *mitzvot*. I have to keep the *mitzvot*, he would have replied, because God has ordered me to so to do. If I am especially intrepid I may go on to try to discover why God did so. But the pressing question the modern Jew asks is, what is the authority for my observance of those *mitzvot* for which no reason can easily be discerned? He cannot fall back on the simple answer given by the mediaeval Jew. Once it is recognised that there is a human element in the Torah it must be seen that there is no simple method by means of which this can be distinguished, as it were, from the divine element. One cannot take a pencil and mark this verse in the Pentateuch human, this divine. In a sense it is all human (in that the record was produced by human beings and can be studied and examined by the methods by which other works of human genius are studied). In another sense it is all divine (in that it is a unique record of God's encounter with man). What, then, are our criteria to be? Granted that there is not too much difficulty in seeing that, for all the recognition of the human element, God really did command us to love our neighbour, how can we be sure that He also commanded us to observe the dietary laws or keep the traditional Sabbath? On the whole, in the modern world, there are five attitudes towards our problem. I propose to call these: (1) Fundamentalism, (2) Classical Reform, (3) The Attitude of the Historical School, (4) Folk-ways, (5) The Theological Attitude. We must examine each of these in turn and try to show why the fifth—the attitude we have sketched in this and in the previous chapter—is the most satisfactory.

Fundamentalism

The simple answer to our problem is to deny that it exists. The fundamentalist does precisely that. He would say that all the talk about a different attitude on the part of the modern Jew is so much hot air. Nothing has happened, he protests, to make us reject the attitude as laid down by Maimonides eight hundred years ago. The famous representative of this point of view is Samson Raphael Hirsch; a thinker in whom there is much to admire but who has been venerated in some fundamentalist circles to the point of idolatry. Hirsch put the fundamentalist position very clearly and eloquently in an essay written in 1854 entitled: "Judaism Up To Date". This is what he had to say:[2]

"If the Bible is to be for me the word of God, and Judaism and Jewish law the revealed will of God, is it possible for me to ask my belly, my sensual enjoyment and comfort, my temporary advantage, whether it is also sweet or easy, or profitable or agreeable? Is it possible for me to take religion, my religion, which has been given to me by God as a standard with which to measure myself, my generation, and all my action and inaction, and trim it to fit the meanness, the sensuality, the petty-mindedness of my own desires at any particular time?"

Hirsch goes on to say:

"Let us not deceive ourselves. The whole question is simply this. Is the statement 'And God spoke to Moses saying', with which all the laws of the Jewish Bible commence, true or not true? Do we really believe that God, the Omnipotent and Holy, spoke thus to Moses? Do we speak the truth when in front of our brethren we lay our hand on the scroll containing these words and say that God has given us this Torah, that His Torah, the Torah of truth and with it of eternal life, is planted in our midst? If this is to be no mere lip-service, no mere rhetorical flourish, then we must keep and carry out this Torah without omission and without carping, in all circumstances and at all times. This word of God must be our eternal rule superior to all human judgement, the rule to which all our actions must at all times conform; and instead of complaining that it is no longer suitable to the times, our only complaint must be that the times are no longer suitable to it."

These are brave and fighting words, presenting an either/or with a vengeance. The present-day followers of Hirsch thrive on this either/or. Either you accept the view that every word of the Pentateuch was dictated by God to Moses or you might as well give up Judaism altogether. More than one of the members of this School has said: "If I believed in a human element in the Bible I would not go to the Synagogue, I would not keep the *mitzvot*, I would see no purpose in living as a Jew"; as if Judaism had no value in itself, as if the *mitzvot* were only an irksome burden, as if the whole range of Jewish religious experience is invalidated unless we accept a particular theory of how God communicated His demands at a certain period in human history.

The followers of this School claim to be modern and let us say in all fairness that it has produced men who have risen to the top of their profession, who have participated to the full in Western life. Yet it is not without significance that the theme of studies these people generally prefer belongs to the realm of the safe. Physics and mathematics are safe subjects. Classics are innocuous and there is no great danger even in philosophy. History, particularly Jewish history, and the scientific study of the Jewish sacred words, are far from being safe subjects. History lets the past speak for itself and once you allow the past to do that you see that there can be no successful building of a philosophy of Judaism on unsound theories as to what happened in the Jewish past.

Hirsch wrote long before the more acute of the critical problems came to the fore. But not only his followers but Orthodoxy in general still adopt the fundamentalist position, i.e. that the present text of the Pentateuch was conveyed by God to Moses. Of course it is impossible to deny on *a priori* grounds that this is so but there is no real awareness that Biblical (and Rabbinic studies) have succeeded in presenting a new picture which, to say the least, make the traditional view extremely difficult to uphold. There is hardly any awareness in this camp of the problems raised by textual variants in the ancient versions, by the evidence of compositeness in the Pentateuch even if one does not accept the Documentary Hypothesis, by the parallels in the ancient mythologies to which we have called attention in the previous chapter, to say nothing of the findings of geology, anthropology and ancient history which occasioned the fierce debates on fundamentalism in the last century. In the *Commentary* symposium: *The Condition of Jewish Belief* none of the Orthodox Rabbis show the slightest appreciation of the real difficulties, with the exception of Emanuel Rackman. Rackman in *Judaism*, Spring 1969: *A Challenge to Orthodoxy* presents a liberal understanding of Orthodoxy but can still write (151): "Even with regard to doctrine, such a divergence of opinion has prevailed among the giants of the Tradition that only one dogma enjoys universal acceptance: the Pentateuch's text was given to the Jewish people by God." And again (p. 153): "Similarly, there is no substantial agreement with regard to the manner in which God communicated with Israel, its Patriarchs and Prophets. Somehow the Tradition preferred never to demand of Jews more than that they believe in the text of the Pentateuch to be divine in origin. Otherwise, the widest latitude in interpretation was not only permitted but often encouraged. Even the authorship of the Five Books of Moses was not beyond the scope of the diversity. Several Sages held that Moses himself wrote the book of *Deuteronomy* but God dictated its inclusion with the earlier books. Moreover, much in the earlier books started also as the work of man. In their dialogues with God the Patriarchs spoke their own words. Jacob composed his own prophecy for his offspring. Moses sang his own song of triumph on the Red Sea. In the final analysis, then, the sanctity of the Pentateuch does not

derive from God's authorship of it all but rather from the fact that God's
is the final version. The final writing by Moses has the stamp of divinity—the
kiss of immortality. So stated, the dogma is a much more limited one than
one would be led to believe it is when one listens to many an Orthodox
teacher today." Rackman says nothing of the evidence for a post-Moasic
authorship of many of the passages in the Pentateuch or, indeed, of any of
the real problems raised by modern Biblical scholarship. The sober fact is
that no Orthodox thinker has yet come forward with a view other than
that the present text of the Pentateuch is the direct word of God to Moses
and this includes the words "And the Lord spoke unto Moses". All this is
to say nothing of the problems raised by the researches of men like Frankel,
Weiss, Ginzberg and Lieberman into the Rabbinic literature which provide
sufficient evidence that the whole concept of a static tradition reaching back
to Moses is a myth. There is no escaping the problems raised by the new
picture of Judaism as a developing religion which has been uncovered by
modern Biblical and Rabbinical scholarship.

Classical Reform

As an alternative to Fundamentalism there is the attitude of
Classical Reform. Classical Reform declares that we cannot convincingly answer the question why we should keep the dietary laws
and the like. On this view Judaism is an ethical religion, a prophetic
religion. The prophets, it is claimed, did not advocate the observance
of ritual but they did stress the need for practising justice, loving
mercy and walking humbly with God. This is what the Reform
leaders had to say in the well-known "Pittsburgh Platform" in
1885:[3]

"We recognise in the Mosaic legislation a system of training the
Jewish people for its mission during its national life in Palestine,
and today we accept as binding only its moral laws, and maintain
only such ceremonies as elevate and sanctify our lives, but reject all
such as are not adapted to the views and habits of modern civilisation. We hold that all such Mosaic and Rabbinical Laws as
regulate diet, priestly purity, and dress originated in ages and under
the influence of ideas entirely foreign to our present mental and
spiritual state. They fail to impress the modern Jew with a spirit of
priestly holiness; their observance in our days is apt rather to
obstruct than to further modern spiritual elation".

3. See W. Gunther Plautt: *The Growth of Reform Judaism*, p. 34.

This was formulated a long time ago, since then a good deal has happened. Among other things a certain Viennese doctor has had much of importance to say about the complexities of the human mind. Apart from the distinctiveness of Judaism, we know that life is deeper than logic, that Judaism is more than assent to theological propositions, that you cannot simply reduce it to ethics, even to ethics infused with a spirit of religion. There are depths in the human soul which only ritual can reach. It is no accident that, during the Roman period, when thousands of Gentiles were flocking to become converts to Judaism, it was not so much the Jewish ethic which attracted them, glorious and challenging though this was, but the fascination of Jewish ritual. They longed to observe *kashrut*, to keep the sabbath and the other distinctive Jewish institutions. Modern man is as much a creature of human needs as ancient man. It is simply untrue to say that these things are not adapted to the views and habits of modern civilisation or that they are entirely foreign to our mental and spiritual state. For man cannot live in Heaven. Judaism has always urged upon him to bring down his ideals from Heaven to give them concrete expression on earth, to make them fruitful in daily living. It is highly significant that here and there in the Reform world of today one finds a new appreciation of the value of *Halakhah*. It is now widely acknowledged that the Classical Reform position results in an impoverishment of Judaism. Jews need a faith which sustains the soul in its quest for the divine and provides opportunities for man's elevation to God in the day-to-day business of living.

A remarkable example of the new appreciation on the part of Reform Rabbis of the legal side of Judaism is the acclaim afforded to the work of Solomon B. Freehof. In his: *Current Reform Responsa*, p. 3. Freehof writes: "All these new voices express a strong feeling which grows from many roots. There was first a realisation that Judaism had always been a religion of law and that Reform somehow had lost a great deal of inner strength when it veered away from the old sense of a religiously organised life and put its sole emphasis on the less specific ethical ideals. Then also these newer feelings rise from a sense of a greater appreciation of the rabbinic past. Since modern biblical criticism has shown the Bible to be a human book, it deprived it of a special uniqueness. It was not necessarily different in status from the confessedly human, argumentative Talmudic literature. Since God speaks in 'the language of human beings', He may be speaking through both literatures. If hitherto God had revealed Himself through the writers of the Bible by the flame of the human conscience then

He revealed Himself through the debating scholars of the Talmud, by the light of the human intellect; and it may well be that the intelligence is as worthy a vehicle of revelation as the conscience." It is a pity that these fine words of Freehof are somewhat vitiated by his limitation of the legal approach to those institutions which Reform Jews accept as of value, e.g. the Synagogue and its services. The *Halakhah* of the traditional sabbath seems to be completely ignored apparently on the grounds that people have no interest in it!

The Historical School

An attitude, which while rejecting Fundamentalism, has a vivid appreciation of the significance of the *mitzvot* in their traditional form, is that of the Historical, or Bresslau, School. Among its representatives were Zechariah Frankel, the historian Graetz and Solomon Schechter. The story is told of Greatz, with what accuracy I cannot say, that during a visit in England Graetz attended Synagogue and read the *Haftarah* on the Sabbath before the fast of Ab. Graetz, it is said, proceeded to read the traditional section, the first chapter of Isaiah, but did so with his own textual emendations. After the service, however, the great historian was seen to wrap his handkerchief around his wrist. Bible critic though he was, he belonged to the Historical School, which upholds the need for observing the Sabbath in the traditional manner, including the prohibition of carrying out any object into the public domain. Louis Ginzberg, one of the most outstanding Talmudists of modern times and a Bible critic to boot, was a disciple of these men. Like them he was in his private life a strictly observant Jew. In an address Ginzberg delivered on Frankel's life and thought[4] he pointed out that neither for Frankel nor for Graetz was the Law identical with the Bible. One could have a free attitude towards the investigation of the Bible and the other sources of Judaism without this affecting practical observance in its traditional form. Ginzberg said:

"The dietary laws are not incumbent upon us because they conduce to moderation, nor the family laws because they further chastity and morals. The law as a whole is not the means to an end, but the end in itself; the law is active religiousness, and in active religion must lie what is specifically Jewish. All men need tangible expression to grasp the highest ideas to keep them clearly before them,

4. *Students, Scholars and Saints*, pp. 195–216.

to say nothing of the ordinary masses for whom abstract ideas are merely empty words. Our need of sensuous expressions and practical ceremonies bring with it the necessity for the material incorporation of religious conceptions, and varying people have given them varying forms. The Law is the form in which the Jewish spirit satisfies this need. In the precepts which are the dramatic representation of the inward feeling, Judaism found a material expression of its religious ideas; through them its abstractions became realities and in them the essential needs themselves, reverence and recognition of the divine will, were expressed. Every form became thus spiritualised and living, bearing within itself a lofty conception."

There is no doubt that the Historical School has achieved great things. Jüdische Wissenschaft has transformed our knowledge of the Jewish past and there can be no over-looking its findings. But it is not unfair and irrelevant to note that the members of this School were more interested in the past than in the present and the future. The questions they tried chiefly to answer were questions regarding the history of Judaism. What did the Bible, The Talmud, Saadia and Maimonides really say? You can only discover this, they rightly argued, by having, in the first instance, accurate texts. And so a good deal of their activity was devoted to the establishment of proper texts. You can only discover this if you know the languages in which the thought of the past is conveyed and so they engaged in the careful study of Semitic philology. You can only discover this if you know much about the background to the thought of the past. And so they examined with keen insight the history of the different civilisations in which Jews moved. Men have only a limited quota of energy. Few can be both theologians and historians and the members of this school decided that they could best make their contribution as historians. The result was that their occasional excursions into theology were not always too profound and, to their credit, they generally recognised this. The theologian of today cannot afford to neglect their massive achievements but, as a theologian, he must build on them and go beyond them.

Soloman Schechter saw the problem. Schechter writes:[5]

"The historical school has never, to my knowledge, offered to the world a theological programme of its own. By the nature of its

5. *Studies in Judaism, First Series*, Introduction, p. xvii.

task, its labours are mostly conducted in the field of philosophy and archaeology, and it pays but little attention to purely dogmatic questions. On the whole, its attitude towards religion may be defined as an enlightened Scepticism combined with a staunch conservatism which is not wholly void of a certain mystical touch."

Schechter goes on to develop his famous theory of Catholic Israel, that is, the source of Jewish authority is not in the Bible but in the historical experience of the people of Israel. It is in this conception that whatever theology there is in the Historical School inheres. But Schechter continues:

"How long the position of this school will prove tenable is another question. Being brought up in the old Low Synagogue, where, with all attachment to tradition, the Bible was looked upon as the crown and climax of Judaism, the old Adam still asserts itself in me, and in unguarded moments makes me rebel against this new rival of revelation in the shape of history. At times this now fashionable exaltation of Tradition at the expense of Scripture even impresses me as a sort of religious bimetallism in which bold speculators in theology try to keep up the market value of an inferior currency by denouncing loudly the bright shining gold which, they would have us believe, is less fitted to circulate in the vulgar use of daily life than the small cash of historical interpretation. Nor can I quite reconcile myself to this alliance of religion with history, which seems to me to be both unworthy and unnatural. The Jew, some writer aptly remarked, was the first and fiercest Nonconformist of the East, and so Judaism was always a protesting religion. To break the idols, whether of the past or the present, has always been a sacred mission of Judaism, and has indeed been esteemed by it as a necessary preliminary to the advent of the kingdom of God on earth."

It is not altogether clear what Schechter is getting at, but he is in any event reminding us, and surely he is right, that Judaism is not antiquarianism, that an adherence to Judaism involves far more than an investigation into our history. Judaism is a living religion. Jews do not only want to know what the Rabbis believed or what Maimonides believed but what present-day Jews can and are expected to believe. The Synagogue Jew is naturally interested in the Jewish past but his burning need as a human being is to know what Judaism says to him now. He needs to know over and above what Maimonides taught long ago how much of relevance is there in Maimonides' teachings for him in his predicament.

Folk-ways

It is to the credit of Mordecai Kaplan that he, probably more than any other contemporary Jewish thinker, has made us face squarely this question of relevance. Kaplan, in his attempt to deal with this problem describes the *mitzvot* as "folk-ways". Kaplan argues that Judaism is a civilisation. It is a whole order of existence, a complete way of life. The precepts of the Torah are life-enhancing. To observe them is not at all a matter of living with the past, it is far removed from ancestor worship. It is rather a determined attempt to live richly and rewardingly in the present with a full realisation of all the dignity and nobility inherent in the term "Jew". To ask why the *mitzvot* should be kept is, on this view, a betrayal. The *mitzvot* are a privilege, they have intrinsic value, they are anything but a burden. The Jewish ceremonies are beautiful, they endow life with meaning and significance. The Sabbath, for example, can give the modern Jew so much, as it gave his ancestors, in terms of spiritual nourishment and refreshment. The dietary laws can provide him with anchorage in his glorious past and help to keep the Jewish ideal alive. And so throughout the whole range of the *mitzvot* there is ample justification for their observance unless we wish to deprive our lives of poetry, feeling and striving after the highest we know. This, indeed, Kaplan would say, is the purpose of religion. It exists to foster human values at their highest and best and summon men to gaze deeper into life's meaning.

Our objection to this solution of the problem is to excessive emphasis on human values as the true aim of religion. What has become of the Jew's eternal quest for God with the *mitzvot* as the means for its realisation? Is it not true that, for all the laxity in the matter of observance today, the modern Jew still wishes to observe the *mitzvot* as *mitzvot* (the word means, after all, "divine commands")? The believing Jew wishes to know how his Creator wishes him to behave. The whole point of the Jewish emphasis on Torah and *mitzvot* is that there is splendour in the idea of submission to the will of God. Rabbi S. J. Sevin once observed that the "folk-ways" attitude tends to suggest that the Torah of Israel is *minhag*—the Torah of Israel is really the custom of Israel. But Israel needs the idea of the Torah as the will of God. Much as we value the insights of this school we cannot stop there. We must try to discover if it is possible to depart from Fundamentalism, as we must if we are to preserve our intellectual integrity, and yet preserve the idea of keeping the *mitzvot* because they are the commands of God, because this it is that God would have us do. This leads to the fifth approach which, for want of a better name, we propose to call the Theological.

The Theological Approach

A sound theological approach will not fail to build on the findings of the Historical School. It will acknowledge that there is a *history* of Jewish observances and that these did not drop down ready made from Heaven. It will recognise, for instance, that the dietary laws were not dictated in all their details by God to Moses but evolved gradually, frequently in response to outside stimuli. It will see the whole area of Jewish observances as growing naturally out of Israel's experience. But it will see the hand of God in all this, will see the "tree of life" that is the Torah as yielding no less nourishing fruit because it began its existence as an acorn. We believe in the God who speaks to us out of Israel's experience; Israel, the covenant people, dedicated to God's service and the fulfilment of His purpose. We believe in the God who, as Frankel said, reveals Himself not alone to the prophets but through Kelal Yisrael, the Community of Israel, as it works out and applies the teachings of the prophets. Yes, it is true, in a sense that the whole of the Torah is *minhag*, custom, growing through the experiences of human beings and interpreted by them in response to particular conditions in human history. But we go on from there to say that since this happened, since this is how God revealed Himself then the *minhag* of Israel is Torah.

Either one sees power in the idea of submission to God's will or one does not see it. If one does, and very many sensitive religious people do, then there can be no greater value than the idea of a *mitzvah* as an opportunity of doing God's will. The Sabbath, for example, whatever its origins, is still the institution by means of which the Jew acknowledges God as his Creator and Creator of the whole world. Louis Ginzberg is right when he says that it is quite possible for a scholarly Jew to have exactly the same opinion as a German Protestant Professor as to how the Sabbath came into Jewish life, but come it did and he can find it to be binding on him because it can bring him nearer to God as it brought his ancestors. Search the Bible from beginning to end and you will find there no command for Jews to build synagogues. And yet Jews do build synagogues and pray in them in their conviction that this is the will of God, since this is how Jews have expressed their religious strivings. We need a vocabulary of worship and this is provided by the *mitzvot*. That is their sanction.

These are the five attitudes. We have adopted the fifth because it seems the best way of understanding the meaning of Judaism for the modern Jew. We reject the first attitude because we cannot believe that Judaism wishes us to be obscurantist. We reject the second attitude because we see Judaism as something more even than ethics. We cannot accept the third attitude as it stands because we see Judaism as more than history. We do not adopt the fourth attitude because we see Judaism as more than sociology. But we believe that the fifth attitude that Judaism is a religion and a religious approach must see the *mitzvot* as ways to God. The sanction for the *mitzvot* is that they succeed in bringing men to God. Because they do this they are commanded by God.

While the approach to the *mitzvot* sketched here seems adequate in general terms it cannot be denied that numerous problems arise when it comes to practical details. The problem of discovering a viable philosophy of the *Halakhah*—the legal side of Judaism—is acute. To consider in anything like a comprehensive fashion the whole range of *Halakhah* is really beyond the scope of a work on theology. It would require an investigation into Jewish law in all its ramifications. But some few suggested guidelines may perhaps be here attempted.

This approach we have adopted proceeds on the justifiable assumption that certain spiritual goods or values have become enshrined in Halakhic institutions, irrespective of their origins, and it is these which give the *Halakhah* its validity today. In this way the concept of *mitzvah* as divine command, giving *Halakhah* its spiritual power, can still be preserved even in a non-fundamentalist approach. But it surely follows that where the *Halakhah*, as it has developed, either does not promote such goods or is opposed to them, its claim on our allegiance is considerably weakened. It may then have to be relinquished entirely in loyalty to the good as taught by Judaism itself. The best way of seeing how this might work out in practice is to examine some of the instances where the *Halakhah* seem to promote no values or to be opposed to Jewish values. From this point of view Jewish observances can be divided into three categories: (a) the significant, (b) the meaningless, (c) the harmful.

(a) *The Significant*

Under this heading some observances such as the dietary laws and the Sabbath, *tallit*, *tefillin* and *mezuzah*, Yom Kippur and the other festivals. By significant in this context we do not understand a utilitarian approach to Jewish observance, that the dietary laws are hygienic and the like, but that the religious ideals of holiness and life's spiritual enrichment are enhanced by the observances. One can argue quite consistently that even if the dietary laws evolved out of primitive taboos and even if the Sabbath came originally from Babylon (and the world was not created in six days with God resting on the seventh) these institutions have become, through the historical experiences of the Jewish people, powerful vehicles for promoting holiness in daily living. The Jew who disciplines his appetites in obedience to a system developed in the service of holiness and who keeps the Sabbath as an affirmation that God is Creator, is loyal to a basic principle of Judaism, the sanctification of human life through action. Nor is it inconsistent for a Jew who argues in this way to be *totally* observant, to keep the Sabbath and the dietary laws as found in the *Shulhan Arukh* in all their details (*be-khol peratehem ve-dikdukehem*), but the likelihood is that he will be less scrupulous than the fundamentalist since, on his view, the fear of transgressing a direct divine command does not affect his choice of what and what not to keep.

Such a Jew may, for instance, decide that switching on electric lights on the Sabbath is not an offence against the prohibition of making "fire". His argument is that even from the point of view of the traditional *Halakhah* there is room for permissiveness here (on the grounds that no *de-oraita* infringement is involved and that some authorities would favour a relaxation of the *de-rabbanan* prohibition for the sake of *oneg shabbat*, see the sources quoted in *Proceedings of the Rabbinical Assembly of America*, Vol. XIV, 1951, pp. 135-137) and the fear of a *risk* of infringement (*safek*) which plays such a large role in the fundamentalist approach (perhaps rightly so, granted the fundamentalist premise) is considerably weakened, if not entirely neutra-lised, for the non-fundamentalist. Moreover, the motive for such a lenient interpretation is not pure expediency but to make the Sabbath less a day of gloom and discomfort and more a day of light and joy. This latter consideration will carry no weight at all with the fundamentalist, for whom the *Halakhah* expresses the direct voice of God. For the non-fundamentalist (horrid term, but what other is there?), however, operating within the categories of the religiously significant, a lenient interpretation of the *Halakhah* in order to enhance the Sabbath values is perfectly legitimate. Similarly the non-fundamentalist may decide to permit himself *kasher* food in a non-kosher restaurant since the traditional Halakhic objection to this is slight (the objection is to the *kelim* and the question of *noten taam lifegam* is involved, see *Shulhan Arukh, Yoreh Deah*, 103) and he will refuse to see the greater freedom of movement and social intercourse this provides him with as anything like a concession to base appetites in disloyalty to his religion.

(b) *The Meaningless*

What of the prohibition of shaving with a razor and of *shaatnez* (a mixture of wool and flax)? On the fundamentalist view these are very far from meaningless. God commanded them and that is suffi-cient. But from the non-fundamentalist viewpoint it is more difficult to find meaning in these observances than in the Sabbath and the dietary laws, partly because these laws of shaving and *shaatnez* have never occupied so prominent a place in Jewish practice. To a far lesser extent can they be said to belong to the vocabulary of Jewish worship. It would, however, be precarious to argue that no meaning at all can be found in these laws. They can be interpreted, without distortion, as expressions of the priestly people idea, the people of God's covenant distinguishing themselves in matters of dress. If, as seems possible, these laws were ancient protests against idolatrous practices,[6] a comparison would be with a regiment wearing with pride a uniform worn by the soldiers of that regiment in a great heroic battle of old.

Fundamentalism can be an attitude adopted towards the Talmud as well as to the Bible. The traditional *Halakhah* sometimes demands that laws of Rabbinic origin be obeyed even when the reason for which they were ordained no longer obtains (see I. H. Weiss: *Dor Dor Ve-Doreshav*, Vol. II,

6. See Maimonides, *Guide* III, 37 and *Yad, Aku,,* 12: 7; Martin Noth: *Leviticus*, p. 143; Hastings' *Dictionary of the Bible*, s.v. *Hair.* p. 359.

pp. 61f and Hayim Tchernowitz: *Toledot Ha-Halakhah*, pp. 194ff). The fundamentalist argument here is that laws laid down by the Talmudic Rabbis without dissenting voice have to be obeyed. The doctrine of the successive deterioration of the generations shows its influence here. "If the earlier scholars were like angels then we are like men. But if they were like men then we are like donkeys" (Sabb. 112b). The only good or value preserved by such an attitude is that of reverence for the past but many of us today would question whether a slavish subservience to the past is, in fact, a value. The two most relevant instances are the prohibition of Gentile wine and of food cooked by Gentiles. Already in the middle ages some of the legal authorities argued for a relaxation of some of these laws on the grounds that the Gentiles among whom the Jews then lived were not pagans. If the test of religious significance is applied it is difficult to defend the continued prohibition of Gentile wine and cooked food.

(c) *The Harmful*

There are (not surprisingly), in fact, very few of these, and they are largely in the area of women's rights. The most serious problem in the Halakhic sphere for the non-fundamentalist is where the present *Halakhah* is unjust. On any reading justice is a basic imperative of Jewish life. How, then, can one countenance Jewish laws which themselves promote injustice? For the fundamentalist, again, there is no problem. On his view, all the laws were God-ordained and God is just. Somehow the apparent injustices in the law are compatible in ways we cannot see in this life with God's justice, in the same way as the instances of evil in the universe are compatible, in ways we cannot at present see, with God's goodness. The non-fundamentalist refuses this refuge. For him the laws were formulated by human beings in response to human conditions, under the guidance of God, to be sure, but subject to error like all other human institutions. The rationale for present-day loyalty to the law is that it preserves values, among them those of justice and equity. Where it patently does the opposite it can have no claim on the allegiance of the Jew.

The main instance of this kind of injustice is the case of the *agunah*, particularly when the couple have been divorced in civil law and the husband refuses to give his consent to the *get* (the bill of divorce) or will do so only if paid a large sum of money. It is true that a husband can find himself in the same position but in that case legal remedy is to hand (the dispensation of 100 Rabbis and divorce without the wife's consent) so that, in this matter, the wife is in an inferior position.

What is to be done by the non-fundamentalist loyal in general to the *Halakhah* but painfully aware of this very hard case? The problem is, of course, a modern one because in Rabbinic times the Rabbis had the power of coercing the husband to give the *get* and, until recently, civil marriage and divorce were not available for Jews.

See the discussion in Kidd. 50a. Rabbi Louis Epstein: *Le-Sheelot Ha-Agunah*, p. 22, states that this resort to coercion is a modification of the original law in which full consent of the husband was essential. The Rabbis introduced the new notion of compelling the husband to agree to the *get* because "life and justice could not tolerate, even in the days of the *Gemara*, a situation in which a wife remains tied to her husband against her will like a slave who can never be free if the husband refuses to grant her freedom willingly". Historically considered Epstein is no doubt right but the notion of this kind of development is foreign to the traditional *Halakhah* and without doubt to the Rabbis themselves who almost certainly believed that the principle of coercion, which they introduced, had, in fact, Scriptural warrant. This is as good an example as any of how the non-fundamentalist approach differs from the fundamentalist.

Tied up with it all is the problem of the *mamzer*. According to the Rabbinic interpretation of Deut. 23:3 the *mamzer* is a child born of an adulterous or incestuous union. This includes a child born to a woman and her present husband in civil law if she has not received a *get* from a previous husband. The *mamzer* may not marry (except if it be to one with the same status as himself) and his children and their children are in the same position. This law is in conflict with the basic principle of justice that children should not be punished for the sins of their parents, and, indeed, apart from this case, the *Halakhah* knows nothing of such punishment. Even if it be argued that the unfortunate status of the *mamzer* acts as a deterrent against adultery it is surely stretching the matter beyond the limits of justice to apply the law to the case of failure to obtain a *get*, quite apart from the extremely dubious nature of a deterrent which operates by penalising innocent children.

It is true that all Halakhists are concerned with these problems and various attempts at alleviation have been suggested so far without conspicuous success. The non-fundamentalist should add his voice to the demand for more determined efforts to deal with an unjust situation.

To sum up, Halakhic rules can be classified as significant, meaningless and harmful. The non-fundamentalist Halakhist will seek to deepen understanding of the significant, try to discover possible meaning in the apparently meaningless, and endeavour to mitigate the effects of the harmful without destroying the system as a whole. He will not necessarily be less scrupulous in his observance than the fundamentalist but if so will see gain in this rather than loss. He still has serious problems on his hands but they are less acute than the problems of those who try to have Judaism without *Halakhah* or those who try to live as fundamentalists.

CHAPTER SIXTEEN

JEWISH ETHICS

THE final chapter of Kaufmann Kohler's *Jewish Theology* is entitled: *The Ethics of Judaism and the Kingdom of God*. The inclusion of this topic in a work on Jewish theology is thus supported by the linking together of the ethical life with God's sovereignty. As Kohler says at the beginning of the chapter: "Jewish ethics, then, derives its sanction from God, the Author and Master of life, and sees its purpose in the hallowing of all life, individual and social." The relationship between religion and ethics has been discussed at length by religious thinkers. Many would disagree nowadays with the virtual *identification* of the *holy* with the *ethical*. But in any reading of Judaism the ethical dimension is of supreme importance. Judaism has always taught that God wishes man to pursue justice and mercy, to have a proper regard for his fellows, to make his contribution towards the emergence of a better social order. This is a constant theme in the Bible and in the Rabbinic literature and over the centuries there has been produced a Jewish moralistic literature which draws on the Bible and Talmud to depict Jewish ethical life in its ideal form. The aim of this literature is to promote sound norms of good conduct and a noble character as the inspiration of the good life. Not that all the Jewish ethical teachers are in agreement on the basis of the ethical life or the details of what constitutes sound ethical conduct. These matters are extremely complex and there is ample room for differences due to individual temperament and background.

Two surveys of Jewish ethics are: Moritz Lazarus: *The Ethics of Judaism* and Simon Bernfeld: *The Foundations of Jewish Ethics*. Samuel E. Karff in his Introduction to the Ktav edition of the latter work rightly calls attention to the fact that the prevailing tone of urbane rationalism and gentle meliorism evident in this and similar works by German Jewish liberals has been shaken to the core by the events of the last few decades. The idea of man as more or less automatically progressing towards the Messianic age, conceived of in terms of natural improvement by such means as education and social advancement, has been dealt a blow, from which it can never recover, by the gas-chambers, global wars, the inhumanity of man, all of which have come to the fore on a particularly brutal scale in this century. An anthology which seeks to redress the balance by relying on classical sources in which the evil in man is not overlooked is provided by Arnold J. Wolf: *What Is Man?* For a short history of Jewish moralistic literature Dov Katz: *Tenuat Ha-Musar* (Vol. I, Introduction, pp. 21–53) should be consulted. This work is also a useful introduction to the thought of the strongly ethical orientated Musar movement, which originated in Lithuania in the last century. This movement has hardly received the attention it deserves, study of it being eclipsed by the interest in Hasidism of which, to some extent, it was a rival. Hardly any of the works of the Musar leaders have found their way into print. See: Kopul Rosen: *Rabbi Israel Salanter and the Musar Movement* and the bibliography on p. 16; D. Zeritzki: *Torat Ha-Musar*; Simhah Züssel of Kelm: *Hokhmah U-Masar*; Joseph Horwitz of Navaradok: *Madregat Ha-Adam*; E. Dessler: *Mikhtav Me-Elijahu*; Joseph Laib Bloch: *Shiure Daat*. In the Jewish moralistic works generally duties are divided into those between man and God and those between man and his fellows. The suggestion that Judaism also knows of a third category, duties a man has to himself is comparatively late, see e.g. *Maharsha* to B.K. 30a and Phineas Elijah b. Meir Hurwitz: *Sefer Ha-Berit*, Part II, *Maamar* 13, Chapter 25, pp. 330–331. Maimonides (*Guide*, III, 35) does refer to the aim of self-improvement and self-protection as the aim of many of the *mitzvot* but identifies these *mitzvot* with the Rabbinic category of *mitzvot* between man and God.

A perhaps not unhelpful way of studying Jewish ethics is to examine in detail the formulation of the Jewish ethical life as it appears in the writings of Moses Maimonides and to note this teacher's special bias and how it differs from the treatment of the same theme in the works of other Jewish moralists. Maimonides attaches so much significance to this aspect of Judaism that he devotes a whole section of his gigantic Code, at the beginning of the work, to its systematic exposition. The seven chapters of this section—*Hilkhot Deot*—draw freely on Rabbinic teachings but Maimonides' own attitudes are powerfully influenced by Greek ideas so that what we have, in fact, here is an attempted synthesis between the Jewish ethical ideal and the Greek.

Maimonides (*Deot* 1: 1) begins by observing that human beings differ in temperament; one man is choleric, flying easily into a rage, while another is so serene in mind that he never loses his temper. One man is vain and conceited, another extremely modest. One man is lustful, his appetites always unsatisfied; another has a pure heart so that even his immediate physical appetites awaken in him no strong desire. One man is greedy for gain; another is perfectly content with the little he has. One man is miserly, prepared to go hungry rather than spend his money; another is a spendthrift, utterly careless about his finances. Similar, with regard to other character traits: for example, frivolity and melancholy; generosity and the lack of it; cruelty and kindliness; timidity and courage. In all these men differ.

Deot 1 : 2. There are, too, traits of character in which a balance is achieved between the two extremes. Character traits are partly inherent in man; he may be born with them, or he may have a natural propensity for them. But it is also possible for a man to acquire character traits by learning from the example of others or by reflection and training.

Deot 1 : 3-4. The two extremes of every character trait should be avoided. If a man finds that either by nature or through habit he has a tendency towards one of the extremes he should try to come nearer to the right way, the middle way. In order to be whole a man should always assess where he stands, striving always to avoid extremes of character. For instance, he should not allow himself to be readily provoked to anger but should at the same time avoid the cultivation of a corpse-like indifference to insult. He should only have strong desires for those things his body needs for survival and should only toil in order to satisfy his immediate wants. He should be neither miserly nor over-generous but should give to charity as much as he can afford. He should be neither frivolous nor sad but quietly serene. This is the way of the wise.

Deot 1 : 5. A man whose character is nicely balanced in this way is called a sage. But he is not a saint. The saints do tend to go to the extreme to a certain degree and it is in this that their saintliness consists.

Deot 1 :6. Man is obliged to follow the middle way. As the Rabbis say[1] in teaching the imitation of God: "Just as God is called 'gracious' be thou gracious; just as He is called 'compassionate' be thou compassionate; just as He is called 'holy' be thou holy." This is why the prophets speak of the attributes of God, calling Him longsuffering, abounding in lovingkindness, just, upright, perfect, strong and so forth, in order that we might recognise these as worthwhile. Man

1. *Sifre, Ekev,* 49.

234 A JEWISH THEOLOGY

is obliged to make these traits his own so as to come to resemble his Maker so far as this is humanly possible.

Maimonides relies here on the Rabbinic ideal of *Imitatio Dei* but it is, of course, extremely doubtful if the Rabbis had in mind anything like the cultivation of the golden mean of which Maimonides speaks. It might be here remarked that in the Kabbalah the doctrine of *Imitatio Dei* is taken far more literally. Since man is mirrored on the pattern of the worlds on high[2] each of his character traits is the counterpart on earth of some entity in the Sefirotic realm. By bringing it into play in a spirit of devotion to God he really does *imitate* God and causes particular illuminations to flow from on high. For example, when man practices lovingkindness he mirrors forth the *Sefirah* of *Hesed* and assists it, as it were, to function for the benefit of creation. When he strives for wisdom he resembles the *Sefirah* of *Hokhmah* and so forth. R. Moses Cordovero's little book of devotion: *Tomer Devorah* ("The Palm Tree of Deborah") is the classical statement of the Kabbalistic view on ethics. In the chapters of this book Cordovero describes how man is to live on the pattern of the Sefirotic realm.

Deot 1: 7. The performance of good deeds is the key to character formation. By acting upon a particular mood of character one acquires this mood for oneself so that eventually it becomes part of the character and eventually the deeds it normally gives rise to follow automatically and without effort.

Deot 2: 1–2. Defects of character, like physical ailments, may at times require drastic methods of treatment. Although extremes are normally to be rejected, the only way a man with a natural tendency towards one extreme can heal himself is to go for a time to the opposite extreme until the balance is achieved. Maimonides' commentators give the illustration of a bamboo cane that is bent. The only way to make it straight is to bend it in the opposite direction.

Deot 2: 3. However, valuable though the middle way is, it is to be rejected with regard to anger and pride. Here it is not enough for man to avoid the extremes of anger and pride but he should avoid any semblance of these ugly traits. Even when it is necessary for a parent, for example, to display anger in order to train his children in the right way, it should be a simulated not a real anger. This is why Scripture says of Moses not simply that he was humble but that he was *very* humble. (Num. 12: 3).

2. See *supra*, p. 29.

Deot 2: 4–5. The cultivation of silence is extremely helpful and is essential if wisdom is to be acquired. A man should train himself to speak only when it is absolutely necessary, i.e. to satisfy his needs or in order to impart wisdom. Even when imparting wisdom, a man should see to it that what he says has much content but little quantity. Where the quantity exceeds the content it is folly.

Deot 2: 6. A man should be sincere and mean what he says. He should never fool others by indulging in pretence. For instance, he should not invite guests to his home knowing full well that they will not come. He should not pretend to his guests that he has opened a barrel of wine in their honour when it was his intention to open it in any event. Even a single false word is forbidden. A man should always have true lips, a firm spirit and a heart free of all deceit and trickery.

Deot 2: 7. A man should neither be frivolous and lightheaded nor sad and miserable but always in a joyous frame of mind, welcoming others with a cheerful countenance. He should not be too ambitious but neither should he be lazy that he does no work. He should do a little work or business in order to earn a living and devote the rest of his time to the study of the Torah, rejoicing all the while in the little he has. He should not be cantankerous nor envious nor lustful nor should he run after fame. The Rabbis say[3] that envy, lust and ambition take a man from the world. To sum it all up, a man should always go in the middle way and all his character traits should be nicely balanced. As Solomon said: "Balance the path of thy feet and let all thy ways be established" (Prov. 4: 26).

Deot 3: 1. A man should not say, however, that since envy, lust, ambition and so forth are bad he will live as a hermit apart from the world, abstaining from meat and wine, living a celibate existence in a frugal dwelling and wearing sackcloth and ashes. This way is bad, too, and one who follows it is called a sinner. It is enough if man abstains from those things that are forbidden by the Torah. He should not afflict his body by fasting. Concerning this Solomon said: "Be not righteous overmuch; neither make thyself overwise; why shouldest thou destroy thyself" (Eccl. 7: 16).

Deot 3: 2–3. Whatever man does should be God–orientated.[4] Even when he attends to his physical needs it should not be solely for the

---

3. Avot 4: 21.   4. See *supra*, pp. 167–173.

sake of pleasure, but for the purpose of having a healthy body with which to serve God. Consequently, a man should look after his health and not indulge his appetites when to do so will harm him. One who follows this way serves God all the time. Maimonides then appends a further chapter which treats of the kind of conduct conducive to health. Naturally the details are based on the state of medicine in Maimonides' day. He concludes by citing the Talmudic saying[5] that a scholar must not reside in a town which has no resident doctor.

Deot 4. This chapter is devoted to the special type of conduct expected of the sage. The sage should behave differently from the ordinary run of men in that everything he does should be refined and perfect. For instance, the sage should never be a glutton. He should eat only to keep himself healthy and should abstain from inessential food. He should try so far as possible only to eat at his own table. It goes without saying that the sage should only drink wine as an aid to the digestive processes, never for the sake of intoxication. He should only have marital relations on the eve of the Sabbath and should be circumspect even then, indulging in no foul conversation. He may sport with his wife in order to awaken her desire but should be shy even when performing the act and should separate himself from it as soon as he can. A scholar who conducts himself in this way will have refined children worthy of attaining to high degrees of wisdom and piety, but one who behaves as do the ordinary folk who walk in darkness will have sons who are like them. The sage should behave modestly even in the privy. The sage should never raise his voice when conversing with others but, on the other hand, he should not speak so softly so as to give the impression that he is too proud to talk to anyone. He should be the first to greet others and should only speak well of others, never ill. He should love peace and pursue it. If he sees that his words of rebuke will be effective he should utter them, otherwise he should remain silent. The sage should have no stain on his garments. He should wear neither splendid clothes nor shabby ones but of a moderate type, clean and dignified. He should avoid the faintest trace of scandal so that, for example, he should not go out alone at night. The right way for the sage is first to acquire a livelihood, then build a house and then marry. He should be prudent in his business dealings. He should not, for example, sell a corn-producing field in order to buy a house or a house in order to buy furniture. His aim in business should be to turn that which goes to waste into permanent capital. All his business dealings should be engaged in with complete honesty. When he says "Yes" or "No" he should mean what he says. He should never cause harm to others and it goes without saying that he should never deprive another of his livelihood. To sum it up, he should be of those who are persecuted not of those who persecute, of those who are insulted not of those who insult others. Of such a sage Scripture says: "And He said unto me: 'Thou art My servant, Israel in whom I will be glorified' " (Is. 49: 3).

Deot 6–7. In these final chapters Maimonides treats of further general rules of ethical conduct. Loving one's neighbour means speaking well of him and having due respect for his property. One who gains fame for himself at the expense of his neighbour's disgrace has no share in the World to Come.[6] Especial care must be taken never to offend strangers, widows and orphans. It is strictly forbidden to speak maliciously of others or to be a tale-bearer or to take revenge or foster hatred. If a man has been wronged by another he should blot out the feelings of resentment from his heart. Only in this way can society be established and men live in peace with one another.

The above survey of Maimonides' ideal of the ethical life serves to demonstrate its power and nobility. It is a picture of life as lived by the Jewish sage; balanced, wise, kindly and life-promoting. Whether this is entirely relevant to the life of the Jew today is another matter. For all his greatness and towering genius, Maimonides was a child of his age. The noble life as conceived by the mediaeval moralists cannot be, as it stands, the ideal for life today and a number of weighty objections can be argued against uncritical emulation.

For one thing Maimonides' "middle way" owes a great deal to Greek influence. The Greek ideal of moderation in all things is based on the idea of harmony. Beauty is the result of a correct harmony in which everything is given its due weight but none to excess. S. D. Luzzatto in the last century went so far as to accuse Maimonides of what he called "Atticism", arguing that the Jewish ethical ideal demands an excess of generosity. It is the ideal of Abraham who sat at the door of his tent ready to welcome the hungry travellers and running out to meet them, not the prudential assessment of how far one should go in extending generosity to others. In fairness to

6. Jer. T. Hag. 2: 1.

Maimonides he has stated that the middle way is not for the saints. But Luzzatto would disagree that it is an ideal at all, to be followed by Maimonides' "sage" for example. The wisdom of Judaism demands an uncalculating type of generosity and a more spontaneous reaction to the call of the needy. In fact, it can be argued that Maimonides' whole attempt to record the ethical life in the form of rules and regulations and as part of a Code of Law is bound to fail precisely because, though idealistic sayings and maxims can act as an inspiration to character formation, by being frozen into unbending rules they destroy the freshness and spontaneity which are of the essence of the free-choosing good character.

Nor is Maimonides free from the idea of a dichotomy between body and soul. For all his rejection of the hermit ideal, the pleasures of the body are for him only a means of keeping body and soul together. The doctrine of doing things "for the sake of Heaven" comes very close, for him, to a rejection of any idea that the bodily appetites are themselves a divine gift. His attitude to sex is especially uncompromising. There is not the faintest trace of any notion of sex as a means of husband and wife expressing their love for one another. In a word Maimonides' attitude is too detached, too coldly inhuman to serve us as the ideal. The Maimonidean ideal, too, has nothing to say about human culture, art, literature and music for example. Maimonides' sage is either occupied in the accumulation of wisdom or engages in business or a profession to keep himself and his family. The question of the use of leisure does not arise for him because evidently he recognises no such concept.

Sagely conduct as described by Maimonides is sublime in its deliniation of the life of wisdom but is at the same time condescending and patronising. There is no suggestion that the sage has anything at all to learn from the simple virtues of the "people who walk in darkness". The sage must keep himself aloof from the common folk, distinguished from them in dress, speech and conduct. A case can perhaps still be made out for the intellectual and spiritual aristocracy favoured by Maimonides, but class distinctions even of this kind are viewed with suspicion today and, on the whole, simply do not speak to our situation. If they move us at all it is to protest.

In short, the Maimonidean ideal may win our admiration. It hardly succeeds in attraction. Maimonides would no doubt say that this is because we are "sick of soul". As he writes at the beginning of this section: "Those who are sick in body taste the bitter as sweet and the sweet as bitter. Some are so sick that they long for uneatable things such as dust and charcoal and they loathe in proportion to their malady good food such as bread and meat. In the same way those who are sick in soul love false opinions and long to hold them. They hate the good way and are too lazy to walk in it and in proportion to their degree of sickness find it exceedingly hard to walk therein." But for many today Maimonides' ideal is too narrow. It stresses too much the conflict between the world and the soul and tends too much to imply that God is at war with His creation.

If the Maimonidean sage were alive today he might occasionally watch television but only the educational programmes. He might even go to the theatre and cinema but only if the performance promised to raise significant moral issues never if the prospect were that of entertainment pure and simple. He would read scientific treatises and works of edification and erudition but never thrillers or works of humour. It is uncertain if he would ever go to concerts and to the opera. He would have little appreciation of the delights of good food, wine or conversation. It is doubtful if he would ever unbend to tell jokes. His sympathy for the afflicted would be real and sincere and he would sacrifice much to help them in a disinterested way but they would probably miss the warmth which stems from the fellowship of men as equals. He would be in short a prig.

This is precisely the problem in the ethical sphere for moderns. The Jew of today acknowledges the great Jewish values taught in the Jewish classics. He may be prepared to follow these even if they are at variance with the civilisation in which he finds himself. He yields to none in his admiration for the values taught in the Jewish tradition— that justice, compassion, righteousness, kindliness and the pursuit of holiness are divine imperatives. But, at the same time, he knows of another set of values which have been particularly stressed in the Western world: tolerance, artistic creativity, the use of scientific method, social welfare, political endeavour, chivalry and the like, and he does not find that these are always emphasised in the traditional thinkers. What is he to do in order to achieve a life of wholeness and integrity? How is he to do justice both to the demands of the past and the claims of the present? Can there be a successful marriage between a theocratic view of life and the ideals of secular society?

There is certainly no easy solution to these problems. They belong to the tensions with which the modern Jew must live. Ultimately we all make up our minds on ethical questions by means of the general attitude we have towards life's meaning and this in turn is an amalgam of complex ideas we have inherited as part of our cultural background. But the Jewish tradition is still a powerful guide containing an abundance of wisdom and stressing those values which have imparted quality to Jewish life at its best. A not too unsatisfactory way of trying to make this clearer is to examine how an ethical problem is actually dealt with in the Responsa literature. We take as one example among many a recent Responsum by Rabbi M. J. Breisch of Zurich.[7]

The following question was put to Rabbi Breisch by an Orthodox Jewish doctor. A young man of twenty, suffering, unknown to him or to his family, from cancer, became engaged to be married. Should the doctor inform the young woman of the truth? Rabbi Breisch came to the conclusion that the doctor is obliged to tell the young woman the truth. The verse: "Neither shalt thou stand idly by the blood of thy neighbour" (Lev. 19: 16) teaches, according to the Rabbis,[8] that if one sees a neighbour floundering in the sea one must save him. Consequently, Maimonides[9] rules: "If a man sees his neighbour drowning in the sea or that robbers are making ready to attack him or that a wild beast is about to pounce on him and is able to save him, either by his own efforts or by hiring others to help, and does not do so he offends against the verse: 'Neither shalt thou stand idly by the blood of thy neighbour'." Surely, argues Rabbi Breisch, this covers our case. Furthermore, there is the prohibition of placing a stumbling-block before a blind man, i.e. by allowing the girl to enter blindly into a marriage which is bound to cause her severe distress. These prohibitions override any considerations of professional etiquette.

Now the argument of Rabbi Breisch seems most reasonable and we can accept it as supported entirely by our commonsense and general ethical outlook. But in that case what is added by finding the rule in the Jewish tradition? The answer is surely that it is encouraging to know that whatever we decide on such matters has a long history and that we are following in a rich tradition of questing for the will of

7. *Helkat Yaakov*, Vol. III, No. 136, pp. 257–258.
8. Sanh. 73a.
9. *Yad, Rotzeah* 1: 14.

God. Our "commonsense" view itself is partly fashioned, partly reinforced, by the truth as taught by the tradition.

What we are touching on here, is, in fact, the perennial question of the relationship between religion and ethics. Modern man asks: "Why is it necessary for a revealed religion to tell me to do good; do I not understand this for myself? While admitting that it is often difficult to live under the requirements of moral duty, would I not still strive to do so even if I had no belief in revelation?"

This argument amounts to the assertion that man's innate moral sense is a sufficient guide for life's conduct. To make the same demand in the name of religion is superfluous.

There are many moves open to the believer in revealed religion. One is to claim the futility of referring to good deeds without consideration of God's revealed will since good deeds *are* good because God has so declared. Revelation is needed to define the good.

The objection to this approach is that it empties the term "good" of all its content. If a course of action is to be followed because God wills it, nothing is gained by calling such a cause "good".

The believer may reply that it is good to carry out God's will. But this can only mean that the "good" is not identical with God's will for otherwise it would be tautologous to say "it is good to do God's will". There is no escaping the conclusion that a thing is not good because it is in the Torah. It is in the Torah because it is good.

But in that case what is gained by having it in the Torah, the record of revelation? At this stage the believer may reply that although revelation does not function in order to define good conduct, it does serve as its guarantee.

Revelation, it can be argued, provides the momentum for the good life. Without revelation men would know what the good is but would they pursue it? Would not their selfish grasping instincts prevail? The main objection to this is that it seems to imply, what is demonstrably false, namely, that the atheist is always vicious. Not is there much truth in the corollary that the believer is always virtuous.

A less vulnerable version of the argument is that the influence of revelation is to be seen not so much in the ethical life of the individual as in that of society. Religion, speaking in God's name, has created and sustained the background against which moral values can flourish.

The Hebrew Bible, with its strong insistence on justice and mercy, has fostered in Western civilisation a climate of opinion favourable to virtue and hostile to evil. There can, indeed, be a virtuous atheist but he is living on the spiritual capital of believing ancestors.

There is much truth in this yet it does not provide a complete answer to our inquiry. Even in the West, to say nothing of other civilisations, some of the more important social reforms have been achieved through the efforts of avowed secularists, while the social conscience of believers has not always been beyond reproach.

Another reply is to argue that religion has little to do with being good in the ethical sense. Revelation is not for the purpose of teaching men how to behave well towards their fellow-men but how to worship God. Religion, in this view, is chiefly a matter of prayer and ritual, of meditation and contemplation, of a soul alone with God.

This kind of answer cannot possibly be acceptable to the believing Jew. Micah tells us that God does desire men to do justly and to love mercy and this teaching is supported by all the prophetic voices in Israel. The Rabbis constantly remind the Jew that in addition to man's duties towards God there are God-ordained duties to men and that in many respects the latter are the more significant.

The most satisfying argument for the need for revelation in the ethical sphere is to appreciate that it opens up a new dimension for ethical man.

Revelation informs us that by living a life of honesty and integrity, by having a proper regard for his fellows and by practising righteousness and loving mercy, a man comes to have not only a better relationship with other human beings but a deeper relationship with God. To be good one does not need revelation but it is important to know through revelation what God would have us be.

Judaism speaks of the nearness of God as the ultimate aim and it teaches that man is never nearer to God than when he responds in love and sympathy to the needs of others. "Just as He is called 'gracious' be thou gracious. Just as He is called 'compassionate' be thou compassionate."

CHAPTER SEVENTEEN

SIN AND REPENTANCE

IN the Rabbinic scheme sin is *averah*, from the root *avar*, "to pass over", i.e. a rejection of God's will. Man is thought of as being pulled in two different directions; the "good inclination", *yetzer ha-tov*, pulling him in the direction of the good, the "evil inclination", *yetzer ha-ra*, towards evil. Sin is the result of allowing the *yetzer ha-ra* to gain the upper hand. The sinner finds atonement for his sins by repenting of them. The usual Rabbinic word for "repentence" is *teshuvah*, meaning "turning", i.e. from sin to God. Repentence has the power of erasing the sin as if it had not been committed. These ideas had the greatest influence on Jewish thought and they form the vocabulary of all subsequent discussions on these themes in Jewish literature. It is essential that they be examined in detail.[1]

In the legal formulation of the Talmud and Codes there are sins of commission and omission or, in the Rabbinic terminology, the transgression of a negative precept and the failure to perform a positive precept.[2] The former is more serious than the latter.[3] But in certain circumstances a positive precept pushes aside a negative one if this is the only way in which the former can be carried out.[4] If the positive precept has to be carried out at a certain time and that time has passed, the omission cannot be rectified, e.g. failure to recite the Shema on a particular day. To this is applied the verse: "That which is crooked

---

1. On the subject of this chapter see: Kohler: *Jewish Theology*, Part II, pp. 238–255; Schechter: *Some Aspects of Rabbinic Theology*, pp. 219–343; Buchler: *Studies in Sin and Atonement*; G. F. Moore: *Judaism*, Vol. I, Part III, pp. 445–552; Abraham Cohen: *Everyman's Talmud*, pp. 88–110; Montefiore and Loewe: *A Rabbinic Anthology*, pp. 295–333; H. I. Abramovitz: *Hekhal Ha-Teshuvah*; Menahem b. Solomon Meiri of Perpignan: *Book of Repentance (Heb.)*.
2. Mishnah, Yoma 8: 8.
3. Yoma 85b and 86a.
4. Yev. 3b.

cannot be made straight, and that which is wanting cannot be numbered" (Eccl. 1: 15).[5] Sins involving the transgression of negative precepts can be of two kinds—offences against God and offences against one's neighbour. The Day of Atonement brings forgiveness for sins committed against God, i.e. for purely religious offences. It only brings forgiveness for offences against other human beings if the wrong done to the victim has first been put right.[6]

The *yetzer ha-ra* is frequently identified particularly with the sex instinct but the term is used, too, for man's physical appetites in general and for his aggressive desires and ambitions. It is more correctly identified with the force in man which drives him to gratify his instincts and ambitions. Although it is called the "evil inclination", because it can easily lead man to wrong-doing, it is essential to life in that it provides life with its driving power. Were it not for the *yetzer ha-ra*, remarks a Rabbinic Midrash,[7] no man would build a house or marry or have children or engage in commerce. This is why Scripture says: "And God saw everything that He had made and behold, it was very good" (Gen. 1: 31). "Good" refers to the "good inclination"; "very good" to the "evil inclination". It is possible that the meaning of this homily is that life without the driving force of the *yetzer ha-ra* would no doubt be good but it would be a colourless, uncreative, pallid kind of good. That which makes life *very* good is the capacity of man to struggle against his environment and this is impossible without egotistic as well as altruistic, aggressive as well as peaceful, instincts. In similar vein is the curious legend[8] that the "Men of the Great Synagogue" (Ezra and his associates) wanted to kill the *yetzer ha-ra*, who, in this legend is personified. The *yetzer ha-ra* warned them that if they were successful the "world would go down". They, therefore, imprisoned him for three days, and then searched all the land for a new-laid egg and could not find one. Instead of killing him they put out his eyes so that he could no longer entice men to incest.

Demythologising this passage, the very interesting thought emerges that the "Men of the Great Synagogue", despite their mighty efforts to further and establish Judaism were not permitted to be so "successful" in their fight against the evil inclination as to destroy it

5. Ber. 26a.
6. Mishnah Yoma, 8: 9.
7. Gen. R. 9: 7
8. Yoma 69.b.

completely; for then the world itself would die. They, however, succeeded in combating the grosser forms of depravity. Israel is no longer tempted to commit incest or, as the same passage declares, to worship idols. This is, possibly, why the Rabbis refer to the *yetzer ha-ra* as the "leaven in the dough".[9] Although the leaven can be responsible for over-fermentation, without it the dough would be unpalatable.[10]

The Rabbinic view is, then, realistic. Man is engaged in a constant struggle against the evil within him but he can control it if he so desires. The means of control are provided by the Torah and its precepts. One of the most remarkable Rabbinic passages in this connection states that the Torah is the antidote to the poison of the *yetzer ha-ra*.[11] The meaning appears to be that when man submits to the discipline provided by the Torah and when he studies the Torah to avail himself of its illumination, he becomes free of morbid guilt feelings, his life unclouded by the fear that the evil within him will drag him down to bring about his ruin. There is no need for him to flee from life, no need (to use a much-discussed modern term) to reject the "secular city". The famous parable told in this passage is of a king who struck his son, later urging the son to keep a plaster on the wound. While the wound is protected by the plaster the prince may eat and drink whatever he desires without coming to harm. Only if the plaster is removed will the wound fester if the prince indulges his appetites. God has "wounded" man by creating him with the evil inclination. But the Torah is the plaster on the wound, which prevents it from festering and enables him to embrace life without fear.

It follows from the above that for the Rabbis the struggle against the *yetzer ha-ra* is never-ending in this life. Nowhere in the Rabbinic literature is there the faintest suggestion that it is possible for man to destroy the *yetzer ha-ra* completely in this life. (Eschatological references to the destruction of the *yetzer ha-ra* are not, of course, relevant. The "World to Come" is not the world as we know it.) The hero is, for the Rabbis, one who "subdues" his *yetzer ha-ra*,[12]

9. Ber. 17a.
10. See Schechter: *Some Aspects of Rabbinic Theology*, pp. 264f.
11. Kidd. 30b.
12. Avot 4: 1.

one who exercises severe self-control and does not yield to temptation. It is not given to any man to slay the *yetzer ha-ra*.

In the Rabbinic literature there are no references either to "breaking the *yetzer ha-ra*", *shevirat ha-yetzer*. The Zohar (I, 202a) observes that there is nothing which can succeed in *breaking* the *yetzer ha-ra* other than the Torah. In the same passage of the Zohar it is said that if a man is unsuccessful in his struggle with the *yetzer ha-ra* he should reflect on the day of his death in order to acquire a broken heart. The Zohar continues: "For the evil inclination resides only in a place where there is the joy of wine and of pride so that when it finds such a broken heart it departs from man and no longer resides with him. Therefore he should remind himself of the day of the death and he should break (= mortify) his body and then the evil inclination will depart. Come and see! The good inclination wants the joy of the Torah but the evil inclination wants the joy of wine, fornication and pride. Consequently, a man should always be in dread of that great day, the day of judgement, the day of reckoning when nothing can act as a shield for a man except the good deeds he performed in this world." For the Hasidic view see the lengthy discussion in R. Schneor Zalman's *Tanya*, Part I, Chapters 1–16. Here it is stated that the perfectly righteous man (*tzaddik gamur*) has no *yetzer ha-ra* "because he has killed it by his fasting" (Chapter 1, p. 10). But even R. Schneor Zalman considers such a stage to be quite extraordinary. Only a very few saints have ever attained to this degree of "righteousness". Most men belong to the category of "average men" (*benonim*) in whom the *yetzer ha-ra* is a fully active as the *yetzer ha-tov*.

Do the Rabbis know anything of the doctrine of original sin? It has been said in this connection that the difference between Judaism and Christianity is that Christianity teaches that man sins because he is a sinner while Judaism teaches that man is a sinner because he sins. Whether such a distinction is much more than a clever play on words is doubtful. It is perhaps true that Judaism places less emphasis on man's sinfulness (though even this requires considerable qualification[13]) and it is true that the Christian doctrine of the Fall[14] and the

13. On this see especially the remarks of A. J. Heschel: *A Hebrew Evaluation of Reinhold Niebuhr*.
14. That Chapter 3 of the book of Genesis begins with the words: "Now the serpent . . ." only means that an artificial division has been imposed on the narrative. Classical Judaism knows nothing of the present chapter divisions of the Bible. These were taken over from the Christians for the purpose of convenient reference in disputations, see S. Weingarten's article in *Sinai*, Vol. XXI, Feb. 1958, pp. 281f. The two passages sometimes quoted for Rabbinic parallels to the doctrine of original sin are: "Four died through the serpent's machinations" (Shab.

need for a Saviour have no place in the Jewish scheme. But it is surely a mistaken view of Judaism that it has an over-optimistic notion of man's capacity for avoiding sin. That the *yetzer ha-ra* is a potent force from which no man is free is at the heart of the Rabbinic teachings on sin and repentance and, after all, the idea that man's heart is "evil from his youth" is found in the Hebrew Bible.

Although the word *teshuvah* is not found in the Bible words formed from the same root and expressing the same idea of return to God are numerous. The prophetic appeal is for Israel to give up its sins and return to God. "Yet the Lord forewarned Israel, and Judah, by the hand of every prophet, and of every seer, saying: 'Turn ye from your evil ways, and keep My commandments and My statutes, according to all the laws which I commanded your fathers, and which I sent to you by the hand of My servants the prophets'" (2 Kings 17: 13). The call for Israel to return to God is found in Jeremiah (3: 12–14; 22; 4: 1; 15: 19; 18: 1; 25: 5; 26: 3; 35: 15; 36: 3; 7); in Ezekiel, who stresses in particular individual repentance (3: 17–18; 13: 22; 14: 6; 18: 21–23; 27–28; 30–32; 33: 7–19; 36: 31–32; 42: 10); in Deutero-Isaiah (44: 22; 55: 6–7); in Hosea (3: 5; 6: 1; 12: 7; 14: 2–3) in Joel (2: 12–14); in Zechariah (1: 3–4); in Malachi (3: 7). The book of Jonah is devoted chiefly to this theme. Even the men of Nineveh are called upon to repent and their repentance is accepted by God. The call to repent is sounded especially in the book of Deuteronomy (4: 29–30; 30: 1–14). The book of Lamentations concludes with a cry to God to bring about a reconciliation between Him and Israel (5: 21, see 3: 39–42). There are numerous penitential prayers in the Bible (Ex. 32: 31–32; 34: 9; Num. 14: 17–20; Deut. 9: 18–20 and 25–27; 21: 8; Ps. 19: 13–14; 25: 7–8 and 11 and 15; 32: 1–5; 38: 2–4; 41:5; 51: 3–19; 65: 3–4; 79: 8–9; 85: 1–8; 130; Kings 8: 30–50; 2 Chron. 6: 21–40; Is. 64: 8; Micah 7: 18–20; Daniel 9: 4–20; Ezra 9: 6–15; Neh. 1: 4–11; 9: 17–33).

There occurs in the Jerusalem Talmud[15] the following penetrating account of how the Rabbis saw the efficacy of repentance. "They asked of wisdom: What is the punishment of the sinner? Wisdom replied: 'Evil pursueth sinners' (Prov. 13:21). They asked of prophecy: What is the punishment of the sinner? Prophecy replied: 'The soul that sinneth it shall die' (Ezek. 18: 4). Then they asked of the Holy

---

55b) and "the serpent copulated with Eve and infected her with his filth" (Shab. 146a) but in these Israel is explicitly excluded from the serpent's machinations and his filth and the passages may be an intentional polemic against Christian views. See Urbach: *Hazal*, pp. 371–392.
15. Makk. 2: 6.

One, blessed be He: What is the punishment of the sinner? He replied: Let him repent and he will find atonement."

For the philosopher repentance is an irrational concept. Wrong-doing contains the germs of its own dissolution. Inexorable laws of cause and effect operate in the universe and the doom of the sinner is pronounced when he sins by the sinner himself. "Wisdom" must declare that "evil pursueth sinners". The prophet sees things in the starkest terms of good and evil. The prophet can in no way compromise with falsehood. The prophet can only warn against the severe consequences of sin. "The soul that sinneth it shall die." But God in His infinite mercy, so the passage implies, forgives the repentant sinner, disregarding, as it were, the rigor of the philosopher and the moral condemnation of the prophet. "Let him repent and he will find atonement."

The Rabbis have much to say on what constitutes repentance. Their views are thus summarised by Maimonides[16] with several additions of his own.

"If a man transgresses, wittingly or unwittingly, any precept of the Torah, whether a positive precept or a negative, and repents and turns away from his wrongdoing, he is obliged to confess his sins to God, blessed be He . . . Confession of this kind is a positive precept. How does a man confess his sins? He says: 'O God! I have sinned, I have committed iniquity, I have transgressed before Thee by doing such-and-such. Behold now I am sorry for what I have done and am ashamed and I shall never do it again.' This basically is what is involved in repentance but the more one confesses at length the better it is . . . Nowadays when the Temple no longer stands so that we do not have the altar of atonement (i.e. we can no longer bring a sin-offering) only repentance remains. Repentance atones for all sins. Even of a man who has behaved wickedly all his life, nothing of his wickedness is mentioned if he repents at the end . . . The Day of Atonement brings pardon to those who repent . . . What constitutes true repentance? If the sinner has the opportunity of committing once again the sinful act and it is quite possible for him to repeat it and yet he refrains from so doing because he has repented—for example, a man cohabited unlawfully with a woman and after a time found himself alone with her again and he still loves her and is still as healthy as ever and it takes place in the same province in which he had previously sinned with her

16. *Yad, Teshuvah* 1–2.

and yet he refrains from repeating the transgression—he is a true penitent . . . But if he only repents when he is old and when he is no longer in any event able to do what he had done previously, even though this hardly qualifies as the best form of repentance, yet it is still effective and he is considered to be a penitent. Even one who had sinned all his days but repented on the day of his death so that he died in a state of repentance, all his sins are pardoned . . . What is repentance? It is that the sinner relinquishes his sin, removing it from his thoughts and resolving never to do it again . . . and he should feel remorse for his past misdeeds . . . so that the One who knows all the heart's secrets can testify that never again will he commit this sin . . . And it is necessary for the sinner to confess with his lips, expressing verbally those matters upon which his heart has resolved . . . It belongs to the way of repentance that the penitent cries out constantly to God in weeping and supplication, giving alms as much as he can afford, keeping himself far from the sinful thing, changing his name, as if to say, I am another, not the one who did these things, changing all his deeds for good deeds and for the righteous way, and exiling himself from his home since exile atones for sin in that it forces the exile to humble himself and to be modest and self-effacing. It is very praiseworthy for the penitent sinner to confess his sins in public, informing others of the offences he has committed against his neighbour, saying to them: 'Verily, I have sinned against So-and-so and have done such-and-such to him but now I am sorry and I repent.' Whoever is too proud to confess his sins to others but keeps them to himself is not a true penitent . . . This does not apply to offences against God. Here it is brazen if one reveals them to others. He should repent before God, declaring his sins in detail to Him alone, confessing in public only that he has sinned against God without giving any details . . . Repentance or the Day of Atonement can only win pardon for offences against God such as eating forbidden food or illegal cohabitation and so forth. But there is no forgiveness for offences against one's neighbour such as assault or injury or theft and so forth until the wrong done is put right. Even after a man has paid the restitution due to the victim he must beg his forgiveness. Even if all he did was to taunt his neighbour he must appease him and beg his forgiveness. If the victim does not wish to forgive him he should go to him in the company of three friends and they should beg him to grant his pardon. If their efforts were of no avail he should repeat the procedure with a second

and a third group but if the victim still persists in his attitude he
should be left alone and the victim is then sinful in refusing his
pardon . . . It is forbidden for a man to be so cruel as to refuse to
forgive those who have wronged him but he should forgive them
wholeheartedly and willingly. Even if they have wronged him
grieviously he should not take revenge or foster hatred. This is the
way of the seed of Israel and their trusted heart. But the heathen of
uncircumcised heart are different, their wrath being preserved for
ever . . . If the victim has died in the meantime he should bring ten
men to his grave and declare: 'I have sinned against the Lord God of
Israel and against this person whom I have wronged in such-and-such
a way.' If he owed him money because of the wrong done he should
return it to the victim's heirs. If these are unknown he should hand
over the money to the Court."

Maimonides here states the classical Rabbinic view that repentance
is effected by a sincere resolve to give up the sin and by confession and
restitution. There is no mention of physical mortification in order to
win pardon. The need for such mortification as a part of the act of
repentance came into Jewish thought in the circle of Judah the Saint
of Regensburg in the twelfth or thirteenth centuries. The self-tortures
required are detailed, for example, in the ethical work *Rokeah* by
Eleazar of Worms (d. 1238). Baer and others have noted the strong
influence of Christian monasticism of the period on the men of this
circle.[17] Among other practices they used to roll naked in the snow in
the depths of winter, smear their bodies with honey and allow themselves to be stung by bees, and fast for days on end.

While it is not unknown down to the present day for Rabbis to
impose penances on repentant sinners, the general tendency is to be
content with sincere and unconditional repentance. The teachers of
the Hasidic movement were especially opposed to the mortification
of the flesh as a means of repentance.

17. See the Chapter on *Hasidism in Mediaeval Germany* in Scholem's *Major Trends*,
pp. 80–118. Cf. the list of works given in *Magen Avraham* to *Orah Hayim* 203.
The Rokeah, I, mentions four types of *teshuvah*: (1) *ha-baah*, "coming", i.e. when
the sinner comes across the same opportunity as before to sin but refrains from
so soing; (2) *ha-gader*, "the fence", in which the sinner abstains even from legitimate things which are in some way connected with his sin: (3) *ha-mishkal*, "the
balance", i.e. the sinner balances his pleasure in the act of sin by suffering pain
in mortification of the flesh: (4) *ha-katuv*, "scripture", the sinner torments himself
with tortures which have affinities to that type of punishment which Scripture
records for his sin.

The eighteenth century Halakhic authority R. Ezekiel Landau of
Prague has a Responsum on this question,[18] much-quoted in the
subsequent literature on the subject. A man who had committed a
serious sin repeatedly for three years turned to the Rabbi for advice
on how to find pardon. The Rabbi's reply is interesting: "You have
asked me a hard question since it is not my habit to reply to questions
put to me unless I can find the principles discussed in the Talmud and
the Codes. It is only in the moralistic literature that one finds references to these matters and most of what they have to say comes
from theories which are from the belly and have no foundation, each
work relying on the others without any basis whatsoever. It is not
my practice to peruse these works but I recall them from the days of
my youth. Hence I say that all this would be relevant only if repentance cannot be achieved except through fasting. But the truth of the
matter is that fasting is only secondary and basically repentance consists of relinquishing the sin, confessing with a broken heart, and
sincere remorse." Rabbi Landau does not, however, reject entirely
the opinions of the *Rokeah* (discussed above) but adds that physical
mortification is not an end in itself but no more than a means of
attaining a broken heart, i.e. of expressing true remorse. He advises
the sinner to fast but especially to give charity which has great saving
power.

In a much more recent Responsum, Rabbi J. J. Weinberg[19]
discusses the case of a man who gave a lift in his automobile to a friend
who was killed in an accident to the automobile. Is the owner obliged
to subject himself to the kind of mortification mentioned by the
Rokeah? Rabbi Weinberg follows various predecessors in stating
that "nowadays" we do not have the physical strength to engage in
mortification of the flesh as atonement for sin. The man should redeem
his sin by giving a sum of money to the victim's heirs if they are poor;
otherwise he should donate the money to the Shaare Zedek hospital
in Jerusalem.

In addition to the many references to repentance in the writings of
the mediaeval Jewish teachers, there are, at least, two complete thirteenth century works devoted entirely to this theme. These are: *Shaare
Teshuvah*, "Gates of Repentance," by R. Jonah b. Abraham Gerondi
(d. 1263) and *Hibbur Ha-Teshuvah*, "Book on Repentance," by R.

18. *Noda Bihudah, Orah Hayim*. No. 35.
19. *Seride Esh*, Vol. III, No. 88, pp. 280–281.

Menahem b. Solomon Meiri of Perpignan (1249–1306). Meiri's book was in manuscript until its recent publication by Abraham Schreiber. It has been surmised,[20] though this is extremely unlikely, that Gerondi compiled his work as an act of personal penance for his part in the anti-Maimonides controversy. A brief summary of these two works can here be attempted.

Gerondi lists no less than 20 essential features of a sincere repentance.[21] These are: (1) remorse; (2) relinquishing the sin; (3) pain for the sin; (4) affliction of the body in fasting and weeping; (5) fear of the consequences of the sin and of repeating it; (6) shame for the sin; (7) submission to God in humility and contrition; (8) gentleness in future conduct; (9) breaking the physical lusts by asceticism; (10) the use by the sinner of that organ with which he sinned to do good, e.g. the mouth guilty of slander should utter words of Torah and prayer; (11) constant self-scrutiny; (12) reflection by the sinner on the punishment he deserves; (13) the treatment of minor sins as major; (14) confession; (15) prayer, especially for God to help the sinner to keep his resolve not to sin again; (16) putting right the sin, e.g. by compensating the victim of the sinner's malice; (17) almsgiving; (18) the sinner should ever be conscious of his sin; (19) to refrain from repeating the sinful act when the opportunity presents itself in exactly the same circumstances as before; (20) leading others away from sin.

Gerondi's asceticism is much in evidence throughout the book. Man should reflect on his approaching death and do all the good he can while there is still time, recognising that the pleasures of the world are vanity.[22] A man whom God has given understanding should consider that God has sent him into the world for no other purpose than to keep His commandments. He should, therefore, not open his eyes to do anything else than to carry out the tasks for which he has been sent here. Then when his end arrives he can return to God with song and everlasting joy. A faithful servant of a great king, sent by the king to perform a task for him in a distant land, has no thought for anything else until he returns to his master the king.

Gate III of the *Shaare Teshuvah* is devoted to a catalogue of all the sins a man can commit in order of severity. It is noteworthy that the

20. See *Jewish Encyclopedia*, Vol. V., p. 638 but see Y. Baer: *A History of the Jews in Christian Spain*, Vol. I. pp. 401–402.
21. *Shaare Teshuvah*, I, 10–50.
22. II, 15–34.

author calls attention and at length to the extreme seriousness of
the sins of speech, malicious slander and gossip, tale-bearing, insulting
others and embarrassing them and the like. Gate IV deals with how to
find pardon for sin. Some sins are so severe that atonement can only be
found for them in suffering. The sinner should rejoice in his sufferings,
accepting them in love. However, no excessive self-torment or
mortification is required. Instead of too much fasting for his sins the
sinner should help others and bring joy into their lives. He should
spend more time in the study of the Torah. He should practise self-
denial. If he does these things his sins will be pardoned.

Meiri, describing[23] his reason for compiling the work, observes
that a Christian scholar informed him that Christian authors express
their astonishment that Jews appear to have neglected entirely the
whole subject of repentance. Jews do not seem to be moved to
repentance by the sufferings which befall them, their hearts remain
unaffected, and they know nothing of confession. Among themselves the Christians attribute this neglect to the lack in Jewish
literature of any complete work on repentance. The Jewish teachings
on repentance are, indeed, many but they are scattered among the
classical works of the Jewish faith and no one has seen fit to collect
these in a comprehensive work on the subject. Meiri states that this
moved him to compile such a work even though he is aware of his
personal inadequacy for such a gigantic task.

The work is divided into two parts. Part I, entitled "Restoring the
Soul", deals with the mechanics of repentance. It is sub-divided into
two sections (maamarim), the first dealing with the main principles of
repentance, the second with the special season of repentance, the ten
days from Rosh Ha-Shanah to Yom Kippur, the first ten days of the
New Year. Part II, entitled "The Fall of Pride", deals with man's
sufferings, which lead him to repent of his sins. This is also divided
into two sections, the first dealing with the practice of fasting, the
second with the laws of mourning for departed relatives. Each section
is further sub-divided into chapters.

According to Meiri[24] four conditions are essential to repentance;

---

23. Introduction p. 2. While Meiri is correct in his observation that there was no
   complete work on *teshuvah* before his day, there are sections on the theme in
   Maimonides (as above) in Saadia *Beliefs and Opinions*, V. 5–8, and in Bahya,
   Duties of the Heart, Gate 7.

24. Part I, 1, Chapter 8, p. 183.

lacking any one of them repentance is incomplete. These are: (1) remorse for the sin committed; (2) resolve not to commit it again; (3) confession of the sin to God; (4) with regard to offences against other people, restitution and righting of the wrong. Meiri states that some authorities (Gerondi, for example, though Meiri does not refer to him by name) count giving up the sin as an essential condition of repentance but Meiri takes issue with this. Giving up the sin is not a condition of repentance but a synonym for it. The fulfilment of the four conditions Meiri records is what is involved in giving up the sin.

At the end of his lengthy work[25] Meiri gives the following short summary of the meaning of repentance as described in detail in the rest of the book. The first thing the sinner must know is that since he has been given free will he is responsible for the sins he has committed and will be punished for them in this world and the next. But if he repents sincerely, no matter how numerous and how severe his sins, his repentance will save him. Not every form of repentance is of equal value. The general principle is that the more repentance is the result of an authentic self-realisation that one has sinned and the less of external circumstances the higher the form of repentance. Even a deathbed repentance is efficacious if performed sincerely but no man should postpone repentance to the time when he is no longer capable of sinning. Nothing is a greater obstacle to repentance than pride. Before a man can sincerely repent he must be humble enough to admit his faults. The sinner must feel remorse for his sins. He must resolve never to repeat them. He must confess to God and, if they are sins against others, must make adequate restitution. He should pursue the good life and accustom himself to new habits of good conduct so as to create for himself a pure heart and firm spirit. Although repentance is of value at any time the penitential season is especially appropriate for this purpose. During this season a man should set aside much time for serious reflection on his conduct. During this period, too, he should give alms generously, offer much prayer and reflect long on the vanities of the world. Another time for repentance is when a man meets with sufferings. His heart is then broken and he is moved to repent of his sins. The way of repentance is God's precious gift to man and through repentance man can attain to eternal bliss.

25. Part II, 2, Chapter 12, pp. 670f.

R. Isaac Alfasi gives the following list of 24 things which act as a barrier to
repentance. (Yoma 8, ed. Vilna, p. 6a. This appears to be a quote but the
source is unknown, see the commentators to the *Rif* and *Responsa of
Maimonides*, ed. Blau. Vol. I, No. 121, pp. 216–217 and Blau's note 2.)
(1) slander and tale-bearing: (2) anger; (3) evil thoughts; (4) association
with wicked men; (5) partaking of meals so as to deprive the host of his
full share; (6) gazing lustfully at women; (7) sharing the spoils of robbery;
(8) sinning with the intention of later repenting; (9) acquiring fame at the
expense of others; (10) separating oneself from the community; (11) holding
one's parents in disgrace; (12) holding one's teacher in disgrace; (13) cursing
the public; (14) preventing the public from doing good; (15) perverting a
neighbour from a good to an evil way of life; (16) using a pledge taken from
the poor; (17) receiving bribes in order to pervert justice; (18) keeping a lost
article one has found; (19) seeing one's son choosing an evil way of life without
preventing it; (20) eating the spoil of widows and orphans; (21) disagreeing with
the sages; (22) suspecting the innocent of doing wrong; (23) hating rebuke;
(24) scoffing at the precepts. Maimonides (*Yad, Teshuvah* 4: 1) explains these,
not as being the most serious offences, but as especially a hindrance to repentance,
e.g. separating oneself from the community so that when there takes place
public repentance one is not involved or hating rebuke so that one cannot
be moved to repent. Meiri (*Book on Repentance*, Part I, *Maamar* 1, 4)
similarly observes that of these 24 some are so severe that repentance is very
difficult; others are so slight that the sinner will not be moved to feel remorse;
others, like cursing the public, are of such a nature as to prevent effective
repentance since it is impossible to appease all who have been wronged;
and others again are of such a nature as to act as a barrier before the whole
idea of repentance.

The matter is debated among the third century Palestinian Rabbis
whether the repentant sinner is greater than the man who has never
tasted sin or whether the latter is greater,[26] R. Johanan holding that
those who have never sinned are greater, R. Abahu that the sinners
who repent are greater. The third century teacher Resh Lakish said,
according to one version, that when the sinner repents his sins are
accounted as if he had committed them unintentionally, but, in
another version, his sins are accounted as virtues! The Talmudic
reconciliation of the two versions is that one refers to repentance out
of fear, the other out of love.[27]

One of the very few philosophical discussions in our sources of the
problem of repentance is that of Joseph Albo.[28] How can we understand, asks Albo,[29] the Rabbinic statement that when a man repents

26. Ber. 34b.   27. Yoma, 86b.
28. Ikkarim, IV, 25–28.   29. Iv, 25.

out of love his sins are converted into virtues? Where is the justice in
this? Surely it is enough that they are not counted as sins, why should
they be turned into merit? His answer is that if justice were to be the
determining factor there would be no room for repentance at all.
Justice demands that the wrong having been done it cannot be righted
and the sinner should receive his deserts. But repentance is due to
God's grace and this is infinite. When a man repents out of love he
responds to God in love and so God's grace can flow in love to him
even to the extent of converting his sins into merits. This passage in
Albo makes it clear that, contrary to the accepted view, Judaism
also knows of the concept of divine grace for the sinner, though
it is not impossible that Albo has been influenced by Christian
thought.[30]

Yet Albo is still bothered by the whole idea of repentance. Grace,
to be sure, affords some notion of how repentance operates but there
must be some justice in the idea. As Albo formulates the objection,[31]
the transgression has been carried out in practice whereas repentance
is only in the form of regret and verbal confession. How, then, can
one wipe out the other? If a man takes a life can the victim's life be
restored to him? If a man profanes the Sabbath is the sabbath observed
simply because the profaner is sorry? Is it not like a person who
demolishes a building and then rebuilds it with his mouth? Antici-
pating Kant, Albo argues that only voluntary acts are deserving of
moral praise and blame. It is notoriously difficult to define a voluntary
act but for an act to be classed as voluntary rather than compulsory it
is necessary for the one who does it to wish it to stand afterwards.
Thus sincere repentance demonstrates that the sin was not committed
voluntarily but in error. The sinner would erase it if he could and he
thereby demonstrates that he did not really wish it to be done. The
same principle applies, of course, to the good deed. If the one who has
done it regrets having done it the deed is not considered to have been
done voluntarily and no merit accrues to the one who has done it.[32]
Thus repentance serves to erase the sin. When the repentance is out
of love this brings God's grace into play and then the sinner's transgressions can even be counted as merits.

There is a further discussion of repentance in Moses b. Joseph di

---

30. But see Ber. 7a, saying of R. Meir.   31. Iv, 27.
32. Kidd. 40b.

Trani's (*Mabit*): *Bet Elohim.*[33] *Mabit's* definition of repentance is:[34] "Drawing near to God from the distance of sin." The two main essentials of repentance for *Mabit* are[35] remorse and resolve: remorse for the sin which has been committed and resolve never to repeat it. Remorse is invalid without resolve in that it indicates that the remorse is insincere. Resolve without remorse is invalid in that it is suspect. The resolve to sin no more might simply be due to the fact that the sinner no longer finds the sin attractive.

Reference has earlier been made to confession as an essential condition for repentance. Here some further details regarding confession can be noted. (See *Jewish Encyclopedia*, Vol. IV, pp. 217–219; *Universal Jewish Encyclopedia*, Vol. 3, pp. 328–329; *Encyclopedia Talmuit*, Vol. II, pp. 412–455.) Confession of sin is mentioned in the Pentateuch (Lev. 5:5; 16:21; Num. 5:6–7) as a religious duty. The High Priest's confession on the Day of Atonement was: "I have sinned, I have transgressed, I have rebelled" (Mishnah Yoma 3:8; 4:2). It is frequently said that Judaism knows nothing of confession of sins to a priest or spiritual mentor only to God. This is not too exact. We have noted earlier Maimonides' discussion, based on the Talmudic sources, of when public confession of sin is advocated and when frowned upon. There have been groups of Jews who knew, too, of the idea of confessing sins to a spiritual guide, a "father-confessor" who would give the sinner a penance to perform. This became a special feature of the circle of German pietists known as the *Haside Ashkenaz* to whom reference has earlier been made. (See especially Y. Baer's article: *Religious Social Tendency of the Sefer Hasidim.*) The *Sefer Hasidim* (No. 38, ed. Wistinetzki p. 40), after quoting the Talmudic passage (Ber. 34b) in which confession to others is frowned upon, remarks that this does not apply when the confession is made to a discreet sage who can instruct the sinner how to do penance for his sins and so bring him to eternal life. There is almost certainly a Christian influence here. Joseph Dan (*The Esoteric Theology of Ashkenazi Hasidim*, p. 37) is far too sweeping when he writes that the *Hasidim* rejected completely the Christian forms of confession even though their doctrine of repentance was influenced by Christian customs. In fact the *Sefer Hasidim* (No. 43, ed. Wistinitzki p. 41) even goes so far as to give instructions to the mentor (*ha-moreh*) when the sinner confesses his sins to him: "First the mentor should ask the sinner if he regrets having sinned. If he answers in the affirmative, the mentor should say to him if the sin was with a woman: 'If you are truly sorry you must keep away from that woman, never seeing her or speaking to her for a whole year. First do this and if you can keep to it then I shall tell you what to do in order to erase your sin' for no sin

33. Part II, *Shaar Ha-Teshuvah*, pp. 28f.   34. Chapter 1, p. 28.
35. Chapter 2, pp. 30–32.

can be removed without mortification, as it is said: Lo, this (the burning coal) has touched thy lips; and thine iniquity is taken away, and thy sin expiated (Is. 6: 7). If the sinner says: 'Give me a different penance, this one is beyond me' he is not heeded for repentance is only possible when the sinner turns from his former deeds and makes a fence around them . . . After this the mentor should give him the penance to which I referred earlier, i.e. to forbid him to enjoy anything which is by the hand of a woman except his own wife. When the sinner fasts for his sins the mentor should flog him severely in private for all voluntary pain the sinner accepts upon himself is accounted as suffering which brings pardon in its wake. Therefore, fasting is good for it breaks the body and alms giving to ward off punishment. Since he is deserving of death he should gain pardon by bringing new life to the souls of the hungry and he should revive them." While the Hasidism of the Baal Shem Tov is far removed from many of the ideas of the *Sefer Hasidim* and while it generally frowns on mortification of the flesh and, indeed, on any undue preoccupation with sin, this movement, too, knows of confession to a mentor, in this case the Hasidic master, the Tzaddik. The Hasidic master Elimelekh of Lizensk writes (*Noam Elimelekh, Tzetil Katan*, No. 13): "A man should tell his mentor (*moreh*, the same word is used in the *Sefer Hasidim*) who teaches him God's way, or even a trustworthy friend, all the evil thoughts he has which are in opposition to the holy Torah, which the evil inclination brings into his head and heart, whether while he is study- ing the Torah or offering his prayers or when he lies in his bed or at any time during the day. He should conceal nothing out of shame. The result will be that by speaking of these matters, by bringing the potential to the actual, he will break the hold of the evil inclination so that it will have far less power to entice him on other occasions, quite apart from the sound spiritual guidance, which is the way of the Lord, that he may receive from his friend. This is a marvellous antidote to the evil inclination." Another Hasidic master, R. Nahman of Bratzlav, in his compendium of moral maxims, *Sefer Ha-Middot*, writes (*hirhurhim*, 3, p. 55): "Good thoughts are the result of confession of sin to scholars." ("Scholars"—*talmide hahamin*— are, of course, in this literature the Hasidic masters. On this topic see Wertheim: *Halakhot Va-Halikhot Ba-Hasidut*, pp. 22–23). It is difficult to know how widespread this form of confession was in Hasidism. In the nature of the case it cannot have been the regular practice of the *Hasid* if only because the average *Hasid* only journeyed to his master's "court" at intervals and was not in a position to confess his sins to the Tzaddik as a regular pattern in his religious life. For the confession on a deathbed see Singer's Prayer Book, pp. 419–420 and Abrahams: *Companion*, pp. 225–226. That a man is told to make confession when he is sick and near to death is mentioned in the Talmud (Sabb. 32a) but no special form of confession is there recorded. Nahmanides (*Torat Ha-Adam in Collected Writings*, ed. Chavel, Vol. 2, pp. 45–47) quotes a form virtually the same as ours as a tradi- tion "from the saints and men of good deeds". Nahmanides' formula is quoted in the *Shulhan Arukh, Yoreh Deah*, 338: 2.

From all that has been said in this chapter it can be seen that the teachings regarding sin and repentance as these appear in the sources strike on the whole a balance between childish irresponsibility and softness, for which saying "sorry" is enough, and morbid guilt, for which nothing one does to repair the wrong is enough. The need to find peace in one's soul, shedding the guilt load by constructive means, namely, by making good the harm that has been done, renewal of one's personal life, reconciliation with God and with one's fellows—these, far from being infantile, are tests of a mature personality.

Special emphasis is given to these themes in the Jewish tradition on the Day of Atonement and the days preceding it—the Ten Days of Penitence. It remains to be said that repentance is not a seasonal matter; yet there is point in setting aside a special period in which the prayers and the ritual can succeed in reminding man, at the beginning of the New Year (the first of the ten days), to lead a new life in the presence of God.

CHAPTER EIGHTEEN

REWARD AND PUNISHMENT

THE highest ideal in Judaism is to do the will of God "for the sake of Heaven", i.e. out of love and without thought of reward or punishment. Yet all the classical sources of Judaism teach that virtue is rewarded by God and vice punished by Him. The mediaeval thinkers considered the doctrine of reward and punishment to be a fundamental principle of the Jewish faith.[1]

There are four levels at which the doctrine of reward and punishment operates. Many of us today would argue that not all of these levels are of the same relevance. The Jewish teachers of the past accepted them all as equally true, though no doubt they, too, would have used terms like "higher" and "lower" in speaking of these levels. The highest of these is that virtue is its own reward, vice its own punishment. "The reward of a good deed (*mitzvah*) is a good deed, the recompense of sin (*averah*) is sin."[2] There are three other levels apart from this self-compensatory idea of virtue and vice. These are: (1) Rewards and punishments, especially the latter, meted out by the Court acting on behalf of society; (2) Reward and punishment by God in this life; (3) Reward and punishment in the Hereafter.

(1) *Reward and punishment by society.* There are very few instances of the ancient Jewish society apportioning rewards for doing good. The examples we do have belong in the area of respect for students of the Torah. The *talmid haham*, the Torah scholar, was exempt from the payment of certain taxes,[3] people were to rise whenever he passed by,[4] he was to be assisted in his business dealings,[5] and it was held to be

---

1. Maimonides: *Commentary to the Mishnah*, Sanh. 10: 1 beg.; Duran: *Magen Avot*, Introduction, end, p. 2b; Albo: *Ikkarim*, Book IV.
2. Avot 4: 2.
3. B.B. 8a; Ned. 62b.
4. Kidd. 32b–33a.
5. Ber. 34b and freq.

meritorious to marry into his family.⁶ But the privileges of the scholar were not really rewards in the proper sense. They were rather means of encouraging learning and increasing men's regard for the Torah. To obtain direct benefit, financial or otherwise, from the Torah, for studying or teaching, was considered to be sinful.⁷

Punishments by the Court acting on behalf of society abound both in the Bible and in the Rabbinic literature. Among the punishments mentioned in the Bible⁸ are the death penalty not alone for the crime of murder but for adultery and incest, for idolatrous worship, the profanation of the sabbath and flagrant disrespect for parents. There are numerous references in the Rabbinic literature to physical punishments meted out by the Court. There are the four death penalties, stoning, burning, decapitation and strangulation;⁹ flagellation, involving 39 stripes with an ox-hide strap, administered on the naked body, for each separate offence;¹⁰ and, in certain circumstances, the placing of the offender in a cell where he is given barley to eat "until his stomach bursts".¹¹ All these were to be meted out to women as well as to men.¹²

It is true that our embarrassment at these barbaric punishments is considerably lessened when it is realised that for the most part they were only theoretical. The majority of the passages in the Talmudic literature in which these are mentioned belong to a period when the Jewish Courts had power to inflict neither capital nor corporal punishment so that consideration of them was all purely academic. For all that, enough is left of physical coercion by the Courts to make us aware that the world of the Rabbis and the mediaeval thinkers is not our world. Religious toleration is the hard-won achievement of those intrepid souls responsible for the modern world as we know it and few would wish to turn the clock back. Similarly, new methods of penal reform have transformed our whole approach to the problem of crime and the community. That the ancient punishments are now a dead letter even theoretically is surely no cause for regret.

6. Pes. 49b.
7. Avot 1: 13 and 4: 5, see Commentary of Maimonides ad loc.
8. See the article *Crimes and Punishments* in Hastings' *Dictionary of the Bible*, 2nd ed., ed. Grant and Rowley, pp. 189–190.
9. Mishnah Sanh. 7: 1.
10. Makk. 3.
11. Mishnah Sanh. 9: 5.
12. Kidd. 35a.

(2) *Reward and punishment by God in this life.* The Bible is full of promised rewards for obeying God's law and punishments threatened for disobedience. The promised rewards include health, many children, rainfall in its season, a good harvest, peace and prosperity. The punishments threatened include disease, war, pestilence, failure of crops, poverty and slavery. But two things require to be stated right away. The first is that, as modern Biblical scholarship sees the Bible,[13] many of the passages in which these rewards and punishments are recorded are not in the nature of anticipatory warnings, as they appear to be, but reflections on national disasters after the event. They are more in the nature of pious acceptance of God's decree than theological statements about how God actually operates, as it were, in the world He has created. Secondly, in the Biblical books themselves, there is sufficient indication of an awareness that there is no tidy scheme of reward and punishment that can adequately explain the sufferings of the righteous and the prosperity of the wicked. The books of Job and Ecclesiastes, for instance, both grapple with this very problem. Israel suffers in Egypt and Moses pleads for them without any suggestion that they deserve to suffer because of their sins. The Rabbis are similarly aware of the tremendous problem. In one passage it is said that Moses asked God why some of the righteous suffer and others prosper, why some of the wicked prosper and others suffer, and, according to one version, the reply is simply that God wills it so and even a Moses cannot know why.[14] A second century Rabbi said that we do not know the answer to why the righteous suffer and the wicked prosper.[15] The Rabbis, in fact, develop the idea that sometimes it is the righteous in particular who are visited with sufferings because they can bear these "sufferings of love" in love.[16] When visiting people in affliction it is forbidden, according to the Rabbis, to suggest that they are suffering because of their sins and if one does so it is the offence of "wronging with words".[17] Clearly the doctrine of reward and punishment in this life contradicts experience if it is interpreted to mean that all suffering is the result of sin and all prosperity and well-being the fruit of virtue.

(3) *Reward and punishment in the Hereafter.* There are hardly any references to this in the Biblical record, as we shall see in the chapter

13. See *supra*, pp. 203–210. 14. Ber. 7a. 15. Avot 4: 15.
16. Ber. 5a–b. 17. B.M. 58b.

on the Hereafter. But in Rabbinic Judaism the doctrine of reward in Heaven and punishment in Hell looms very large. In fact, a good part of the Rabbinic theology of suffering is based on the idea that the righteous suffer in this life but are rewarded in the World to Come while the wicked prosper here but are punished in Hell.[18] This must be examined more closely in the chapter on the Hereafter but here it is sufficient to note that all the Rabbinic teachers believed implicitly in the doctrine of reward and punishment in the Hereafter. One who says that God is, as it were, easy-going and lets people off lightly forfeits his life, is a typical Rabbinic saying.[19] Life, for the Rabbis, was grim. Man is presented with the stark choice of ultimate bliss or ultimate ruin, or, at least, a disastrous existence in the Hereafter until his sins have been purged.

What are we to make of the doctrine of reward and punishment? Any interpretation of the doctrine which thinks of God as vindictive, bent on enforcing His will in tyrannical fashion, presents an unworthy concept of Deity. The many Rabbinic ideas on this subject are better understood as spontaneous preachment rather than systematic theological presentation. For instance, the Rabbis say that a man should always regard himself as though he were half-guilty and half-worthy of merit. If he carries out one further good deed he weighs himself down in the scale of merit, if he commits one further sin he weighs himself down in the scale of guilt. R. Eleazar b. R. Simeon added that the world as well as the individual is weighed in the scale of merit. It is therefore possible that when an individual performs one good deed he may, by virtue of that deed, cause the whole world to be weighed in the scale of merit, whereas one evil deed may have the opposite effect.[20] This is surely much more in the nature of a vivid piece of sermonising rather than an attempt to work out a theological scheme.

It is true that the mediaeval thinkers, whose views we must note here, did not see it in this way. On the basis of passages such as the foregoing they did try to construct a detailed scheme of reward and punishment but we are hardly bound by their opinions. In his statement of the scheme Maimonides[21] begins by observing that every human being has both merits and sins. One whose merits exceed his sins is a righteous man. One whose sins exceed his merits is wicked.

18. See e.g. Kidd. 39b and 40b and freq.   19. B.K. 50a.
20. Kidd. 40a–b.   21. *Yad, Teshuvah* 3: 1–4.

The man whose merits and sins are equally balanced is an average man. The same applies to a country or province. If its inhabitants possess collectively more merits than sins it is a righteous country. If the collective sins exceed the merits it is a wicked country. Where the two are equally balanced it is an average country. Finally, the test is applied to the world as a whole. If at a given period there are more virtues than vices in the world then that age is a righteous age. If the vices exceed the virtues it is a wicked age. Where the two are equally balanced the age is average. As soon as the sins of an individual outweigh his merits he dies for his sins. Similarly, as soon as the sins of a country or province outweigh its virtues it is destroyed. And when the whole world is wicked, in the sense that in the world as a whole there are more sins than virtues, the world is destroyed, as in the days of the Deluge.

Maimonides, is, however, too acute a thinker to be satisfied with this simple, mathematical assessment. Obviously it is not true to experience that the man with a preponderence of sins dies immediately. To cope with this difficulty Maimonides suggests that not all sins and merits are treated in the same fashion. It is not the quantity of the deeds which matters but their type and quality. It is possible, for instance, for an otherwise good man to be guilty of so evil a deed that it succeeds in outweighing all the good he has done. Conversely, an otherwise wicked man may carry out a good deed of such heroic proportions that it succeeds in outweighing all the evil he has done. Only God can make the true assessment. Following a famous Talmudic passage,[22] Maimonides goes on to say that each New Year's day is the time when God makes this assessment. If as a result man emerges as righteous he is "sealed" in the Book of Life. If he emerges as wicked it is decreed that he should die. If he emerges as an average person he is given time to repent until the Day of Atonement. If he repents he is "sealed" in the Book of Life. If he does not repent death is decreed for him.

It is clear from all this that Maimonides takes the Rabbinic sayings in this connection quite literally. As for the question of our experience —good people do die after the New Year and the wicked people do live on—Maimonides, as we have seen, refers to the quality of the deeds and this can only be known to God Himself. The problem of experience, which contradicts the Rabbinic teaching regarding the

22. R.H. 16b.

New Year assize, was a constant source of embarrassment to those thinkers in the middle ages who took the Rabbinic sayings literally.

Nahmanides[23] attempts to get round the difficulty in a way different from Maimonides. According to Nahmanides, following Rabbinic parallels, it is possible that death or suffering is decreed for the good man in order that his sufferings here on earth might atone for the sins he has committed so that he can go to Heaven purged of his sins. Conversely, it is possible that a wicked man, whose fate is Hell, has nonetheless carried out good deeds for which he deserves to be rewarded here on earth. Consequently, at the New Year assize, God assesses whether the individual is to have suffering or death, perhaps because he is righteous and requires this purgation, or to enjoy happiness and success, perhaps because he is wicked and requires to be rewarded here on earth. It is, of course, also possible that the good man may be rewarded with prosperity here on earth and the wicked punished here on earth. The result of it all is that the terms "righteous" and "wicked" and "average" are not used here in an absolute or general sense but refer to each particular New Year assize. One who, for whatever reason, is to be acquitted on the New Year is called "righteous" since at this trial he has been acquitted. Similarly, one who, for whatever reason, is to be condemned on the New Year is called "wicked" since at this trial he has been declared guilty.

What bothers moderns perhaps more than anything else about these mediaeval schemes is their frightening certainty, their claim to know in precise detail the way in which God works. The book of Job might never have been written. The Kabbalistic author R. Joseph Ergas[24] is even more explicit. There is a complete scheme of reward and punishment which man can fully grasp and even observe in operation. If, for instance, good men suffer in a national catastrophe this is because once the decree has gone forth it must embrace all without exception, unless it be that of the man so righteous that he deserves to be saved. But one who is partly to blame, i.e. because he failed to rebuke the others for their misdeeds will perish with them. It is also true that an especially great saint may have the power to save even the wicked. A wicked man may be blessed with prosperity in order that he might serve as an instrument for the fulfilment of God's

23. *Torat Ha-Adam, Shaar Ha-Gemul*, in *Collected Writings* ed. Chavel, Vol. II, pp. 264f.
24. *Shomer Emunim*, II, 81, pp. 91–96.

purpose. He may, for example, have a righteous son who will inherit his wealth and use it for good purposes. When a woman miscarries this is because of her own sins but also because the embryo deserves the punishment because of the sins he had committed in a previous existence. This explains, too, why innocent children suffer. They are not, in fact, innocent but are guilty of sins committed in a previous incarnation.

The doctrine of reward and punishment is discussed, with reference to the earlier sources, by the eighteenth century teacher R. Moses Hayim Luzzatto (*Mesillat Yesharim*, Chapter 4, ed. Kaplan, pp. 29f). Luzzatto observes that men of great intelligence need no incentive to lead the good life. For them it is sufficient that perfection is the only thing worth striving for and failure to attain perfection the greatest calamity. Those of more limited intelligence need ambition as an incentive, hence the appeals of ambition, especially spiritual ambition, in the Rabbinic literature. "Would they in this world, which is only transient", asks Luzzatto, "bear with equanimity the sight of one of their comrades attaining greater honour and rank than they, and acquiring domination over them, especially one of their own servants, or some beggar whom they hold in contempt? Would they not feel chagrin? Would not their very blood boil with indignation? . . . Now, since men find it unbearable to be inferior to others in a world in which differences in rank are but illusory and deceiving, where inferiority is only an appearance of things and high rank futility, how can they bear to find themselves in a lower class than those whom they looked upon as their inferiors, and that in a world where differences in rank are real, and glory eternal?" For the masses, continues Luzzatto, the only incentives are reward and punishment. Luzzatto quotes a number of Rabbinic passages in which God's severe judgement is spoken of in trepidation. Even the frivolous talk between a man and his wife is held against him on Judgement Day (Hag. 5b). God is as exacting with His saints even to the extent of a hair's breadth (Yev. 121b). Even the Patriarchs were punished by God whenever they deviated from the right path. "In the same manner as the Holy One, blessed be He, allows no good deed, however inconsiderable, to go unrewarded, so He allows no evil deed, however trivial, to pass unjudged and unpunished. This should be a warning to those who delude themselves with the thought that the Lord, blessed be He, does not take into account matters of small importance, and does not include them in His reckoning." If it be argued, observes Luzzatto, that all this fails to consider that God is merciful, the reply is that God's mercy never has the effect of setting justice aside completely. Mercy provides a respite before punishment is executed. It also has the effect of softening the punishment and it is because of God's mercy that repentance is possible. For all that, divine punishment is a stern reality. Though God be long-suffering, He exacts payment (Jer. T. Taan. 2: 1).

There are three reasons why many moderns find the mediaeval formulations of the doctrine of reward and punishment unsatisfactory. These formulations are too neat, too cruel and too vindictive for our tastes and because of this represent what is for us an inferior concept of Deity. There are surely gains in our greater reticence in these matters. We cannot presume to know how God works. The all too tidy schemes of the mediaeval thinkers leave us unmoved. Their frequent quotes from earlier Rabbinic teaching have no power to convince, partly because we recognise the organic, unsystematic nature of Rabbinic (and Biblical) thought, partly because we no longer see the Rabbis as infallible supermen (and we recognise a human element in the Bible, too, so that a Biblical text does not necessarily clinch an argument). We are, moreover, more sensitive to cruelty. This might seem a very strange assertion in the age of the concentration camp but it is true that far less cruelty is tolerated in civilised countries today than anywhere in the middle ages and, at least, we hesitate to adopt any theological scheme in which cruelty appears to be ascribed in some way to God. And modern emphasis on reforming the criminal rather than punishing him vindictively has made us very wary of any doctrine of retribution which seems to ignore reformation.

Yet if the doctrine of reward and punishment is not interpreted in tit-for-tat terms but of natural processes it still has power. Evil is evil and is hateful in God's eyes. Unless this is affirmed we reduce religion to a vague sentimental feeling for the divine. A God who tolerates a Hitler would not be deserving of our worship. The principle of reward and punishment means for us that *ultimately* it is better for us to lead a good life, to obey God's will, and to reject an evil life, even though we must leave the details to God. When we pursue evil we are at variance with God's purpose and this can never succeed in any ultimate sense. When we pursue the good we are doing God's work and for all the suffering this may entail we find complete reassurance in the knowledge that there is no other purpose ultimately for man than to be on God's "side", as it were, in the struggle against evil.

Although the idea of collective guilt and responsibility is difficult to accept, postulating an inferior concept of the Deity and His justice (hence the protest of the prophet Ezekiel, for example), yet even this idea is not entirely dead. Two aspects of the doctrine have become especially relevant in our day, in ways inconceivable to the ancients.

First, the increase of communications has made the world one to an extent beyond the imagination of former ages. For better or for worse all men are today involved with one another. A minor squabble in some obscure trouble spot can result in global war. The kind of life we choose to lead is not without its repercussions everywhere. It requires neither doctrinal narrowness nor dogma incapable of proof to perceive that the sin of nuclear warfare, or even of the testing of nuclear weapons, is visited upon posterity. Secondly, modern psychological studies and researches have shown beyond doubt that the character of parents or grandparents is in some measure transmitted to their offspring; that it is more difficult for people with bad hereditary influence and environment to lead decent, useful lives and far easier for the descendents of righteous ancestors to do so. The old Rabbinic doctrine of *zekhut avot*, "the merit of the fathers", is sound psychology. It is not suggested that the Rabbis anticipated modern psychology, nor is it suggested that the older doctrine was always free from the notion of a semi-magical transmission of virtue. But moderns who dismiss the whole idea are guided by sentimentality rather than clear insight into life's realities.

It can, of course, be asked why God who is good should have made us this way as part of one another. In reply—unless we wish to repeat the mistake of the mediaevals—all we can say is that this belongs to the wider question of why the good God tolerates evil in His creation and that however little we can understand His mysterious ways the facts are that He has made us so that for good or ill our deeds have their influence on the lives of others. We can only see a faint glimmer of light in illuminating why the world should be so constituted that our deeds affect others and theirs ours, but is not this fact a constant reminder that God wants man to belong to his fellows and possess a strong sense of responsibility to them?

CHAPTER NINETEEN

THE CHOSEN PEOPLE

IN view of the importance the doctrine of Israel as God's chosen people assumes in the Bible, its central role in Rabbinic thought and the emphasis placed upon it by many modern Jewish thinkers, it comes as a shock to discover that it features in none of the mediaeval classifications as a basic principle of the Jewish faith. In all probability the reason for the omission is that the mediaeval thinkers did not see the chosenness of Israel as a separate dogma but as implied in other principles of the faith, especially those concerning the Torah, which were given to Israel. But it is also very plausible to suggest that the influence of Greek thought, which gave a universalistic cast to mediaeval thinking, made the doctrine of a chosen people something of an embarrassment. Maimonides, for example, when he does discuss the question of why God revealed His law to one particular nation and at one particular time can only reply that God willed it so.[1] The "scandal of particularism" is always a problem when this idea of God choosing is examined. The "oddness' in God's choosing is not in His choice of the Jews but in the choice itself. Why did God have to make a *choice* among peoples, why not convey the truth to all mankind?

It cannot be denied that some Jewish thinkers have interpreted the doctrine to mean that there is a qualitative difference between Jews and other peoples, that the Jews are spiritual supermen, endowed with rare qualities of soul by virtue of their descent from the Patriarchs. In the mediaeval world the representative of this type of thinking was Judah Ha-Levi. Ha-Levi builds his philosophy on the view that the Jew is not simply a superior type of human being but belongs, in fact, to a different category altogether. The difference between Israel and the other peoples of the world is one of kind, not of degree, just as humans are different from animals, animals from plants, and plants

1. *Guide*, II, 25.

from minerals.[2] Aware of the moral difficulty in such a view, Ha-Levi observes[3] that since, however, Israel is the "heart' of the nations" it can be the most healthy and the most sick of peoples. A bad Jew is more thoroughly bad than the worst Gentile. Ha-Levi's "racism" is, of course, limited. He cannot reject the Rabbinic view that Gentiles can be converted to Judaism and hence belong to the Jewish people. But, for Ha-Levi, the higher reaches of the religious life such as prophecy are not possible for those born outside the people of Israel.[4]

The qualitative interpretation of Jewish chosenness is especially pronounced in the Kabbalah. Here the Jewish people on earth has its counterpart in the *Shekhinah* in the Sefirotic realm. The *Sefirah Malkhut*, "Sovereignty", is, in fact, known as the *Community of Israel*. It is the archetype of the physical community of Israel on earth. Israel's exile among the nations mirrors the cosmic disharmony in which the *Shekhinah* is exiled, as it were, from the *Holy One, blessed be He*, i.e. the *Sefirah Tiferet*, "Beauty". The drama of Israel's exile and eventual restoration reflects the realities in the "upper worlds" (see *supra*, pp. 28–34; Scholem: *Major Trends*, pp. 229–330; Tishby: *Mishnat Ha-Zohar*, Vol. I, pp. 265–231). It is no accident that the Kabbalah came into its own after the expulsion from Spain when Jews needed desperately the reassurance that despite their lowly situation when viewed by appearances God really cared and that their role was the most significant of all. In *Habad* thought, with antecedents in the earlier Kabbalah, the Jew has two souls: the "animal soul", *nefesh ha-behamit*, the vital force, that which keeps men alive and provides the driving force of their lives, and the "divine soul", *nefesh ha-elohut*, a "divine spark" which is in reality part of God, as it were, deep in the recesses of the human psyche. But this "divine soul" is possessed only by Jews. Gentiles are not endowed with a "divine soul". Moreover, even the "animal soul" of Israel derives from the "Shell" (*kelipah*) known as *Nogah*, which is not wholly bad but which contains an admixture of good and evil. The "animal soul" of the Gentiles, on the other hand, derives from the wholly unclean "Shells" (*kelipot*) so that, for example, no Gentile is capable of performing a completely unselfish and disinterested good deed. (See R. Schneor Zalman: *Tanya*, Part I, pp. 5f and especially pp. 10–11 and my article: *The Doctrine of the 'Divine Spark' in Man* in *Jewish Sources in Studies in Rationalism, Judaism and Universalism*, ed. R. Loewe, pp. 87–114.) These ideas are sometimes expressed in the crudest terms by suggesting, for example, that there are real physical differences between Jews and Gentiles, the counterpart on the Jewish side of the accusation that Jews have horns or tails. (See, for example, the very curious remark that Jews have a tooth

2. See *Kuzari*, I, 102–111.   3. *Kuzari*, II, 36–44.   4. *Kuzari*, I, 115.

fewer than Gentiles and the whole discussion in Elijah b. Abraham's
Midrash Talpiot, p. 12, s.v. *evarim* and Israel Lipschütz's remarks that the
"Jewish face" is different because of the "divine spark", in his *Commentary*
to the Mishnah, Avot, VI, 10, note 157, p. 264b.)

In modern times a qualitative interpretation of Jewish chosenness
has been advocated by thinkers like Abraham Geiger who believed
that the Jewish people has a special genius for religion and is far more
sensitive than others to the call of the religious life.[5]

At the opposite extreme are those Jewish thinkers who would
reject the whole notion of chosenness as unworthy. On the theological level it has seemed to some to have an inadequate concept of
Deity to say that God shows favouritism to any one group and it
seems unjust that the children of righteous forebears should be
singled out not through any merit of their own but by accident of
birth. One of the most vigorous protagonists of the view that all
peoples are "called" by God to fulfil His purpose but none are
"chosen", not even the Jews, is Mordecai Kaplan.[6] Not that Kaplan
fails to consider the special nature of Jewish religious forms. Kaplan
is a great believer in preserving and furthering the distinctive patterns
of Jewish life as enriching and rewarding. But he steadfastly refuses
to formulate this in terms of "chosenness" which suggests privilege.
To the stock answer that the "choice" of Israel is not for privilege but
for service, Kaplan retorts that to be chosen for service is the greatest
privilege of all. Hugo Bergman, after studying carefully the various
moves of modern Jewish thinkers to defend the doctrine of chosenness, finds none of them completely convincing and comes to the
conclusion that the doctrine, in whatever form it is presented, is
difficult to reconcile with the idea of God's justice.[7]

Between the two extremes is the view, followed here, that while
chosenness should not be interpreted in qualitative terms it should
not be given up entirely. On the contrary it is still valid and, para-
doxical though this may seem, is still the most powerful way of
expressing the universal ideal. Jewish history has demonstrated that
truths originally the possession of a particular people have become,

5. See J. B. Agus: *Modern Philosophies of Judaism*, pp. 5–11.
6. For a helpful summary of Kaplan's views see his *Questions Jews Ask*, Index:
Chosen People.
7. See Bergman's essay: *Israel and the Oikoumene* in *Studies in Rationalism, Judaism
and Universalism*, ed. R. Loewe, pp. 47–65.

through the efforts of that people to live by them, the property of millions beyond the confines of the people to whom the truth was originally revealed. Ethical monotheism is the supreme example of this. The rest of this chapter is devoted, then, to a defence of the doctrine of the chosen people always with the *proviso* that the doctrine is conceived of in non-qualitative terms. The following points require especially to be made in defence of the doctrine.

1. The Biblical conception of the election of Israel has nothing in common with the idea of a tribal god protecting his people, responding to their attempts to buy his favour and capable of suffering defeat at the hands of a more powerful deity. The relation of a tribal god to his people is a "natural" one. He does not "choose" his people any more than they are members of the tribe by choice. In the Bible it is the universal God who "chooses". As I. Heinemann has pointed out[8] the Biblical references to the choice are in a universalistic context and the election of Israel is only possible within a universalistic framework. "Now, therefore, if ye will obey My voice indeed, and keep My covenant, then ye shall be a peculiar treasure unto Me above all people: *For all the earth is Mine*" (Ex. 19: 5). "Why sayest thou, O Jacob, and speakest O Israel, my way is hid from the Lord, and my judgement is passed over from my God? Hast thou not known? hast thou not heard, *that the everlasting God, the Lord, the Creator of the ends of the earth*, fainteth not, neither is weary? there is no searching of His understanding" (Is. 40: 27-28). "Thus saith God the Lord, *He spread the heavens, and stretched them forth, He spread forth the earth and that which cometh out of it, He that giveth bread unto the people upon it, And spirit to them that walk therein*; I the Lord have called thee in righteousness, and have taken hold of thy hand, and kept thee, and set thee for a covenant of the people, For a light of the Nations; to open the blind eyes. To bring out the prisoners from the dungeon. And them that sit in darkness out of the prison-house" (Is. 42: 5-7).

2. The doctrine is not of a Herrenvolk whom others must serve but on the contrary of a folk dedicated to the service of others. The prophet Amos declares: "You only have I known of all the families of the earth, therefore I will visit upon you all your iniquities" (Amos 3: 2). The constant castigations of their people by the prophets, their steadfast demands that the people live up to their vocation in which they are failing lamentably, their frequent warnings of divine

8. *The Election of Israel in the Bible.*

displeasure, are hardly ideas one associates with divine favouritism. Zangwill once said that the Bible is an anti-Semitic book! In a typical Rabbinic passage we read:[9] "It is written: 'It was not because you were greater than any people that the Lord set His love upon you and chose you for you are the smallest of all peoples' (Deut. 7: 7). The Holy One, blessed be He, said to Israel, I love you because even though I bestow greatness upon you, you humble yourselves before Me. I bestowed greatness upon Abraham, yet he said to Me, 'I am dust and ashes' (Gen. 18: 27); upon Moses and Aaron, yet they said, 'And we are nothing' (Ex. 16: 8); upon David, yet he said, 'But I am a worm and no man' (Ps. 22: 7). But with the heathen it is not so. I bestowed greatness upon Nimrod, and he said, 'Come let us build us a city' (Gen. 11: 4); upon Pharaoh, and he said, 'Who is the Lord' (Ex. 5: 2); upon Sennacherib, and he said, 'Who are they among all the gods of the countries?' (2 Kings 18: 35); upon Nebuchadnezzar, and he said, 'I will ascend above the heights of the clouds' (Is. 14: 14); upon Hiram king of Tyre, and he said, 'I sit in the seat of God, in the heart of the seas'" (Ezek. 28: 2).

3. The doctrine has no affinity with such notions as that of Aryan racial superiority. Jewish particularism is never exclusive: anyone can become a Jew by embracing the Jewish faith. Some of the greatest of the Rabbis are said to have been descended from converts to Judaism. In one Talmudic passage it is said that the proselyte is dearer to God than the born Israelite. Another passage teaches that Israel was scattered among the nations only that they might make proselytes. The proselyte is regarded as a Jew in every respect. He should recite in his prayers the formula: "Our God and the God of our fathers", for he is a spiritual child of Abraham. It is strictly forbidden to taunt a proselyte with his background or former behaviour.[10]

4. The choice was reciprocal—God choosing Israel and Israel choosing God. The idea of a covenant between God and Israel is basic to the whole conception. "Thou has avouched the Lord this day to be thy God, and to walk in His ways, and to keep His statutes, and His commandments, and His judgements, and to hearken unto His voice; And the Lord hath avouched thee this day to be His peculiar people,

9. Hull. 89a.
10. A full treatment of this topic is to be found in *Encyclopedia Talmudit*, Vol. VI, pp. 254–289.

as He hath promised thee, and that thou shouldest keep His commandments" (Deut. 26: 17–18). "And Joshua said unto the people, Ye are witnesses against yourselves that you have chosen you the Lord to serve Him. And they said, we are witnesses"(Josh. 24:22). The Rabbis had something of this in mind when they told of God offering the Torah to all the other nations, who refused it, before giving it to Israel who accepted its yoke and cheerfully proclaimed: "We will do and we will hear".[11]

5. If the empirical test is applied it becomes obvious that we are not discussing a dogma incapable of verification but the recognition of sober historical fact. The world owes Israel the idea of the One God of righteousness and holiness. This is how God became known to mankind and clearly God used Israel for this great purpose. When Judaism declares that the covenant is still in force it reaffirms that Israel still has a special role to play.

From what has been said it is clear that the Chosen People idea is not a narrowly exclusive one, that it is universalistic, that it invokes duty rather than bestows privilege, that it is a doctrine of reciprocity, and that it bears the stamp of historical truth.

Yet there is also no doubt that this doctrine, perhaps more than any other, is so easily distorted and may even be dangerous. The suggestion or implication that it means that God is exclusively concerned with Jews or even that they are His special concern is surely at variance with the universalistic doctrine of Judaism that God is the Father of all mankind. Undoubtedly, less worthy interpretations of the doctrine are found in the Jewish sources but the nobler view is also found there and that in abundance.

The Jew of today is the heir to the whole tradition and this means that here, as in other areas, there are tensions with which he has to learn to live. As a powerful spur to Jewish survival, as providing a sense of destiny, as a reaffirmation of the covenant with its demands, responsibilities and obligations, the doctrine of the chosen people still possesses much value. As a temptation to narrowness and exclusiveness it still has its dangers. The modern Jew must learn to avail himself of the values inherent in the doctrine while taking due caution against its degeneration. To attempt to live without such tensions is to deprive life of its creativity. It is altogether right and proper that Jews should

---

11. *Sifre* to Deut. 33: 2.

be concerned with the difficulties in the doctrine of Israel's chosenness. It may be that the Jew never comes closer to the truth in the doctrine of chosenness than when he is severely critical of why and how God can choose the Jewish people.

CHAPTER TWENTY

PEOPLEHOOD AND STATEHOOD

JEWISH peoplehood, from the destruction of the Temple until the nineteenth century, was understood by Jews in a religious, not a nationalistic, sense. It could hardly have been otherwise. An ethnic group settled in many different lands, with neither a land of its own nor a common language except for prayer, could only find its cohesiveness in the religious faith professed by the majority of its members. It is equally clear that in the earlier period the Jews were a nation—in the Biblical idiom "a holy nation" but a nation nonetheless. With the rise of modern Zionism the question was naturally posed: were the Jews a nation or were they the adherents of a religion?

Opposition to Zionism on the part of some Jews came from a number of different directions. Many Reform leaders thought of Jewish nationalism as a betrayal of universalism. It was a divine boon, they argued, not a calamity, that Jews had no land of their own and so were able to keep their religion unsullied by particularistic national ideas which tend to frustrate the wider hope of a mankind united in the service of God. Many Orthodox thinkers shared the Reform suspicion of a revival of Jewish nationalism and these added the fear that a return to the holy land by human effort in the pre-Messianic age amounted to a denial of the Messiah for whose coming Jews were to wait patiently. According to the classical scheme, the Jews, exiled from their land because of their sins, had to wait until God sent the Messiah to redeem them from bondage and bring them back to the land of Israel. It was positively impious to anticipate the divine intervention by human endeavour on the political level, although the religious duty of settling in the holy land (*yishuv eretz yisrael*) was still binding on individual Jews who should, if this were possible, go to live in Palestine.

The whole question was further complicated by the fact that the Zionist movement was inspired by the rise of nationalistic movements of a secular nature in Europe and that many of the most prominent Zionist leaders were secularists. The fierce denunciations of Zionism were not always based on distrust of the new but on a real apprehension that Judaism itself was being redefined in secular nationalistic terms. Jewish nationalism was sometimes seen as a kind of idolatry, the nation being accorded the place previously reserved for God alone.

A typical Reform statement is contained in the "Pittsburgh Platform" in 1885. "We recognise in the modern era of universal culture of heart and intellect the approach of the realisation of Israel's great Messianic hope for the establishment of the kingdom of truth, justice and peace among all men. We consider ourselves no longer a nation but a religious community, and therefore expect neither a return to Palestine, nor a sacrificial worship under the administration of the sons of Aaron, nor the restoration of any of the laws concerning the Jewish state."[1] In 1911 Felix Goldman observed:[2] "If Zionism frankly admits that in the sense of nationalism one can be a good Jew and at the same time an atheist who is contemptuous of religion, then in the same moment Zionism would be condemned to death in the eyes of all thinking Jews. The spread of Zionism under such conditions would mean death for Judaism. We non-Zionists frankly declare that we have no interest in a Judaism in which religion is not the first, highest and most important part. Therefore we have no interest in a mere nationalism, and not merely because of the purely theoretical reason that we believe the progress of civilised humanity will occur only by lessening nationalism and chauvinism. We therefore see no advantage for us or for anybody else if we add another nation to the world, a nation which in importance, capacity of cultural development and power would only be equal to the robber states of the Balkans." However, this opposition to Zionism on the part of Reform Judaism eventually yielded not alone to a tolerant acceptance but to strong advocacy on the part of some of the most distinguished and influential Reform Rabbis who became, indeed, leaders in the Zionist movement.[3]

From the Orthodox side the following typical comment[4] by Rabbi Shalom Dov of Lubavitch can be quoted as an illustration among

1. W. Gunther Plaut: *The Growth of Reform Judaism*, p. 34.
2. Plaut op. cit. p. 147.
3. See Plaut op. cit. Chapter X: Zion: *The Great Debate*, pp. 144–158.
4. Quoted by I. Domb: *The Transformation*, pp. 225–226.

many of how a large number of European Rabbis saw Zionism as a menace to the Jewish religion: "From all these articles written by Zionists we can clearly see that their main aim and activity is to make —and unfortunately they do—the impression among the people of Israel that the whole purpose of the Torah and the commandments is merely to strengthen collective feeling. This theory can easily be adopted by young people who regard themselves as instruments prepared for the fulfilment of the Zionist ideal. They naturally regard themselves as completely liberated from Torah and the commandments for now, they think, nationalism has replaced religion, and is the best means for the preservation of society."

Material in English on the Orthodox opposition to Zionism is to be found in I. Domb: *The Transformation* and Emile Marmorstein: *Heaven at Bay*. An early Reform statement on the value of the dispersion at the Conference in Philadelphia in 1869 (Rall and Cohon: *Christianity and Judaism Compare Notes*, pp. 91–92) reads: "We look upon the destruction of the Jewish commonwealth not as a punishment for the sinfulness of Israel, but as a result of the divine purpose revealed to Abraham, which, as has become even clearer in the course of the world's history, consists in the dispersion of the Jews to all parts of the earth, for the realisation of their high priestly mission, to lead nations to the true knowledge and worship of God." An interesting illustration of how events have a habit of overtaking theory is the note of Rabbi Herzog (*Main Institutions of Jewish Law*, Introduction, note 3, pp. xxii–xxiv) who later became the Israeli Chief Rabbi. Writing in 1936 Rabbi Herzog deals with the question of the death penalty in a Jewish State and notes the theoretical difficulties but goes on to remark: "But, of course, in view of the actual position the idea of a Jewish State in Palestine (as distinct from a National Home), quite irrespective of the restoration of the Temple, is, in itself, rather a *Messianic* hope than a question of practical politics" (*italics* the author's). Standing apart from both Reform and extreme Orthodoxy, Franz Rosenzweig believed that the peoplehood of Israel in its classical form demands the conception of the land as a *holy* land and the language as a *holy* language, i.e. as beyond the actual limitations of a real spot on earth and a real living language. Israel must be a world people. It will only be a completely eternal people when it will be free of the ever-changing conditions of political life, and when its language will be free of the temporal developments which are the heritage of other languages. Israel cannot affirm its eternity without concomitant lack of ties to any external conditions. Instead of Israel losing its distinctiveness as an eternal people in exile, its existence is there brought to its highest point. See Julius Guttmann: Philosophies of Judaism, pp. 394–395.

Many religious Jews, however, warmly embraced the Zionist philosophy seeing in it not a foe of religion but the greatest aid to religious loyalty on the part of the Jew tempted to abandon his faith. There are enough passages in the classical literature regarding the duty of populating the holy land to have provided ammunition to religious Zionists who argued that Zionism in the contemporary world was a *religious* obligation. The Mizrachi movement in particular advocated religious Zionism with its slogan: "The land of Israel for the people of Israel according to the Torah of Israel." There are also enough passages in the classical literature on the idea that God uses human effort in order to fulfil His purpose to make specious the argument that the return of the Jews to the holy land must be by supernatural means. Judaism does not advocate quietism in such matters as earning a livelihood. Why, then, the religious Zionists argued, should it be considered impious to engage in human effort for the amelioration of Jewish suffering that would result from the realisation of the Zionist ideal? Rabbi A. I. Kook, the Chief Rabbi of Palestine, even went so far as to declare that the Jewish people had become too "spiritual" and that the secular was to be used as the stepping-stone to higher things. According to this teacher even the atheists who were making tremendous sacrifices in reclaiming the land and developing the Hebrew language were doing God's work without knowing it. Solomon Schechter, in a statement on Zionism published in 1906, similarly said:[5] "The reproach that Zionism is unspiritual is meaningless. Indeed, there seems to be a notion abroad that spirituality is a negative quality. Take any ideal and translate it into action, any sentiment of reverence and piety, and give it expression through a symbol or ceremony, speak of human yearning after communion with God, and try to realise it through actual prayer, and you will at once be denounced as unspiritual. However, the imputation is as old as the days when the name Pharisee became a reproach, and it is not to be expected that the Zionists would be spared. In general, it is the antinomian who will tell you that he is the only heir to the rare quality of spirituality, whereas the real saint is in all his actions so spontaneous and so natural that he is entirely unconscious of possessing spirituality, and practically never mentions it. The Zionists are no saints, but they may fairly claim that few movements are more free from the considerations of convenience and comfort, and less tainted with worldliness and other worldliness than the one they serve.

5. *Seminary Addresses*, pp. 98–99.

Nothing was to be gained by joining it. All the powers that be, were, and still are, opposed to it, whether in their capacity as individuals or as wealthy corporations. The Zionists are just beginning to be tolerated, but I remember distinctly the time when adhesion to the cause of Zionism might interfere with the prospects of a man's career, the cry being, 'no Zionist need apply'. The classes from which the Zionists were recruited were mostly the poorest of the poor. College men and university men, more blessed with enthusiasm and idealism than with the goods of this world, also furnished a fair quota. But their lack of means did not prevent them from responding most generously to every appeal made on behalf of the cause. They taxed themselves to the utmost of their capacity, and beyond. I myself have witnessed cases in which men and women joyfully contributed their last earnings, foregoing their summer vacations, for which they had been saving a whole year."

Two factors have combined to make all this debate a dead letter. The holocaust, in which six million Jews perished, brought in its wake a fierce and completely justified resolve on the part of Jews everywhere to put an end to the kind of Jewish homelessness which had made such horror possible. The creation of the State of Israel which resulted made academic the whole Zionist question. The State of Israel is a reality. It has won by its achievements the goodwill of the majority of Jews everywhere. The State of Israel is a reality and it has influenced Jewish thinking in a way that makes nonsense of the claim that Jews are *only* the adherents of the Jewish religion. In Israel, at least, the Jews are a nation.

This is not to say, of course, that there should be no theological concern with the implications of the State of Israel for Judaism. On the contrary, the reality of Jewish nationalism poses in far more acute form than ever before the problem of how to reconcile Jewish nationalistic aspirations with universalism, the secular with the sacred, belief in God's providence with human endeavour, justice for the Jews with the rights of the Arabs, love for the holy land with the loyalty the Jews outside Israel owe to the lands in which they reside. There are no easy solutions but theology can help by stressing, as it must, that the God Jews worship is the God of all the earth and all mankind and so guard against any narrowing of the Jewish vision. We can now see with the hindsight of history that those Rabbis who protested against Zionism were wrong. But they were not wrong when they saw that an unbridled nationalism is a form of idolatry, that no state, no matter how noble its aims, is to be worshipped, that the individual counts because he is unique, possessing a fraction of the divine light which only he can reveal.

Theology cannot provide detailed practical solutions to the problems facing Jews now that the State of Israel is a reality. But it can help in seeking to foster certain attitudes which, from the theological point of view, are sounder than others. Some of these attitudes can be stated.

1. God alone is to be worshipped, not the Jewish people

The more one admires the astonishing achievements of the State of Israel in reclaiming the desert, building a viable society based on justice and equity, in democratic government, in technical know-how, in the revival of the Hebrew language and literature, in the progress of learning and education; the more one loves the holy land, the Jewish way of life, the folk-ways of the Jews; the more one respects the heroism of Israel's soldiers, the devotion of Israel's statesmen, the sincere endeavours of the Israelis to find peace for themselves and their neighbours; and these things are all deserving of great admiration; the more must one guard against the apotheosis of the Jewish nation. No creature is to be worshipped. Only God is to be worshipped. These are basic principles without which there is no Judaism.

2. Jewish nationalism is no substitute for religion

Religion is *sui generis*. It is not "for" something else. Its aim is the worship of God. There is a tendency, nowadays, even among religious Jews to argue that Judaism is of value *because* it ensures Jewish survival. But this makes Jewish survival the ultimate instead of God and His service. Needless to say, service in this context is not confined to prayer or ritual but embraces all that God requires of man. The religious believer will struggle as hard for the right of his people to survive, make as many sacrifices, give as much time and effort, as his non-believing fellow-Jew but he will do these things themselves for God and as part of what he understands by the worship of God. He will see in the survival of the Jews a means to an end and not the end in itself.

3. God is the Father of all mankind

Judaism has long taught that the God of Israel is no tribal god but the Father of all men. To be sure, a man's first duty is to his own group and no reasonable person would require, for instance, that Israel sacrifice itself to Arab hate, greed or sheer stupidity. But God's world is wide and all men are His children. Judaism, now as ever, must continue to be taught as a universalistic faith with the aim of justice for all.

4. There should be no crude interpretation of the notion of "sacred soil"

The location of divinity in certain spots belongs to a primitive mode of thought. While there are traces of the idea in the Bible, Judaism nonetheless teaches that God is omnipresent and that He transcends the universe. Yet Judaism knows, too, of places especially hallowed: the synagogue, the Temple site, Jerusalem and the land of Israel as a whole. For modern Jews the most refined understanding of the idea of sacred places is not in the semi-magical way of seeing God as "present" in one place rather than another but in terms of psychological association. The land of Israel does have, according to the *Halakhah*, more "holiness", *kedushah*, than other lands but this should be interpreted in terms of the richer historical associations it has with the men who found God there. The land in which the Patriarchs lived and the prophets taught is the idea which should be stressed. The same applies to the other sacred spots. Superstitious reverence for a particular piece of soil in itself should be rejected. The Hebrew language is, similarly, the "holy tongue" not because it is God's special language. Historically considered Hebrew is an ancient Semitic tongue with the strongest affinities to other Semitic languages such as Aramaic and Arabic and was not originally spoken only by the Israelites. Hebrew is the "holy tongue" by association, because it is the language of the Bible, the form in which the covenant between God and Israel first was expressed, the instrument by means of which the seers and prophets of Israel poured out their hearts to God, the key with which to unlock the spiritual treasures of the Jewish people.

5. Hebrew culture is not Torah

The Torah is God's word in that, for all our recognition of its human side, its concern is with the ongoing process of the covenant between God and Israel. In our world it is futile to deny the claims of secular literature nor would anyone wish to do so. One can be an admirer of Ahad Ha-Am, Bialik and Tchernichowsky as one can be an admirer of Shakespeare, Milton and Matthew Arnold. But the demarcation lines between Torah and culture must be preserved. In our kind of world it can without contradiction be claimed that the study of say a Reform Rabbi's writings in German or English on Judaism is Torah while the secular essays or novels of a brilliant modern writer in Hebrew are not. This is not an appeal for a narrow view of Jewish culture. As William Temple once said, God is interested in many things apart from religion. But Judaism knows of *havdalah*, of the distinction between the sacred and the secular. The secular has its role to play in God's world, and it is an important role, but the secular is not sacred any more than the days of the week are the sabbath.

The problems of Jewish peoplehood and statehood are many. It is too soon after the establishment of the State of Israel for anyone to attempt to offer precise solutions. Much is in a state of flux and will remain so for some time. But these problems should be approached by religious Jews in the spirit of their faith, which attaches the greatest significance to what has happened in Israel and entertains the highest hopes for Israel in the future, but which has God alone as its "ultimate concern".

CHAPTER TWENTY-ONE

JUDAISM AND OTHER RELIGIONS

I N the Biblical record the conflict between the religion of Israel
and other religions is expressed chiefly in terms of Israel's loyalty
to God and its apostasy in worshipping strange gods. Elijah's
confrontation with the prophets of Baal (1 Kings 18) is the best-known
example of the ruthless war the prophetic teachers waged against the
"gods of the nations". The pagan deities are everywhere in the Bible
described in the most derisory terms. They are *elilim* (1 Chron. 16: 26),
literally "non-entities"; "loathsome" and "abominable" (Deut.
7: 26). Israel's worship of strange gods is compared to harlotry (Hos.
2: 7). The worship of God is alone true: the other religions are false.
This thought pervades the whole of the Biblical teaching. E. L.
Allen[1] is right: "The Hebrew prophets, faced with the licence of
Baal worship, the magic practices of Babylon, and the superstitions
of the Hellenistic world, swept them away as false and called men to
acknowledge the true God." Yehezkel Kaufmann has argued that the
Biblical authors had so little truck with the pagan religions that they
were ignorant of the pagan mythologies and never refer to them.[2]

However, one of the most striking things to be noticed in connection with the prophetic condemnation of pagan worship is that
where this is directed against the nations it is for the atrocities such as
child sacrifice not for the worship itself. Nowhere in the Bible is an
appeal made for the nations to give up their own gods, though, of
course, in the ideal state envisaged in the future all men will worship
the true God (Is. 12: 9; 66: 23; Zech. 14: 9). Indeed, it is implied that
God permits the nations to worship their own gods: "These the Lord
your God allotted to the other peoples everywhere under heaven"
(Deut. 4: 19). It is even suggested that when the heathen nations
worship their gods they are really worshipping God without knowing

1. *Christianity Among the Religions*, p. 120.   2. *The Religion of Israel*, pp. 7-59.

it: "For from the rising of the sun even to the going down of the same My name is great among the nations; And in every place offerings are presented unto My name, Even pure oblations; For my name is great among the nations, saith the Lord of hosts" (Mal. 1: 11). The prophet Micah declares: "For let all the peoples walk each one in the name of its god, But we will walk in the name of the Lord our God for ever and ever" (Micah 4: 5).

The Rabbis continued unabated the struggle against pagan idolatry—*avodah zarah*, "strange worship", as they called it. A whole tractate of the Talmud, bearing this name, is devoted to the laws concerning total rejection of anything which smacks of idolatrous worship. The Rabbis had in mind here chiefly the Greek and Roman pantheon but there are to be found frequent polemics, too, against Zoroastrianism, Christianity and Gnostic dualism, all of which are generally lumped together as the heresy of affirming "two powers", i.e. that there is more than one god.[3] For the Rabbis, while the Torah in its totality is for Israel alone, there is a Torah for Gentiles—the seven precepts of the sons of Noah, the usual classification of which is: (1) Not to worship idols; (2) Not to commit murder; (3) Not to commit adultery and incest; (4) Not to eat a limb torn from a living animal; (5) Not to blaspheme; (6) Not to steal; (7) To have an adequate system of law and justice.[4] There is evidence that in the early Rabbinic period Judaism was a missionary religion which strove to win converts to the Jewish faith.[5]

In the middle ages the two rival faiths to Judaism were her daughter religions Christianity and Islam. The general argument of the mediaeval Jewish thinkers was that since both these religions acknowledged that Judaism was once the true religion but had now been superseded, it was up to them to prove that this was so, not for Judaism to prove that it was true. The onus of proof was on them and it was not forthcoming. Generally speaking Islam was not considered to be idolatry but with regard to Christianity there was much debate.[6] The Far Eastern religions were completely unknown. It is

---

3. See *supra*, pp. 23–27.
4. Full details are given in the comprehensive article *ben noah* in *Encyclopedia Talmudit*, Vol. III, pp. 348–362.
5. See B. J. Bamberger: *Proselytism in the Talmudic Period* and W. G. Braude: *Jewish Proselytizing in the First Five Centuries of the Common Era*.
6. See Katz's excellent study: *Exclusiveness and Tolerance*.

not unusual in this period to find Jewish teachers quoting teachings of Muslims and Christians if these were helpful to the religious life as understood by Judaism. Bahya Ibn Pakudah, to quote one example, not only relies extensively on Sufi teachers but defends vigorously his right to use Gentiles as teachers of religion and refers to them as "saints", *hasidim*.[7] There is no doubt, however, that all the mediaeval Jewish thinkers considered both Islam and Christianity to be false and Judaism alone the true religion.

This is not to say that the mediaeval thinkers necessarily saw no value in the rival religions. In uncensored editions of Maimonides' Code there occurs this passage (*Yad, Melachim* 9: 3–4): "Even of him (Jesus) who imagined that he was the Messiah but was put to death by the Court, Daniel had previously prophesied, as it is said: 'Also the children of the violent among thy people shall lift themselves up to establish the vision; but they shall stumble' (Dan. 9: 14). Has there ever been a greater stumbling than this? For all the prophets declared that the Messiah will be the deliverer of Israel and their saviour, gathering their dispersed ones and confirming their commandments. But he caused Israel to perish by the sword, their remnant to be dispersed and humbled. He induced them to change the Torah and led the greater part of the world to err and serve another beside God. No human being, however, is capable of fathoming the designs of the Creator, for their ways are not His ways, neither are His thoughts their thoughts. All these events (relating to Jesus) and even those relating to him who succeeded the one referred to (Mohammed), were nothing else than a means for preparing the way for the King Messiah. It will reform the whole world to worship God with one accord; as it is said, 'For then will I turn the peoples a pure language that they may all call upon the name of the Lord to serve Him with one consent' (Zeph. 3:9). How will this be? The entire world has been fitted with the doctrine of the Messiah, the Torah and the Commandments. The doctrines have been propagated to the distant isles and among many peoples, uncircumcised of heart and flesh. They discuss these subjects which contradict the Torah. Some declare these Commandments were true, but are abrogated at the present time and have lost their force; while others assert that there are occult significations in them and they are not plain of meaning—the King has already come and revealed their hidden significance. But when the (true) king Messiah will in fact arise and succeed, be exalted and lifted up, they will immediately all recant and acknowledge the falsity of their assertions." At a much later date, Jacob Emden (*Preface to Seder Olam*, quoted by M. Goldstein: *Jesus in the Jewish Tradition*, p. 221) is more emphatic; "The founder of Christianity conferred a double blessing upon the world: On the one hand he strengthened the Torah of Moses, and emphasised its eternal obligatoriness. On the other hand he conferred favour

7. *Duties of the Heart*, Introduction, end.

upon the heathen in removing idolatry from them, imposing upon them
stricter moral obligations than are contained in the Torah of Moses. There
are many Christians of high qualities and excellent morals. Would that all
Christians would live in conformity with their precepts! They are not
enjoined, like the Israelites, to observe the laws of Moses, nor do they sin
if they associate other beings with God in worshipping a triune God. They
will receive a reward from God for having propagated a belief in Him
among nations that never heard His name: For He looks into the heart."
Jacob Emden wrote this in the eighteenth century by which time it was very
widely held among Jews that Christians and Muslims were in no way
included in the harsh condemnations voiced against the heathen in the
classical sources. The standard response seems to have been to say that these
condemnations applied only to the ancient heathen and to the contemporary
idolators, about whom Jewish authors at this time had very little knowledge.
See e.g. the remarkable universalistic section in Phineas Elijah Hurwitz's
Sefer Ha-Berit, Part II, *Maamar* 13 but Hurwitz (pp. 310–311) goes on to say
that Jeremiah's: "Pour out Thy wrath upon the nations that know Thee
not" (Jer. 10: 25) refers to nations that do not know God "like the men of
India and Japan who worship fire and water and who are called 'heathen'."
The legal authorities all treat the Far Eastern religions as idolatry, see e.g.
Rabbi Ezekiel Landau, *Noda Biyudah, Tinyana, Orah Hayim*, No. 10,
dated 1777 in a reply to a question from London. A Cohen married a pagan
woman in India with a ceremony according to Hindu rites. The Cohen
later divorced the woman and repented of his actions but the rule is that a
Cohen who had once worshipped idols is not permitted to bless the people
even after his repentance. Rabbi Landau permits the Cohen to bless the people,
arguing that participation in a marriage ceremony does not constitute
idolatrous worship since it is only a formality. Cf. the ruling of the famous
twentieth century Halakhist Rabbi Pesach Zevi Frank: *Har Tzevi*, No. 118,
pp. 106–107. The practical question addressed to Rabbi Frank from India
was whether it is permitted for Jews to drink the milk of "sacred cows"
since these are worshipped. The Rabbis reply that an animal which has been
worshipped was not offered as a sacrifice to God in Temple times but it is
permitted to eat of its meat and drink of its milk.

So much for the historical background. There are three attitudes
among Jews today on the relationship between Judaism and other
faiths.

1. *Judaism is true: all other religions are false*

This is, in fact, the mediaeval view. But a number of factors militate
against its acceptance nowadays in this stark form. First, we know
today much more about the religions of the world than the mediaeval
writers did. With the opening up of the Far East it was seen that the
peoples of the Far East have their own religious traditions and their

own sacred scriptures and that these contain much of spiritual value. It is now very difficult to believe that the Bhavagadgita or Zen or Confucianism or Taoism can simply be dismissed entirely as *avodah zarah* without acknowledging that these also contain truth. Secondly, so far as Christianity and Islam are concerned, once polemical distortions have been removed Jews are able to see these faiths in a far more favourable light and to appreciate to a greater extent than ever before the spiritual resources of these religions. Thirdly, the new discipline of Comparative Religion has made us more aware of the ideas common to all the great world religions, e.g. that there is a Ground of being and that man is able by virtue of something within his own soul to transcend his narrow ego and reach out to that Ground. Fourthly, the critical investigation into the sources of Judaism, historical investigation and the like, have enabled us to see Judaism itself as a developing religion, containing a "higher" and "lower" teaching so that a simple Judaism truth formula is no longer feasible in quite the way it was in the middle ages.

2. *All religions are equally true (or false)*

This is the relativist attitude, sometimes expressed as: it does not matter which religion you profess as long as you profess a religion or as long as it inspires you to lead a good life. The classical statement of this position is Lessing's *Nathan the Wise*. None of the three sons in the play knows who possesses the true ring but each can live as if he possessed it. The trouble with a relativistic approach is, however, that hardly any religious believers really think of their religion in this way. It appears to be an essential feature of religious belief that those who hold it consider it to be true, that for them questions of truth are involved. Furthermore, it is simply not true to the facts to say that all religions are basically the same. For all the things they have in common, the religions of the world affirm as basic principles ideas that are simply not compatible with one another. If certain forms of atheistic Buddhism are true then Hinduism with its many gods and Judaism and her daughter religions with their One God must be false. When Judaism denies that God can ever assume flesh it rejects thereby Christianity. If the "way" of the Buddha is alone "true" for all men then the way of the Torah cannot be true for Jews. For this reason the dream of one religion for all mankind, comprising the highest "insights" of all religions, is doomed to failure from the start because it is meaningless. Many of the "highest insights" of each particular religion are incompatible with those of other religions.

Again, existentialist emphasis on religion seen in the context of the personal makes it well-nigh impossible to treat religion as an idea alone from which other abstract ideas can be distilled to form a new amalgam. Syncretism in religion is as little possible in any enriching way as syncretism in language.

3. *There is more truth in Judaism than in other religions*

Sweeping though it may seem, there is no escaping the truth which Judaism enunciates, and for which Jews have been ready to suffer martyrdom, that there is only One God and that the Torah (for all the many interpretations given to the concept of Torah itself and for all the difficulties we have noted in a previous chapter)[8] has not been superseded by any other religion. This compels us, if we are adherents of Judaism, frankly to declare that the positions other religions take on these questions are false. Far Eastern faiths are either polytheistic or atheistic. The Christian concept of God is false from the Jewish point of view. Judaism similarly denies that Mohammed received a revelation from God which made him the last of the prophets with the Koran in the place of the Torah. Yet for all the lack of compromise in such an attitude it should not lead Jews to conclude that God has not revealed Himself to others or that the religions of the world have no truth in them. The position one ought to adopt is that there is *more* truth in Judaism than in other religions. Such an attitude is free alike from the dogmatism of the first views we have considered and the vagaries of relativism.

Certain conclusions would seem to follow from the adoption of such an attitude. Since the realities of the situation are that hardly anyone born in the Far East, for example, is likely to have Judaism presented to him as a live option and since even in the West very few Christians or Muslims are likely to embrace Judaism, then it must follow that while Judaism will continue to accept converts and while it will not give up its Messianic hope of an eventual conversion to the truth by all men, it must believe that the good man of whatever faith (or, for that matter, of none) will be counted among what the Rabbis call "the righteous of the nations of the world". The Rabbis of the early second century debated whether Gentiles have a share in the

8. See *supra*, pp. 211–218.

World to Come but the view adopted was that of R. Joshua who taught that the righteous of the nations of the world have a share in the World to Come.[9] Maimonides' formulation of this is as follows:[10] "Whoever accepts upon himself the seven precepts (of the sons of Noah) and keeps them belongs to the saints of the nations of the world and has a share in the World to Come. But this only applies if he accepts them and keeps them because the Holy One, blessed be He, commanded them in the Torah and informed us through Moses our teacher that the sons of Noah of old had been commanded to keep them. If, however, he keeps them because his reason tells him so he is not a 'proselyte of the gate' and is neither of the saints of the nations of the world nor of their sages."[11] To adopt this exceedingly narrow view which, incidentally, is Maimonides' own and finds no support in the Rabbinic sources, would mean that for Judaism the majority of mankind is denied spiritual bliss in the Hereafter. Even if Maimonides' view is rejected and the "righteous of the nations of the world" means those who keep the "seven precepts of the sons of Noah", even if they keep them because it seems right to do so not because of a belief in their revealed character, it would still rule out all polytheists and presumably all atheists and agnostics since one of the seven is aimed against idolatry and polytheism. But even according to the traditional Halakhah, there is the notion, helpful here, that a child brought up among heathen is not held responsible for pagan acts he performs when an adult because he has been trained to do them and cannot help himself. This doctrine of the "child captured by heathen" is applied in the Rabbinic sources to a Jew[12] but by the same token it would apply to anyone brought up in a polytheistic faith or an atheistic background who cannot be held responsible unless he had the opportunities of knowing the truth and wilfully rejects it and this

9. Tosefta Sanh. 13:2. It should be noted that the original reading here is *tzaddikim*, "righteous" of the nations not *hasidim*, "saints". This latter term is much later e.g. in Maimonides, *Yad, Melakhim*, 8: 11 and Bertinoro to Sanh. 10: 2.

10. *Yad, Melakhim* 8: 11.

11. In other texts the reading is: "is not of the saints of the nations of the world *but* of their sages." Rabbi A. I. Kook (*Letters*, Vol. I, No. 89, pp. 99–100) accepts this reading as the correct one and argues either that the "stage" of the "sage" is even higher than that of the "saint" or that there are "stages" for the sage which though not the "World to Come" represent a spiritual elevation of their own. This undoubtedly does credit to the learned Rabbi's heart but is hardly what Maimonides means.

12. Sabb. 68b.

is known only to God. In any event it seems reasonable to conclude that the "good man" of the nations is to be understood in the purely ethical sense and that in this sense, therefore, it does not matter whether a man has been brought up in this religion or the other or in no religion at all provided that he leads a good ethical life. Admittedly this is speculative but Judaism does, after all, affirm that God is the Father of all mankind and it is very hard to believe that He will deprive any of His children of spiritual bliss because, by an accident of birth, there were no opportunities of fully knowing the truth. Indeed, it would seem to be necessary, granted our premiss, to make the even bolder suggestion that the religious classics of mankind, insofar as they are monotheistic, or, at least, not polytheistic, are themselves God's way of teaching His truth to some of His children. One would presumably have to go even further than this and admit that Jews can learn from the religious classics of other faiths as they can learn from secular works. There is an old Jewish tradition to this effect. As we have noted, for instance, Bahya was prepared to accept Sufi teaching where it did not conflict with the Torah but produced a deeper understanding of the Torah.

CHAPTER TWENTY-TWO

THE MESSIANIC HOPE

THE doctrine of the Messiah, who will be sent by God to redeem Israel and usher in a new era in which all mankind will worship the true God, is one of the most distinctive of Judaism's teachings. With the strongest antecedents in the Bible, the doctrine was developed, elaborated upon, and given a variety of interpretations throughout Jewish history, but its basic affirmation is that human history will find its culmination and fulfilment here on earth. Ultimately, the doctrine declares, God will not abandon His world to moral chaos. Eventually He will intercede directly in order to call a halt to tyranny, oppression and the pursuit of evil so as to restore mankind to the state of bliss here on earth that is described at the beginning of the book of Genesis, when Adam and Eve lived in the Garden of Eden. The whole of human history is seen as reaching from the Paradise Lost of Adam to the Paradise Regained in the Messianic Age.[1]

The term *Mashiah*, from the root *mashah*, "to anoint", means "the anointed one". It is interesting that the term itself is not applied to the redeemer sent by God to release Israel from bondage, earlier than in the Apocalyptic literature, but the idea behind it is much earlier. In the Bible the term *Mashiah* refers not to a person who will come in the future to redeem Israel but to any person actually anointed with sacred oil for the purpose of high office, e.g. the king or the high priest. The term is also applied to any person for whom God has a special purpose; to Cyrus King of Persia, for instance (Is. 45: 1). It would be totally erroneous, however, to conclude from

---

1. For the subject of this chapter see especially: J. Klausner: *The Messianic Idea in Israel*; G. Scholem: *Shabbatai Zevi*; Julius H. Greenstone: *The Messiah Idea in Jewish History*; Steven S. Schwarzschild: *The Personal Messiah—Towards the Restoration of a Discarded Doctrine*; Joseph Sarachek: *The Doctrine of the Messiah in Mediaeval Jewish Literature*.

this that the whole idea of a personal Messiah is post-Biblical. While not referring to him as the Messiah, some of the prophets do speak of the future redemption as being ushered in by a scion of the house of David, although other prophets speak only of the bliss of that future state without any reference to a charismatic personality who will bring it about. In other words both doctrines are found in the Bible, that of the personal Messiah and that of the Messianic Age.

Klausner[2] thus describes the difference between what he calls the *Messianic expectation* and the more explicit *belief in the Messiah*. His definition of the Messianic expectation is: *The prophetic hope for the end of this age, in which there will be political freedom, moral perfection, and earthly bliss for the people of Israel in its own land, and also for the entire human race.* His definition of the belief in the Messiah is: *The prophetic hope for the end of this age, in which a strong redeemer, by his power and his spirit, will bring complete redemption, political and spiritual, to the people of Israel, and along with this, earthly bliss and moral perfection to the entire human race.* The prophets Isaiah, Micah, Jeremiah and Zechariah all speak of an ideal human leader possessed of lofty spiritual and ethical qualities. He is not, however, a redeemer (as the Messiah became in the later literature). God alone is the redeemer and the Messiah-King is only the leader of the redeemed people, who will execute justice and righteousness upon earth. In Nahum, Zephaniah, Habbakuk, Malachi, Joel and Daniel, on the other hand, there is no human leader at all but the Lord alone is the redeemer. In other books (Amos, Ezekiel, Obadiah) there is only a collective "Messiah", the kingdom of the house of David.[3]

As Klausner points out the Biblical ideas were embellished in the Apocrypha and Pseudepigrapha so that there was forged a complete chain of Messianic speculation. Although the separate links are not found in all the books of the Apocrypha and Pseudepigrapha they are found in the literature in a definite order and they reappear in this

2. *The Messianic Idea in Israel*, p. 9.
3. The major Biblical references of Messianic import are: Gen. 12: 2–3; 26:4; 28: 14; Ex. 19: 5–6; Lev. 26: 3–45; Num. 24: 17–19; Deut. 28: 1–68; 30: 3–10; Amos 5: 18–20; 8: 11–12; 9: 8–15; Hos. 6: 1–3; 3: 4–5; 14: 6–8; Is. 9: 5f.; 11: 1f; 30: 26; Micah 5: 9–13; Zeph. 1: 15–16; 2: 3; 3: 9–12; Jer. 4: 9; 6: 23–27; 16: 14–15; 23: 7–8; 30: 16; 31: 12; 33: 14–26; Ezek. 20: 32–34; 36: 25–33; 37: 1–14; 34: 23–24; 46: 2–13; Obad.; Is. 40–66; Hag., Zech., Joel 2: 17; 3: 5; 4: 18; Mal. 3: 17–21; 22–24; Dan. 2: 6–9; 12; Ps. 89; 132: 11–18; 102: 14–17; and Ps. 12; 46; 66; 68 and 117.

order in the Rabbinic literature. The links are: the signs of the Messiah; the birth pangs of the Messiah; the coming of Elijah; the trumpet of the Messiah; the ingathering of the exiles; the reception of proselytes; the war with Gog and Magog; the Days of the Messiah; the renovation of the world; the Day of Judgement; the resurrection of the dead; the World to Come. Klausner also notes that there is no mention of the personality of the Messiah in any book of the Apocrypha. The house of David is mentioned but not the son of David. In the apocalyptic literature, on the other hand, the idea of a personal Messiah again comes into prominence.[4]

All these speculations are reflected in the vast amount of material on the Messiah contained in the Rabbinic literature. The general view in this literature is undoubtedly that of a personal Messiah. The sole exception is that of the Amora R. Hillel who declared: "There shall be no Messiah for Israel, because they have already enjoyed him in the days of the Hezekiah"[5] whereupon R. Joseph rebuked him: "May God forgive R. Hillel." Rabbi Akiba recognised Bar Kochba as the Messiah even though he had performed no miracles.[6] The third century Babylonian Amora, Samuel, taught: "The days of the Messiah do not differ from the present at all except for the fact that in that age Israel will no longer be in bondage to the kingdoms of the world."[7] The prophet Elijah is frequently mentioned in the Rabbinic literature as the herald of the Messiah.[8]

All the mediaeval thinkers believe in a personal Messiah but they differ on whether the advent of the Messiah and the Messianic Age generally are to be conceived of in naturalistic or supernaturalistic terms. Maimonides' formulation[9] with which he concludes his great Code, repays study.

4. The main passages of Messianic import in the Apocrypha and Pseudepigrapha are: Eccl. 35: 22–26; 36; 45: 6–7; 47: 22; 48: 10; 1 Macc. 2: 27; 4: 46; 2 Macc. 7: 9–11; 14: 46; 36; Judith 16: 17; Tobit 13: 9–16; 14: 5–7; Baruch 2; 24–35; 4: 36–5; 4; 5: 5 to end; Wisdom of Solomon 3: 1–4; 5: 15–16; The 'Ethiopic' Book of Enoch; Jubilees 1: 8–18; 23; Testament of the Twelve Patriarchs: Simeon 6; Levi: 17 and 23; Judah 24; Psalms of Solomon 16; 17; 28: 3–91; Assumption of Moses 10; the Syriac Book of Baruch; IV Ezra; Biblical antiquities 3: 10; The Sibylline Oracles.
5. Sanh. 99a. Rashi ad loc. is probably correct that R. Hillel does not deny the Messianic hope as such, only the belief in a personal Messiah.
6. Jer. T. Taan. 4: 5; Lam. R. to 22: 2.
7. Ber. 34b.
8. e.g. in Ed. 8: 7.
9. *Yad, Melakhim,* 11–12.

King Messiah, begins Maimonides, will restore the kingdom of David to its former state. He will rebuild the Temple, gather in the dispersed ones of Israel and restore all the laws of the Torah that were in abeyance such as the sacrificial cult. Whoever does not believe in him or does not hope for his coming denies not alone the prophets but the Torah of Moses. Maimonides quotes Numbers 24: 17–18; Deuteronomy 30: 3–5; Zechariah 9: 10 and Obadiah 1: 24.[10]

The King Messiah will not be obliged to perform miracles in order to establish his identity. Rabbi Akiba acknowledged Bar Kochba as the Messiah even though he performed no miracles. It was only when Bar Kochba suffered defeat that it was seen that he was not, in fact, the Messiah.[11]

How, then, is the Messiah to be identified? Maimonides replies:[12] "If a king arises of the house of David, meditating in the Torah and performing precepts like his father David, in accordance with the Written Torah and the Oral Torah, and if he will compel all Israel to walk in the way of the Torah and repairs its breaches, and if he will wage the wars of the Lord, it can be assumed that he is the Messiah. If he succeeds in rebuilding the Temple and gathering the dispersed ones of Israel, it will then be established beyond doubt that he is the Messiah who will perfect the whole world to serve God together, as it is said: 'For then will I turn to the peoples of a pure language, that they may call upon the name of the Lord, to serve Him with one consent'" (Zeph. 3: 9).

It should not be imagined, continues Maimonides,[13] that a different order will prevail in the world in the days of the Messiah or that nature will change. The apparent references in the prophetic writings to the marvels which will take place at that time are not to be understood literally but figuratively, e.g. the lamb dwelling with the wolf refers to the "lamb" of Israel living at peace undisturbed by the Gentile "wolves", who themselves will embrace the true religion and rob and plunder no more.

Especially significant is Maimonides' attempt to discourage speculation on the detailed order of events in the Messianic Age.[14] The

10. *Yad, Melakhim*, 11: 1.
11. *Yad, Melakhim*, 11: 3.
12. *Yad, Melakhim*, 11: 4.
13. *Yad, Melakhim*, 12: 1.
14. *Yad, Melakhim*, 12: 2.

Rabbis, he says, had no definite tradition regarding these details and simply tried to interpret the relevant Scriptural verses. This is why differences are to be found among the sages themselves regarding the details. Such details are not fundamental and speculation regarding them is simply a waste of time. Similarly, it is wrong to try to guess the "end", i.e. trying to unravel the secret of when the Messiah will come from the references to the event in Scripture. All that man has to do in this connection is to believe in a general sense that the Messiah will come and to hope for the event to happen.

There is no contradiction between what Maimonides says here and his earlier detailed description of what is to happen in the Messianic Age. The distinction he makes is between truth handed down by tradition or taught in the Torah and pure speculation. Those aspects of the Messiance belief which Maimonides states in detail, e.g. the personal Messiah, the rebuilding of the Temple, that the Messiah is a descendant of David, are, for him, either taught explicitly in the Torah or are known by tradition so that none dissents from them. The other details found in the Rabbinic literature are simply speculative and on these it is possible, even desirable, to have an open mind.

The Messiah, by means of the holy spirit which will rest on him, will inform each Israelite to which tribe he belongs, declaring, for example, who is a *kohen* and who a *Levite*.[15]

Finally, Maimonides[16] declares his view on the purpose of the Messianic Age: "The sages and prophets desired the days of the Messiah neither that they might rule over the world nor that they might lord it over the nations nor that the nations should elevate them nor that they might eat, drink and be merry, but that they might be free to engage in the study of the Torah and its wisdom, without any tyrant preventing them from so doing, so that they might attain to the life of the World to Come. At that time there will be neither famine nor war, neither envy nor competition, for goodness will be freely bestowed and delicacies will be as abundant as dust and there will be no other occupation among all mankind than to know the Lord. Consequently, at that time the Jews will be great sages, knowing secret things, and apprehending as much of the knowledge of God as the human mind is capable, as it is said: "For the earth shall

15. *Yad, Melakhim*, 12: 3.   16. *Yad, Melakhim*, 12: 4–5.

be full of the knowledge of the Lord, as the waters cover the sea'"
(Is. 11:9).

After the expulsion from Spain Messianic longing became particularly
acute and was reflected especially in the Lurianic Kabbalah at the heart of
which is the doctrine of "restoration". Every act of man performed in a
spirit of devotion succeeds in reclaiming the "divine sparks" which were
scattered at the "breaking of the vessels", see *supra*, pp. 32–34. G. Scholem
has traced with great skill how the doctrine of the "divine sparks" played its
part in the Shabbatai Zevi movement. The false Messiah managed to retain
some of his followers even after his conversion to Islam because they
believed that it was the function of the Messiah to reclaim even those
"sparks" which had fallen into the domain of the "other side". For this in
detail see Scholem's work: *Shabbatai Zevi*. Modern thinkers are divided as
to whether the Hasidic movement was Messianic in an acute sense. For a
summary and study of the whole question see I. Tishby: *The Messianic
Idea and Messianic Trends in the Growth of Hassidism*. But Scholem has
recently argued that while it is undoubtedly true that the early Hasidim were
Orthodox Jews and hence certainly held to the belief in the coming of the
Messiah, they "neutralised" to a large extent the intense Messianic longing
released by the Shabbateans. Thus in Hasidism the ideal of *devekut*, "cleaving
to God", is a personal ideal capable of realisation even without the advent
of the Messiah and in some Hasidic texts the term *geulah*, "redemption",
always referring in the older sources to the redemption of Israel, now refers
to the personal redemption of the individual soul. A particularly original
turn was given in early Hasidism to the "divine sparks" doctrine. For the
Baal Shem Tov and his disciples man can only lift up such sparks as belong
to what the Kabbalists call the "root" of his soul. "All that belongs to a man,
his servants, and animals, even his household effects, his business transactions,
his wife and his contemporaries—they all contain sparks of his own soul
which he has to lift up." This is a personalistic interpretation of the Lurianic
doctrine and is found nowhere in the earlier sources. For Scholem's views
on all the above matters see his: *The Messianic Idea in Judaism*.

Modern Jewish thinkers were the heirs to all the previous ideas on
the Messianic Age. The fluctuating nature of the doctrine in former
times, the accretion of legends and fanciful details, the debates among
the sages on this or that detail, the possibility of a naturalistic as well
as supernaturalistic interpretation of the doctrine, the emphasis here
on the personal Messiah and there on the Messianic Age, all contributed to make this principle of the Jewish faith the one most fluid of
all in its capacity for reinterpretation. Hardly any Jewish thinkers
were prepared to give up the doctrine entirely. But the variety of

interpretation of its meaning and significance has become bewildering in its diversity.

Even in the earlier period it was recognised that of all the principles of the Jewish faith the belief in the coming of the Messiah is the one less defined than the others and more open to speculation. In addition to Maimonides' views in this connection quoted above it is worth quoting the ideas contained in the formulation of R. Moses b. Joseph di Trani (the *Mabit*) in the sixteenth century. *Mabit* (*Bet Elohim, Shaar Ha-Yesodot*, Chapter 50) remarks that in his treatment of the principles of the Jewish faith he has endeavoured to demonstrate their truth rationally as well as by relying on tradition but since this principle concerns events that are to happen in the future no direct demonstration is possible and it must be ultimately a matter of faith. For *Mabit* in the Messianic Age all men will acknowledge the law of Moses as the true religion and through this God's name will be magnified and sanctified since then only He will be worshipped. This will be brought about by God giving men a new heart, i.e. by direct divine intervention (Chapter 50). The advent of the Messiah will be attended by numerous miracles according to *Mabit* (Chapter 51). Just as at the time of the Exodus the miraculous events were necessary both in order to convince Pharaoh and the Israelites so the miraculous element in the coming of the Messiah will have to be so powerful as to convince the greatest sceptic. Maimonides' "naturalistic" interpretation has been abandoned entirely, even though *Mabit* otherwise bases his views in this and the other chapters of this section of his book on Maimonides.

Maimonides' "naturalism" consists only in his rejection of miracles as the test for the Messiah and his denial that the order of nature will change in the Messianic Age. Many modern thinkers have gone much further, interpreting the whole Messianic idea in purely naturalistic terms. The two main modern naturalistic interpretations of the Messianic Age are those of classical Reform and Zionism. Diametrically opposed though these two movements were on the question of Jewish nationalism and the return to the holy land,[17] they were in agreement in seeing the realisation of the Messianic hope in terms of natural processes. The early Reformers believed that the Messianic Age was beginning to dawn in their own day since mankind was evidently taking rapid strides towards a new world of sound education for all, social progress, greater liberalism in theory and practice, and more comprehensive opportunities for a decent human existence. There is no need to repeat what has been so frequently said, that the

17. See *supra*, pp. 276–280.

events of the twentieth century have dashed these hopes. Perhaps
Naziism is no argument against the nineteenth century idea of auto-
matic progress in all spheres including the moral. Nonetheless, it is
clear to most thinking people nowadays that the "new heart" which,
according to the tradition God will provide in the Messianic Age,
means the emergence of a better type of human being. There is no
evidence that this is happening or can happen without divine intervention. Naturally, the classical Reform position rejects the belief
in a personal Messiah.

Many Zionists similarly saw the Zionist movement as the realisation of the Messianic hope, rejecting, too, the doctrine of the personal
Messiah but embracing warmly the idea of the restoration of Israel.
Yet this naturalistic interpretation of the doctrine remains totally
inadequate on a number of grounds. There is the greatest danger in
identifying the State of Israel, for instance, and its achievements—
though these are of the most impressive kind—with the Messianic
Age because mankind is still the same and capable of behaving in the
same old unregenerate way. Realised eschatalogy is a hindrance to
the Jewish hope of a new world in which the Kingdom of Heaven is
established. Traditionally there is a powerful numinous quality to
the Messianic hope. In the words of the Rosh Ha-Shanah and Yom
Kippur prayer it is the hope that God will "impose His awe on all
creatures". To identify this with the present state of human society is
ridiculous. Nor is the attempt of some religious Zionists to have the
best of both worlds by seeing the emergence of the State of Israel as,
in the current term, "the beginning of 'redemption' ", *athalta di-geula*,
very helpful. Either redemption is the natural result of Israel's determination to survive as a nation, in which case it is not the Messianic
"redemption" at all, albeit the achievements of the State are altogether
worthy of our enthusiasm and loyal support; or the redemption is
not yet, in which case nothing is gained by introducing the traditionally dubious conception of a "beginning". It is extremely hard to
accept that the dream of Judaism since the days of the prophets of a
perfected world has been in error. We may not be able to see fully
the purpose of the Messianic Age but we can still see the power of a
divine summing-up of the whole human enterprise by inaugurating
a period of life at its most elevated level here on earth.

If one is prepared to go so far why not accept the traditional view
in its entirety? But the doctrine of a personal Messiah is hard to believe

in not because it is in itself philosophically unrespectable—after all it cannot be denied on *a priori* grounds that God may choose this way of bringing about His purpose—but because of other considerations. First, as we have noted, not all the prophets think of a personal Messiah. Then again the whole idea is bound up with the idea of the promise to the house of David. A Maimonides is obliged to accept this as the direct promise of God which must be fulfilled. Our view of the Bible is altogether different.[18] We no longer appeal to Biblical texts as evidence in this way for what is to happen in the future. It cannot also be denied that democratic ideas have had an influence on our thinking. The purpose of a special royal person, elevated above all others by reason of birth, to *rule* over all others, is hard for us to fathom. Maimonides, as we have seen, associates the work of King Messiah with the recognition by him of each of the 12 tribes. Such a *motif* has no place in our thinking. Nor, once the appeal to Biblical texts is discarded, does the idea of a rebuilt Temple in which animal sacrifices are offered seem to us the highest to which our religion can aspire. We simply do not see the matter at all in this way and do not believe it will ever happen in this way.

A degree of religious agnosticism is called for here. We must be frank enough to admit that we simply do not know what will happen in the Messianic Age. Relying on Maimonides' boldness in his day and going beyond it for good reason in ours, we affirm our belief that God will one day intervene, that no good deed goes to waste, that the human drama will somehow find its fulfilment here on earth, that we do right to long and pray for God's direct intervention. More than this we cannot say. We must leave it to God who alone knows all secrets.

18. See *supra*, pp. 204–210.

CHAPTER TWENTY-THREE

THE HEREAFTER

THE doctrine that this life is not all but that after here on earth there is another state of existence is a basic principle of the Jewish faith. One of the most remarkable features of Jewish belief in the Hereafter is the absence of any kind of definite information in the Bible. Naturally, Jewish believers in the doctrine wished to find it referred to in the Bible. Salo Baron is undoubtedly correct when he writes:[1] "Entire libraries could be filled with writings on the Old Testament doctrine of the Hereafter, even more than ordinarily contrasting with the paucity of the biblical statements themselves. This is not altogether surprising when one considers the enormous role this doctrine was to play in the subsequent world outlook of Judaism and its daughter religions."

In order to study the little Biblical material there is on the subject it is essential to examine the views prevalent in the two great ancient civilisations of Egypt and Babylon, which formed the background to a good deal of Biblical thought.

The official Babylonian religion[2] had no belief in a Hereafter but there were "popular" beliefs reaching back to hoary antiquity according to which man could become immortal as the gods were immortal. There are references to this idea in such sources as the Gilgamesh epic and many tombs have been discovered in which various articles were placed to help the deceased in his progress in the next world. Similar beliefs were entertained by the ancient Arabs. It is possible that these two types of belief were found also among the ancient Hebrews, i.e. a "popular", very old belief, attended with

1. *A Social and Religious History of the Jews*, Vol. I, p. 357, note 5, see the bibliographical references in this note and in note 9, end, p. 358.
2. On Babylonian beliefs as a background to Biblical considerations of the Hereafter see Oesterley and Robinson: *Hebrew Religion*, Chapter VIII, pp. 79–97; Chapter XXI, pp. 243–253; Chapter XXXVI, pp. 352–365.

superstitions, and an "official" belief which frowned on all speculation regarding the Hereafter. This would help to explain why, on the one hand, in the Bible there are found such popular stories as that of the witch of Endor and, on the other hand, there is "official" silence on the whole question. The concept of *Sheol*, the abode of the dead, was probably originally a "popular" belief which later became "officially" accepted, with *Sheol* as a nebulous region. At a later stage still the possibility of the soul having a vital relationship with God even in *Sheol*, was accepted, as is evidenced in the Psalms.

In the Egyptian religion, of course, the belief in the Hereafter was part of the "official" religion. The Egyptian doctrine was founded on the belief that Osiris was slain by his brother Set, raised up again and justified before the gods against the accusations of Set and made god and judge in the underworld. Those who believed in him shared the same destiny. Chapter 154 of the *Book of the Dead* reads:

> "Homage to thee, O my divine father
> Osiris! Thou hast thy body with thy
> members. Thou didst not decay . . . thou
> didst not become corruption. I shall
> not decay . . . and I shall not see
> corruption . . . I shall have my being,
> I shall live, I shall germinate, I
> shall wake up in peace."[3]

Of the persistent Egyptian practice of burying all kinds of objects in tombs for the use of the dead, W. B. Emery[4] wittily remarks that the Egyptians believed that "you could take it with you".

Summing up the differences between the two civilisations on this matter G. F. Moore observes:[5] "A striking difference between Egypt and Babylon is the paucity in the latter, through all periods, of material from the tombs. The 'eternal houses' of the dead in Egypt, with their inscriptions and decorations and the funerary texts written on the walls or deposited in coffins, reveal to us in much detail the life of this world as well as the notions of the other world. To all this there is no counterpart in Babylonia. The fact itself is significant; the hereafter never occupied the imagination of the Babylonians as it

---

3. See Hastings' *Encyclopedia of Religion and Ethics*, Vol. IV, pp. 243–244.
4. *Archaic Egypt*, p. 129.
5. *History of Religions*, Vol. I, pp. 228f.

did that of the Egyptians, and their notions about it never got beyond
a very primitive stage."

Thus, the "official" Egyptian view was based on the idea that the
realm of death was the realm of the gods. This may well be why, as
Y. Kaufmann has argued, "the realm of the dead, the rites connected
with death and burial, as well as the destiny of the soul in the other
world, play no part in the religion of YHWH".[6] Since man in the
ancient religions could only become immortal by identifying himself
with the gods and becoming in some ways a god himself, the realm
of death was bound to be considered in the Hebrew religion the realm
of the impure, hence the idea in Biblical law of the corpse as source of
ritual contamination. "What distinguishes the faith of later Judaism",
writes Kaufmann,[7] "from that of the Bible is not, then, the idea of
immortality. It is rather that the biblical age had not succeeded in
forming a conception of a judgement of the soul and its deliverance
from death that would not be vitiated by the images of an infernal
god, a dying god, or the apotheosis of the dead. Having surrounded
death with impurity, it was unable to find a way to introduce holiness
into that realm. And because the holy, the divine, has no place among
the dwellers of Sheol, there is no judgement, no reward, and no
punishment there. It was not the belief in immortality that came
later, but the breakthrough of the soul to God from the realm of
death. This transformation occurred only after many centuries."
Kaufmann is probably right but the breakthrough of which he speaks
took place in the (late) Biblical period:

> "Whither shall I go from Thy spirit?
> Or whither shall I flee from Thy presence?
> If I ascend into heaven, Thou art there;
> If I make my bed in Sheol, behold Thou art there"
>
> (Ps. 139: 7-8)

The derivation of the word Sheol is uncertain. The two most
frequent suggestions are that it is derived from the root *shaal*, "to ask"
(possibly, the place where inquiry is made of the dead) or from the

---

6. *The Religion of Israel*, p. 311. In the Heb. original (*Toledot Ha-Emunah Ha-Yisreelit*,
   Vol. II, Book 2, Chapter 17, pp. 544-556), Kaufmann remarks that it is imprecise
   to say that the immortality of the soul is unknown in Biblical religion. It is
   known but is not brought into association with the official religion.
7. *The Religion of Israel*, pp. 315-316.

root *shaal* (with an *ayin*) meaning "to be hollow". The general association of Sheol is with vagueness. It is apparently a nebulous, shadowy region. Something is going on there but what it is remains uncertain. Sheol is contrasted with heaven, hence it is the "underworld":

> "Though they dig into Sheol,
> Thence shall My hand take them;
> And though they climb up to heaven,
> Thence will I bring them down" (Amos 9: 2)

Similarly: "But if the Lord made a new thing, and the ground open her mouth, and swallow them up, with all that appertain unto them, and they go down alive to Sheol, then ye shall understand that these men have despised the Lord" (Num. 16: 30). Though the Psalmist (Ps. 139: 7–8), as above, thinks of a meeting with God even in Sheol, the prophet declares:

> "For Sheol cannot praise Thee,
> Death cannot celebrate Thee;
> They that go down into the pit cannot hope for Thy truth,
> The living, the living, he shall praise Thee.
> As I do this day;
> The father to the children shall make known Thy truth"
> (Is. 35: 18–19).

Possibly of relevance to Biblical notions regarding the Hereafter is the punishment (found only in the source known as "P", the 'Priestly Code') known as *karet*, "to be cut off". Some scholars have understood this to mean a form of excommunication. In a number of passages, however, *karet* is equated with the death penalty, e.g.: "For whosoever shall do any of these abominations, even the souls that do them shall be cut off from their people" (Lev. 18: 29). But in Lev. 20: 10, 11, 12, 13, etc., the penalty for the same offences is death. (Cf. Ex. 31: 14: "Ye shall keep the sabbath therefore, for it is holy unto you; every one that profaneth it shall surely be put to death; for whosoever doeth any work therein, that soul shall be cut off from among his people.") A possible explanation is that *karet* means divine punishment; perhaps the guilty person is to be "excommunicated" and then left to receive his divine punishment (cf. Lev. 20: 4–5).[8] It is, however, possible that *karet* does not refer to a punishment in this life at all but to one in the Hereafter. The soul is cut off from its "people" and this may perhaps be connected with the idea of one who dies as being, in the Biblical idiom, "gathered unto his people". But all this remains very uncertain.

The following are the main Biblical passages relevant to the theme of immortality. They are not arranged chronologically. Apart from the very difficult problem of dating, it would be absurd to try to trace the development of the idea in neat sequence since earlier ideas frequently persist until a much later period and, conversely, ideas, later to be fully developed, appear in rudimentary form much earlier. (1) Eccl. 9: 4–10 seems to contradict the verse: "Then shall the dust return to the earth as it was: and the spirit shall return unto God who gave it" (Eccl. 12: 7). This latter verse, however, may mean that man's individuality is absorbed back into God (there is obviously a reference to the creation narrative (Gen. 2: 7). In any event, this belongs to the much-discussed problem of the contradictions in Ecclesiastes. (2) Dan. 12: 2–3. This is a very late passage. It clearly refers to the resurrection of the dead, a doctrine that was widely held at the time when the book of Daniel was written. (3) Job. 19: 25–26 has frequently been understood as expressing a belief either in the resurrection of the dead or in the immortality of the soul (depending on whether *mi-besari* means "*from* my flesh" or "*without* my flesh", see E. C. S. Gibson: *The Book of Job*, pp. 99–100). But the passage is in any event difficult. Although the book of Job is late and although the idea of immortality is strictly relevant to the theme of the book, there is, in fact, no clear reference to the idea in the book. This almost certainly means that although in the author's day the belief was already widely held he himself did not share it. (4) 1 Sam. 28, especially verses 13–19, the story of the witch of Endor. Some of the mediaeval Jewish commentators treat the passage as suggesting sheer fraud on the part of the woman but the plain meaning clearly implies a belief in the possibility of raising the dead and that the dead are still in existence in the other world. (5) 1 Sam. 25: 29. In the (late) Talmudic literature the "bundle of life" refers to the Hereafter, as does the "sling"—*kaf ha-kela*, but, as some of the mediaeval Jewish commentators suggest, the references can easily be to this life. "Soul", *nefesh*, here, of course, simply means, as generally in classical Hebrew, the vital force, the life, the person. (6) Gen. 47: 29–30. The meaning appears to be that Jacob would still enjoy existence after death so that the kindness done should be *to him* after his death. The mediaeval Jewish commentators are divided on the meaning of the first part of the

8. In the Rabbinic literature *karet* is a divine punishment where, because of the absence of certain technicalities or because it is too severe, the full death penalty of the Court cannot be carried out.

second verse but the plain meaning appears to be that dying itself is called "sleeping with the fathers", i.e. the reference is to the gathering of the tribe in the other world not to the burial of the body in the place of the fathers. In this connection it is worth noting that the similar expression used of Abraham at his death (Gen. 25: 8) cannot refer to burial in the family sepulchre since he was, in fact, buried elsewhere. (7) Jer. 31:14-15. Rachel weeps and is comforted by God. She is still aware of the sufferings of her children. Rachel is described as being near her grave in Ramah. (8) Is. 26: 19. This is a difficult verse of uncertain date which seems to refer either to individual resurrection or the resurrection of the people, in which latter case it is merely a figurative statement of national rebirth. (9) Ps. 48: 15. According to the Midrash (Lev. R. 11; Jer. T. Meg. 2: 4; Eccl. R. 1: 11) Aquilas translates *al-mut* in the verse as *athanasia*. But many moderns do not consider this to be part of the Psalm at all and, in any event, it may refer only to the continued existence of the people in their national life. On balance it does seem as if the translation "He will lead us beyond death" is homiletical. (10) Lev. 19: 31. The meaning of *ovot* and *yiddeonim* mentioned in the verse is not clear but they occur in the singular in Deut. 18: 10-11 governed by the verb *shaal*, "to ask" and, moreover, there is a definite reference in Deut. to the necromancer—*doresh el ha-metim*, "one who seeks the dead". The mediaeval Jewish commentators were divided as to whether the verse implies a belief in the efficiency of necromancy but the plain meaning seems to be that it was possible, though strictly forbidden, for a living person to make contact with the dead. The witch of Endor is described (1 Sam. 28: 7) as *baalat ov* so that the English translation of *ov* and *yiddeoni* as "ghosts" and "familiar spirits" is not far off the mark (see Driver's notes on these terms in his *Deuteronomy*, pp. 223-226). (11) Is. 57: 1-2. This is not very definite but does seem to imply that there is a Hereafter in which the righteous are rewarded.

The Biblical references, then, to the Hereafter are not very definite. It is generally held that the doctrine of the Hereafter came into full prominence during the Maccabean period when many good men were dying for their faith and the older view of reward and punishment in this life became untenable. But, as we have seen, some doctrine of a future life, was held previously. It is really a question of a deepening of the doctrine, especially among the ranks of the warrior saints of the Maccabean period, the Hasidim.[9]

From this period, at least, there are to be found three connected eschatological ideas: (1) The immortality of the soul; (2) The doctrine of the Messiah; (3) The resurrection of the dead. The immortality of the soul doctrine, as it developed, owes much, in all probability, to

6. On the beliefs regarding the Hereafter in the post-Biblical period see Charles: *A Critical History of the Doctrine of a Future Life*, Chapters V-VIII, pp. 162-305.

Greek beliefs; the resurrection of the dead to Persian beliefs. The Messianic belief is entirely of Jewish origin. Basically there is a contradiction between the two doctrines of the immortality of the soul and the resurrection of the dead. The doctrine of the immortality of the soul teaches that when the body of the individual dies his soul still lives on. The resurrection, on the other hand, is national and universal, taking place on earth after the advent of the Messiah. According to this latter doctrine in its original meaning, when the individual died he was truly dead and there was no separate soul to live on in Heaven after the death of the body. The resurrection of the dead was exactly what the name implies. Later in Judaism the two doctrines were, however, combined and this helps to explain the tensions in this matter in the Rabbinic literature and the ambiguities in the Rabbinic term "the World to Come".[10] Once the two were combined the three beliefs formed the Jewish eschatological scheme. In this the individual does not lose his soul at death. This lives on in Heaven. Some time after the coming of the Messiah the body is resurrected and the soul returns to it here on earth.

Josephus[11] states that the Sadducees denied the doctrine of the immortality of the soul. The Mishnah,[12] too, states that the Sadducees said that there is only one "world". It is generally assumed that the debate between the Sadducees and the Pharisees concerned both the immortality of the soul and the resurrection; the Pharisees accepting both doctrines, the Sadducees denying both. David Neumark,[13] however, has argued, not very convincingly, that the Sadducees only denied the resurrection of the dead but believed in the immortality of the soul, which, he claims, is what one would have expected of the Greek influenced Sadducees.[14]

10. In the middle ages it was debated whether *Olam Ha-Ba*, "the World to Come", refers in the Rabbinic literature to the resurrection or to immortality of the soul, see *infra*, pp. 312–315, and Albeck's note in his *Commentary to the Mishnah* on Sanh. 10: 1. Albeck holds that *Olam Ha-Ba* always refers to the resurrection. For the immortality of the soul, i.e. the soul in its abode in Heaven after the death of the body, the Rabbis use the term *Gan Eden*. The terms "Heaven" and "Paradise" are, of course, never found in this connection in the Rabbinic literature.
11. *Antiquities*, Book XVIII, Chapter 2, cf. ARN V.
12. Ber. 9: 5.
13. *Toledot Ha-Ikkarim be-Yisrael*, Chapter 6, pp. 165–175.
14. The main references to the Hereafter in the Apocrypha are: Wisdom of Solomon 3: 4; II Macc. 7: 9 and 36 and 12: 43–44.

The Greek influence is especially marked in Philo's treatment of the doctrine of the immortality of the soul.[15] Wolfson[16] observes that among the Palestinian Jews the primary belief was in resurrection whereas among the Hellenistic Jews it was primarily in immortality of the soul. Taking as his proof-text Gen. 15: 15 Philo remarks: "He here clearly indicates the incorruptibility of the soul, when it transfers itself out of the mortal body and returns as it were to the metropolis of the fatherland, from which it originally migrated into the body."[17] Wolfson[18] says of Philo: "Throughout his writings Philo speaks of the immortality of the soul rather than of the resurrection of the body. No direct or indirect reference to resurrection as distinguished from immortality is ever made by him, though the belief in resurrection was common among the Egyptians of his own native country and though also it is mentioned in the Sibylline Oracles. But it is quite evident that all the references to resurrection found in the traditional literature of his time were understood by him as being only a figurative way of referring to immortality. It is on account of this, we imagine, that he constantly draws upon the traditional vocabulary of resurrection to express his view of immortality." Charles[19] is even more emphatic: "As matter was (for Philo) incurably evil there could of course be no resurrection of the body. Our present life in the body is death; for the body is the 'utterly polluted prison' of the soul: nay, more, it is its sepulchre . . ."

The Rabbinic literature is so full of references to the Hereafter that many a large volume would be required to list them all. Here we note some of the main ideas first as they appear in the Tannaitic period (to the beginning of the third century C.E.) and then as they appear in the Amoraic period (200–500 C.E.). We have noted earlier a certain ambiguity about the term "the World to Come" in the Rabbinic literature. The terms for the abode of the souls of the righteous after the death of the body is *Gan Eden*, "the Garden of Eden";[20] for the place of torment for the wicked *Gehinnom*, "Hell".[21] The wicked are judged in Gehinnom for 12 months.[22]

15. See Wolfson: *Philo*, Vol. I. Chapter VII, 5: *The Immortality of the Soul*, pp. 395–413.
16. Op. cit., p. 396.
17. *Qu. in Gen.* III, 11.
18. Op cit., p. 404.
19. Op. cit., p. 260.
20. Avot 5: 20.
21. Avot 5: 19 and 20; Kidd. 4: 14.
22. Ed. 2: 10.

A teacher is superior to a father because a man's teacher brings him to the World to Come whereas his father only brings him into this world.[23] This world is like a vestibule before the World to Come. "Prepare thyself in the vestibule, that thou mayest enter into the hall of the palace."[24] The typical Tannaitic statement about the relationship between the two worlds (so that Rabbinic Judaism is *both* this-worldly and other-worldly) is: "Better is one hour of repentance and good deeds in this world than the whole life of the World to Come; and better is one hour of blissfulness of spirit in the World to Come than the whole life of this world."[25] All Israel has a share in the World to Come with certain exceptions.[26] But the righteous of the nations also have a share in the World to Come.[27]

One of the most significant sayings regarding the Hereafter in the Amoraic literature is that of Rab: "In the World to Come there is no eating nor drinking nor propagation nor business nor jealousy nor hatred nor competition, but the righteous sit with their crowns on their heads feasting on the brightness of the *Shekhinah*."[28] In this context there is a further illustration of the possibility of having both a this-worldly and other-worldly form of Judaism. The same Rab who is so eloquent on the purely spiritual nature of bliss in the Hereafter is reported as saying that in the World to Come man will have to give an account and reckoning before the judgement seat of God for every legitimate pleasure he denied himself in this world![19] Very striking is the saying that three things afford a foretaste in miniature of the bliss of the World to Come: the sabbath, sexual intercourse and a sunny day.[30] Students of the Torah have rest neither in this world nor in the World to Come.[31] The third century teacher Resh Lakish said that there is no Hell in the future but God will bring the sun out of its sheath to shine in all its brilliance; the wicked will be punished thereby, the righteous will be rewarded thereby.[32] The meaning of this much discussed saying is probably not that Resh Lakish denies that there is a Hell *now* but he holds that *in the future* (*le-atid lavo*), i.e. in the Messianic Age the sun will be the substitute for Hell. R. Joseph the son of R. Joshua b. Levi went into a trance in which he was

23. B.M. 2: 11.   24. Avot 4: 16.   25. Avot 4: 17.
26. Sanh. 10: 1–2.   27. Tosefta Sanh. 13: 2, see *supra*, pp. 289–290.
38. Ber. 17a.   29. Jer. T. Kidd. 4: 12 end.
20. Ber. 57b but see comment of the Gemera to this.
31. Ber. 64a; M.K. 29a.   32. Ned. 8b; A.Z. 3b.

transported to the World to Come. On his return his father asked him: "What did you see?" He replied: "I saw a topsy-turvy world. Those who are here high are there low. Those who are here low are there high." "You saw a clear world," replied the father.[33]

Saadia Gaon has much to say on the Hereafter in his *Beliefs and Opinions*. Saadia does not believe in a pre-existent soul. The soul of man is created simultaneously with his body. When the body dies the soul remains separated from it until the number of souls requiring to be created has been reached. The soul is then reunited with the body and both together are rewarded or punished.[34] During their time of separation from the body the pure souls are preserved on high under the Throne of Glory but the turbid souls wander aimlessly below. Like the former inhabitant of a ruined home the soul has no fixed abode until the decomposition of the body and suffers from the contemplation of the body's fate. Hence the Rabbis say[35] that worms in the decaying body are as painful to the dead (i.e. to the soul) as needles in living flesh.[36] Saadia emphatically rejects the doctrine of metempsychosis or the transmigration of souls.[37]

"All our nation", states Saadia,[38] agree in holding the belief in the resurrection of the dead. Since the Jew accepts the doctrine of *creatio ex nihilo* he can find no difficulty in holding belief in the resurrection. For Saadia there are, in fact, two resurrections; one for the virtuous of Israel at the time of Messianic redemption, the other for all men in the World to Come.[39] Saadia poses a number of problems with regard to the resurrection.[40] If a man is eaten by a lion, the lion by a fish, the fish by another man whose body is burned, how will the first be resurrected? The answer is that nothing is lost and God can reconstitute the body of the first man. The men who are resurrected will eat and drink and marry. If their wives had died and they had remarried will they live with their former wives at the resurrection? We can safely leave such questions to the prophets who will then be alive. Those brought back to life in the first resurrection will not return to dust. All these will eventually be transferred to the place reserved for the other resurrected dead (i.e. at the second resurrection)

33. Pes. 50a. On the question whether the dead know what transpires on earth see the passage in Ber. 18a–19a.

34. *Beliefs and Opinions*, 6: 1.   35. Sabb. 152a.   36. *Beliefs and Opinions*, 6: 7.

37. *Beliefs and Opinions*, 6: 8.   38. *Beliefs and Opinions*, 7: 2.

39. *Beliefs and Opinions*, 7: 1–7.   40. *Beliefs and Opinions*, 7: 7.

and in that place there will be no eating, drinking, etc.; the resurrected dead then living in the state described of Moses (Ex. 34: 28).

Who will be resurrected? All virtuous Jews and Jewish sinners who have repented will enjoy the first resurrection in this world; all mankind the second in the World to Come. The purpose of the special privilege granted to Israel is a boon proportionate to their trials. But how will the earth be able to contain them all? Saadia works out that it will be quite possible.[41]

Some further questions are:[42] will people recognise their kinsfolk? The answer is in the affirmative. Will blemishes he healed? Yes. Will the people who have been resurrected be capable of rebellion against God? If not, they are not free, if yes, what will happen if they do? The answer is that theoretically they can rebel against God but God knows that in fact they will not do so. Is there any reward at that time for God's service? Again the answer is in the affirmative. What of those who are already alive at the time of the resurrection? They will live for a very long time, say 500 years, and then they will die to be resurrected together with the rest of mankind at the second resurrection.

There will be two luminous substances in the World to Come formed of the essence of light and these will provide illumination for the righteous and burning for the wicked. A fine "preservative substance" will enable the wicked to endure so that they might receive further punishment. This reward for the righteous is called *Gan Eden*, this punishment for the wicked *Gehinnom*.[43] All this will happen in a special place created for the purpose. Why not on the old earth? Because the conditions of amelioration will no longer be required. There will be endless time, all of it illumined, with neither sun nor moon, neither day nor night.[44]

Saadia believes that both reward for the righteous and punishment for the wicked are eternal.[45] Only limitless reward and punishment can provide proper incentives for God's worship. But is not eternal punishment contrary to God's mercy? The answer to this is that since only the strongest possible deterrent is effective this must be provided and once God has provided it He cannot go back on His word. In reality even eternal punishment is due to God's kindness in

41. *Beliefs and Opinions*, 7: 8.   42. *Beliefs and Opinions*, 7: 9.
43. *Beliefs and Opinions*, 9: 5.   44. *Beliefs and Opinions*, 9: 6.
45. *Beliefs and Opinions*, 9: 7.

His desire to make men more virtuous. But if creatures are to enjoy being with God for all eternity in the future why could they not have enjoyed this in the past? The answer to this is that the Creator must precede His creatures but once creatures have come into existence they are eternal. The differences in degree of reward and punishment are not in duration—all reward and punishment is eternal but there are variations in content and intensity.[46] However, eternal punishment is only for non-believers, polytheists and perpetrators of grave sins.[47] Will people meet one another in the Hereafter? The wicked will meet with the righteous for the purpose of comparison but the righteous will only meet among themselves those of similar rank while the wicked will be doomed to a solitary existence.

Will there be opportunities then for God's service? Yes, there will be service of a purely contemplative nature, i.e. the acknowledgement of God and there will also be appointed seasons for pilgrimage (ls. 66: 23). The reward for such service will be additional happiness. But the wicked will have no opportunities for service, otherwise they might earn a transfer to Heaven which will not do.[48]

Saadia's description has been quoted at length as a typical example of mediaeval speculation on this mystery. It suffers, from our point of view, from all the defects of mediaeval dogmatism. With frightening certainty Saadia presents the doctrine of eternal torment and describes the whole scheme in the Hereafter as if he had just been there. It should be noted that evidently Saadia does not believe in either Heaven or Hell as places. Nor does he believe that any soul is annihilated. He also introduces the novel idea of two resurrections and he believes that the body will exist for ever together with the soul but in a specially created "place" in which there are no bodily appetites. The modern Jew is bound to be repelled by mediaeval dogmatism of this description and prefers to leave the details of the Hereafter to God. If man is to enjoy God for ever the reality must be so sublime that it is literally indescribable.

Maimonides has theories of his own on the whole question of the Hereafter. The following points are especially to be noted.

Maimonides' doctrine of the Hereafter is highly spiritual. His theory of immortality is based on the Aristotelian view in its Arabic garb that only that part of man's intellect which he has acquired, as it

---

46. *Beliefs and Opinions*, 9: 8.　　47. *Beliefs and Opinions*, 9: 9.
48. *Beliefs and Opinions*, 9: 10.

were, through metaphysical thought (the "acquired intellect") is immortal. This alone, through its contact with the "Active Intellect", survives the death of the body.[49] Maimonides was obviously embarrassed by the doctrine of the resurrection. In his Commentary to the Mishnah, in which he formulates the 13 principles of the Jewish faith,[50] he counts belief in the resurrection as the 13th principle but refers to it in a most casual manner. In his code[51] he refers to it only once and that in a section in which he speaks of the Hereafter in purely spiritual terms. In fact, Maimonides was accused in his lifetime of denying the resurrection of the dead so that he was compelled to write a special treatise on the resurrection.[52] Here he argues that there will be a resurrection of the body but that the body will endure only for a time. Ultimately, it is the soul alone that is immortal in the World to Come. In this he disagrees with Saadia without mentioning him. For Saadia the final resurrection is also for the body and is for all eternity whereas for Maimonides the final aim is the immortality of the soul after the resurrected body has once again returned to dust. Maimonides evidently could not bring himself to believe in the idea of a body inhabiting eternity.

Maimonides seems to equate Hell with the annihilation of the sinner's soul not with actual torment,[53] though here and there in his writings he does seem to touch on the idea of Hell as an actual place of torment.[54] In his Commentary to the Mishnah[55] Maimonides is at pains to reject the various folk-beliefs and superstitions which have grown up around the doctrine of the Hereafter. Maimonides was severely criticised for his figurative interpretation of apparently less spiritual passages on the Hereafter in the Rabbinic literature.[56]

The theme of the Hereafter exercised a powerful fascination on the minds of the mediaeval thinkers. Nahmanides, too, has a lengthy treatise, entitled Shaar Ha-Gemul, "Gate of Recompense", in his Torat Ha-Adam, a book dealing with the laws connected with sickness,

49. Guide III, 27; 51–52; 54; Yad, Teshuvah 8: 3.
50. Sanh. 10: 1.   51. Yad, Teshuvah 3: 5.
52. Maamar Tehiat Ha-Metim ed. Finkel. For Teicher's denial of the authenticity of the Maamar and Sonne's reply see Salo Baron: Social and Religious History, Vol. VIII, note 17 (4), p. 308.
53. Yad, Teshuvah 8: 5.
54. See Yad, Teshuvah 3: 6 and Commentary to the Mishnah Sanh. 10: 1.
55. Commentary to the Mishnah, Sanh. 10- 1.
56. See strictures of Raabad to Yad, Teshuvah 8: 2, 4, 8.

death, burial and mourning.[57] For Nahmanides Hell is an actual place
and not annihilation of the soul, as Maimonides would appear to have
it. There is no justice in having the same punishment for all classes of
the wicked. In the Rabbinic literature the precise measurements of
Gehinnom are stated[58] which shows that the Rabbis thought of it as
an actual place. They also forbid the cooking of food on the sabbath
in the hot springs of Tiberia since these cross the gates of Hell,[59]
hence the physical existence of Hell is recognised even by the
Halakhah.[60] Since physical fire does not have the requisite properties
for burning a soul, the fire of Hell is a very refined and subtle form of
fire appropriate for this purpose.[61] The soul itself is an extremely
refined and spiritual substance and there is no reason why God should
not have created a similar substance for the purpose of punishing the
erring soul.[62] As for the argument of the philosophers that a soul
cannot occupy space and therefore Hell cannot be a *place*; although
these thinkers argue that the soul, which is spiritual, is not *in* the body
in any physical sense, there must be some association with the particular body of A so that it can be said, at least, that in some way the soul
of A is more intimately associated with A than with B. And by the
same token the soul can be associated with the place called Hell to be
punished there in that specially refined form of fire. Our Rabbis, too,
believed in the soul's spiritual nature. Indeed, for the Rabbis the soul
is far more spiritual than for the philosophers, yet the Rabbis saw no
incompatibility between this and their belief in Hell as a place.[63]
Souls are never annihilated. When the Rabbis speak of certain souls
being "lost"[64] they do not refer to the destruction or annihilation of
the soul but to a species of punishment in which the soul is "lost" to
its Source, longing to return to God but unable to do so because of
its sins.[65]

In his treatment of Heaven as the blissful state of the righteous soul
after the death of the body,[66] Nahmanides observes that this is called
Gan Eden by the Rabbis generally in contradistinction to *Gehinnom*.
It is a place on earth as in Gen. 2: 10–14.[67] Stories are even told of
human travellers coming near to it but being driven away by the

57. In *Collected Writings*, ed. Chavel, Vol. II, pp. 264–311.
58. Taan. 10a; Eruv. 91a.   59. Sabb. 39a.   60. pp. 283–285.
61. pp. 285–286.   62. pp. 286–287.   63. pp. 287–288.
64. Sifra to Lev. 14: 14.   65. p. 288.   66. pp. 294–299.
67. Cf. Nahmanides *Commentary* to Gen. 3: 22.

flaming sword. But there is also a "higher *Gan Eden*." Just as Jacob had his tremendous dream at a specially sacred spot, so, too, the soul, by virtue of its residence in the earthly *Gan Eden*, can rise in contemplation to the purely spiritual stage known as the "higher *Gan Eden*" Nahmanides concludes that the words of the Rabbis regarding *Gan Eden* as a place on earth are to be taken literally but, for all that, there are many stages of spiritual comprehension one higher than the other.

The term "the World to Come" means, for Nahmanides, not *Gan Eden* but the world at the time of the resurrection of the dead.[68] In the time of the resurrection the body will be reunited with the soul but there will be no eating nor drinking nor any of the other physical appetites. But how can a body exist without food? The Israelites lived on manna, which is to be understood as spiritual light in its material form. Moses lived for 40 days without food. But of what use is a body there? One answer is that since the body was needed in this life God preserves it in His mercy. Another answer is that the human body mirrors the Sefirotic realm and its mysteries. Nahmanides sums it up as follows. As soon as the body dies the virtuous soul receives its reward in *Gan Eden*. The Messianic Age is in this world on earth. Then there comes judgement day when the soul is reunited with the body. This is "the World to Come" when the body itself becomes soul-like, the soul soaring in the world of souls, and so it will be for ever.

Reference should be made to two later full-scale speculations on the Hereafter, those of Moses b. Joseph di Trani (the *Mabit*) in the sixteenth century (*Bet Elohim*, Gate III, *Shaar Ha-Yesodot*, Chapters 53–62, pp. 130–147) and Manasseh ben Israel (c. 1604–1657) entitled: *Nishmat Hayim*. Mabit, after stating in detail (Chapter 59) the questions put by Saadia, as above, poses problems of his own (Chapter 60) which he seeks to answer. Will the resurrected dead wear the shrouds they rise up in for ever? The answer is in the affirmative. God surely has the power to make these everlasting as He has the power to reconstitute them after they have returned to dust in the grave. The shrouds of resurrected children will grow with them as, according to the Rabbis, the garment of infants grew with them during Israel's 40 years in the wilderness. The food of the resurrected dead will be the fruit of *Gan Eden* which Adam ate before his expulsion. This is extremely subtle, far more refined and spiritual than the manna the Israelites ate in the wilderness. The bodies of the resurrected dead will be especially

68. pp. 299–311.

refined and pure so that they will require very little even of this pure food. There will be sleep and rest even in that time since it is impossible for man to use his senses without giving them rest. Moreover, all men at that time will be prophets and they will require to sleep so that God can communicate to them His truths in their dreams. All the prayers we recite now will still be recited then with the exception of those which long for the coming of the Messiah. Manasseh b. Israel writes in his Introduction to the *Nishmat Hayim* that he was inspired to write a book on the immortality of the soul since critics of Judaism say that Scripture is incomplete because it contains no reference to immortality. The reference is, of course, to the Christian argument that the Old Testament is inadequate on these grounds and requires the "fulfilment" of the New. (See Albo: *Ikkarim* and Isaac Arama's: *Akedat Yitzhak*, ed. Pollak, p. 144b. Arama observes that both Christians and Muslims assert on these grounds the superiority of their religion over Judaism.) The author believes that immortality is mentioned in the Bible (*Maamar* I, Chapters 2–9) e.g. in the promises of life which cannot refer to life here on earth since those who keep the Torah do not live longer on earth than others. The references to one being "gathered unto his people" (Gen. 15: 15; Gen. 25: 8) can only refer to the immortality of the soul and *karet* to the punishment of the soul. Other references quoted are: Ex. 32: 33; Mal. 3: 16; Ps. 56: 9; 139: 5 and especially 69: 29. Joseph commanded his brothers to take up his bones from Egypt (Gen. 50: 24). The sons of Aaron were burned in fire (Lev. 10: 2) and unless their souls were immortal it would have been unjust for God to have done this to Aaron on the great day of his rejoicing. Enoch (Gen. 5: 24) ascended alive to Heaven. Isaac went willingly to be sacrificed because he knew that he had an immortal soul and death was not the end. Even in their lifetime the Israelites enjoyed attachment to God (Ex. 24: 17; Num. 14: 14; Deut. 4: 4 and 33) which is of the essence of the spiritual bliss of the Hereafter. There are two *Gan Edens*, one on earth, the other, purely spiritual, in Heaven. The Greeks knew of the place on earth which they called the *Elysian fields*, from Elijah who ascended to Heaven while still alive [*sic*]. The soul must first reside here in order to become accustomed to spiritual delights and it can then ascend to the higher *Gan Eden*, Maamar I, Chapter 10. Manasseh (*Maamar* I, Chapter 11) discusses the nature of heavenly bliss. Even in Heaven it is impossible for man to "see" God Himself but the *Sefirot* known as God's "face" will there be seen by the virtuous soul. There is only joy in Heaven, never sorrow. Gersonides has argued that there can be no intellectual progress in Heaven but this is not so. Hard though it is for man to acquire wisdom on earth in Heaven it will be easy. Some sinners are punished eternally in Hell but are granted a respite on the sabbath (*Maamar* I, Chapter 14). The time of the resurrection is the time of judgement. But have not the souls already been judged and rewarded or punished? The answer is that, indeed, those who died long before the resurrection will not be judged again, only those who died recently. Manasseh (*Maamar* I, Chapters 15–17) observes that the Kabbalists interpret the Rabbinic references to the great

banquet that will be held for the righteous at that time in a figurative
sense. Manasseh believes in ghosts. The dead are sometimes given permission to appear in this world (*Maamar* II, Chapter 22). When a son recites
Kaddish for his parent the soul of the parent is elevated to a higher stage in
Heaven (*Maamar* II, Chapter 27). There are proofs from experience for the
immortality of the soul. Man alone of all creatures walks upright because his
soul is immortal and reaches Heavenwards. This is why Jews sway their
bodies (see *supra*, pp. 191–192) when praying or studying the Torah. The
Torah is the life of the soul and the soul moves like a tree which moves
when rain comes down from Heaven (*Maamar* III, Chapter 1). Moreover,
it can be seen that no two individuals are exactly alike and this is because
their souls are different, each soul finding a body to suit it (*Maamar* III,
Chapter 2). Telepathy and precognition are known to happen and this
affords proof of man's immortal soul (*Maamar* III, Chapter 4). Having
proved the existence of the immortal soul from tradition and experience
Manasseh (*Maamar* IV, Chapters 1–5) proceeds to demonstrate proofs from
human reason. Thus, unless man has a soul how can he ever grasp intellectual
matters? The older a man is the wiser he becomes even though his bodily
faculties are on the decline. Man has the idea of infinity, e.g. an infinite
series of numbers, which shows that there is more to him than his finite
body. Why else does man desire wisdom unless he has an immortal soul
and how else can he have free-will? All men, moreover, strive for immortality, wishing to leave something of themselves behind. Finally, all
men have this belief. It is axiomatic. Manasseh (*Maamar* IV, Chapters 6–21)
concludes with a lengthy defence of belief in the transmigration of souls—
Gilgul—which, he says, is accepted by all Jewish thinkers except Saadia.
For the doctrine of the transmigration of souls or metempsychosis see the
articles in *Jewish Encyclopedia*, Vol. XII, pp. 231–234 and in *Encyclopedia
of Religion and Ethics*, Vol. XII, pp. 435–440. The three different types are:
(1) *gilgul* = "transmigration"; (2) *ibbur* = "impregnation", in which a
soul assists another soul in a body here on earth (this was first introduced
in the Lurianic Kabbalah); (3) *dibbuk* (this is late and generally means
a guilt-laden soul which invades a human body in order to escape the
demons pursuing it and which has to be exorcised). *Gilgul* was unknown in
Judaism until the eighth century when it began to be adopted by the
Karaites (perhaps under the influence of Islamic mysticism). The first reference
to it is, as above, in Saadia (*Beliefs and Opinions* IV, 7). Saadia states that the
doctrine is held by some "who call themselves Jews" and he ridicules it.
For the Zoharic view see e.g. Zohar II, 99b. Albo: *Ikkarim*, IV, 29, attacks
the doctrine as superstitious. Abarbanel in his *Commentary to the Pentateuch*
on Deut. 25: 5 accepts it. Loewe's suggestion (*Rabbinic Anthology* pp. 660–663)
that the doctrine was known to the Rabbis is very questionable. Manasseh
b. Israel (Chapter 21) notes that the doctrine was "invented" by Pythagoras
after it had been known to Adam, Seth, etc. Pythagoras, he says, was a Jew (!)
who received the doctrine from the prophet Ezekiel. (On this see Ginzberg: *Legends*, Index Pythagoras.) For the Kabbalistic view see Aaron Roth's

Shomer Emunim, Vol. I, pp. 141f and Elijah of Smyrna's *Midrash Talpiot*, pp. 120–127 and Jacob Zevi Jolles: *Kehillot Yaakov.* s.v. *gilgul.*

What can a modern Jew believe on this whole question of the Hereafter? It depends on which type of modern Jew we mean. Some modern Jews clearly have no use for any doctrine of a Hereafter and, oddly enough, this includes some religious Jews. But it is surely a very curious religious outlook which limits man's opportunities for encountering God to the brief span of this life. The strongest argument for immortality is provided for the theist by his basic theistic affirmation. Can it be believed that God has created only to destroy, that all man's hopes and dreams of a higher life are doomed to frustration? Nor is it much use speaking of individuals living on in their children or in the lives they have influenced or in their deeds and works. To say that Shakespeare is immortal in the sense that his plays will always be read is not really to speak about the man Shakespeare at all but about his ideas. The quality of this life is quite different if it is seen as a school for eternity as well as being good in itself. Surely the idea that man's deeds have eternal significance is not to be treated lightly as a kind of optional belief or pious opinion. Belief in the Hereafter is deeply rooted in Judaism and to reject it is to impoverish and despiritualise Judaism itself.

The general tendency among modern Jews who do believe in an After-life is to place the stress on the immortality of the soul rather than on the resurrection of the dead. We can see why this should be so. Already in the middle ages, as we have seen, the difficulties of the *purpose* of the resurrection and in the idea of a body inhabiting eternity were recognised. In more recent years some Jewish thinkers[69] have tried to defend the doctrine of the resurrection and to prefer it, in fact, to that of the immortality of the soul. The argument runs that the doctrine of immortality is Greek, not Jewish, and that it fails to consider the survival of the whole person. To prefer the doctrine of the resurrection to that of immortality on the grounds that the latter is Greek is to overlook the evidence that the doctrine of the resurrection is in all probability Persian in origin. Why should this matter? It is all a question of studying ideas which have come into Judaism

69. See the discussion in my *Principles of the Jewish Faith*, pp. 413–420; Joseph Seliger: *Collected Writings*, pp. 71–96; Will Herberg: *Judaism and Modern Man*, p. 229; I. Epstein: *The Faith of Judaism*, pp. 323f.; Reinhold Niebuhr: *The Resurrection* in his: *The Nature and Destiny of Man*, Vol. II, pp. 304–309.

from without to see how a viable Jewish theology can be constructed.
One can see the point about the whole human personality surviving
but, unless we are prepared to accept the biological details of an actual
recomposition of the physical body, we are still affirming a version of
the immortality of the soul even when we affirm the doctrine of the
resurrection. To speak of a spiritual body or an especially refined body
is really to use only different words for the same thing. We ought to
be frank enough to admit that all the speculations regarding life here
on earth after the resurrection simply do not "ring a bell" for us
whereas the more spiritual interpretation of a Maimonides does. It all
comes back to the former point we have made. The modern religious
Jew can see the tremendous power of belief that there is a Hereafter
but beyond affirming that the virtuous soul will find its God in a
manner so rich and so sublime as to be utterly beyond all our comprehension, he is prepared to leave the rest to God. He will not wish to
explore the "geography of Heaven". He will say with Maimonides[70]
that for human beings in this world to try to grasp the nature of the
Hereafter is like a man born blind trying to grasp the nature of colour.

We have noted more than once Maimonides' elevated spiritual
interpretation of the Hereafter in which, in fact, Heaven is not a place
but a state of soul. One should speak of man *becoming* Heaven rather
than *going* to Heaven. The mystical idea of the "eternal Now"[71] is
also relevant here. Eternity should not be thought of as endless
duration in time but as outside time altogether, although, admittedly,
this is an extremely difficult idea for us to grasp.

The modern Jew who prefers to speak of the immortality of the
soul is not obeying a fad of his own. As we have seen, there are enough
Jewish thinkers, from Philo onwards, who have held this view of the
matter to make it completely respectable from the Jewish point of
view. A few passages from Maimonides' formulation[72] can profitably
be quoted in this connection. "There are neither bodies nor bodily
forms in the World to Come but only the disembodied souls of the
righteous who have become like the ministering angels. Since there
are no bodies there is no eating or drinking there nor is there anything
which the human body needs in this world. Nor do there occur
there any of the events which occur to the human body in this world
such as sitting, standing, sleep, death, distress, laughter and so forth

70. *Commentary to Mishnah* Sanh. 10: 1.
71. See *supra*, pp. 86–92.   72. *Yad, Teshuvah* 8.

. . . You may be repelled by this, imagining that the only worthwhile reward for keeping the commandments and for a man being perfect in the ways of truth is for him to eat and drink well and have beautiful women and wear garments of fine linen and embroidery and live in marble palaces and have vessels of silver and gold . . . But the sages and intellectuals know that these things are vain, stupid and valueless and only are greatly attractive to us in this world where we do have bodies and bodily form. All these things have to do with the needs of the body. The soul only longs for them because the body needs them if it is to remain healthy and thus perform its function. But all these things cease when the body no longer enjoys existence. There is no way at all for us to comprehend the great goodness which is the experience of the soul in the World to Come, for in this world we know only of material pleasures and these we desire. That goodness is great beyond measure and can only be compared to that which we consider to be good in this world by analogy but in reality there can be no way of comparing the good of the soul in the World to Come with the physical goods of food and drink in this world. That good is great beyond all our understanding and incomparable beyond all our imagination . . . The ancient sages have already told us that man is incapable of truly comprehending the good of the World to Come and that only the Holy One, blessed be He, knows its greatness, beauty and nature and that all the goods the prophets foretold for Israel refer only to the material pleasures that will be theirs in the days of the Messiah when Israel will once again enjoy sovereignty. But there is nothing to which the life of the World to Come can be compared and it is beyond the human imagination. The prophets did not try to imagine it lest their imagination made it less than it really is . . . When the sages call it the World to Come this does not mean that it is not in existence now so that when this world is destroyed that World will come into being. Not so. It is in existence all the time, as it is said: 'Which Thou has laid up for them that fear Thee' (Ps. 31 : 20). They only called it the World to Come because that type of life only comes to man after he has first experienced the life of this world in which we exist with a body as well as a soul."

What of Hell? The Reform 'Pittsburgh Platform' declared:[73] "We reassert the doctrine of Judaism, that the soul of man is immortal, grounding this belief on the divine nature of the human spirit, which

73. W. Gunther Plaut: *The Growth of Reform Judaism*, p. 34.

forever finds bliss in righteousness and misery in wickedness. We reject as ideas not rooted in Judaism the belief both in bodily resurrection and in Gehenna and Eden (hell and paradise), as abodes for eternal punishment or reward." But if the doctrine of the immortality of the soul is accepted, why, apart from sheer sentimentality, should it be assumed that the soul which wilfully chose evil here on earth should immediately enjoy the spiritual bliss of communion with God simply because of the death of the body? To be sure the doctrine of *eternal* punishment is monstrous, at complete variance with all the ideas we have inherited about God's mercy and His justice. But how can we be so dogmatic as to reject the idea that the soul of the sinner requires some kind of purgation until it can be admitted into God's presence? We may not call this "Hell" but this is simply a matter of nomenclature. Morris Joseph,[74] though he, too, has an extreme reluctance to use the word "Hell", wisely writes: "For him (the modern Jew) punishment in the future life affects the soul only. He thinks of it as akin to the remorse which tortures the guilty even in this existence. Some of the Talmudic Rabbis adopted this view. After death, they say, temptation seems like a mountain to the good, as a threat to the wicked; the one weeps for joy because he has passed over it, the other for grief because he has allowed it to bother him.[75] After death, they say elsewhere, the body and the soul come before the Divine judgement-seat. Each lays upon the other the blame for the sins of the past. But God decrees that the soul alone shall pay the penalty; for having come from heaven, it alone is responsible.[76] Very striking is the idea of a later teacher that the punishment in the future life consists in the torment of the soul torn by conflicting desires—by its own sinful longings, which it can no longer gratify, and by its yearning after the higher joys which it is not yet pure enough to attain. And agony such as this, he adds, far surpasses all earthly pain."[77]

Religious agnosticism in some aspects of this whole area is not only legitimate but altogether desirable. As Maimonides says we simply can have no idea of what pure spiritual bliss in the Hereafter is like. Agnosticism on the basic issue of whether there is a Hereafter would seem narrowness of vision believing what we do of God. But once the basic affirmation is made, it is almost as narrow to project our poor, earthly imaginings on to the landscape of Heaven. Bliss beyond all

74. *Judaism as Creed and Life*, pp. 144–149. 75. Sukk. 52a.
76. Lev. R. 4, to Lev. 4: 4. 77. Albo: *Ikkarim*, IV, 33.

human conception in which God is enjoyed, bliss dependent for its intensity on how man acquits himself in freely chosing the good in this life, this is sufficient a programme and a goal for the man with visions of eternity. And the vision must not be exclusive. Very moving is the legend told by the Jews of Eastern Europe in the last century.[78] When R. Hayim of Volozhyn died he was told that he would be admitted immediately to Heaven so rich was he in good deeds. R. Hayim refused to enter until a guarantee had been given him that the pupils and teachers of the great Yeshiva would also be admitted without further ado. After all, he argued, the success of the Yeshiva is their achievement not mine. When this was acknowledged, R. Hayim argued further for the admission of all Jews since Jewish householders everywhere contribute to the Torah. But even this did not satisfy R. Hayim. After all, he argued further, the Gentiles have provided a home for the Jews. They, too have a share in the Torah. In short, R. Hayim refused to enter unless he were given a guarantee that all men would be allowed to enter. He was told that at that time this was not possible since it had not yet been decreed that the Messiah would come. And so R. Hayim refused to enter Paradise and there his great soul still waits patiently at the portals, praying for the ultimate redemption of all mankind.

78. This legend is told in Fischel Schneorsohn's novel *Hayim Gravitzer*, pp. 293-298.

BIBLIOGRAPHY

ONLY WORKS REFERRED TO IN THIS BOOK ARE INCLUDED

ABARBANEL, DON ISAAC, *Commentary to the Pentateuch*, Venice, 1579: *Rosh Amanah*, Constantinople, 1505.

ABBA MARI b. MOSES OF LUNEL, *Minhat Kenaot*, Presburg, 1838.

ABELSON, J., *The Immanence of God in Rabbinical Literature*, Lond., 1912.

ABRAHAM IBN DAVID, *Emunah Ramah*, ed. Weil, Berlin, 1919.

ABRAHAMS, ISRAEL, *A Companion to the Authorized Daily Prayer Book*, N.Y., 1966.

ABRAMOVITZ, H. I., *Hekhal Ha-Teshuvah*, Benai Berak, 1961.

AGUS, J. B., *Guideposts in Modern Judaism*, N.Y., 1954: *Modern Philosophies of Judaism*, N.Y., 1941.

ALBECK, H., *Commentary to the Mishnah*, Tel-Aviv, 1957.

ALBO, JOSEPH, *Sefer Ha-Ikkarim*, ed. and trans. I. Husik, Philadelphia, 1946.

ALEXANDER SÜSSKIND b. MOSES OF GRODNO: *Yesod Ve-Shoresh Ha-Avodah*, Jer., 1965.

ALLEN, E. L., *Christianity Among the Religions*, Lond., 1960.

ALMOSNINO, MOSES, *Tefillah Le-Mosheh*, Cracow, 1805.

ALTIZER, T. J. J., *The Gospel of Christian Atheism*, Lond., 1967; with William Hamilton: *Radical Theology and the Death of God*, Indianapolis, 1966.

ALTMANN, A., *Studies in Religious Philosophy and Mysticism*, Lond., 1969; *Saadya's Theory of Revelation, Its Origin and Background* in Saadya Studies, ed. I. J. Rosenthal, Manchester, 1943, pp. 4–25.

ANATOLI, JACOB, *Malmad Ha-Talmidim*, Lyck, 1866.

ANSELM, ST., *Proslogion*, trans. S. W. Deane in *St. Anselm: Basic Theology*, Illinois, 1962.

ARAMA, ISAAC, *Akedat Yitzhak*, ed. H. J. Pollak, Presburg, 1849.

AQUINAS, THOMAS, *Summa Theologica*, var. eds.

ASHKENAZI, ZEVI, *Teshuvot Tzevi Ashkenazi*, Lemberg, 1900.

AZIKRI, ELEAZAR, *Sefer Heredim*, Jer., 1958.

BACHER, W., *Shem Ha-Meforash* in *Jewish Encyclopedia*, Vol. XI, pp. 262–264.

BAECK, LEO, *The Essence of Judaism*, trans. Victor Grubwieser and Leonard Pearl, Lond., 1936; *This People Israel: The Meaning of Jewish Existence*, trans. Albert H. Friedlander, Lond. 1965.

BAELZ, P. R., *Prayer and Providence*, SCM, Lond., 1968.

BAER, Y., *A History of the Jews in Christian Spain*, trans. L. Schaffman, Philadelphia 1961; *Religious Social Tendency of the Sefer Hasidim* (Heb.) in *Zion*, Vol. III (1938). pp. 1–50.

BAHYA IBN ASHER, *Commentary to the Pentateuch*, ed. C. B. Chavel, Jer., 1966–68.

BAHYA IBN PAKUDAH, *Duties of the Heart* (*Hovot Ha-Levavot* ed. A. Zifroni, Jer., 1928; trans. Moses Hyamson, Bloch. N.Y. 1945.

BAMBERGER, BERNARD, *Proselytism in the Talmudic Period*, Cincinnati, 1939.

BARBOUR, IAN G., *Issues in Science and Religion*, N.J., 1966.

BARON, SALO W., *A Social and Religious History of the Jews*, 2nd ed., N.Y. 1952.

BARR, JAMES, *Names of God in the Old Testament* in Hastings' *Dictionary of the Bible*, 2nd rev., ed., pp. 334–335.

BEDERSI, JEDAIAH b. ABRAHAM, *Behinot Olam*, ed. Stern, Vienna, 1847.

BELKIN, SAMUEL, *Essays in Traditional Jewish Thought*, N.Y., 1956; *In His Image*, N.Y., (n.d.).

BERNFIELD, SIMON ed., *The Foundations of Jewish Ethics*, Ktav, N.Y., 1968.

BERTOCCI, P. A., *Introduction to the Philosophy of Religion*, N.Y., 1951.

BLACK, MATTHEW, AND ROWLEY, H. H. Ed., *Peake's Commentary on the Bible*, Lond., 1962.

BLOCH, JOSEPH LAIB, *Shiure Daat*, Tel-Aviv, 1953.

BOETHIUS, *The Consolation of Philosophy*, trans. Richard Green, N.Y., 1962.

BOROWWITZ, EUGENE B., *A New Jewish Theology in the Making*, Philadelphia, 1968; *How Can a Jew Speak of Faith Today?*, Philadelphia, 1969.

BOUQET, A. C., *Sacred Books of the World*, Lond., 1963.

BRAUDE, W. G., *Jewish Proselytizing in the First Five Centuries of the Common Era*, Boston, 1940.

BREISCH, M. J., *Helkat Yaakov*, Vol. III, Benai Berak, 1966.

BRIGHTMAN, E. S., *The Problem of God*, N.Y., 1930; *The Philosophy of Religion*, Lond., 1940.

BROAD, C. D., *Time* in Hastings' *Encyclopedia of Religion and Ethics*, Vol. 12, pp. 334–335.

BUBER, MARTIN, *I and Thou*, trans. Ronald Gregor Smith, N.Y., 1937; *Biblical Humanism*, ed. Nahum N. Glatzer, Lond., 1968; *The Philosophy of Martin Buber*, ed. Schilpp and Friedman, Illinois, 1967; *Tales of the Hasidim*, Schocken, N.Y., 1947.

BÜCHLER, A., *Studies in Sin and Atonement in the Rabbinical Literature of the First Century*, Lond., 1928.

CAHN, STEVEN M., *Fate, Logic and Time*, Yale University Press, 1967.

CALDECOTT, A. AND MACKINTOSH, H. R., *Selections from the Literature of Theism*, 3rd ed. Edinburgh, 1931.

CAMPBELL, JOSEPH ed., *Man and Time: Papers from the Eranos Yearbook*, Lond., 1958.

CARLYE, T., *Sartor Resartus*.

CARMEL, L., *The Problem of Evil: The Jewish Synthesis* in *Proceedings of the Association of Orthodox Jewish Scientists*, Vol. I, N.Y., 1966, pp. 92–100.

CASSUTO, M. D. (U.), *Shemot Elohim Ba-Mikra* in *Encyclopedia Mikrait*, Vol. I, Jer., 1950, pp. 301–321; *From Noah to Abraham*, trans., I. Abrahams, Jer., 1964.

CHARLES, R. H., *A Critical History of the Doctrine of a Future Life*, Lond., 1899.

Cohen, Abraham, *Everyman's Talmud*, Lond., 1949.

COHEN, ARTHUR A., *The Natural and the Supernatural Jew*, Lond., 1967.

COHEN, SIMON, *God, Names of* in *Universal Jewish Encyclopedia*, Vol. 5, pp. 6–8.

COHON, SAMUEL S., *Theology* in *Universal Jewish Encyclopedia*, Vol. 10, pp. 242–244; *Theology Lectures*, mimeographed, Cincinnati, 1933; *Jewish Theology*, Assen, The Netherlands, 1971.

COLLINS, JAMES, *God in Modern Philosophy*, Lond., 1960.

Commentary, ed. of, ed., *The Condition of Jewish Belief*, N.Y., 1966, originally published in *Commentary* magazine, Aug. 1966, Number 2, Vol. 42.

CORDOVERO, MOSES, *Pardes Rimmonim*, Lemberg, 1862; *Elimah Rabbati*, Brody, 1881; *Tomer Devorah*, Petah Tikveh, 1953.

Cox, H., *The Secular City*, N.Y., 1966.

CRESCAS, HASDAI, *Bittul Ikkare Ha-Notzerim*, ed. Deinard, Kearny, N.J., 1894; *Or Adonai*, Vienna, 1859.

CROSS, FRANK M. JR., *The Priestly Tabernacle* in *Old Testament Issues* ed. Samuel Sandmel, SCM, Lond., 1969, pp. 39–67.

Dadistani Dinik in *Sacred Books of the East* ed. F. M. Muller, Oxford, Vol. XVIII, 1880.

DAN, JOSEPH, *The Esoteric Theology of Ashekenazi Hasidism* (Heb.), Jer., 1968.

DAVID b. SOLOMON IBN ABI ZIMRA *(Ridbaz): Responsa*, Sedilkow, 1836.

DAVIDSON, ROBERT E., *Rudolf Otto's Interpretation of Religion*, Princeton University Press, 1947.

DENTAN, R. C., *The Knowledge of God in Ancient Isreal*, N.Y., 1968.

DESSLER, E., *Mikhtav Me-Elijahu*, Lond., 1955.

DODD, E. R., *Proclus: The Elements of Theology*, Clarendon Press, Oxford, 1933.

DOMB, I., *The Transformation*, Lond., 1958.

DOV. BAER OF LÜBAVITCH, *Tract on Ecstasy*, trans., L. Jacobs, Lond., 1963.

DRIVER, S. R., *Deuteronomy* in the ICC Series, 3rd ed., Edinburgh, 1920; *Genesis* in Westminster Commentaries, 12th ed., 1954.

DUBNOW, S., *Toledot Ha-Hasidut*, 2nd ed., Tel-Aviv, 1960.

DURAN, SIMON b. ZEMACH, *Magen Avot*, Leghorn, 1785.

ECKSTEIN, JEROME, *The Fall and Rise of Man* in *Journal for the Scientific Study of Religion*, Vol. V, 1, 1965.

EISENSTEIN, IRA ed., *Varieties of Jewish Belief*, N.Y., 1966.

EISENSTEIN, J. D., *Otzar Vikhuhim*, 1928; *Names of God: In Rabbinical Literature* in *Jewish Encylcopedia*, Vol. IX, pp. 162–165.

ELEAZAR OF WORMS, *Rokeah*, Fano, 1505.

ELIJAH b. SOLOMON ABRAHAM OF SMYRNA, *Midrash Talpiot*, Warsaw, 1875.

ELIMELECH OF LIZENSK, *Noam Elimelekh*, Lemberg, 1788.

EMDEN, JACOB, *Preface to Seder Olam*, Hamburg, 1757.

EMERY, W. B., *Archaic Egypt*, Pelican Books, 1961.

ENELOW, H. G., *Kawwanah: the Struggle for Inwardness in Judaism* in *Studies in Jewish Literature in honor of Kaufmann Kohler*, Berlin, 1913, pp. 82–107.

EPSTEIN, BARUCH, *Torah Temimah*, Tel-Aviv, 1955.

EPSTEIN, ISIDORE, *The Faith of Judaism*, Lond., 1954.

EPSTEIN, LOUIS, *Le-Sheelot Ha-Agunah*, N.Y., 1940.

ERGAS, JOSEPH, *Shomer Emunim*, Jer., 1965.

FACKENHEIM, EMIL L., *Quest for Past and Future; Essays in Jewish Theology*, Indiana University Press, 1968.

FELDMAN, DAVID M., *Birth Control in Jewish Law*, N.Y., 1968.

FRANK, PESACH ZEVI, *Har Tzevi*, Jer., 1964.

FRASER, J. T., ed., *The Voices of Time*, Lond., 1968.

FREEHOF, SOLOMON B., *A Treasury of Responsa*, Philadelphia, 1963; *Current Reform Responsa*, Heb. Union College Press, 1969.

FRIEDLANDER, ALBERT H., *Leo Baeck, Teacher of Theresienstadt*, N.Y., 1968.

FRIEDLÄNDER, M., *The Jewish Religion*, 2nd ed., Lond., 1900.

GABBAI, MEIR IBN, *Derekh Emunah*, Berlin, 1950.

GABIROL, SOLOMON IBN, *Keter Malkhut*, "The Kingly Crown", trans. Bernard Lewis, Lond., 1961.

GALE, RICHARD ed., *The Philosophy of Time*, Lond., 1968.

GALLOWAY, GEORGE, *The Philosophy of Religion*, Edinburgh, 1951.

GERONDI, JONAH b. ABRAHAM, *Shaare Teshuvah*, Vilna, 1895.

GERSONIDES, *Milhamot Adonai*, Riva di Trento, 1560.

GIBSON, E. C. S., *The Book of Job* in *Westminster Commentaries*, Lond., 1905.

GIKATILA, JOSEPH, *Shaare Orah*, Mantua, 1561.

GILKEY, LANGDON B., *The Concept of Providence in Contemporary Theology* in *Journal of Religion*, xiiii, July, 1963, pp. 171-192.

GINZBERG, L., *The Legends of the Jews*, Philadelphia, 1942; *Students, Scholars and Saints*, Philadelphia, 1928; Meridian Books, 1958.

GOLDMAN, SOLOMON, *Crisis and Decision*, N.Y., 1938; *From Slavery to Freedom*, N.Y., 1958.

GOLDSTEIN, M., *Jesus in the Jewish Tradition*, N.Y., 1950.

GORDIS, ROBERT, *Judaism for the Modern Age*, N.Y., 1955.

GREENBERG, SIMON, *Foundations of a Faith*, N.Y., 1967.

GREENSTONE, JULIUS H., *The Messiah Idea in Jewish History*, Philadelphia, 1943.

GRUNBAUM, ADOLF, *Philosophical Problems of Space and Time*, Lond., 1964.

GUTTMANN, JULIUS, *Philosophies of Judaism*, trans. David W. Silverman, N.Y., 1964.

HA-LEVI, JUDAH, *Kazari*, Warsaw, 1880; trans. H. Hirschfeld, London, 1931; *Selected Poems*, trans. Nina Salamon, Philadelphia, 1946.

HARTSHORNE, CHARLES AND REESE, WILLIAM L., *Philosophers Speak of God*, Chicago University Press, 1953; *Man's Vision of God*, N.Y., 1941.

Hastings' Dictionary of the Bible, 2nd ed., ed. Grant and Rowley, Edinburgh, 1963.

HAYIM OF VOLOZHYN, *Nefesh Ha-Hayim*, Vilna, 1937.

HEIDEL, ALEXANDER, *The Gilgamesh Epic and Old Testament Parallels*, Chicago University Press, 1963.

HEINEMANN, ISAAC, *Ahadut Ha-Elohim* in *Encyclopedia Mikrait*, Vol. I, Jer., 1950, pp. 202-205; *Taame Ha-Mitzvot*, Jer., 1949; *The Election of Israel in the Bible* (Heb.) in *Sinai*, Vol. 8, 1944-1945, pp. 17f.

HERBERG, WILL, *Judaism and Modern Man*, N.Y., 1959.

HERRERA, ABRAHAM, *Shaar Ha-Shamayim*, Warsaw, 1864.

HERZOG, ISAAC, *The Main Institutions of Jewish Law*, Lond., 1965.

HESCHEL, A. J., *Man's Quest for God*, N.Y., 1954; *God in Search of Man*, Lond., 1956; *Who is Man?*, California, 1966; *Between God and Man: From the Writings of Abraham J. Heschel* selected and edited by Fritz A. Rothschild, N.Y., 1959; *The Spirit of Prayer* in *Proceedings Rabbinical Assembly America*, Vol. XVII, 1953, pp. 151-238; *Torah Min Ha-Shamayim*, Lond., Vol. I, 1962; Vol. II, 1965; *A Hebrew Evaluation of Reinhold Niebuhr* in *Reinhold Niebuhr: His Religious, Social amd Political Thought*, N.Y., pp. 391-410.

HICK, JOHN, *The Existence of God*, N.Y., 1964; *Evil and the God of Love*, Lond., 1966; *God, Evil and Mystery* in *Religious Studies*, April, 1968, pp. 539-546.

HIRSCH, S. R., *Horeb*, trans. I. Grunfeld, Lond., 1962; *Judaism Eternal*, ed. and trans. I. Grunfeld, Lond, 1956.

HOROWITZ, ISAIAH, *Shene Luhot Ha-Berit*, Jer., 1963.

HORWITZ, JOSEPH OF NAVARADOK, *Madregat Ha-Adam*, N.Y., 1947.

HUME, DAVID, *The Natural History of Religion*, 1757; *Dialogues Concerning Natural Religion*, 1779; *An Inquiry Concerning Human Understanding*, 1748.

HURWITZ, PHINEAS ELIJAH b. MEIR, *Sefer Ha-Berit*, 2nd ed., Warsaw, 1881.

HUSIK, ISAAC, *A History of Mediaeval Jewish Philosophy*, N.Y., Philadelphia, 1958.

HUXLEY, ALDOUS, *The Perennial Philosophy*, Fontana Books, 1958.

ISAAC b. SHESHET BARFET, *Sheelot U-Teshuvot Ribash*, Constantinople, 1546-1547.

ISRAEL MEIR KAGAN, *Hafetz Hayim*, Warsaw, 1877; *Shemirot Ha-Lashon*, Warsaw, 1892; *Ahavat Hesed*, Warsaw, 1885.

JABEZ, JOSEPH, *Maamar Ha-Ahadut*, Lublin, 1597.

JACOB b. ASHER, *Baal Ha-Turim* in *Mikraot Gedolot* ed. Lond., N.Y., 1948.

JACOB, EDMOND, *Theology of the Old Testament*, Lond., 1958.

JACOB ISAAC, the "Seer" of Lublin, *Sheloshah Sefarim Niftahim*, Yafeh, Germany, 1947.

JACOB JOSEPH OF PULNOY, *Toledot Yaakov Yosef*, Warsaw, 1881.

JACOBS, LOUIS, *Faith*, Lond., 1968; *Principles of the Jewish Faith*, Lond., 1964; *Seeker of Unity*, Lond., 1966; *The Via Negativa in Jewish Religious Thought*, 3rd Allan Bronfman Lecture, Judaica Press, N.Y., 1967; *Jewish Thought Today*, Behrman House, New York, 1970.

JASTROW, M., *Dictionary of the Talmud*, N.Y./Berlin, 1926.

JENKINS, DANIEL E., *Guide to the Debate about God*, Lond., 1966.

JOLLES, JACOB ZEVI, *Kehillat Yaahov*, Lemberg, 1870.

JOSEPH MORDECAI OF IZBICA, *Me Ha-Shiloah*, Vienna, 1860.

JOSEPH, MORRIS, *Judaism as Creed and Life*, Lond., 1903.

JUDAH b. SAMUEL HE-HASID, *Sefer Hasidim*, ed. Wistinietzki, Frankfurt, 1924.

KADUSHIN, MAX, *The Rabbinic Mind*, 2nd ed., N.Y., 1965; *A Conceptual Approach to the Mekilta*, N.Y., 1969.

KALONYMOUS KALMAN OF CRACOW, *Maor Va-Shemash* in *Humash Rav Peninim*, Jer., 1969.

KALONYMOUS KALMISH OF PIATZENA, *Hakhsharat Ha-Avrekhim*, Jer., 1962.

KANT, I., *Critique of Pure Reason*, 1781; *Critique of Practical Reason*, 1788.

KAPLAN, MORDECAI M., *Questions Jews Ask*, N.Y., 1958; *Judaism as a Civilization*, N.Y., 1936; *The Meaning of God in Modern Jewish Religion*, N.Y., 1947.

KARO, JOSEPH, *Bet Yoesf*, Warsaw, 1882.

KASHER, M. M., *The Concept of Time in Rabbinic Literature* (Heb.) in *Talpiot*, Vol. V., 1952, pp. 799–827.

KASHER, M. S., *Ha-Gaon Ha-Ragadshovi Ve-Talmudo*, Jer., 1958.

KATZ, DOV, *Tenuat Ha-Musar*, Tel-Aviv, 1958–1963.

KATZ, JACOB, *Martyrdom in the Middle Ages* (Heb.) in *Baer Jubilee Volume*, Jer., 1960, pp. 318–337; *Exclusiveness and Tolerance*, Clarendon Press, Oxford, 1961.

KAUFMANN, WALTER, *Critique of Religion and Philosophy*, N.Y., 1961.

KAUFMANN, Y., *The Religion of Israel*, trans. and abridged by Moshe Greenberg, Lond., 1961; *Toledot Ha-Emunah Ha-Yisreelit* (orig. of above), Tel-Aviv, 1952.

KIERKEGAARD, S., *Concluding Unscientific Postcsript*, N.J., 1944.

Keter Shem Tov, Podgorze, 1898.

KLAUSNER, J., *The Messianic Idea in Israel*, trans. from 3rd ed. W. F. Stinespring, Lond., 1956.

KOHLER, KAUFMANN, *Jewish Theology*, N.Y., 1918; Ktav. ed. 1968.

KOHN, EUGENE: *Prayer and the Modern Jew* in *Proceedings Rabbinical Assembly America*, Vol. XVII, 1953, pp. 151–238.

KONOVITZ, ISRAEL, *Ha-Elohut*, N.Y., 1905.

KOOK, A. I., *Letters*, 2nd ed., Jer., 1961; *Orot Ha-Kodesh*, Jer., 1938.

LAMM, NORMAN AND WURZBURGER, W. S., ed., *A Treasury of Tradition*, N.Y., 1967; *The Religious Implications of Extraterrestrial Life* in *Tradition*, Vol. 7, No. 4–Vol. 8, No. 1, Winter 1965–Spring 1966, pp. 5–56.

LANDAU, E., *Die dem Raume entnommenen Synonyma für Gott in der neu-hebraischen Litteratur*, Zurich, 1888.

LANDAU, EZEKIEL, *Noda Bihudah*, Stettin, 1861.

LAUTERBACH, J. Z., *Theology* in *Jewish Encyclopedia*, Vol. XII, pp. 128–137.

LAZARUS, MORITZ, *The Ethics of Judaism*, trans. Henrietta Solzd, Philadelphia, 1900.

LEVI YITZHAK OF BERDITCHEV, *Kedushat Levi*, Jer., 1964.

LEVIN, B. M., *Otzar Ha-Geonim*, Jer., 1931.

LEVY, JACOB., *Wörterbuch uber die Talmudim und Midraschim*, Berlin, 1924.

LEWIS, C. S., *Christian Reflections*, ed. Walter Hooper, Lond., 1967; *The Problem of Pain*, Lond., 1940.

LIPSCHUTZ, ISRAEL, *Tiferet Yisrael*, Vilna, 1911.

LOEWE, RAPHAEL, ed., *Studies in Rationalism, Judaism and Universalism: Im Memory of Leon Roth*, Lond., 1966.

LUZZATTO, M. H., *Derekh Ha-Shem*, Tel-Aviv, 1949; *Mesillat Yesharim*, ed. Kaplan, Philadelphia 1936; *K'lah Pithe Hokhmah*, Jer., 1961.

MACDONALD, JOHN, *The Theology of the Samaritans*, Lond., 1964.

MAIMONIDES, *The Guide of the Perplexed*, Lemberg, 1866, trans. S. Pines, University of Chicago Press, 1963; *Responsa, ed.* J. Blau, Jer., 1957; *Yad Ha-Hazakah*, Warsaw, 1882; *Commentary to the Mishnah* in *Vilna* ed. of the Talmud; *Sefer Ha-Mitzvot*, ed. Warsaw, 1883; *Maamar Tehiat Ha-Metim*, ed. Finkel, American Academy for Jewish Research, Vol. IX, 1939.

MALTER, HENRY, *Life and Works of Saadia Gaon*, Philadelphia, 1942.

MANASSEH b. ISRAEL, *Nishmat Hayim*, Stettin, 1751.

MARMORSTEIN, A., *The Old Rabbinic Doctrine of God*, Lond., 1927, Ktav. ed. 1968.

MARMORSTEIN, EMILE, *Heaven at Bay*, Lond., 1969.

MARTIN, BERNARD, ed., *Contemporary Reform Jewish Thought*, Chicago, 1968.

MASCALL, E. L., *Christian Theology and Natural Science*, Lond., 1956.

MAYBAUM, IGNAZ, *The Fate of the Jewish Diaspora*, Lond., 1962; *The Face of God After Auschwitz*, Amsterdam, 1965.

McLAUGHLIN, J. F., *Names of God: Biblical Data* in *Jewish Encyclopedia*, Vol. IX, pp. 160–162.

MEIRI, MENAHEM b. SOLOMON OF PERPIGNAN, *The Book of Repentance* (Heb.), ed. Abraham Schreiber, N.Y., 1950.

MENAHEM MENDEL OF LÜBAVITCH, *Derekh Mitzvotekha*, Poltava, 1913.

MILL, JOHN STUART, *Three Essays in Religion*, Lond., 1874.

MILNE, E. A., *A Modern Cosmology and the Christian Idea of God*, Lond., 1952.

MODENA, LEON DE, *Magen Va-Herev*, ed. S. Simonsohn, Jer., 1960.

MONTEFIORE, C. G. and LOEWE, H., *A Rabbinic Anthology*, Lond., 1938.

MOORE, G. F., *Judaism*, Harvard University Press, 1958; *History of Religions*, Edinburgh, 1950.

MORRELL, SAMUEL, *The Halachic Status of Non-Halachic Jews* in *Judaism*, Vol. 18, No. 4 (Fall, 1969) pp. 448–457.

MOSES b. JOSEPH DI TRANI (*Mabit*): *Bet Elohim*, Warsaw, 1872.

MOULE, C. F. D., and others, *Faith, Fact and Fantasy*, Fontana Books, 1964; ed. *Miracles—Cambridge Studies in Their Philosophy and History*, Lond., 1965.

MOWINCKEL, S., *The Old Testament and the Word of God*, trans. Reidar B. Bjornard, Oxford, 1960.

NAHMAN OF BRATZLAV, *Likkute Maharan*, Benai Berak, 1965; *Sefer Ha-Middot*, Warsaw, 1912.

NAHMAN OF TCHERIN, *Leashon Hasidim*, Tel-Aviv, 1961; *Derekh Hasidim*, Jer., 1962.

NAHMANIDES, *Commentary to the Pentateuch* ed., B. Chavel, Jer., 1959–1960; *Collected Writings* ed., B. Chavel, Jer., Vol I, 1963; Vol. II, 1964.

NEUMARK, DAVID, *Toledot Ha-Ikkarim Be-Yisrael*, Odessa, 1912.

NIEBUHR, REINHOLD, *The Nature and Destiny of Man*, Lond., 1943.

NOTH MARTIN, *Leviticus*, Lond., 1965.

NOUY, DECOMTE DU, *Human Destiny*, N.Y., 1947.

OESTERLY, W. O. E. and ROBINSON, T. H., *Hebrew Religion*, 2nd ed., Lond., 1937.

ORR, J., *English Deism: Its Roots and Fruits*, Grand Rapids, 1934.

OSHLAG, J., *Talmud Eser Sefirot*, Jer., 1957.

OTTO, RUDOLF, *The Idea of the Holy*, trans. J. W. Harvey, 2nd ed., Lond., 1957.

PERL, JOSEPH, *Meggale Temirin*, Lemberg, 1864.

PETUCHOWSKI, J. J., *Ever Since Sinai*, N.Y., 1961; *The Theology of Haham David Nieto*, 2nd ed., Ktav, N.Y., 1970; *Can Modern Man Pray?* in *Central Conference American Rabbis Yearbook*, Vol. LXXVII, 1967, pp. 168–176.

PHILLIPS, D. I., *The Concept of Prayer*, Lond., 1965.

PHILO, *Legum Allegoria*, Loeb Classical Library, Vol. I, 1949; *De Fuga et Inventione*, Loeb, Vol. V, 1949; *De Specialibus Legibus*, Loeb, Vol. VIII, 1950; *Vita Mosis*, Loeb Vd. VI, 1935.

PIKE, NELSON, *God and Timelessness*, London, 1970.

PLATO, *The Laws*, trans. A. E. Taylor, Lond., 1960; *Timaeus* in *Dialogues of Plato*, trans. Jowett, 2nd ed., Oxford, 1875.

PLAUT, W. GUNTHER, *Judaism and the Scientific Spirit*, N.Y., 1962; *The Growth of Reform Judaism*, N.Y., 1965.

PLOTINUS, *The Enneads*, trans. Stephen Mackenna, 2nd ed., rev. B.S. Page, Lond., 1956.

POLLARD, WILLIAM G., *Chance and Providence*, N.Y., 1958.

PUCCETTI, ROLAND, *The Loving God—Some Observations on John Hick's Evil and the Love of God* in *Religious Studies*, April, 1967, 1967, pp. 255–268.

RACKMAN, EMANUEL, *A Challenge to Orthodoxy* in *Judaism*, Vol. 18, 2, Spring 1969, pp. 143–158.

RAHNER, KARL, *Theological Investigations*, Vol. 4, Baltimore, Lond., 1966.

RALL, H. R. and COHON, S. S., *Christianity and Judaism Compare Notes*, N.Y., 1927.

RAMSEY, MICHAEL, *Images Old and New*, Lond., 1963.

RANKIN, O. S., *Jewish Religious Polemics*, Edinburgh, 1956.

RASHDALL, HASTINGS, *Philosophy and Religion*, Lond., 1914.

RATNER, I. S., *Le-Or Ha-Kabbalah*, Tel-Aviv, 1961.

RAWIDOWICZ, SIMON, *Saadya's Purification of the Idea of God* in *Saadya Studies*, ed., Erwin I. J. Rosenthal, Manchester University Press, 1943, pp. 139–165.

ROBINSON, CHARLES K., *Biblical Theism and Modern Science* in *Journal of Religion*, XLIII, 1963, pp. 118–138.

ROBINSON, JOHN A. T., *Honest to God*, Lond., 1963; with David L. Edwards, *The Honest to God Debate*, Lond., 1963; *The New Reformation*, Lond., 1965; *Exploration into God*, Lond., 1967.

ROBINSON, H. WHEELER, *Inspiration and Revelation in the Old Testament*, Clarendon Press, Oxford, 1962.

ROSEN, KOPUL, *Rabbi Israel Salanter and the Musar Movement*, Lond., 1945.

ROSENZWEIG, FRANZ, *Franz Rosenzweig His Life and Thought* presented by Nahum N. Glatzer, N. Y., 1953; *On Jewish Learning*, N.Y., 1955; *The Star of Redemption*, trans. William W. Hallo, London, 1971.

ROTH, AARON, *Shomer Emunim*, Jer., 1964.

ROTH, CECIL, *Anglo-Jewish Letters*, Lond., 1938.

ROTH, LEON, *Judaism, A Portrait*, Lond., 1960; *The Guide for the Perplexed: Moses Maimonides*, Lond., 1948.

ROWLEY, H. H. ed., *The Old Testament and Modern Study*, Clarendon Press, Oxford, 1951; *From Moses to Qumran*, Lond., 1963.

RUBENSTEIN, RICHARD L., *After Auschwitz*, Indianapolis, 1966; *The Religious Imagination*, Indianapolis, 1968.

RUBIN, S., *Heidenthum und Kabbala*, Vienna, 1893.

SAADIA GAON, *The Book of Beliefs and Opinions*, many Heb. editions, trans. from the Arabic by Samuel Rosenblatt, Yale University Press, 1948.

SARACHEK, JOSEPH, *The Doctrine of the Messiah in Mediaeval Jewish Literature*, N.Y., 1932.

SARNA, NAHUM N., *Understanding Genesis*, N.Y., 1966.

SCHATZ, R., *Contemplative Prayer in Hasidism* in *Studies in Mysticism and Religion presented to Gershom G. Scholem*, Jer., 1967, pp. 209–226.

SCHECHTER, SOLOMON, *Seminary Addresses*, N.Y., 1959; *Studies in Judaism*, Philadelphia, 1945; *Aspects of Rabbinic Theology*, N.Y., 1961.

SCHLESINGER, G. N., *Divine Benevolence* in *Proceedings Association Orthodox Jewish Scientists*, Vol. I, N.Y., 1966, pp. 101–103.

SCHNEOR ZALMAN OF LIADY, *Tanya*, Vilna, 1930.

SCHNEORSOHN, FISCHEL, *Hayim Gravitzer*, Tel-Aviv, 1957.

SCHOLEM, GERSHOM G., *Shabbatai Zevi*, Tel-Aviv, 1957; *Major Trends in Jewish Mysticism*, 3rd ed., Lond., 1955; *On the Kabbalah and Its Symbolism*, trans. Ralph Manheim, Lond., 1965; *Reshit Ha-Kabbalah*, Tel-Aviv, 1948; *Devekuth or Communion with God* in *Review of Religion*, 1950, pp. 115–139; *The Messianic Idea in Judaism*, Schochen Books, New York, 1971.

SCHWARZSCHILD, STEVEN S., *The Personal Messiah—Towards the Restoration of a Discarded Doctrine* in *Judaism*, Vol. V, 1956, pp. 123–135.

SEGAL, SAMUEL b. YEHUDAH LAIB, *Likkute Yekarim*, Lemberg, 1792.

Sefer Baal Shem Tov, Lodz, 1938.

SELIGER, JOSEPH, *Collected Writings* (Heb.) ed., Leah Seliger, Jer., 1930.

SEVIN, S., *Ha-Moadim Ba-Halakhah*, 2nd ed., Tel-Aviv, 1949.

SHERWIN, BYRON L., *Elie Wiesel and Jewish Theology* in *Judaism*, Winter, 1969, pp. 39–52.

SHESTOV, LEV, *Athens and Jerusalem*, trans. Bernard Martin, Ohio University Press, 1966.

Siddur Ishe Yisrael, following the Gaon of Vilna, Tel-Aviv, 1968.

SIMHAH ZÜSSEL OF KELM, *Hokhmah U-Musar*, Vol. I, N.Y., 1957; Vol. II, Jer., 1964.

SIMON, ULRICH, E., *A Theology of Auschwitz*, Lond., 1967.

SINGER, S., *Authorised Daily Prayer Book*, new ed., Lond., 1962.

SKINNER, J., *Genesis in the ICC Series*, Edinburgh, 1951.

SLONIMSKY, HENRY, *Essays*, Hebrew Union College Press, Cincinnati, 1967.

SMART, NINIAN, *Philosophers and Religious Truth*, Lond., 1964.

SMETHURST, ARTHUR F., *Modern Science and Christian Beliefs*, Lond., 1955.

SPEISER, E. A., *Genesis*, Anchor Bible, N.Y., 1964.

SPIRA, ZEVI ELIMELECH, *Derekh Pikkudekha*, Lublin, 1865; new ed., Jer., n.d.; *Bene Yisakhar*, Stuttgart, 1947.

STEINBERG, MILTON, *Anatomy of Faith*, ed. Arthur A. Cohen, N.Y., 1960.

SWINBURNE, RICHARD, *Space and Time*, Lond., 1968.

TAKU, MOSES, *Ketav Tamin*, ed., R. Kircheim in *Otzar Nehmad*, Vol. III, Vienna, 1860, pp. 54–99.

TCHERNOWITZ, HAYIM, *Shaar Ha-Tefillah*, *Toledot Ha-Halakhah*, N.Y., 1934. Sedilkov, 1837.

TEILHARD DE CHARDIN, P., *The Phenomenon of Man*, Lond., 1959.

TEITELBAUM, M., *Ha-Rav Mi-Ladi*, Part I, Warsaw, 1910; Part II, Warsaw, 1913.

TILLICH, PAUL., *Systematic Theology*, Chicago, 1951; *Dynamics of Faith*, Lond., 1957.

TISHBY, I., *Torat He-Ra Ve-Ha-Kelipah Be-Kabbalat Ha-Ari*, Jer., 1942; *Mishnat Ha-Zohar*, Vol. I, 2nd ed., Jer., 1951, Vol. 2, Jer., 1961; with J. Dan, *Torat Ha-Hasidut Ve-Sifrutah*, offprint Hebrew Encyclopedia, Vol. 17, Jer., 1966; *The Messianic Idea and Messianic Trends in the Growth of Hassidism* (Heb.) in *Zion* Vol. XXXII (1967) pp. 1–45.

TORREY, N. L., *Voltaire and the English Deists*, Yale University Press, 1930.

TRACHTENBERG, JOSHUA, *Jewish Magic and Superstition*, N.Y., 1939.

Tzavaat Ha-Ribash, Warsaw, 1913.

UNDERHILL, EVELYN, *Worship*, Lond., 1958.

URBACH, EPHRAIM E., *The Sages Their Concepts and Beliefs* (Heb.) (*Hazal*), Magnes Press, Heb. University, Jer., 1969.

URBACH, S. B., *Pillars of Jewish Thought* (Heb.), Vol. I, Jer., 1953.

VAJDA, GEORGES, *L'amour De Dieu Dans La Theologie Juive Du Moyen Age*, Paris, 1957.

VIDAS, ELIJAH DE, *Reshit Hokhmah*, Venice, 1593.

WAXMAN, MEYER, *The Philosophy of Don Hasdai Crescas*, N.Y., 1966.

WEINBERG, J. J., *Seride Esh*, Vol. III, Jer., 1966.

WEINSTOCK, I., *Be-Maagale Ha-Nigleh Ve-Ha-Nistar*, Jer., 1969.

WEISS, I. H., *Dor Dor Ve-Doreshav*, Berlin, 1924.

WEISS, J. G., *The Kavvanoth of Prayer in Early Hasidism* in *Journal of Jewish Studies*, Vol. IX, 1958, pp. 163–192; *The Religious Determinism of Joseph Mordecai of Izbica* in *Baer Jubilee Volume*, Jer., 1960, pp. 447–453.

WERBLOWSKY, R. J. Z., *Joseph Karo: Lawyer and Mystic*, Clarendon Press, Oxford, 1962.

WERTHEIM, A., *Halakhot Va-Halikhot Ba-Hasidut*, Jer., 1960.

WHITEMAN, MICHAEL, *Philosophy of Space and Time*, Lond./N.Y., 1967.

WOLF, ARNOLD J., *What is Man*, B'nai B'rith, 1968; ed., *Rediscovering Judaism: Reflections on a New Theology*, Chicago, 1965.

WOLFSON, H. A., *The Philosophy of the Church Fathers*, Harvard University Press, 1956; *Philo*, Harvard University Press, 1948.

WOLLHEIM, RICHARD, *Hume on Religion*, Fontana Books, 1963.

WOUK, HERMAN, *This is My God*, Lond., 1960.

WRIGHT, WILLIAM K., *A Students' Philosophy of Religion*, rev., ed., N.Y., 1950.

WURTHWEIN, E., *The Text of the Old Testament*, trans. P. R. Ackroyd, Oxford, 1957.

YARNOLD, G. D., *The Moving Image*, Lond., 1966.

YISRAELI, SAUL, *Perakim Be-Mahashevet Yisrael*, 3rd ed., Pardes-Hannah, 1964.

ZERITZKI, D., *Torat Ha-Musar*, Tel-Aviv, 1959.

ZEVI ELIMELECH OF DINOV, *Derekh Pikkudekha*, Jer.

ZUNZ, L., *Ha-Derashot Be-Yisreal*, trans. and ed., Albeck, Jer., 1947.

ZWEIFUL, E., *Shalom Al Yisrael*, Zhitomer, 1868–1869.

INDEX

Aaron, 83, 132, 161, 273, 316
Aaron Ha-Levi of Barcelona, 47
Aaron Starosselje, 36, 191
Abahu, 25, 255
Abarbarnel, 9, 317, 323
Abba, 33
Abba Mari of Lunel, 9, 323
Abba Saul, 141
Abelson, J., 60, 61, 63, 323
Abin, 47
Abraham, 72, 147, 153, 158, 162, 193, 273, 278, 306
Abraham Ibn David I, 4, 127, 128, 134, 155, 174, 176, 323
Abraham Ibn David II, 50, 314
Abrahams, Israel, 111, 323
Abramovitz, H. I., 243, 323
absurd, 5, 19, 74
acosmism, 34
Adam, 100, 292, 315, 317
Adam Kadmon, 32–34
Adonai, 137, 139, 140, 141, 147, 148
Africa, 181
agnosticism, 14, 15, 300, 321
Agus, J. B., 7, 271, 323
Ahad Ha-Am, 283
Ahriman, 23, 25
Akkadian, 146
Albeck, H., 111, 307, 323
Albo, 2, 4, 9, 10, 16, 27, 41, 42, 73, 74, 75, 85, 86, 94, 147, 148, 176–177, 196, 255–256, 260, 316, 317, 323
Akiba, 77, 165, 202, 206, 207, 294
Allen, E. L., 284, 323
Alexander, 83
Alexander Süsskind, 164–165, 323
Alexandria, 10, 17, 83
Alfasi, 255
Almighty, 139
Almosnino, Moses, 80, 86, 323
Altizer, T. J. J., 51, 232
Altmann, A., 47, 95, 232
Ammishaddai, 138
Amoraim, 23, 294, 308
Amos, 202, 272, 293
Amsterdam, 65
Anatoli, Jacob, 110, 111, 232
'Ancient of Days,' 140
angels, 49, 103, 107, 109–113, 115, 128, 138, 147, 157, 158, 196
Ani, 146
animals, 95, 107–109, 114–115, 183
Anselm, 17, 86, 232
anthropomorphism, 46, 54, 126, 142

Antioch, 83
Antiochus, 83
Apocrypha and Pseudopigrapha, 293–294, 307
Apollo, 44
Aquilas, 140, 306
Aquinas, 5, 74, 323
Arabic, 4, 5, 11, 146, 187, 282, 312
Arabs, 280, 282, 301
Arama, Isaac, 9, 232, 316
Aramaic, 5, 68, 143, 144, 145, 282
Ari, see Luria, Isaac
Arikh, 33
Aristotle, 4, 94, 147, 148, 312
Arnold, Matthew, 283
asceticism, 156, 164, 165, 168–172, 236–239, 244–246, 250–251, 252, 258, 308
Ashhenazi, Zevi, 65–66, 232
Ashterot, 21
Asia, 5
Asler Ha-Kohen, 168
astronomy, 15, 35, 50, 77, 193, 289
atheism, 14, 15, 300, 321
Athens, 45, 74
'Atticism,' 237
Attik Yomin, 140
Augustine, 133
Auschwitz, 135
Avinu Malkenu, 144
Azariah, 138
Azriel of Gerona, 43

Baal, 21, 284
baale hem, 149
Baal Shem Tov, 115, 149, 157, 166, 167, 179, 189, 190
Babylon, 23, 61, 62, 109, 111, 146, 167, 183, 226, 284, 301–303
Bacher, W., 141, 323
Baeck, Leo, 7, 10, 13, 84, 323
Baelz, P. R., 51, 194, 323
Baer, Y., 252, 257, 323
Bahya Ibn Asher, 26, 86, 323
Bahya Ibn Pakudah, 4, 10, 12, 27, 39, 40, 41, 43, 146, 147, 152, 155, 156, 175, 188, 189, 253, 286, 291, 323
Balaam, 117
Bamberger, B. J., 285, 323
Bampton lectures, 98
Barbour, I. G., 122, 323
Barfet, Isaac b. Sheshet, 30–31, 326
Bar Kappara, 167, 171
Bar Kochba, 294
Baron, S. W., 27, 301, 313, 324
Barr, James, 156, 324

Barth, 122
bat kol, 62
Bedersi, 2, 324
behaviourism, religious, 6
Beliefs and Opinions, 2, 4, 27, 46, 49, 62, 73,
    87, 94, 104, 108, 110, 155, 253, 310–313,
    317
Belkin, Samuel, 7, 324
Bergman, Hugo, 271
Berkeley, Bishop, 70
Bernfeld, S., 231, 324
Bertinoro, 171
Bertocci, P., 76, 324
Bethel, 10, 138
Bhavagadgita, 288
Bialik, 283
Bible, 5, 10, 11, 15, 22, 36, 41, 44, 47, 49, 57,
    59, 60, 61, 72, 77, 81, 82, 83, 93, 94, 98,
    109, 112, 114, 117, 119, 123, 124, 125, 126,
    135, 136–140, 144, 149, 150, 152, 157, 174,
    175, 180, 187, 191, 199, 201, 202, 203, 205,
    208, 215, 219, 220, 221, 231, 240, 247, 261,
    262, 267, 269, 272, 282, 284, 293, 301–306,
    316
"big bang" theory, 96
Binah, 26, 28–34, 43, 44
biophysics, 6
Blau, J., 255
Bloch, J. L., 88, 232, 324
Boethius, 86, 324
Book of the Dead, 302
Borowitz, E. G., 8, 186, 324
Boswell, 201
Bouqet, A. C., 45, 324
Brahma, 30
"bread of shame," 130
Breisch, M. J., 240, 324
Bresslau, 220
Brever, I., 208
Brightman, E. S., 76, 77, 324
Broad, C. D., 85, 324
Browning, Elizabeth Barrett, 69
Brunner, E., 214
Buber, M., 7, 10, 13, 52–55, 71, 192, 208, 324
Buber, S., 62
Büchler, A., 243, 324
Buddhism, 288

Caesarea, 25
Cahn, S. M., 90–91, 324
Cain, sons of, 99
Caldecott and Mackintosh, 18, 324
Calvin, 78
Campbell, J., 88, 324
Canaan, 123, 138
Carlyle, 7, 64, 324
Carmel, L., 135, 324
Cassuto, U., 136, 204, 324
Catholicism, 18, 88
Catholic Israel, 222
Chaldeans, 72
chance, 114–124
Charles, R. H., 306, 308, 324

Chavel, B., 149, 183, 258, 265, 314, 323, 328
cherubim, 110
Chesterton, G. K., 11
chosen people, 7, 8, 106, 269–275, 276–283
Christianity, 17, 22–27, 100, 101, 102, 108,
    121, 135, 137, 186, 194, 246, 247, 250, 256,
    257, 285–291, 316
Christians, 5, 17, 25, 26, 30, 72, 98, 99, 214,
    253
Church Fathers, 27, 29, 137
confession, 248–259
Confucionism, 288
Cohen, A., 95, 109, 243, 324
Cohen, Arthur A., 7, 324
Cohen, Simon, 136, 324
Cohon, Samuel S., 5, 7, 8, 278, 324
Collins, James, 76, 324
commandments, 9, 12, 206, 211–230, 232, 252,
    286
Commentary, 7, 217, 324
Conservative Judaism, 7
consistency, 5
Constantine, 83
Constantinople, 83
Cordovero, Moses, 10, 52, 96, 108, 149, 150,
    234, 324
cosmological proof, 17, 18, 19
covenant, 206
Cox, H., 51, 324
creatio ex nihilo, 2, 9, 94–97
Creatures on other planets, 98–107
Crescas, 4, 10, 27, 40, 41, 49, 51, 78, 79, 80,
    85, 114, 324
Cross, F. M., 61, 325
cycles, 96
Cyrus, 292

Daat, 29
Dadistani Dinik, 143, 325
Daniel, 109, 117, 174, 293, 305
Dan, Joseph, 47, 69, 257, 325
Darwin, 120
David Ibn Abi Zimra, 9, 325
David, King, 82, 143, 144, 158, 172, 175,
    273, 293–297
Davidson, R. E., 180, 325
Day of Atonement, 141, 181, 243, 248, 249,
    253, 257, 259, 299
Dead Sea Scrolls, 140
Deane, S. W., 86
decatheism, 29, 30
de Chardin, 7, 121, 330
Defter, 9
deism, 15, 56, 63–71
demons, 33, 102, 107, 111–113, 129, 163, 317
Dentan, R. C., 136, 325
Descartes, 75
Dessler, E., 88, 135, 232, 325
deus absconditus, 42
deus revelatus, 42
Deutero-Isaiah, 23, 57, 58
Deuteronomy, 21, 22, 217
devekut, 157, 197, 297

dibbuk, 317
dimension, third, 91–92
Dinah, 163
divorce, 228–229
Documentary Hypothesis, 203–210, 317
Dodd, E. R., 45, 325
dogmas, 8–10, 214, 312
Domb, I., 277, 278, 325
Dov Baer of Lübavitch, 191
Driver, S. R., 22, 60, 203, 325
dualism, 15, 22–25, 37, 54, 285
Dubnow, S., 68, 189, 325
du Nouy, 118, 328
Duran, Simon b. Zemah, 9, 260, 325
Duties of the Heart, 4, 10, 12, 27, 39, 146, 152, 155, 175, 188, 253, 286, 323

Ecclesiastes, 59, 125, 262, 305
Eckstein, Jerome, 100, 325
ecstasy, 191
Egypt, 20, 30, 62, 184, 262, 301–303, 308, 316
Ehych, 137, 141
Eisensten, Ira, 7, 76, 325
Eisenstein, J. D., 27, 136, 325
El, 138, 141
Eleazar b. Simeon, 263
Eleazar of Worms, 250–251, 325
Elijah, 31, 294, 316
Elijah de Vidas, 163, 164, 177, 178, 331
Elijah of Smyrna, 271, 318, 325
Elimelech Lizensk, 165, 172, 198, 258, 325
Elisha b. Abuyah, 24
Elohim, 138, 141, 147, 150, 151, 166, 200
Elyon, 139
Elysian fields, 316
Emden, Jacob, 286, 325
emanations, 29–34, 95
Emery, W. B., 302, 325
Emunah Ramah, 127, 155, 174, 323
Enelow, H. G., 188, 325
England, 112, 220
English, 83, 136, 139, 142, 181, 283, 306
Enoch, 158
En Sof, 26, 28, 29–34, 42, 43, 44, 57, 68, 104, 130, 149–151, 163, 184, 191
Ephraim, 204
Epstein, Baruch, 47, 325
Epstein, Isidore, 7, 51, 318, 325
Epstein, Louis, 229, 325
Ergas, Joseph, 31, 43, 115, 118, 265, 325
erotic symbolism, 160–164, 192
ESP, 89–90
Esther, Book of, 140, 199
Eternal Now, 80, 86–92, 97, 319
ethics, 225, 231–242
Europe, 201, 277, 278
Eve, 100, 163, 247, 292
evil inclination, 109, 153, 242–247
evil, problem of, 8, 15, 24, 33, 76, 107, 116, 120, 125–135, 228
existentialism, 12–13, 17, 19, 75, 89, 105, 111, 122, 205, 208

Exodus, 61
Ezekiel, 267, 293, 317
Ezra, 174, 244

Fackenheim, E. L., 7, 325
Fall of Man, 133, 246
Falstaff, 101
Far Eastern religions, 5, 34, 285–291
fatalism, 116
"Father," 144
Feldman, David M., 97, 325
Finite God, 75–80, 130
Finkel, J., 313
foreknowledge, 77–79, 86–88, 89, 90, 91, 116
Fortune, 118
France, 7
Frank, P. Z., 289, 325
Frankel, Z., 218, 220
Fraser, J. J., 88, 325
Freehof, S. B., 66, 109, 219, 220, 325
Freewill, 77–79, 91, 99, 128, 133
Friedlander, Albert H., 325
Friedländer, M., 7, 11, 325
Fundamentalism, 206–230

Gabriel, 109, 325
Gale, R., 88, 325
Galloway, George, 64, 325
Gamaliel, 95
Gaon of Vilna, 44, 68, 111, 168
Garden of Eden, 292, 301–322
Gavoah, 145
Geiger, A., 271
Gemara, 23, 201, 229, 309
Generation of the wilderness, 68
Genesis, 57, 81, 94, 96, 142, 150, 175, 203, 204, 246, 292
Gentiles, 99, 168, 212, 219, 228, 270, 271, 286–291, 309
Gerizim, Mount, 9–10
German, 5, 186, 225, 231
Germany, 7, 208
Gersonides, 4, 10, 76, 78, 80, 89, 91, 94, 114, 316, 325
gestures in prayer, 191–192
Gevurah, 26, 28–34, 145, 179
Gibson, E. C. S., 305, 325
Gikatila, Joseph, 30, 325
Gilgamesh Epic, 204
gilgul, 14, 132, 168, 178, 266, 318–319
Gilkey, L. B., 120, 326
Ginzberg, L., 99, 218, 220, 317, 326
"Given," 77
Gnosticism, 31, 84, 285
God:
    attributes of, 3, 27, 39, 40, 47, 139–140
    approach to, 8, 147, 148, 242
    concept of, 1, 2, 3, 21–22, 155
    as Creator, 2, 9, 15, 16, 20, 23, 28, 32, 65, 66, 67, 75–76, 77, 78, 81, 84, 85, 93–113, 116–117, 119, 125, 130, 142, 146, 148, 150, 158, 194, 226, 239

God, (contd.)—
   death of, 7, 17, 51, 81, 83
   eternity of, 9, 15, 40, 76, 80, 81–92
   existence of, 9, 15–20, 36, 40
   goodness of, 15, 40, 125–135, 142, 228
   incorporeality of, 9, 27, 50, 52
   in manifestation, 2, 28, 49, 62, 149–151,
      184
   nature of, 1, 3, 38, 41, 94, 125, 148
   omnipotence and omniscience of, 9, 15,
      49, 72–80, 89, 91, 94, 122, 126–135,
      138–139
   transcendence and immanence of, 15,
      18, 56–71, 118, 122, 123, 142–143,
      145, 189, 193, 194, 282
   as unknowable, 2, 3, 28, 38–52, 155
   will of, 10, 33, 76, 111, 130, 173, 210,
      224, 240, 260
   worship of, 2, 8, 9, 10, 126, 162, 167–
      173, 183–198, 205, 206, 210, 225,
      278, 280, 281
Gog and Magog, 294
Goldman, Felix, 277
Goldman, Solomon, 11, 136, 326
Goldstein, M., 26, 286, 326
Gordis, Robert, 7, 326
Gospels, 214
Graetz, H., 220
Great Britain, 12
Greek, 5, 10, 11, 57, 72, 74, 99, 137, 140,
   146, 232, 237, 285, 307, 308, 316, 318
Greenberg, S. 7, 326
Greenstone, J. H., 292, 326
Grunbaum, A., 88, 326
Guide for the Perplexed, 2, 4, 40, 41, 47, 48,
   85, 94, 104, 108, 110, 114, 128, 146, 147,
   227, 232, 269
Guttmann, Julius, 79, 278, 326

Habad, 34–37, 66–71, 190–192, 210
Habbakuk, 293
Hagiographa, 43, 60, 199, 201
Hai Gaon, 150
Ha-Kadosh Barukh Hu, 143–144
Halakhah, 104, 105, 219, 220, 225–230, 287,
   290, 314
Ha-Levi, Judah, 4, 20, 47, 107, 110, 146, 147,
   158, 191, 269, 269, 270, 326
Hallel, 42
Hallelujah, 138
Hamilton, William, 51
Hamnuna, 97
Hanina, 117
Hartshorne, Charles, 76, 91, 326
Hasidism, 34–37, 66–71, 79, 86, 96, 115–116,
   135, 149, 157, 165, 166, 168, 171, 179, 180,
   188–192, 197–198, 213, 232, 250, 257, 297
Hayim of Sanz, 115
Hayim of Volozhyn, 10, 35, 68, 105–106,
   168, 189, 191, 213, 322, 326
"Heaven," as name of God, see Shamayim
Hebrew, 4, 5, 72, 74, 114, 125, 136, 138, 140,
   143, 150, 152, 205, 279, 282

Heidel, A., 204, 326
Heilsgeschichte, 123, 204
Heinemann, I., 212, 273, 326
Hell, 175, 177–179, 181, 262, 301–322
Hellenism, 141, 284, 308
henotheism, 15, 22
Herberg, Will, 7, 318, 326
Hereafter, 8, 88, 108, 177, 260, 262, 301–322
hermit, 164
Herodotus, 143
Herrenvolk, 272
Herzog, I., 278, 326
Heschel, A. J., 7, 192–193, 206, 246, 326
Hesed, 26, 28–34, 179
Hesse, Mary, 123
Hezekiah, 294
Hick, John, 18, 108, 133–135, 326
High Priest, 140, 141, 191, 257
Hillel, 95, 146
Hillel, R., 294
Himmelfarb, Milton, 7
Hinduism, 288
Hiram, 273
Hiroshima, 131
Hirsch, S. R., 97, 208, 215–218, 326
history, 1, 6, 7, 8, 14–15, 31, 123, 124, 136,
   150, 187, 201, 202, 204, 215, 220–230, 271,
   287
Hitler, 267
Hobbes, T., 89
Hod, 29–34
Hokhmah, 26, 28–34, 43, 44, 234
Hollywood, 206
"holy beasts," 110
holy land, 201, 279, 280
holy spirit, 199
Honi, 144
Horowitz, Isaiah, 42, 165, 185, 326
Horwitz, Joseph, 232, 326
Horus, 30
Hu, 140, 146
Hume, David, 18–19, 71, 116, 122, 326
Hurwitz, Phineas Elijah, 99, 232, 287, 326
Husik, Isaac, 2, 42, 129, 326
Huxley, Aldous, 89–91, 326
Huxley, Julian, 121
hygiene, 9, 212

ibbur, 317
Ibn Ezra, Abraham, 48, 94, 112
Ibn Gabirol, Solomon, 27
ideas, 1, 164
idolatry, 22, 109, 277, 281, 290
Ikkarim, 2, 4, 9, 16, 27, 41, 42, 73, 75, 85, 94,
   147, 176, 196, 255, 260, 316, 317
Imitatio Dei, 233–242
Imma, 33
immortality, 308–322
impossibility, 72–80, 94, 127
Incarnation, 25, 27, 98, 99, 100, 101, 102
India, 30
intellectual honesty, 4
intolerance, 14

Irenaeus, 133
Isaac, 190, 193, 316
Isaac of Acre, 164
Isaiah, 60, 139, 202, 203, 214, 293
Ishmael, R., 206
Isis, 30
Islam, 17, 72, 98, 99, 116, 214, 285–291, 316
Israel, 15, 20, 22, 62, 82, 109, 110, 111, 117, 118, 124, 136, 137, 140, 142, 144, 147, 151, 165, 201, 202, 206, 207, 224–230, 237, 247, 250, 262, 269, 270–275, 278, 285, 292, 294, 309, 315
Israel Salanter, 180
Israel, State of, 8, 276–288
Italy, 178
I-Thou, 53–55, 192

Jabez, Joseph, 9, 326
Jacob, 60, 111, 138, 140, 163, 193, 305
Jacob b. Asher, 140, 326
Jacob, E., 136, 326
Jacob Isaac, the "Seer," 197, 327
Jacob Joseph of Pulnoy, 166, 180, 327
Jacob of Neboria, 47
Jacobs, Louis, 327
Jael, 168
Jastrow, M., 48, 327
Jehoiakim, 138
Jehovah, 137
Jenkins, D. E., 31, 327
Jeremiah, 72, 287, 293
Jerusalem, 74, 83, 282
Jesse, 293
Jesus, 25, 100, 286
Job, 58, 125, 174, 262, 265, 305
Joel, 293
Johanan, R., 60, 95, 255
Johanan, R. b. Zakkai, 84, 167
Jolles, J. Z., 318
Jonah, 117
Jonah, of Gerona, 47, 170, 171, 251–253
Jonathan of Lubtsh, 197
Jose, R., 167, 171
Joseph, 204, 316
Joseph, Ibn Shoshan, 30
Joseph Mordecai of Izbica, 79, 327
Joseph, Morris, 7,'321, 327
Joseph, Yossel, 157, 326
Josephus, 307
Joshua, b. Levi, 309
Joshua, R., 290
Josiah, 22
Judah, 204
Judah, the Prince, 108
Judah, R., 167
Judah, the Saint, 51, 63, 250
Judaism, 1, 4, 6, 7, 8, 9, 10, 11, 12, 15, 24, 26, 27, 37, 50, 63, 64, 73, 76, 79, 103, 104, 107, 108, 152, 158, 181, 182, 187, 202, 212, 215, 217, 219, 223, 225, 226, 230, 232, 244, 246, 256, 257, 260, 277, 280, 282, 284–291, 299, 301, 303, 307, 309, 316, 318
Judge, 97

Judgement Day, 9–10, 266
Jüdische Wissenschaft, 221
justice, 231–242

Kabbalah, 10, 12, 14, 24, 26, 27, 28–34, 42, 43, 44, 45, 46, 62, 85, 86–92, 95, 96, 104–107, 112, 115, 121, 129–131, 134, 136, 148–151, 161, 162, 163, 167, 177, 178, 179, 184–185, 186, 188–192, 212, 213, 234, 265, 270, 316, 317
Kaddish, 317
Kadushin, Max, 10, 63, 117, 327
Kagan, Israel Meir, 197
Kalonymous Kalman of Cracow, 96, 327
Kalonymous Kalman of Pictzena, 198, 327
Kant, I., 18–19, 36, 71, 256, 527
Kaplan, M. M., 7, 50, 223–230, 271, 327
karet, 304–306, 316
Karf, S. E., 231
Karo, Joseph, 47, 165, 327
Kasher, M. M., 83, 327
Kasher, M. S., 88, 327
Katz, D., 180, 232, 327
Katz, J., 26, 166, 285, 327
Kaufmann, Walter, 17, 327
Kaufmann, Y., 15, 123, 284, 303, 327
kavvanah, 187–191
Keats, 133
Kelipot, 129–130, 270
Keter, 28–34, 43
Khazars, 147
Kierkegaard, 19, 75, 327
Kircheim, R., 49
"King," 144
Kingdom of God, 135, 231, 299
"kiss of death," 161
Klausner, J., 292, 293, 294, 327
Kohler, Kaufmann, 7, 10, 64, 117, 135, 136, 180, 231, 243, 327
Kohn, Eugene, 192–193, 327
Konovitz, I., 22, 117, 136, 327
Kook, A. I., 10, 121, 173, 279, 290, 327
Koran, 98, 214, 289
Kuzari, 4, 20, 47, 107, 110, 146, 147, 158, 191, 270, 326

Lady Macbeth, 101
Lamm, N., 7, 103–107, 327
Landau, E., 136, 142, 143, 144, 145, 146, 327
Landau, Ezckial, 30, 108–109, 251, 287, 327
language, religious, 6, 12–13, 36–37, 49, 120
Latin, 5, 180
Lauterbach, J. Z., 8, 327
Lazarus, M., 231, 327
Leah, 163
leap of faith, 17
Leon de Modena, 27
Lessing, 288
Levi, b. Hama, 201
Levi Yitzhak of Berditchev, 69–71, 179, 327
Levin, B. M., 150, 327
Levy, J., 48, 327
Lewis, C. S., 101, 102, 108, 181, 328

Liebersman, Saul, 218
linguistic analysis, 6, 12, 41, 90, 91, 92, 193–194, 195
Lipschutz, Israel, 271
Lithuania, 88, 180, 232
liturgy, 181, 187
Loewe, H., 8, 117, 243, 317, 328
Loewe, R., 270, 271, 328
logic, 36, 37, 70, 74, 75, 78, 79, 90, 91, 92, 106
London, 64, 287
love and fear of God, 152–182, 198
Luria, David, 25
Luria, Isaac, 10, 30, 32–37, 67, 96, 129–130, 150, 188, 317
Luzzatto, M. H., 32, 130, 178–179, 266, 328
Luzzatto, S. D., 237

Maalah, 145
Mabit, 9, 196, 200, 256–257, 298, 315–316, 328
Maccabees, 306
Macdonald, John, 9, 328
Mackenna, S., 44
McLaughlin, J. F., 136
Maggid of Meseritch, 185
magic, 111–112, 141, 148, 149
Magus, 24
Maimonides, 2, 3, 4, 7, 9, 10, 13, 14, 27, 40, 41, 42, 47, 48, 49, 50, 51, 78, 79, 80, 85, 86, 91, 92, 93, 94, 104, 108, 110, 111, 112, 114, 115, 122, 124, 128, 129, 131, 134, 146, 147, 148, 150, 151, 157, 158, 161, 162, 164, 168, 169, 170, 171, 188, 195, 199, 200, 202, 207, 213, 215, 221, 222, 223, 227, 232–239, 248–250, 253, 255, 260, 261, 263–265, 269, 286, 290, 294–297, 298, 300, 312–313, 319–320
Makom, 142–143, 145, 151
Malachi, 293
Malkhut, 29–34, 62, 162, 185
Malter, H., 108
Man and God, 33–34, 76, 96, 102, 103, 130, 151, 152, 163, 177, 232
Manasseh b. Israel, 14, 315–317, 328
manna, 315
Marmorstein, A., 136, 141, 142, 143, 144, 145, 146, 328
Marmorstein, E., 278, 328
Martin, B., 76
martyrdom, 21, 26, 132, 147, 153, 157, 164–166, 197, 289
Mascall, E. L., 98, 101, 328
matter, 76, 94–95, 101, 129, 191
Maybaum, I., 7, 135, 328
Meir, R., 62
Meiri, 243, 252–254, 255, 328
Meir Ibn Gabbai, 43, 325
Menahem Mendel of Lubavitch, 34, 87
Mendelssohn, Moses, 10, 64
"Merciful," 145
Meroz, 99
Messiah, 8, 9, 79, 100, 231, 276–283, 286, 289, 202–300, 307 310, 315, 316

Metatron, 24
metaphysics, 12
methodology, 13–15
Meynell, Alice, 101
Micah, 285, 293
Michael, 109
Midrash, 11, 61, 62, 63, 68, 103, 108, 153, 154, 172, 184, 244, 306
Milhamot Adonai, 4, 78, 94, 114
Mill, John Stuart, 75, 328
Milne, E. A., 100, 328
Milton, 283
min, 24, 50
miracles, 8, 117, 119, 122, 123–124, 149, 155, 295
Miriam, 161
Mishnah, 4, 9, 23, 62, 76, 84, 97, 109, 111, 116, 117, 141, 143, 146, 152, 153, 201, 271, 307
mitzvah, 158, 172, 210, 211–230, 260
mitzvot, see commandments
Mizrachi movement, 279
Moabite Stone, 205
Mohammed, 289
modern thought, 4, 5, 6, 9, 10, 16, 31, 37, 123, 195–196, 297, 318–322
monasticism, 250
monism, 34–35
monotheism, 15, 21–23, 34–35, 37, 61, 64, 272
Montefiore, C. G., 8, 60, 117, 243, 328
Moore, G. F., 23, 24, 117, 141, 243, 802, 328
moral argument, 17, 19
Moses, 3, 6, 9, 46, 47, 48, 83, 111, 128, 137, 158, 161, 162, 179, 199, 201, 207, 209, 213, 216, 217, 218, 224, 234, 262, 273, 286, 287, 290, 311, 315
Moses of Taku, 49, 51, 112, 330
Moule, C. F. D., 51, 101, 123–124, 328
Mowinckel, S., 204, 328
Muilenburg, J., 203
Musar movement, 180, 232
mysticism, 17, 18, 30, 31, 39, 54–55, 63, 69, 70–71, 89, 90, 154–164, 173, 178, 190–191, 212, 213, 222
mythology, 29, 30, 81, 105, 133, 163, 284

Nahman of Bratzlav, 74, 86–87, 180, 258, 328
Nahman b. Isaac, 167
Nahman of Tcherin, 116, 157, 166, 180, 192, 328
Nahmanides, 149, 157, 158, 183–184, 258, 265, 313–315, 328
Nahum, 293
Names of God, 54, 112, 136–151
Nathan Hirsch of Slabodka, 198
Nathan the Wise, 288
Nationalism, 10, 276–283
naturalism and supernaturalism, 50, 51, 70 192–193, 223–230, 294
Nature, 63–71, 73, 122
Nazis, 131, 299

Nebuchadnezzer, 273
necromancy, 306
nefilim, 98
negation, theology of, 2, 3, 27, 38–52
Nehuniah b. Ha-Kanah, 150
Neo-Platonism, 31, 44, 45, 48, 86, 157, 193
neo-Thomists, 122–123
Netzah, 29–34
Neumark, D., 109, 307, 328
Newton, 123
Niagara Falls, 50
Nicholas of Cusa, 90
Niebuhr, R., 318
Nieto, David, 64–66
Nimrod, 273
Noahide laws, 99, 168, 285, 290
Noth, M., 227, 328
"Nothing" and "Nothingness," 44, 96, 132, 188–189
nukvah, 33
numinous, 180–182

Obadiah, 293
occult, 113
Ofanim, 110
Olan, Levi, 76
ontological proof, 17
Or Adonai, 4, 40, 41, 78, 85, 114
organic thinking, 10
Origen, 140
original sin, 246–247
Ormuzd, 22, 25
Orr, J., 64, 328
Orthodoxy, 7, 14, 97, 208, 217, 218, 240, 276–278
Oshlag, J., 32, 87, 328
Osiris, 30, 302
Otto, R., 180–182, 329

Pahad Yitzhak, 139
Palestine, 47, 109, 117, 201, 255, 276, 279, 308
"Pantocrator," 138
panentheism, 35–37, 56, 63–71
pantheism, 15, 35, 56, 63–71
Pappa, R., 147
para-psychology, 6
partzufim, 33–34
Pascal, 158, 193
Patriarchs, 161
pegam, 12, 177
penances, 250–259
Pentateuch, 43, 60, 199, 200–210, 213, 214, 215, 217, 257
Perl, J., 192, 329
Persia, 22–23, 143, 144, 292, 297, 318
Personal God, 38–55, 94, 151, 192–193
Petuchowski, J. J., 7, 64, 195, 196, 206, 329
phallic symbol, 30 *cf.* erotic symbolism
Pharaoh, 83, 273
Pharisees, 279, 307
Phillips, D. I., 195, 329
Philo, 5, 10, 17, 27, 140, 308, 329

philosophy, 10, 11, 12, 16, 19, 24, 28, 30, 36, 42, 43, 46, 62, 64, 72, 85, 88, 89, 90, 94, 111, 112, 114, 121, 122, 123, 125, 126, 146, 147, 158, 161, 193, 217, 248, 255, 269, 314
Phineas of Koretz, 115
Pike, N., 88, 329
Pines, S., 3, 328
Plato, 17, 85, 94, 95, 129, 329
Plaut, W. G., 102, 103, 202, 218, 277, 320, 329
Plotinus, 44, 329
poetry, 113
politics, 7, 8
Pollak, J., 316
Pollard, W. G., 117–119, 329
polytheism, 15, 17, 21–23, 24, 36, 37, 40, 147, 284, 289, 290, 291, 312
prayer, 2, 30, 31, 111, 116, 144, 165, 183–198, 316
precognition, 317
Priestly Writers, 61, 304
process philosophy, 122
Proclus, 45
prophecy, 9, 10, 46, 51, 110, 111, 155, 157, 199, 203, 205, 247–248, 270, 284
Prophets, Books of, 43, 60, 199, 201
Protestants, 8
providence, 8, 9, 56, 63, 65, 114–124, 143, 147, 194, 198
Psalms and Psalmists, 42, 58, 59, 65, 77, 82, 93, 114, 302, 306
Pseudo-Dionysius, 45
psychology, 6, 111, 268
Puccetti, R., 134, 329
Pythagoras, 44, 178, 317

quantum physics, 118

Rab, 61, 108, 167, 183, 309
Raba, 167
Rabbis and Rabbinic literature, 5, 8, 10, 13, 22, 23, 24, 25, 44, 47, 61, 63, 64, 83, 84, 86, 95, 97, 102, 109, 111, 112, 116, 117, 125, 136, 138, 140–142, 154, 157, 158, 161, 167, 168, 172, 174, 187, 191, 192, 198, 201, 202, 203, 205, 206, 207, 211–230, 231, 232, 233, 235, 240, 242, 243, 244, 245, 246, 247, 248, 255, 261, 262, 265, 267, 268, 273, 274, 285, 290, 294, 307, 310, 313, 314, 315, 316, 321
Rabbenu Tam, 150
Rachel, 306
racism, 273
Rackman, E., 217, 329
Rahmana, 145
Rahner, K., 88–89, 329
Rall, H. R., 278, 329
Ramsey, M., 51, 329
Rankin, O. S., 26, 329
Rashdall, Hastings, 52, 329
Rashi, 7, 48, 150, 294
Ratner, I. S., 32, 44, 329
Rawidowicz, S., 49, 329
reason, 18, 19, 147, 155, 181–182

Red Sea, 66, 119
Redactor, 208–209
Reese, W. L., 76
Reform, 7, 202, 215–220, 276–277, 283, 298–300, 320
religions, other, 8, 284–291, 301
religious experience, 18, 180–182
repentence, 242–259
Resh Lakish, 255, 309
Responsa, 30, 66, 240, 287
resurrection, 9, 73, 294, 306–322
revelation, 7, 9, 11, 31, 39, 56, 64, 105, 106, 119, 145, 147, 186, 199–210, 214, 241, 242
reward and punishment, 5, 8, 9, 132, 175–180, 260–268, 314, 316
Ribbono Shel Olam, 144, 151
Robinson, Charles K., 118–119, 329
Robinson, H. Wheeler, 207, 329
Robinson, John, 51, 329
Robinson, T. H., 94
Rokeah, 250–251
Roman, 285
Rosen, Joseph, 88
Rosen, K., 232, 329
Rosenblatt, S., 2, 62, 329
Rosenheim, J., 208
Rosenzweig, F., 7, 10, 13, 208, 278, 329
Ross, J. P., 123–124
Roth, Aaron, 317, 329
Roth, Cecil, 65, 329
Roth, Leon, 7, 213, 329
Rowley, H. H., 94, 261, 329
Rubenstein, R. L., 7, 51, 135, 329
Rubin, S., 30, 163, 329
Russia, 100, 102

Saadia, 2, 4, 10, 14, 27, 46, 47, 49, 62, 73, 74, 87, 104, 108, 110, 155, 221, 253, 310–313, 315, 317, 329
sabbath, 88, 97, 116–117, 211, 215, 223, 224, 226, 227, 256, 309, 316
sacred marriage, 29, 94
sacrifices, 189, 295
Sadducees, 24, 307
Safed, 162, 198
saints, 114, 117, 156, 167–173, 178, 179, 196–198, 237, 265, 286, 290
sake of Heaven, 167–173, 260
Salaman, Nina, 63
Samaritans, 9, 208, 209
Sarachek, J., 292, 330
Sarah, 72
Sarna, N., 205, 330
Sassanians, 23
Satan, 23, 24, 135
Schatz, R., 188, 330
Schechem, 163
Schechter, S., 5, 8, 9, 10, 117, 198, 201, 220, 221–222, 243, 245, 279, 330
Schlesinger, G. N., 135, 330
Schneersohn, F., 322, 330
Schneor Zalman of Liady, 10, 34–37, 66–71, 88, 330

Scholem, G., 28, 30, 32, 43, 44, 62, 96, 157, 162, 213, 250, 270, 292, 297, 330
Schwarzschild, S., 292, 330
science, 4, 6, 24, 75, 95, 96–107, 116–124, 135, 158, 161, 194
script, 140
Sefirot, 26, 28–34, 42, 43, 62, 87, 104, 129–130, 149–151, 162, 163, 184, 188, 234, 270, 316
Seliger, J., 318, 330
Semitic languages, 5, 138, 205, 282
Sennacherib, 118, 273
Septuagint, 138
Serafim, 110
serpent, 163, 246
Set, 302
Seth, 317
Sevin, S., 223, 330
Shaatnez, 227
Shabbatai Zevi, 297
Shaddai, 138–139, 141, 142
Shakespeare, 101, 283, 318
Shalom, 146
Shalom Dov of Lubavitch, 277
Shamayim, 143, 144, 145, 151
Shamir, 117
Shammai, 95
Shekhinah, 29, 30–34, 61–63, 68, 145, 153, 157, 162, 163, 177, 190, 192, 197, 270, 309
Shem Ha-Meforash, 140, 141, 148
Shema, 21, 22, 25, 26, 37, 109, 165, 243
Sheol, 302–306
Sherlock Holmes, 36
Sherwin, B. L., 130, 330
Shestov, Lev, 74, 330
shevirat ha-kelim, 32–34
Shir Ha-Kavod, 51–52
Shofar, 142
Shulhan Arukh, 111, 171, 191, 226
Sibylline Oracles, 308
Sifre, 23, 62, 141, 153, 154
Simeon b. Lakish, 201 and see Resh Lakish
Simeon b. Shetach, 144
Simhah Züssel of Kelm, 232, 330
Simon, U., 135, 330
sin, 5, 167–168, 172, 178, 179, 243–259
Singer's Prayer Book, 16, 51, 93, 150, 258, 330
sitra ahara, 24, 34, 129, 163
Siva, 30
Skinner, J., 203, 330
Slonimsky, Harry, 76, 330
Smart, Ninian, 18, 180, 330
Smethurst, A. F., 101, 330
snail, 68
Solomon, 3, 104, 117, 160, 235
Song of Songs, 160, 162
soul, 56, 57, 63, 88, 133, 135, 152, 153, 155, 156, 158, 168, 183, 188, 190, 193, 237, 259, 270, 303, 305–322
space, 32, 56, 57, 86, 88, 110
space exploration, 102–107
Spain, 7, 9, 127, 270, 297

sparks, holy, 33, 297
speculation, 14, 22, 125, 147
Speiser, E., 203, 330
Spinoza, 63, 64, 65, 79
spirituality, 7, 57, 110, 111, 156, 178, 179, 189, 190, 218, 290, 308, 316, 319
statistics, 9
Steinberg, Milton, 7, 330
Stern, 115
suffering, 5, 190, 239
Sufis, 286, 291
superstition, 112, 282, 284, 302
Swinburne, R., 88, 330
symposia, 7
synagogue, 216, 220, 222, 225
synagogue, Spanish and Portuguese, 64
system, 8, 10, 22, 63, 69

Tabernacle, 60–61
Talmud, 8, 13, 14, 22, 23, 24, 30, 47, 48, 49, 50, 56, 60, 62, 63, 79, 99, 108, 111, 112, 143, 144, 150, 157, 165, 197, 201, 207, 219, 220, 221, 228, 231, 236, 243, 247, 255, 285, 305
Tannaim, 308–309
Tanya, 66–71, 88, 246
Taoism, 288
Targum, 140
Tchernichowsky, 283
Tchernowitz, Hayim, I, 30, 330
Tchernowitz, Hayim, II, 228, 330
technology, 75
tefillin, 47
Teicher, J., 313
Teitelbaum, M., 34, 69, 330
teleological proof, 17, 19, 120
telepathy, 317
Telz, 88
Temple, 60, 104, 117, 140, 141, 145, 189, 248, 278, 282, 287, 295, 300
Temple, William, 283
Tent of Meeting, 61
Tetragrammaton, 88, 136–137, 140–142, 146, 147, 148, 150, 166, 197
theism, 15, 17, 39, 51, 56, 64, 76, 77, 92, 125, 193
Throne of Glory, 110
Tiberias, 314
Tiferet, 26, 29–34, 62, 162, 185, 270
tikkun, 33, 96, 188
Tikkune Zohar, 31
Tillich, P., 16, 22, 152
Timaeus, 85, 94
time, 32, 82–92, 97
Tishby, I., 24, 26, 28, 30, 32, 43, 69, 111, 129, 130, 161, 162, 270, 297, 330
Tohu, 95–96
Torah, 7, 9, 11, 35, 69, 95, 98, 99, 106, 107, 110, 121, 149, 153, 154, 158, 160, 162, 163, 164, 166, 167, 168, 170, 172, 176, 184, 191, 197, 199, 200, 201, 202, 205, 206, 208–230, 235, 246, 248, 253, 260, 261, 269, 274, 278, 282, 283, 285, 286, 295, 322

Torah, immutability of, 9
Torrey, N. L., 64, 331
Trachtenberg, J., 111, 149, 331
tradition, 4, 6, 11, 12, 14, 17, 18, 20, 118, 122, 125, 127, 139, 172, 199, 201, 211–230, 240
Trani, Moses, see *Mabit*
transmigration of souls, see *gilgul*
Trinity, 25, 26, 27, 29, 37
Tur, 171
Tyre, 47
Tzevaot, 141
Tzimtzum, 32–37, 67, 87, 96, 129–130, 166

Ugaritic, 138
Ullendorf, E., 187
ultimate concern, 152
unbelievers, 14, 16, 17
Underhill, Evelyn, 186, 331
United States, 7, 12, 102, 202
universe, 15, 16, 19, 31, 35, 36, 56, 57, 66, 85, 96–107, 144, 282
Upanishads, 45
Urbach, E. E., 8, 24, 62, 145, 155, 247, 331
Utnapishtim, 204

Vajda, G., 152, 154, 155, 331
values, 1, 239
van Buren, Paul, 51
via negativa, see God as unknowable, negation, theology of
Vienna, 219
Vishnu, 30
Voltaire, 64
Vulgate, 138

Waxman, M., 41, 79, 331
Weinberg, J. J., 251, 331
Weingarten, S., 246
Weinstock, I., 96, 331
Weiss, I. H., 218, 227, 331
Weiss, J. G., 79, 188, 331
Wellhausen, 208–209
Wells, H. G., 92
Werblowsky, R. J. Z., 145, 165, 331
Wertheim, A., 30, 191, 258, 331
Whiteman, M., 88, 331
Witch of Endor, 302, 305, 306
Wolf, Arnold J., 7, 331
Wolfson, H. A., 27, 305, 331
Wolheim, R., 88, 331
World to Come, 9, 50, 61, 88, 141, 158, 160, 211, 237, 245, 290, 294, 296, 301–322
Worlds, Four, 33–34
Wouk, H., 97, 331
Wright, W. K., 76, 331
Wurthwein, E., 140, 331
Wurzburger, W., 7

Yad Ha-Hazakah, 4
Yah, 137–138
Yarnold, G. D., 90, 331
Yesod, 29–34
yetzer ha-ra, see evil inclination

YHWH, 61, 136–137, 303
Yom Kippur, see Day of Atonement

Zangwill, I., 117, 273
Zechariah, 293
zeer, 33
Zen, 288
Zephaniah, 293
Zeritski, D., 232, 331
Zevi Elimelech Spira, 171–172, 179, 198, 331

Zion, 83
Zionism, 276–283, 298–300
zivvug, 33
Zohar, 26, 29, 30, 32, 43, 44, 46, 47, 88, 96,
    149, 150, 161, 162, 163, 165, 175, 177, 178,
    190, 191, 214, 246, 317
Zoroastrianism, 22–25, 285
Zunz, L., 111, 331
Zurich, 240
Zweiful, E., 35, 68, 331